Liferay in Action

Liferay in Action

The Official Guide to Liferay Portal Development

RICH SEZOV, JR

MANNING
SHELTER ISLAND

To my wife: *Yo Deborah! I did it!*

For online information and ordering of this and other Manning books, please visit www.manning.com. The publisher offers discounts on this book when ordered in quantity. For more information, please contact

Special Sales Department
Manning Publications Co.
20 Baldwin Road
PO Box 261
Shelter Island, NY 11964
Email: orders@manning.com

Manning Publications Co.
20 Baldwin Road
PO Box 261
Shelter Island, NY 11964

Development editor: Lianna Wlasiuk
Copyeditor: Tiffany Taylor
Proofreader: Melody Dolab
Typesetter: Marija Tudor
Cover designer: Marija Tudor

ISBN: 9781935182825
Printed in the United States of America
1 2 3 4 5 6 7 8 9 10 – MAL – 17 16 15 14 13 12 11

brief contents

contents

foreword

During the mid to late 1990s, portals emerged with the promise to help bring together applications seamlessly via a unified user interface. As a result, many software developers today still maintain that preconception of the word *portal*.

Although that definition of a portal still holds true, I believe the meaning has shifted to something more encompassing. My colleagues describe it as a "convergence" in which traditionally horizontally separated web applications are now beginning to converge within the portal as components of the portal. Portals like Liferay are now comprehensive, ready-to-deploy solutions that include adjacent capabilities, such as social collaboration, content management, and business process management. And in parallel with that shift, portals are taking on the critical infrastructural role of a platform on which a broad range of sophisticated enterprise web applications can be developed.

That's where this book comes in. If you're new to portal technology, you'll find Rich Sezov's writing style easy to follow as he guides you through the fundamentals of portlets. Rich not only teaches you how to integrate into the portal existing applications you may already have, but also helps you develop new ones using the tools and components provided by Liferay. Most important, because this book helps you learn to develop the right way with Liferay Portal, it may very well save you weeks of development time. Part 2 of this book provides an in-depth look at portlet development, and Rich's excellent coverage of hooks and extensions in Part 3 includes conventions and techniques that are vital to advanced developers who want to customize Liferay Portal. You'll find this to be *the* flat-out best guide both for Liferay 6.0 and the upcoming 6.1 release.

Liferay in Action represents the culmination of many people's dreams at Liferay. We always knew that we wanted to write a comprehensive book on Liferay Portal development, and Rich's dual background in technology and writing combined with his extensive knowledge of Liferay made him the perfect candidate to be its author. Rich has invested years collecting the intricate details of Liferay Portal, many of which have never been documented before, and put them on paper—no easy task.

On behalf of Liferay, for all the hard work and sweat that Rich has poured into this book, I want to say to Rich, thank you. Who knew we could find an engineer with an English degree? And to you, the reader, enjoy this book; we hope it means as much to you as it means to us.

BRIAN KIM
CHIEF OPERATING OFFICER
LIFERAY, INC.

preface

I was sitting in the back of the Liferay Car (yes, Liferay owns an old, beat-up Toyota Corolla), and Brian Kim, Liferay's Chief Operating Officer, was sitting next to me, giving me a hard time. I was already uncomfortable in the back seat: I'm 6'2", and my knees were up next to my ears. But it was only a short trip from the Liferay Symposium hotel in Anaheim, CA, to Brian Chan's house (where we and the other occupants of the car were staying), so I wouldn't have to endure the cramped quarters for long.

You see, I'd written a couple of editions of Liferay's *Administrator's Guide*, but its companion volume, the *Developer's Guide*, had suffered several aborted attempts at getting off the ground. It had finally achieved some semblance of completion, but it wasn't yet where I wanted it to be. The problem was, I needed to release some developer documentation soon, so I could get to work on the training materials and the documentation for the next release of Liferay. For this reason, I'd resigned myself to publishing what we had and then attempting to make the next edition of the book more complete. We'd been self-publishing the *Administrator's Guide*, so I thought we should do the same with the *Developer's Guide*, particularly because it wasn't going to be as complete as I wished.

Brian wasn't giving me a hard time because of that: Liferay was in a period of rapid growth, and we often found ourselves in the position of having more work than we had hands to complete it. Instead, Brian was giving me a hard time, frankly, because he had a bigger vision than I had.

"Why do you want to self-publish again?" Brian asked. "Don't you think it would be better if we worked with a book publisher?"

"Of course it would," I said. "I just think that the material I currently have isn't yet up to the standards that one of the two publishers I'd want to work with would accept."

"Really? Okay, what would it take to get it that way?"

"Well, I'd have to be able to dedicate more time to writing the book, which I can't do right now." I then gave him my sob story about all the work that I had to finish in addition to the *Developer's Guide.*

"Then let's hire some people to help you. One problem solved. Who are the two publishers you'd like to work with?"

I told him. Manning was one of them. The other shall remain nameless.

"Why do you like those guys?" Brian asked.

My only real experience with computer book publishers—before I wrote this book—was as a reader. Because I'm mostly self-educated with regard to the industry I'm in, I've read a lot of computer books (my degree is in English; how I got into programming, Java, and portals is another—longer—story). I answered from that perspective.

"I think the quality from those guys is consistently higher than the rest. And, of course, I'd want Liferay to be represented by that kind of quality. So I'd want to be able to take the time to deliver something that they'd be willing to publish."

"Okay, then why don't we make it a goal to reach out to those publishers, once we get you some help? I think working with a publisher will help provide us with more visibility and fill a real need our community has for some good, polished material to get them up to speed on Liferay."

"All right, I can do that," I replied.

Except I never really got the chance.

By the hand of what can only be described as Providence, not even a month later, *Manning* reached out to *us*. I say *us* because they didn't reach out to *me*; they went after the Liferay rock stars, like Brian Chan, Nate Cavanaugh, and Ray Augé, which makes perfect sense. But those guys were far too busy to write a book: if they spent time doing that, Liferay wouldn't be where it is today. Instead they sent Manning, specifically Mike Stephens, to little old me, who was supposed to be preparing a proposal to send to Manning anyway.

Funny how these things work out, isn't it?

Through a long, circuitous route that I could never have planned, I get to fulfill a dream of being a published author. It's not a novel (that may come someday too, I hope), but I've tried to make what could become a dry subject interesting. To me, there's nothing dry about Liferay: it's an exciting product that can do a ton of things, and I think it's an ideal platform on which to build a web site. I hope that by the end of this book, you'll think so too.

acknowledgments

When I started working on this book, I thought I'd be finished much sooner than I was actually able to do so. I already had material that formed about a third of what the book eventually became, and I figured the rest of it would slide easily into place. Boy, was I wrong! If anyone reading this is considering writing a book, everything other authors tell you about the process is true: it's a lot more work than you think it's going to be. And the people around you are just as key to your success as you are.

First and foremost, I'd like to thank my wife, Deborah, and my daughter, Julia, for their incredible sacrifice. Over the past year, I've been holed up in my office for more hours than I'd like to count, and they've borne the brunt of the effects of a missing husband and father. Thank you, Deborah, for your understanding, patience, kind-heartedness, and support; and thank you, Julia, for your good cheer and your always-diverting games and fun.

No acknowledgments for anything having to do with Liferay would be complete without mentioning Brian Chan, who created Liferay, as well as the other founders of Liferay, Caris Chan, Bryan Cheung, Brian Kim, and Mike Young. You make huge sacrifices of time and talent every day to keep both the company and product moving forward. You trusted me out of the blue (and without prior contact) with a huge responsibility when the company was tiny and vulnerable. Thank you for believing in me. And thanks to Brian Kim for giving me a good kick in the rear (as described in the preface).

Liferay's core engineers are without a doubt some of the smartest people on the planet. In all likelihood, I'd still be working on the code for this book if it weren't for the help of several of them, but the man I want to mention first is Ray Augé. Ray is one of the smartest guys I know, and he's the mind behind many of Liferay's most robust features. He took lots of time out of many of his days to help me puzzle out some undocumented and tricky (at least to me) APIs—which are now documented in this book. He didn't just do this for me, though—he does this for everybody. I have no idea how he gets his own work done, because he's constantly putting himself out for others, yet he consistently delivers on making Liferay better and better with each version. Thanks, Ray, for all of your help with this book.

Jorge Ferrer is another one of these guys who seems to achieve the impossible. Somehow he manages to run the Liferay office in Spain, drive many of Liferay's projects, help other people (like me), contribute to Liferay's core, and heavily involve himself in Liferay's community. Always positive, always energetic—quite frankly sometimes it makes me tired just thinking about all he does. Thanks, Jorge.

Thanks to Mike Young for walking me through Liferay's page composition logic in chapter 9. That was fun to puzzle out and added an important aspect to the book. In many ways I also owe Mike for planting the seeds that got me into Liferay in the first place. Thanks, Mike!

If you've read the preface, you know that we had to hire some help for me in order to make this book possible. That help came in the form of Stephen Kostas. Steve picked up many of my responsibilities of keeping Liferay's training materials up to date and free from error, making it possible for me to make only quick, sideways glances at the training material for the last year. Thanks, Steve, for being so easy to work with and so willing to pick up a wide variety of tasks.

I guess I have to move this along faster, or it'll get to be as long as the book itself. Thanks to all the trainers who helped keep the training material going while I was working on the book: Julio Camarero, Juan Fernandez, Olaf Kock, Jonathon Omahen, Sten Martinez, Alberto Montero, Zsigmond Rab, and Steven Cao. Thanks to Tim Telcik for taking off and running with the PDF tools.

Speaking of training, special thanks to Ed Shin and Jeff Handa for helping me maximize my time on the book by organizing various training tasks. Thanks also to Mike Han for keeping us in line and for your help with my workflow questions.

Thanks to Greg Amerson for the awesome Liferay IDE/Developer Studio and all of your excellent feedback. You're making Liferay development easier every day, man.

To Ivan Cheung and James Min: I wouldn't be in Liferay without you guys. Thanks!

Neil Griffin is to me the (slightly) older brother I never had. Thanks for your encouragement and wisdom, Neil.

Thanks to my many coworkers who were so encouraging over the past year: Josh Asbury, Alice Cheng, Paul Hinz, James Falkner, Michelle Hoshi, JR Houn, Mike Saechang, Scott Lee, Nate Cavanaugh, Aaron Delani, Craig Kaneko, Ryan Park, Cynthia Wilburn, Charles May, Zsigmond Rab, Zsolt Balogh, Jeff Young, Ed Chung, Jerry Niu, Jeff Han, Louis Mui, Juan Fernandez, Thiago Moreira, Ruth Huijser, Joe Shum, and Alex Chow. Thanks to Cecilia Lam for putting up with my hare-brained symposium ideas (a compliments contest?) so people could win copies of this book.

Manning put together a fantastic team for this book. Thank you, Marjan Bace, for such a great bunch of people to work with, and for your hands-on approach. Thanks to Mike Stephens for getting it all started. Lianna Wlasiuk was my developmental editor, and I am grateful to you, Lianna, for all you did to make this book better. I learned a great deal about how to put together a quality book manuscript, and I know it's going to spill over into my other work in the future.

Thanks to Karen Tegtmeyer for managing the review process so well, and thank you to all of my reviewers: Sean Hogg, Armin Dahncke, Davide Piazza, Ashish Sarin, Barbara Regan, Tariq Ahmed, John J. Ryan III, John Griffin, Robert Hanson, Jakub Holy, James M. Denmark, Pete Helgren, Manish Gupta, Tomáš Polešovský, Sopan Shewale, Sumit Pal, and John Stevenson. You made the book stronger by your suggestions. Special thanks to Minhchau Dang for doing a final technical review of the manuscript shortly before it went to press. Thanks also to Mary Piergies, who shepherded the book through production, and to my copyeditor, Tiffany Taylor, and my proofreader, Melody Dolab.

Of course, I also need to thank my mom, Constance Hunter, for believing I could write books from the time I started making science fiction stories out of my spelling sentences in the sixth grade.

Thanks most especially to God for His mercy to me, giving me the strength and stamina to complete the book.

I hope I haven't forgotten anybody. If I have, it was unintentional—please accept my apologies and my sincere thanks.

about this book

Liferay Portal is a fantastic product for building a web site. It's incredibly robust and feature-filled, and this book is designed to help Java EE developers learn to use the platform effectively. It doesn't exhaustively go through every API Liferay has; you are better served by looking at online reference documentation for that. Instead, this book is like a roadmap of practical experience in working with the Liferay platform. I've tried to make the book useful to anyone working with Liferay, from the absolute beginner who wants to read the book from cover to cover, to the experienced Java EE developer who wants to dive into subjects of interest.

In order to do this, I've created an example company whose web site we'll work on together throughout the book. The code examples are purposefully designed to hit many of the most-needed Liferay features and APIs that you'll want to use in your own work, but they stand on their own. Experienced developers should be able to jump in and work with the examples in any order you like.

Who should read this book

If you're familiar with Java web development, this book is for you. You don't need to have any prior experience with portals or Liferay; in fact, I'd prefer that you didn't. That way, you can approach the material with a fresh view of portals and Liferay in particular. But because this is an *In Action* book, we hit the ground running really fast; if you need an introduction to the Portlet API, you may want to read appendix B in between chapter 2 and chapter 3.

If you've done work with other portals before, this book will help you become familiar with Liferay and all it has to offer. Your knowledge of the Portlet API will help you understand the underpinnings of Liferay's platform, and you'll learn how to make use of lots of Liferay-specific APIs that enhance and complement it.

Seasoned Liferay developers will also be served well by this book. Liferay 6.0 and 6.1 introduce many architectural changes that affect developers, and many best practices from previous versions change in more recent releases. You'll also get to see how to work with some of Liferay's newer APIs, such as workflow, in this book.

How to use this book

Naturally, you'll get the most complete view of Liferay development if you read this book from cover to cover. The book has been designed to build on itself, and you'll certainly be well-served by doing that. I do recognize, however, that this is not the way many people approach books like this, so the book has also been designed to allow you to flip through it, find what you're looking for, and apply that information to your own project. I've done this by grouping the chapters into three parts.

Part 1, which includes chapters 1 and 2, contains introductory material about Liferay and Liferay development. Part 2, which includes chapters 3–7, is all about writing applications on Liferay's platform. To round out the discussion of Liferay development, part 3 (chapters 8–10) describes how to customize Liferay to conform to the requirements of your project. Let's take a look at how this works out in detail by viewing a high-level roadmap of the book.

Roadmap

Chapter 1 gets things started quickly by talking about Liferay and how it fulfills the missed promises of the portal platform. You'll get an introduction to what Liferay is, how it structures a web site, how to navigate in Liferay, and how to design a Liferay implementation project.

Chapter 2 picks up from there and dives right in to setting up a development environment and writing your first portlet. This portlet uses just the generic Portlet API, so you can get your feet wet with framework that underlies Liferay.

In chapter 3, you begin using Liferay's development platform, starting with Service Builder. You'll use Service Builder to design and create a data-driven application from a single configuration file.

Moving from the back end to the front end, chapter 4 continues from where we left off in chapter 3. You use the MVC design pattern provided by Liferay's `MVCPortlet` to create the portlet application that depends on the service layer you generated previously. You also start using Liferay's AlloyUI tag libraries to lay out the forms required by the application.

In chapter 5, we take a break from applications and look at Liferay themes. Themes let you completely customize the way Liferay looks, so that your web site can have the look and design that you define. This chapter will prepare front-end developers for working their design magic with Liferay.

We move out of themes and back to Liferay APIs with chapter 6. Here, you learn about Liferay's Social API, so that you can enable users to connect with each other and view their activities on your site. You'll also see how Liferay integrates with existing social networks.

Chapter 7 continues with a focus on the user by looking at Liferay's Collaboration API. In this chapter, you create a new portlet that provides a platform on which users can collaborate: a slogan contest. You'll learn how to create Liferay assets, to use Liferay's Workflow API, to tag and categorize your content, to add discussions and ratings, and to use custom SQL queries in Liferay applications.

From here, we leave the realm of Liferay applications and begin looking at customizing Liferay in chapter 8. This chapter shows you hook plugins, and how hooks can be used to customize properties, JSP files, and services. You use a hook to modify Liferay's Shopping portlet and give it a custom user interface.

We put Liferay customization on steroids with chapter 9. Here, you use Ext plugins to customize *anything* in Liferay. As far as Liferay's development framework goes, this is the ultimate in what you can do to make Liferay your own. We round out this discussion by talking about development best practices, so you know when it's appropriate to use each kind of plugin.

Now that you know all the components of Liferay development, chapter 10 ends the book by showing you seven APIs in Liferay that you can use in various places in your applications. You'll see how to create friendly URLs, use `ActionCommands` for larger applications, use indexing and search, and more.

Code conventions and downloads

Code conventions in the book follow the style of other Manning books in this series. Code always appears in a `monospaced font like this`. Additionally, at times it will be annotated with descriptive numbers or **`bolded`** in order to call out particularly interesting examples. You'll also see class names and other code terms in the text using the same `monospaced` font. *Italics* are used for emphasis. After each code listing, we include the path and filename for that particular piece of code.

Liferay uses particularly descriptive package names, class names, and JSP tags, and these can get pretty long. This is fine when you're looking at code on a screen, but these names don't always translate well to a book. For that reason, I've had to break up some lines in the book that aren't broken in the code. When this happens, you'll see a line-continuation character (➥). This means the code is meant to be on a single line, but for layout purposes it wouldn't fit unless we made the font really small—so small you couldn't read it, which sort of defeats the purpose of printing it in the first place.

One other thing must be mentioned about the code: there's a lot more of it than appears in the book. In the text, I've pointed out only the important code, and left the mundane, obvious stuff as a download only. If I showed everything, the book would be really boring, and you wouldn't want to read it. If you want to look at the complete examples, please download the code. You can find it at Manning's web site at www.manning.com/LiferayinAction or at my profile on liferay.com at www.liferay.com/web/richard.sezov/documents.

Software requirements

One of Liferay's strengths is that it comes from an agnostic philosophy with regard to the environment in which it runs. This means you're free to choose whichever environment you like to work in the most. Because it's Java, of course, JDK 5+ must be able to run on your machine. Further details about this appear in chapter 2, where you install a Liferay development environment. Even more details appear in appendix A, where I show you how to get set up in multiple IDEs.

Because Liferay supports so many deployment combinations, you also have a huge choice of what database or application server you want to use. For simplicity's sake, for the book I used the development configuration that Liferay developers use the most: a Tomcat runtime and a MySQL database. Liferay conveniently supplies a Liferay/Tomcat bundle as a download, so you don't have to worry about installing Liferay yourself into a Java application server. Of course, you're free to use any of Liferay's deployment combinations, but I think this one is the best for developers. It's small, fast, lightweight, and easily configured.

Author Online

Purchase of *Liferay in Action* includes free access to a private web forum run by Manning Publications where you can make comments about the book, ask technical questions, and receive help from the author and from other users. To access the forum and subscribe to it, point your web browser to www.manning.com/LiferayinAction. This page provides information on how to get on the forum once you're registered, what kind of help is available, and the rules of conduct on the forum.

Manning's commitment to our readers is to provide a venue where a meaningful dialog between individual readers and between readers and the author can take place. It is not a commitment to any specific amount of participation on the part of the author, whose contribution to the Author Online forum remains voluntary (and unpaid). We suggest you try asking the author some challenging questions lest his interest stray!

The Author Online forum and the archives of previous discussions will be accessible from the publisher's web site as long as the book is in print.

About the author

RICH SEZOV, JR is an unusual combination of software developer, writer, and trainer. Most of his career has been spent doing software development, but as Liferay's Knowledge Manager, he now has the opportunity to help others do the same by writing about it and teaching it. And man, does he love Liferay. When Rich isn't working, you'll generally find him spending time with his wife and daughter, doing all kinds of interesting things, and (he hopes) not getting into too much trouble.

about the cover illustration

The figure on the cover of *Liferay in Action* is captioned "Staff Officer." The illustration is taken from a nineteenth-century edition of Sylvain Maréchal's four-volume compendium of regional and military dress customs published in France. Each illustration is finely drawn and colored by hand. The rich variety of Maréchal's collection reminds us vividly of how culturally apart the world's towns and regions were just 200 years ago. Isolated from each other, people spoke different dialects and languages. In the streets or in the countryside, it was easy to identify where they lived and what their trade or station in life was just by their dress.

Dress codes have changed since then and the diversity by region, so rich at the time, has faded away. It is now hard to tell apart the inhabitants of different continents, let alone different towns or regions. Perhaps we have traded cultural diversity for a more varied personal life—certainly for a more varied and fast-paced technological life.

At a time when it's hard to tell one computer book from another, Manning celebrates the inventiveness and initiative of the computer business with book covers based on the rich diversity of regional life of two centuries ago, brought back to life by Maréchal's pictures.

Part 1

Working with Liferay and portlets

The first part of this book gives you an introduction to Liferay, showing you what it is, what it does, and how you can use its powerful features to implement your web site.

Chapter 1 introduces the portal landscape and how Liferay leads in that space. You'll learn how Liferay's users, roles, communities, and organizations work and how to navigate its interface. You'll also see how to run a Liferay development project, using best practices that have been proven to work.

Chapter 2 hits the ground running by introducing you to Liferay's development tools. You'll learn how to use the Plugins SDK to create Liferay projects, and you'll write your first portlet using the industry standard Portlet API.

This part of the book prepares you for the nuances of Liferay's development platform. When you finish reading it, you'll understand what Liferay is for and how you can use it to implement any web site.

1 The Liferay difference

This chapter covers

- Understanding portals then and now
- Exploring what Liferay is and how to work with it
- Defining basic portal concepts
- Using Liferay to design a portal

Everybody needs a web site these days. Whether you're building one for a company, for a service organization, or for personal reasons, you need one. And when trying to decide how to build it, you've probably found a dizzying array of choices running on a dizzying array of platforms. How do you go about choosing which platform is best?

If you're anything like me, you've got a list of a bunch of products. You created this list by looking at the feature claims of various software platforms that seem to do something close to what you want to do with your site. Now you're going through that list, testing the products, weighing their strengths and weaknesses against each other, and weighing those against how well those products' underlying platforms will fit into your infrastructure.

If Liferay Portal isn't on your list, you should put it at the top right away. Liferay Portal is a Java-based open source portal, containing an unprecedented number of features that will help you to implement your site in as little time as possible. When you have Liferay on your list, let me respectfully submit that your search can end with Liferay Portal, which is hands down the best platform on which to build a web site.

I feel safe in saying this because I was a Liferay user for some time before I wound up working for the company. Yes, I took the red pill,[1] so to speak, but I've also experienced Liferay from the outside, and so I know what it's like to be doing that search for a platform. I can tell you from experience that you're going to find working with Liferay to be a pleasure, and you'll be happy to know that using the platform that Liferay offers will free you from limitations. It speeds up your development cycle and gives you features that you likely wouldn't have the time or inclination to build yourself. Usually, potential Liferay users focus on Liferay as a product—because it boasts such a huge range of features—but they don't stop to consider the rich development platform it offers. By the end of this chapter, you'll have a good understanding of what Liferay is all about and what it can do for your web site. And I have no doubt that you'll find many reasons to choose Liferay for your next development project.

Choosing Liferay is also safe: you're putting yourself in a group with some of the largest organizations (with the largest web sites) out there that have also chosen Liferay. If I can give you any advice, it would be to end your search with Liferay and begin learning how you can use the platform to build the site of your dreams.

This chapter will go over several important topics. I'll show you why Liferay calls itself a portal, what a portal used to be, and how Liferay pioneered getting past its early limitations. We'll then take a helicopter ride over Liferay's feature set to see what it can do at a high level. After this, we'll delve into how Liferay helps you structure a web site. You'll also get to see what Liferay looks like by default and how you can navigate around it. And finally, using all the information presented, I'll show you how to begin thinking about implementing your site using Liferay Portal.

To get your bearings, let's start by exploring why Liferay calls itself a portal and what that term has come to mean in the industry.

1.1 The Java portal promise: from disappointment to fulfillment

Liferay calls itself a portal. What do you commonly think of when you hear the word portal? As a big fan of sci-fi and fantasy, I tend to think of a doorway to another dimension or time like the portal that Kirk and Spock went through in *Star Trek*, chasing after McCoy to stop him from doing whatever he did to change the timeline. I'll tell you right away: Liferay Portal isn't that elaborate (but you've likely already figured that out). Why do we call it a portal? Let's start with the so-called official definition of a portal.

PORTAL A web-based gateway that allows users to locate and create relevant content and use the applications they commonly need to be productive.

[1] From the 1999 film *The Matrix*.

That definition comes from a bullet on a slide that I've used to teach Liferay to prospective users. I may even have written that bullet, but I'm not sure. Generally, the reaction I get is a narrowing of the eyes, some pursed lips, and then heads nodding up and down. This tells me that people want me to think that what I've just said makes sense, but they're being kind and reserving judgment on my teaching abilities because the definition made no sense at all.

The problem with definitions like that is that they try to say too much in one sentence. Liferay is many, many things, and you can't capture it all in one sentence. But just for fun, let's try it again.

> **PORTAL** A single web-based environment from which all of a user's applications can run. These applications are integrated together in a consistent and systematic way.

That definition is a bit closer when viewed in the context of the web. When we talk about Liferay as a development platform, that's exactly what we mean. At its base, Liferay is a container for integrated applications. Those applications are what make the difference between Liferay and competing products. You're free to use the applications you like, write your own, and disable the rest. And this is what sets Liferay apart. Figure 1.1 shows how you can easily mix and match your applications with Liferay's.

As an analogy, think back to the 1980s and early 90s. If you bought a computer and you needed to use it to write something, you also bought a word processor program. If you then decided you wanted to calculate numbers with the computer, you bought a spreadsheet program. And if you needed to store and retrieve data of some kind (perhaps for a mailing list), you bought a database program. (Nobody created electronic slides back then; they used an overhead projector. And yes, I am dating myself.)

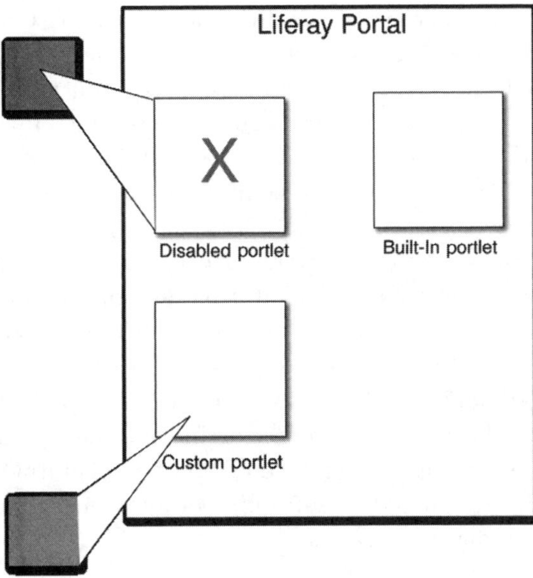

Figure 1.1 Liferay contains many built-in applications called portlets. If there are some you'll never use, you can disable them. You can also write and deploy your own portlets. These custom portlets are indistinguishable from portlets that ship with Liferay Portal.

Most of the time, people chose what was considered the best of whichever program they wanted. One vendor had the best word processor. Another had the best spreadsheet. A third had the best database. If you had to perform all three functions, you probably had three separate programs written by separate entities, but individually each was the best.

Pretty soon, people wanted to create graphs in their spreadsheets that they could insert into a word-processing document and send to a mailing list stored in the database. The problem was that all of these programs were created by different vendors, and they didn't always work together that well. Much effort on users' parts was spent trying to get programs to work together well.

You know the rest of the story. We wound up with office suites, consisting of programs written on the same platform that were designed to work together. Not only did this save us all some money (because buying the separate programs cost a fortune), but it also gave us a level of integration that had so far been unavailable.

The same thing is happening today with software on the web. Liferay is an engine for running web sites. Liferay consists of the base engine as well as the many applications that run on that engine. When you use this platform, your applications can integrate with the rest of Liferay's applications and make your users' experience seamless and smooth. Why? Because the integrated experience is far better than the nonintegrated experience. This is the difference that makes Liferay stand above all the other portals out there. I have to say that because there are some who view the word portal with disdain, sometimes with good reason. Let me explain further.

1.1.1 The Java portal disappointment

When Java portals were first announced, they were hailed as the solution to many of the problems facing enterprises and solution architects. The web had grown up. Instead of using proprietary interfaces, everybody finally standardized on TCP/IP networking and open protocols such as HTTP, SOAP, IMAP, SMTP, and the like. Services, applications, and email operated on these open protocols, and products that once relied on proprietary protocols now opened up to the web. Those products that didn't (or whose vendors delayed doing so) were relegated to the dustbin of history. And when we had all of these siloed services speaking the same language, we needed a way to bring everything together for the end user.

Enter the Java portal. The release of the Java portal specification came with the promise of bringing services together in a single unified web desktop. Not only would it unify everything for a corporation's internal applications, but it would also be the hub of all business to business (B2B), business to consumer (B2C), business to employee (B2E), and even government to public (G2P) communication. It would be the presentation layer for the brand-new service-oriented architecture that we had just finished (or were in the process of) implementing. It could also be a platform for new applications. And it could finally bring together our static web sites and our applications, which resided on separate application servers.

Do you think too much was promised? How's that old saying go? "If it seems too good to be true, it probably is." Well, you're right. What happened? At least three issues emerged that prevented Java portals from achieving widespread acceptance.

First, it was difficult to develop solutions using a portal. The initial Portal API turned out to be something like getting to the least common denominator. Instead of providing all the features developers needed to bring all this stuff together, it defined what seemed like the absolute minimum that vendors could standardize on and left everything else up to the individual vendors. This meant developers had to spend time implementing features that should have been part of the platform in the first place. For example, the initial standard didn't include any way for portlets to communicate with each other.

Second, the portal servers were too big and complex (not to mention hideously expensive), often taking days to set up. For the developer trying to get a development environment going, it was sometimes even worse. I can remember trying to work with one of the first portals (sorry, can't tell you which one it was) and finding it impossible to get a development environment properly configured on my laptop. At the time, I was a team lead and was trying to make the install process a repeatable procedure for the rest of the developers on my team. My solution? I went to a conference, grabbed one of the presenters after his talk, and made him help me install the development environment on my machine. When he heard of my plight, he understood completely: he told me everybody was having this problem and that they had to make this process easier.

Third, other things were happening in the industry at the same time. The Web 2.0 concept was beginning to become popular, and the portlet specification left no room whatsoever for enabling a rich, client-side experience for the end user. In order to compete, portal vendors started to implement their own proprietary extensions to the portlet specification. We all know what this leads to: vendor lock-in, which is precisely what defining a standard is supposed to avoid.

At the same time Java portals were getting a bad rap, sites like Facebook and MySpace came out and pretty much implemented what portals were meant to do all along. As they became more and more popular, suddenly other sites like Amazon.com and other software like JIRA began to implement the social collaboration features of Facebook and MySpace, along with their slick, AJAX-enabled user interfaces. What powered all these new and improved web sites? What enabled them to implement such rich features for the end user so quickly? You guessed it: open source.

Open source solves a lot of the problems inherent in the old Java portal paradigm. Open source projects don't wait around for committees to decide on things; they tend to implement what the users want as fast as possible. There are no barriers to entry with open source; the development tools and the software are made available for free. Open source products also tend to be lighter weight: you don't need a large, dedicated server to start building your solution. Development goes faster, because developers don't have to learn the entire architecture to be effective. And you don't need a huge initial investment to get started using an open source solution—you can start small (free) and then grow your application and hardware as your needs grow. Facebook is the perfect example of this: implemented using PHP (which is an open source web development platform), the site has grown organically as its user base has grown. This is what the market really wanted. And as you're about to see, Liferay Portal provides the same kind of open source platform that has allowed many organizations to do the same.

1.1.2 Liferay keeps the Java portal promises

From the beginning, Liferay Portal has been an open source project. Its whole purpose for existence was to level the playing field so that smaller organizations such as nonprofits, small businesses, and open source projects could take advantage of its platform without having to incur huge expenditures for either software or hardware. Right out of the gate, it did things differently.

An open source project doesn't have the luxury of making it difficult for developers to work on the platform. Instead, developers need to find the platform to be easy to work with, or the project will have major hurdles to community gestation. And if an open source project can't foster the birth and growth of a vibrant community, it's dead. Right away, Liferay was (and continues to be) easy for developers to use, adapting to many different development styles, and not requiring any specific tools to be installed beyond what is already in any Java developer's toolset.

This same philosophy translates to its size. Open source projects also don't have the luxury of being too big or taking up too many system resources; they may be running on new hardware or five-year-old hardware that was donated to a nonprofit that can't afford anything else. Liferay Portal is much smaller and simpler to configure than its competitors. Can you run Liferay on big hardware with a proprietary Java application server? Sure you can. Can you run it on a shared server with a small servlet container like Tomcat? Absolutely. Liferay Portal is provided as a standard .war file—only around 125 MB in size—which can be installed on any application server, or as a bundle, preinstalled in your open source application server of choice. You don't have to go through long installation routines and complex command-line incantations to get it working. If you use a bundle, installing Liferay is as easy as unzipping an archive and editing a text file to point it to your database.

And guess what? Instead of giving you by default an empty portlet container into which portlet applications can be installed, Liferay Portal comes with over 60 portlet applications included. These applications cover about all of the standard functionality you're likely to need in a web site—content management, forums, wikis, blogs, and much more—leaving you to implement only the features specific to your site. And for developers, your setup time will be measured in minutes, not hours. You also don't have to know everything about the architecture to be effective—it's easy to get started.

Open source software also has to be innovative in order to compete with its proprietary competition. Liferay Portal was the first portal to implement that slick, Web 2.0

interface, back in 2006. The first time I saw a portlet being dragged across the browser window and dropped into another spot on the page, I was blown away, because I was used to the old, proprietary solutions that hadn't implemented that yet. Because Liferay Portal was open source, it could respond to market demands faster than the other guys, using the same standards they were using. You'll continue to see that in Liferay Portal, because the open source paradigm works. What users demand gets implemented, without sacrificing adherence to standards.

As far as standards go, Liferay is also based on widely used, standard ways of doing things. It adheres to the JSR-286 portlet standard. In addition to that, it includes utilities such as Service Builder to automatically generate interfaces to databases (something not covered by the standard). Under the hood, Service Builder is just Spring and Hibernate—widely used by Java developers everywhere. You get the benefit of using the platform to get your site done more quickly while taking advantage of standards that keep your code free.

Now that I've spent so much time extolling the virtues of this magical, mystical thing known as Liferay Portal, you're probably anxious to see what this wonderful specimen I've described looks like.

1.2 Getting to know Liferay

Liferay Portal is an open source project that uses the Lesser General Public License (LGPL). This is the GPL license you know and love, with one important exception: Liferay can be linked to software that isn't open source. As long as you use Liferay's extension points for your custom code, you don't have to release your code as open source if you don't wish to. You can keep it, sell it, or do whatever you want with it; it's yours. But if you make a change to Liferay itself by modifying Liferay's source code and want to redistribute the product thereafter, then you need to contribute that change back to Liferay. You get an important exception with the LGPL: you can use Liferay as a base for your own product and either open-source the result or sell it commercially if you wish. Or, if you want to change Liferay directly, you can contribute to the open source project. It's entirely up to you.

You can download the open source version of Liferay Portal for free from Liferay's web site.

Alternatively, Liferay sells an Enterprise Edition of Liferay Portal. This is a commercially available version of the product that comes with support and a hot-patching system for bug fixes and performance improvements. There are web sites running on both versions of Liferay Portal, and both are perfectly appropriate for serving up your site.

In this section, we'll take a quick tour of some of the things you can do with Liferay to begin building a web site. You're going to play around with the interface a bit so you can get to know it better. Figure 1.2 shows the default Liferay Portal 6 user interface.

Okay, I agree; it doesn't look like much, does it? But there's an awful lot of power hidden in the humble interface that Liferay shows you by default. If you're ahead of the game and already have Liferay running, you can follow along. If not, sit back and

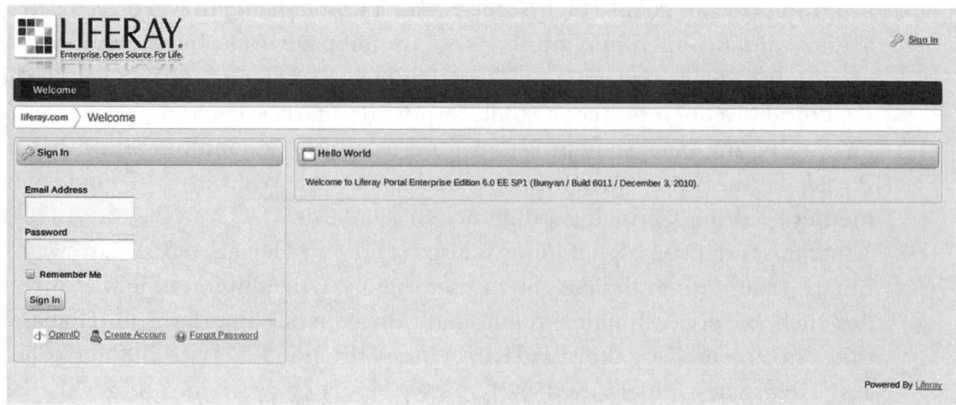

Figure 1.2 Liferay Portal 6, as it looks the first time you start it. It presents a basic interface at first, but as you'll see, you can easily jazz it up.

enjoy the ride: we'll go over how to get Liferay installed and running on your system in Chapter 2.

1.2.1 Liferay is an application aggregator

We've been saying that Liferay Portal isn't just a product; it's a platform. This platform runs applications, and these applications are integrated in ways that separate applications can't be, by virtue of their shared platform.

This means you can take that default Liferay page and load it with integrated applications. Liferay makes doing something like that easy. First, you have to log in as the default administrative user, whose user name is *test@liferay.com* and whose password is *test*. Doing so displays the *Dockbar* (see figure 1.3) at the top of the page, which gives you access to several other functions.

We'll come to all the things you can do with the Dockbar in a moment. For now, all we want to look at is applications, which you can access from the Add menu. Commonly used applications appear directly in the menu, but if you want to see the whole list, choose More. Doing so pops up a fully searchable, categorized view of all the

Figure 1.3 The Dockbar appears when you log in. Hovering the mouse over the Add menu in the Dockbar opens a drop-down menu. To see a full list of available applications, choose More.

applications that have been installed in your Liferay Portal by default. As an aside, by the time you're finished with this book, one of the things you'll be able to do is write your own applications, which can appear in this list.

You're going to fill this page with applications so you can see how Liferay aggregates them. You can browse the applications by opening the categories to which they're assigned. Or if you know the name of the application you're looking for, you can search for it by using the search bar at the top of the Applications window. You can add an application to a specific column by dragging the application off the Applications window and dropping it into the appropriate column, as shown in figure 1.4. Let's pick some cool applications to add to your page. To the left column, add Navigation, Activities, Dictionary, and Translator. To the right column, add Message Boards, Wiki, and Calendar. Note that in a real-world web site, you'd likely never put all of these on one page—you're doing an experiment here to see the concept.

Now you have a single page with a bunch of applications on it. These applications can perform a lot of different functions.

The Message Boards application is a complete implementation of web-based forum software. If you're planning to have discussion forums on your web site, Liferay already has them built in. And the cool thing about it is you don't have to integrate anything. They already work with Liferay's user-management and security features, as do all of Liferay's applications.

You've also added a Wiki application to the page. Again, this is a full-fledged wiki that you can use for whatever purpose suits you. As with the Message Boards application, Wiki is integrated with Liferay's user management and security. But (and this is

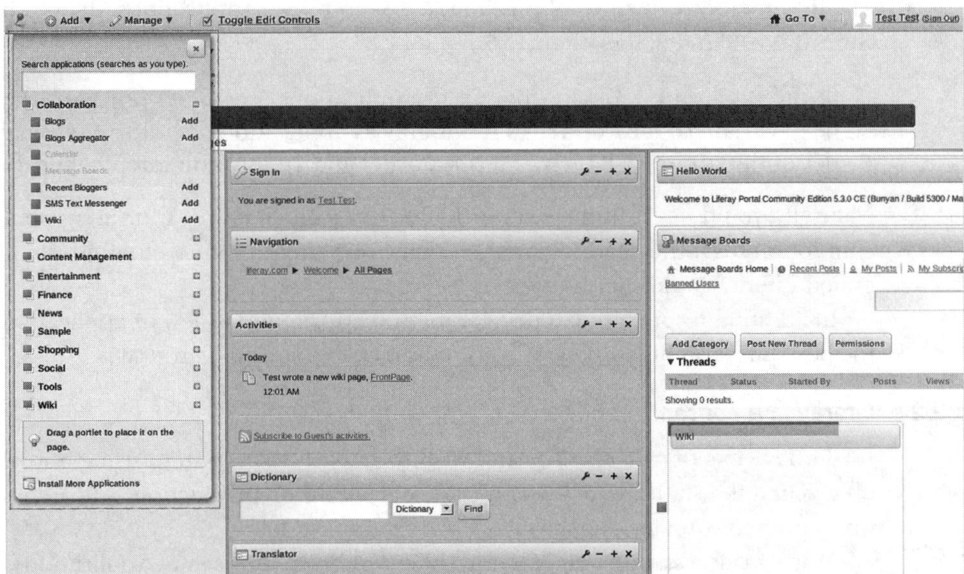

Figure 1.4 Most of the applications have been added. This screen shot was taken while dragging the Wiki application into the column on the right.

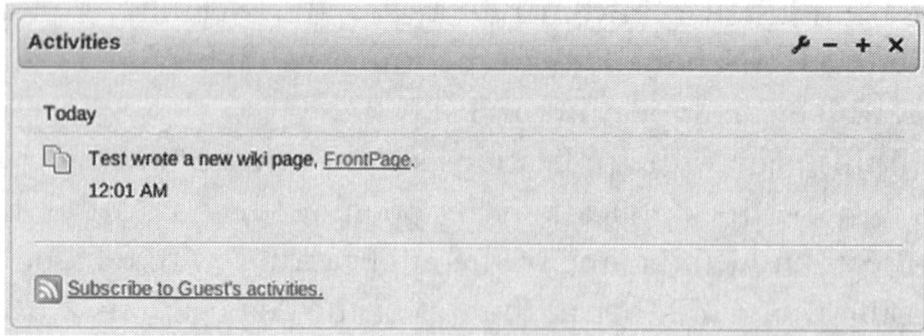

Figure 1.5 Every application in Liferay that uses the Social API can capture activities unique to that application. The Activities portlet displays those activities. Did you really create a new wiki page?

the cool part) Wiki also is integrated with Liferay's Message Boards application, because it borrows functionality from that application to provide comment threads at the bottom of Wiki articles. Those threads use your users' profile information (including pictures) to uniquely identify them in a consistent way throughout your site, which is yet another level of integration.

What about the Calendar application? Again, it's totally integrated, complete with email notifications and more. And it's a full-fledged calendar application that supports export and import of calendar data from other applications.

The other applications are smaller, and I don't want to gloss over them, but you're probably getting the picture at this point. Let me point out one other thing, though: the Activities application. Notice in figure 1.5 what it says.

When you added the Wiki application to your page, you created a top-level wiki page, which is by default called FrontPage. Because the Wiki application uses Liferay's Social API to capture its unique activities, the Activities application can report on what you did (and even provides an RSS feed of activities). If you also use Liferay's Social API, this opens up all kinds of possibilities for your own applications, doesn't it? (We'll cover this API in detail in chapter 6.)

> **NOTE** Because Liferay is a portal, its applications are called portlets. I have been careful so far to refer to them only as applications, but for the remainder of this book, we'll use the terms portlet and application interchangeably.

Naturally, you'd never in the real world create a page like this. Your users would throw conniption fits if they had to navigate such a thing. I just wanted to illustrate how integrated Liferay's applications are.

In addition to providing a development platform and a slew of applications out of the box, Liferay is also a powerful content management system (CMS).

1.2.2 Liferay is a content manager

If you have lots of web content and wish to publish that content using a workflow or on a schedule, statically or dynamically, to staging or production, with templates or without, then you may want to check out Liferay's CMS.

You can access the web-content functions from the same Applications window you've already seen; they're in their own category. But the quickest way to do it is to select Web Content Display from the Add menu. It's on the menu for convenience—if

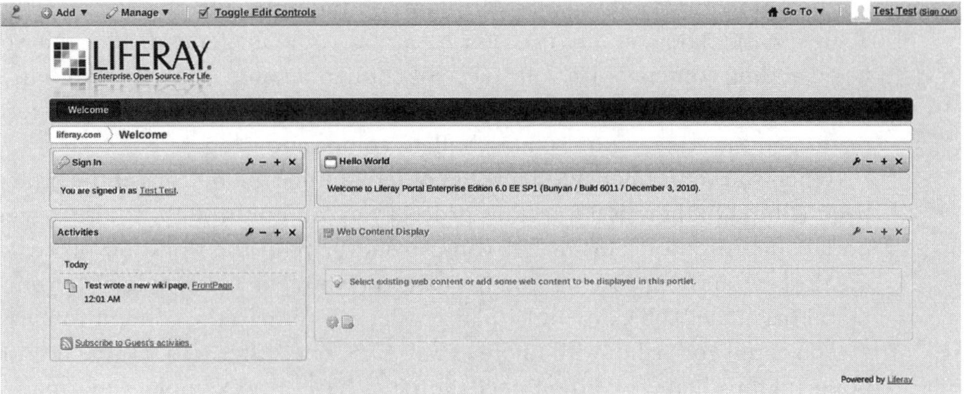

Figure 1.6 The Web Content Display portlet is added, but it has no content (yet). You'll remedy that quickly.

you're building a content-rich web site, you'll use it a lot. After it's added, you can drag it to whatever position on the page you want. Figure 1.6 shows this portlet added to the right column on the page.

The Web Content Display portlet does what its name implies: it displays web content. In order for it to do its job, you'll have to create some web content. You can do that quickly by clicking the Add Web Content icon at lower right. You're then brought to a form where you can add content (see figure 1.7).

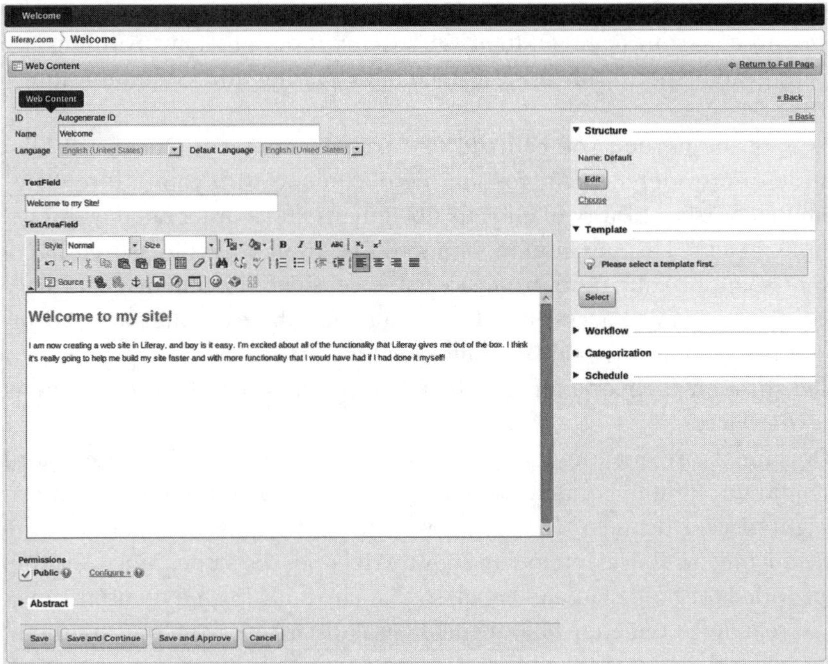

Figure 1.7 Entering content in Liferay's CMS

For now, don't worry about all the options on the right side of the screen (Structure, Template, Workflow, and so on). For basic content management, all you have to do is begin adding content. Give your piece of content a name and a description, and type some content into the editor. Notice in figure 1.7 that you can apply all sorts of formatting in the editor: fonts, tables, bullets, colors, and images.

When you've finished adding your content, notice the buttons at the bottom of the page. Although there is a workflow process you can go through, you're logged in as a portal administrator. This means you can short-circuit the workflow process by clicking the Save and Approve button. Do that, and you'll be brought back to your original portal page; the Web Content Display portlet will contain the content you just added.

You could go further with Liferay's web CMS, but suffice it to say that it's sufficiently powerful for whatever content needs you may have. For example, you can create your own structures with custom fields for your content, as well as templates to go along with your structures to display content exactly the way you want it displayed. You can stage content on a staging server and have it published on a schedule of your choosing. And you can write powerful, scripted templates in XSL, Velocity, or FreeMarker.

You've seen so far that Liferay can be a platform or a UI for your applications, and it can also manage your site's content. The last ingredient that you need, Liferay provides in spades, and that's a way for your users to find and collaborate with each other.

1.2.3 Liferay is a collaboration tool

Liferay Portal is ideal for setting up collaboration environments among workgroups. Whether you call these environments communities or virtual team rooms, Liferay can be used to help your team get their work done. It does this by providing applications that are geared specifically toward document sharing and communicating with one another.

One of the portlets you can add to a page in Liferay is Document Library. This application provides a facility for sharing documents with your entire team. It keeps a complete version history of all your documents and is integrated with Liferay's permissions system. This integration allows you to grant access to shared documents or prevent some of your users from accessing sensitive documents. And if your users need an easier way to access the documents than the web interface provides, Document Library supports WebDAV, allowing documents to be uploaded and downloaded through their operating system's native interface. Figure 1.8 shows both of these interfaces.

Documents are one thing, but what about communication? Liferay's portlets allow for communication in context, so your users can keep all the relevant information in the right place. Document Library allows your users to create discussion threads next to the documents they need to talk about. Wiki does the same thing. And applications are provided for both chat and email, so that currently logged-on users can communicate in real time no matter what their physical distance is from one another.

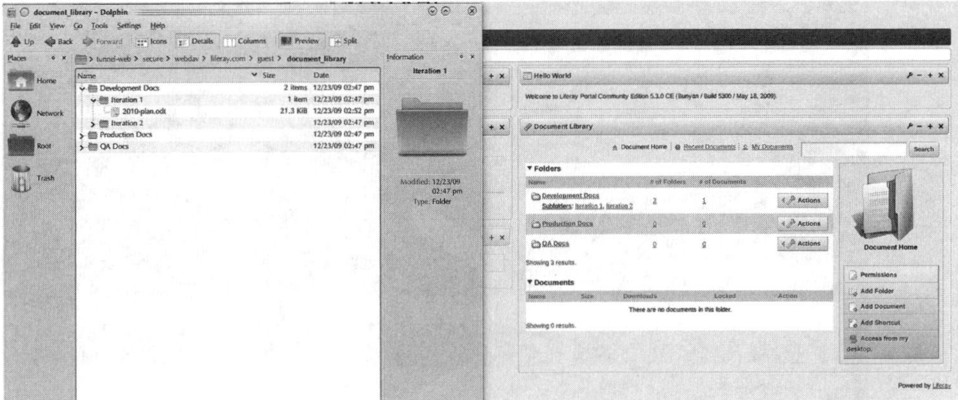

Figure 1.8 Accessing the same folders in Document Library in the operating system via WebDAV or using the browser interface

Need a group calendar? The Calendar portlet can be used for either individuals or for groups. Additionally, users can have their own individual blogs on their own pages, which are then aggregated to the community page using the Blogs Aggregator. This enables you to display a "blog of blogs," allowing your team to stay updated on what everyone is doing. Combining this with Activities makes for a consistent, rolling list of what the team is up to.

All the functionality I've mentioned so far is what is built in to Liferay (and there's more we haven't touched on). But Liferay is extensible, too.

1.2.4 Liferay is anything you want it to be and any way you want it to look

Liferay offers a level of customization that is unparalleled, because you can modify *anything* in Liferay, from simple functionality changes all the way to making your own product out of it.

This book will systematically show you how to write your own portlets so that your applications can be added seamlessly to your Liferay-powered web site's pages in a way that is indistinguishable from the built-in portlets. You'll also learn how to customize Liferay's layout templates so that your page layouts can be what you want them to be. You'll learn about hooks, which let you customize Liferay by substituting your own classes and JSPs in the place of Liferay's. And finally, you'll learn about Ext plugins, which let you override anything in Liferay with functionality of your own.

No discussion of customizing Liferay would be complete without covering themes. Using themes, you can transform Liferay's look and feel to make it look any way you want it to (see figure 1.9). In short, Liferay can be anything you want it to be, and it can look any way you want it to look. This gives you the power and flexibility you need to build your own custom site, with the functionality you need to get it done in a timely fashion.

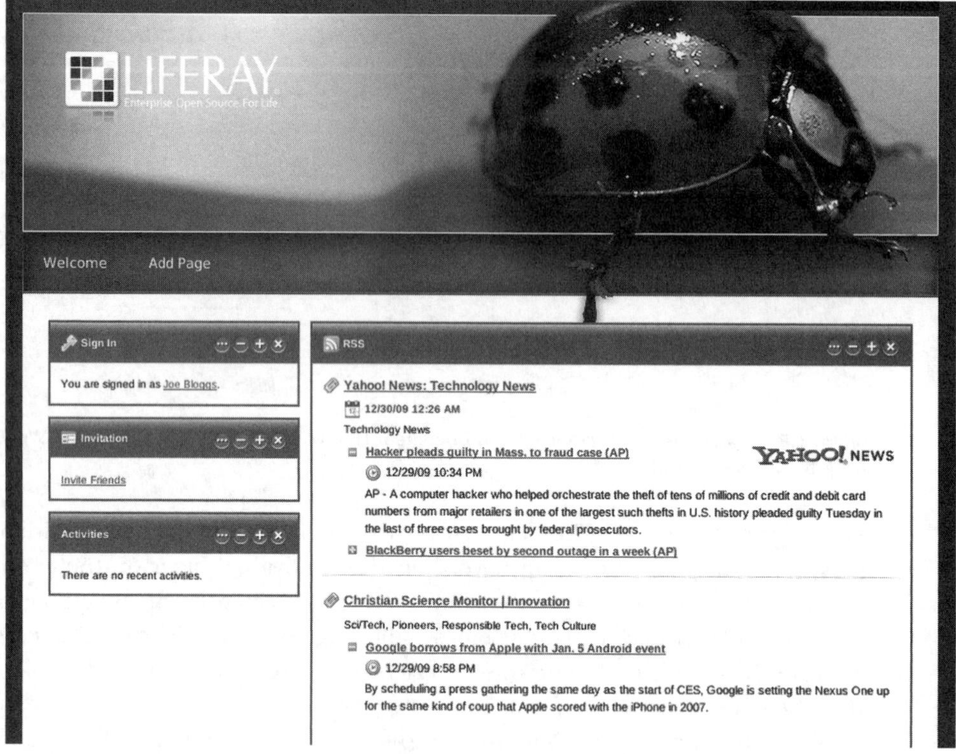

Figure 1.9 Liferay with a custom theme applied. This is just one of many themes in Liferay's community repository.

You can modify Liferay's look and feel using skills you already have. Themes are nothing more than custom HTML and CSS applied to the page. You can design your site just as you would if you were writing the whole thing from scratch—except that you have less work to do, because of Liferay's built-in functionality and rich development platform.

Liferay also comes connected to two repositories of ready-made plugins that extend Liferay's functionality. One of these is a Liferay-provided repository, and the other is a community repository. Figure 1.9 is an example of a theme provided by Liferay's community through the community repository. Liferay's repositories make it easy to both distribute and to install new software that runs on Liferay's platform, as you can see in figure 1.10.

As you can see, a lot of functionality is built in to Liferay Portal, and it's also extremely easy to add functionality to Liferay Portal. You can rest assured that the software you create on Liferay's platform will be easily installed by your users. Let's take a step back now so you can see what you have accomplished with just a few clicks.

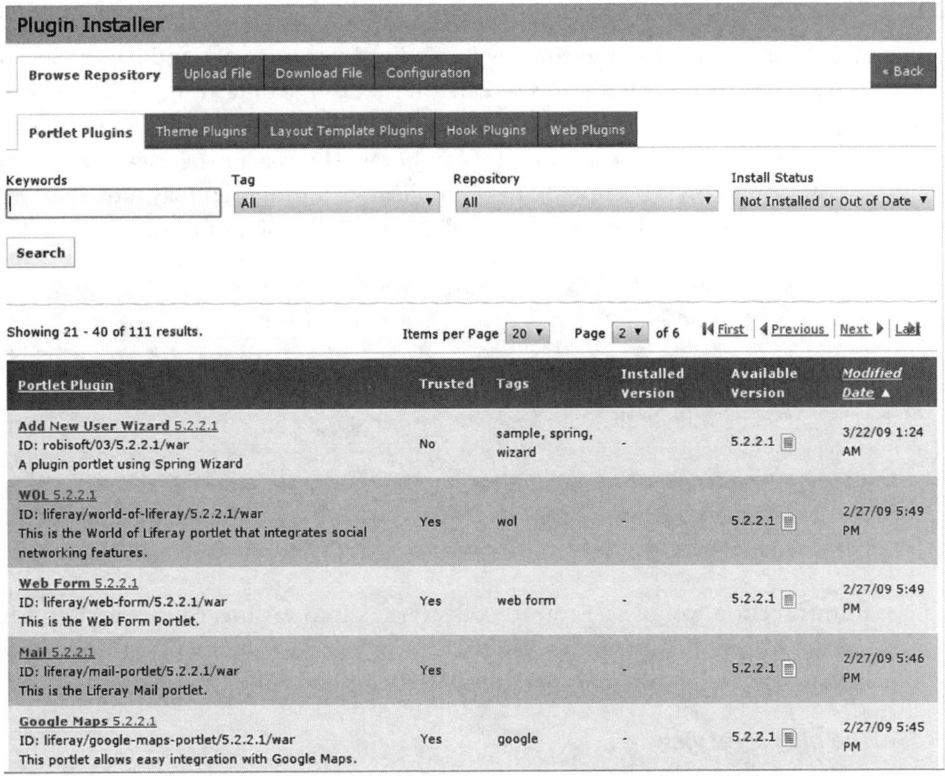

Figure 1.10 Browsing Liferay's plugin repository from within the control panel. Installing any plugin is a simple matter of clicking the plugin and then clicking the Install button that appears with the full description of the plugin.

1.2.5 *What has this little exercise accomplished?*

I hope you see the power that Liferay gives you. In about 10 minutes—and without any additional software—you've created a web site that contains web content, forums, and a wiki; displays users' activities; shares documents; and has a custom look and feel. You didn't have to use separate applications—instead, all that functionality (and more) is included in Liferay. And because you didn't have to use separate applications to implement what you wanted, you didn't have to spend any time integrating those applications. Users get the experience of being able to sign in to your site once and then navigate to the content they have access to, and you don't have to do *anything* to make that work.

Pretty awesome, isn't it?

Obviously, this only scratches the surface. You need ways of organizing and granting permissions to all those users you're going to have. To do this, you'll need to understand the reinforcement beams, foundation blocks, and structures Liferay gives you to support that portal full of users.

1.3 How Liferay structures a portal

Every portal is different in the way it handles users, security, and pages. Because these aspects of a portal aren't covered by the JSR-286 standard, every portal vendor has implemented these concepts differently. If you're going to start developing on Liferay's platform, you'll need to understand how a Liferay portal is configured and organized. Don't worry: it's not all that complicated, although it may look that way at first. When you start using the system, you'll get the hang of it quickly.

> **Liferay 6.0 and Liferay 6.1**
>
> Liferay 6.0 has organizations and communities; Liferay 6.1 has organizations and sites. In the following discussion, I mention organizations and communities quite a bit. If you're on Liferay 6.1, everything I say about communities applies to sites. Organizations don't have pages in 6.1, but sites can be linked to organizations. Sites linked like this in 6.1 are essentially the same as organizations in 6.0. For this reason, the terminology is interchangeable. All 6.1 does is give you a little more flexibility.

In this section, you'll see how to collect users into various categories and what those categories can do for you. You'll also see how Liferay makes it easy to create web pages in your site and how to place content on them.

1.3.1 The high-level view

At its most basic level, a Liferay server consists of one or more portals. Portals have users, and these users can be categorized into various collections. Some of these collections can also have web pages that compose a portion of your site.

You can define many portals per portal server, and each portal has its own set of users and user collections. Figure 1.11 displays this graphically. As shown in the figure, each portal has users, and those users can be organized into several different types of

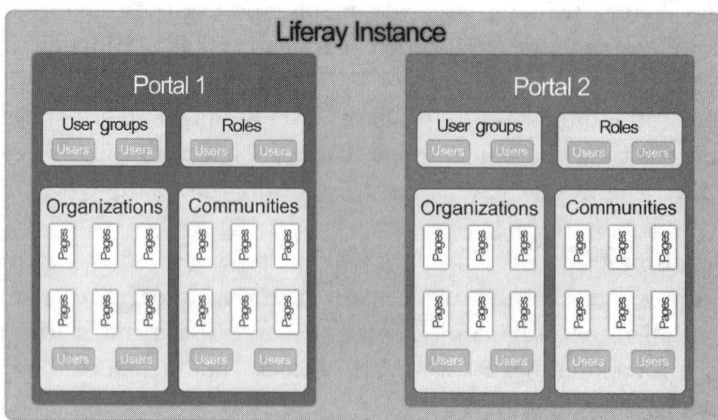

Figure 1.11 A single Liferay Portal installation can host many different portals, all with separate users and content.

collections: roles, organizations, communities, user groups, and any combination of those collections within that portal. Table 1.1 lists the collection types Liferay offers.

Table 1.1 Liferay collection types

Collection type	Description
Role	Collects users by their function. Permissions in the portal can be attached to roles.
Organization	Collects users by their position in a hierarchy. Organizations can be nested in a tree structure. You use organizations to represent things like a company's organizational chart.
Community	Collects users who have a common interest. Communities are single entities and can't be grouped hierarchically. By default, users can join and leave communities whenever they want, although you can administratively change this so users are assigned to communities (or invited) by community administrators.
User group	Collects users for purposes that cut across the portal. User groups are defined by portal administrators.

Roles are inherently linked to permissions. You use a role to collect users who have the same permissions. A good example is a Wiki Administrator role: this role contains users who have permission to administer wikis.

Organizations are hierarchical collections of users. Users can be members of one or many of them, up and down the hierarchy. Membership in organizations gives users access to the pages of that organization. If you picture a hierarchical structure that represents a company called Inkwell, some users might belong to Inkwell, Sales Department, Mid-Atlantic Region. This not only denotes the employees' position in the company, but also gives employees access to the content they need to do their jobs.

Communities are ad hoc collections of users. Users can join and leave communities, and membership in communities gives them access to the pages in the communities of which they're members. You may have a community called Photography: users of your site can join this community to share pictures.

User groups are defined by portal administrators. They're used to collect users for purposes that tend to cut across the portal. For example, you may want to grant some users the ability to create a blog on your site. To do so, you create a user group called Bloggers and create a page template for them that contains Liferay's Blog portlet. Regardless of these users' membership in other collections (as part of a hierarchy of organizations or as having joined several communities), user groups provide a separate way of granting specific access to functions that don't depend on membership in other collections or on specific portal permissions.

That's the high-level view of a Liferay portal structure. Although this describes a powerful system for building your web site, it's only the basics. Let's move on to the next level.

1.3.2 Adding content to a collection with pages

Three types of collections can have not only users, but also pages. Pages are, of course, clickable, navigable web pages. Organizations and communities can have any number of pages defined within them. Pages are organized into *layout sets*, which come in two types: public and private. Each organization or community can have public pages, allowing them to configure a public web site which can be used by members and nonmembers of the organization or community. And they can also have private pages, which are only accessible by the members of the organization or community. You can begin to see how you can build out your site and separate functionality by whoever is accessing the site.

User groups don't have pages per se but rather can have *page templates*. These are configured by portal administrators and become useful for users' personal communities. By default, each user gets a personal community, which itself has public and private layouts. This is a personal web site that the end user can configure (or that can be fairly static—or not exist at all, depending on how you've set up the portal). Portal administrators can create page templates for user groups. These page templates can be populated with the portlets that administrators want users to have. When users are then placed into the user group, any page templates are copied into those users' personal communities. If, for example, you want certain users to have a blog, you can create a Blog page with the Blogs portlet on it in a user group called Bloggers. Users you add to this user group will have this page copied automatically to their personal communities, and they can begin blogging immediately.

If you haven't already figured it out, a roles collection has no pages because roles are used solely to aggregate permissions. For example, you can define a role that has permission to view certain pages. This is how roles work together with organizations, communities, and user groups.

Liferay Portal also has the idea of *scope*, the topic of the next discussion.

1.3.3 Configuring a portlet's scope

Scope allows some of the concepts mentioned previously to be refined. One user collection that is refined by scope is roles. As stated earlier, roles are the only collection to which permissions can be attached. For example, you can create a role called Wiki Administrator. This role has permissions to the Wiki portlet, allowing users in this role to create new wikis and add, edit, delete, and move pages. This role can be created under one of two scopes:

- Portal role
- Community/Organization role

If you create this role as a portal role, then any members of the role have the defined permissions across the entire portal, in any community or organization. This allows users in this role to administer wikis in whatever communities or organizations they have access to. But you can define the role in another way, by scoping it only by community or organization. If the role is defined this way, users have the role's permission in only the community or organization in which that role is assigned. As you can see, scope is important when it comes to how permissions are defined.

Scope also comes into play with regard to certain Liferay built-in portlets. If you go back up to the Dockbar and choose Add > More, you'll see that the portlets are marked with different icons. These icons tell you something about the portlets with which they're associated. But before we go over what they mean, let's look at some portal terminology.

Sometimes I feel like Dr. Seuss when I begin to discuss this topic:

If a portlet in a portal on a page in an org,
Has a data-set saved as its own data-store,
And the data would be different for other users' chores,
We call that a non-instanceable portlet!

And...

When a portlet in a portal saves its data on the disk,
And the user hits the data based on membership in this,
If the portlet is configured to have its own instances,
We call that an instanceable portlet!

All of this has to do with scope.

NON-INSTANCEABLE PORTLETS

Let's stick with the wiki example. If you place a Wiki portlet on a page, based on what I've described, where is that page? Yes, it's in a community or organization. That wiki now belongs to that community or organization.

You can't place another Wiki portlet on the same page, because that portlet is what Liferay calls *non-instanceable.* The portlet's set of data belongs to that community or organization. This is in contrast to *instanceable* portlets, where the set of data belongs to the user. But we'll get to those in a minute.

You can place another Wiki portlet on a different page in that community or organization, but that Wiki portlet will display the same data as the first one (that is, unless you place it in another *scope*, which we'll also get to in a minute). Why is that? Because the portlet's data set has already been created, by placing it on a page in that community or organization. In other words, non-instanceable portlets by default all point to the same instance of data (see figure 1.12).

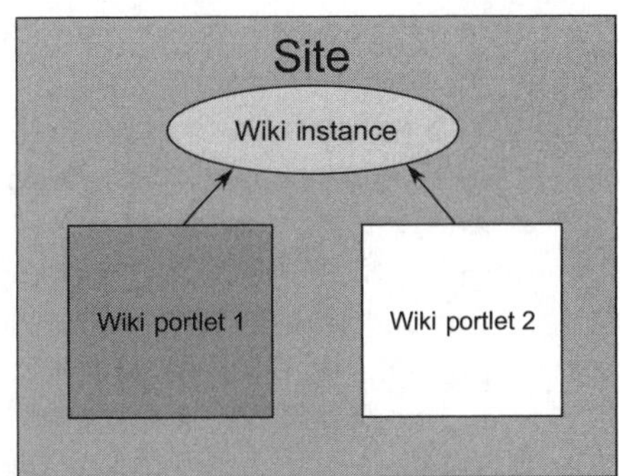

Figure 1.12 A non-instanceable, scopeable portlet has its data scoped by the community or organization to which it belongs. No matter how many times you add it to the community or organization, it points to the same data.

For non-instanceable portlets, the data a portlet contains belongs to the community or organization.

This may seem like a limitation, but it's a powerful benefit. You can have lots of wikis on your site, and they can all be kept completely separate from the others. For example, say you're building a portal for do-it-yourselfers. Your audience likes to build stuff, but the stuff they want to build differs wildly. Your site has communities for many different topics, from home renovation all the way to building model rockets and platforms for model railroads. To serve the needs of these users, you may want to give them a wiki so they can add helpful tips and articles based on their experiences. But the model-rocket group and a home-improvement plumbing group won't have much in common (or maybe they will, depending on the size of the rocket—but that's not what we're focusing on right now). You can easily give them separate wikis in their own communities with Liferay. And, of course, because of Liferay's powerful way of collecting users into communities, all your users will be members of your portal, but not necessarily of the same communities. They will have the freedom to navigate to the content that is most appropriate for them.

INSTANCEABLE PORTLETS

Other portlets in Liferay are *instanceable*. This means you can place as many of them as you like on the same pages in any community or organization, and by default they all have their own configurations. For example, the RSS portlet is designed to show RSS feeds. You can add as many RSS portlets as you want to any page and configure each portlet to display different feeds, because this portlet is instanceable. The Web Content Display portlet is the same way: you can place as many Web Content Display portlets on a page as you wish, and each portlet can display a different piece of web content. When you choose portlets from Liferay's Add > More window, the interface indicates which portlets are instanceable and which are non-instanceable, as shown in figure 1.13.

You can tell which portlet is which in the user interface by looking at the icons in the Add > More window. If there's a green icon with two windows, the portlet is instanceable. If there's a purple icon with one window, the portlet is non-instanceable.

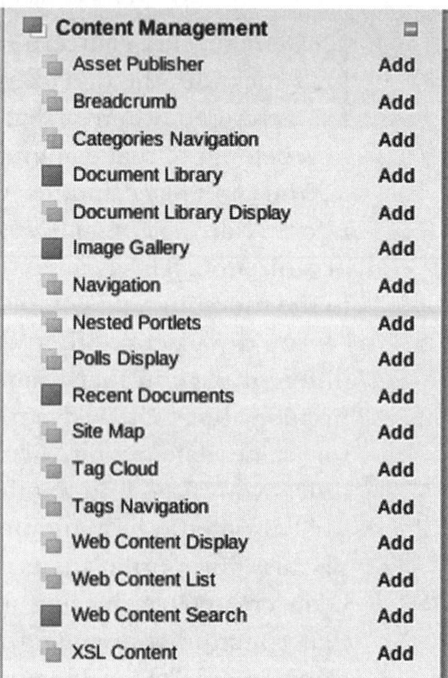

Figure 1.13 Instanceable and non-instanceable portlets in Liferay's Add window. Liferay's UI clearly shows you which portlets can be added multiple times to the same page (instanceable) and which can't (non-instanceable).

PAGE SCOPES

Sometimes, Liferay's default scopes need to be enhanced with more flexibility. I'm going to backtrack a bit on what I said earlier: if you *really* need to have two non-instanceable portlets with different data sets in your

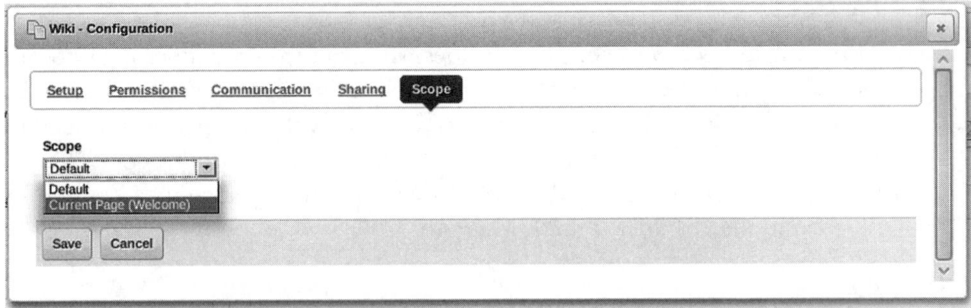

Figure 1.14 Changing the scope in the Wiki portlet

community, you can do that. It's just not configured to be that way by default (and this functionality wasn't available in older versions of the product). This has to be configured on a per-portlet basis.

Still using the Wiki portlet as an example, if you click the configuration icon in the portlet window (which looks like a wrench in the default theme), a menu pops open. Click Configuration in this menu, and all the configuration options for the portlet are displayed. One of the tabs in this window is called Scope (see figure 1.14).

Here, you can change the scope from the default to the current page. This lets you tie the portlet data to the page *in* the community or organization instead of the community or organization globally. What this means is that you can add another page to this community or organization, place *another* Wiki portlet on that page, and set the portlet's scope to *page*, and it will have a different data set than the one on the other page. You can't add multiple wikis to the same page, but you can have multiple non-instanceable portlets per community or organization, all with different data, provided the portlet supports page scopes.

I don't want to delve too much into these concepts at this stage. You'll be taking advantage of scope soon enough in your code. For now, let it all sink in, and we'll turn to something more concrete: how to navigate around Liferay.

1.4 Getting around in Liferay

Liferay's user interface has a philosophy behind it: get out of the user's way. For that reason, it hides a lot of power behind what looks like a simple interface. One of the main UI elements is the Dockbar.

You've already been introduced to some of the functionality of the Dockbar, so let's see what other functions it provides. Figure 1.15 shows the Dockbar in full.

Let's take each element in order from left to right.

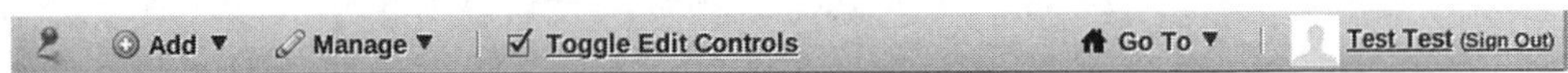

Figure 1.15 Liferay's Dockbar, which appears at the top of every page when a user is logged in

1.4.1 Pin icon

At the far left is a pin icon, which does what you would expect it to do: it pins the Dockbar to the screen so that no matter how far down you scroll, it stays at the top of the screen. This can be helpful if you're working with long pages and need to use the Dockbar's functionality to add portlets to the bottom of the screen. This is a toggle switch, so you can unpin the Dockbar by clicking the icon again.

Next in the Dockbar is the Add menu.

1.4.2 Add menu

You've already seen most of the functionality of this menu for adding applications to the page. It can add pages, too. If you choose Add > Page, a new page is added next to the page you're on, and a field appears, allowing you to name the page. There's a much more powerful page-administration screen, but this function allows you to quickly add pages to your web site as you're working on it.

The next item in the Dockbar is the Manage menu.

1.4.3 Manage menu

Use the Manage menu to manage pages, page layouts, and more. This is where you get access to the interface that lets you group pages in the order you wish—as well as nest them into subpage levels. You can also apply themes to entire layout sets or to single pages. The Manage Pages screen is shown in figure 1.16.

Perhaps the most important item in the Manage menu, however, is the Control Panel.

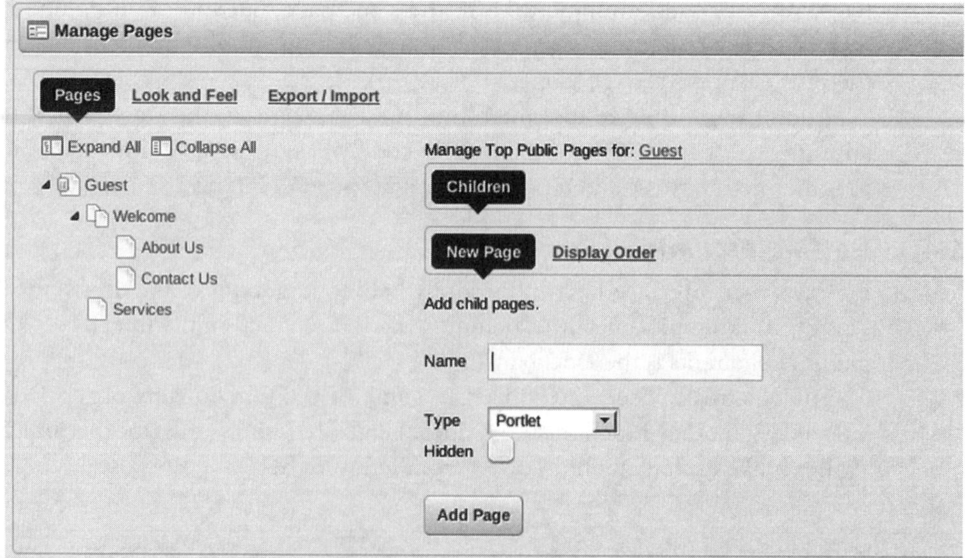

Figure 1.16 The Manage Pages screen allows you to nest pages, change the display order by dragging and dropping pages, change themes, and more.

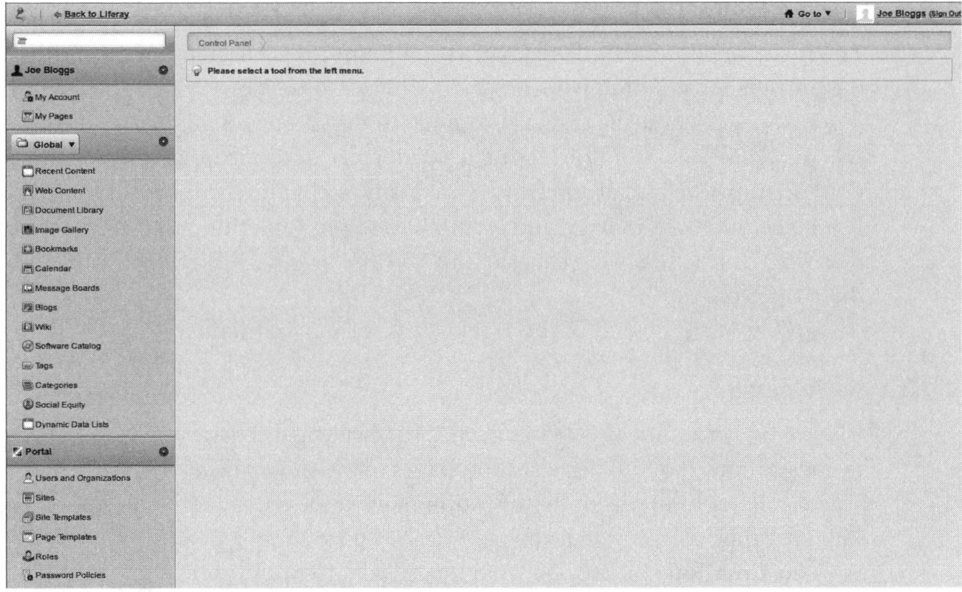

Figure 1.17 Liferay's Control Panel. It's divided into four sections: a section for the current user, a Content section, a Portal section, and a Server section, which isn't visible in the figure.

Liferay's Control Panel is the central location where just about everything can be administered. If you'll be administering a Liferay portal, you'll spend most of your time here. The Control Panel is easy to navigate. On the left side is a list of headings with functions under them. The headings are in alphabetical order, but the functions are in a logical order. Figure 1.17 shows the Control Panel, which purposefully uses a different theme from the default pages so you can instantly tell where you are.

The Control Panel's sections are as follows:

- *User Name*—The first heading is named for the logged-in user (Joe Bloggs in figure 1.17) and is used to manage the user's personal space. Here, you can change your account information and manage your own personal pages.
- *Content*—The Content section contains links to all of Liferay's content-management functions. You can maintain web content, documents, images, bookmarks, and a calendar; administer a message board; configure a wiki; and more. These links are scoped for the particular community from which you navigated to the Control Panel, but this can be changed using the select box.
- *Portal*—The Portal section allows portal administrators to set up and maintain the portal. This is where you can add and edit users, organizations, communities, and roles as well as configure the settings of the portal.
- *Server*—The Server section contains administrative functions for configuring portal instances, plugins, and more.

Next, we'll move to the right on the Dockbar to look at a toggle that becomes very important when you're administering the portal.

1.4.4 Toggle Edit Controls

The next function in the Dockbar isn't a menu; it's a toggle for the edit controls on the portlets. As an administrator, you get to see some icons in the title bars of the portlets on a page. These correspond roughly to the icons you might see in your operating system. There's an icon for closing a portlet, for minimizing it, and for the configuration menu you've already seen (you used this to change the scope of the Wiki portlet). If you're composing a page and would like to see something that more closely resembles what your users will see, you can use the Toggle Edit Controls link to turn off these controls.

Next, toward the end of the Dockbar, is the Go To menu.

1.4.5 Go To menu

Use the Go To menu (shown in figure 1.18) to navigate to the various community and organization pages to which you have access. Each community or organization name appears, along with its public and private layout sets, if they have them.

The final link in the Dockbar takes you to your user account information in the Control Panel.

Figure 1.18 The Go To menu displaying public and private layouts for three communities: the default Guest community, Dog Lovers, and Cat Lovers. Notice that the default community only has public pages, so only one link appears.

1.4.6 User Account

The User Account menu item opens a page where you can change your name and email address, upload a profile picture, and maintain all information about you. You can also sign out of the portal from here.

As you can see, Liferay packs a lot of power in a deceptively simple user interface. The intent of this small tour was to give you an idea of where you can go in Liferay and how to get there as you begin to build your site.

Even though we've now touched on several of the constructs that provide you with the building blocks you'll use to build a web site in Liferay, it's sometimes difficult to begin imagining how your site could be built using these building blocks, because many of the concepts are new and unique to Liferay. So, let's spend a little time figuring out how you can imagine your site running in Liferay Portal.

1.5 Imagining your site in Liferay

Every successful web site does something unique or does something in a way that is better than anyone else has done it before. Although Liferay has tons of functionality out of the box, much of that functionality is a default implementation of features that are under the hood. What do I mean by that? Let me answer by giving you some examples.

Liferay Portal has a collaboration API that contains features allowing users to post discussions, rate items, or tag content. This API has been used to provide everything from the Message Boards portlet, to tagging wiki articles, to rating shopping cart items. This book will introduce you to these APIs so you can consider what kinds of applications you can build with these powerful features.

That, of course, is not the only API we'll cover. You'll also see Liferay's Social API, which gives you the ability to make your applications—indeed, even your entire web site—social. Your users can connect with each other and share content and activities, and even share content and applications on other social networks. Again, the question remains: what will you do when given the power to build such applications?

The point is that when you're finished reading this book, you'll have the ability to make Liferay sing to your tune. And because there's so much power in the Liferay platform, you'll get a head start on building your site because the functionality you need is already built into the platform—all you need to do is use it.

We'll go from the ground up in familiarizing you with Liferay development throughout the course of this book. For now, let's use the information you already have to begin imagining your site from within the Liferay constructs described in the preceding sections. Then later, as you discover the full power of Liferay's development platform, you'll see how easy it is to use Liferay as the foundation of your web site, and you can plan how to integrate the features of your applications with the power of the platform.

Portal design is best done by breaking up your site into small chunks and then designing each chunk individually. That way, you don't get overwhelmed by the largeness of your task, and before you know it, breaking it into smaller chunks has enabled you to design the entire site!

In this section, we'll walk through a design process that is based on a set of forms that I've used with success to design many portals.

> **TIP** For your convenience, you can find the portal design forms as a download along with the book's source code. Print them, and then fill them out as you work through this section.

We'll break the design process into three main portal chunks:

- User groupings
- Organizations and communities
- Content

1.5.1 *Asking the right questions*

The first thing you need to do is figure out how you can divide all your ideas into neat, organized chunks that you can then focus on in more detail. Ask yourself the following questions:

- Will users be given freedom to sign up on the site?
- Will your user groupings be ad hoc, static, or both? (If your user groupings will be ad hoc, you know you'll be creating communities for your users to join and leave.)

- Will some regular users have access to things others won't? (If so, you know you'll be using roles.)
- Will you be delegating administrative tasks to some users? (If so, you may have community or organization administrators.)

When you've answered these questions, go ahead and brainstorm the groupings or collections of users you may have.

1.5.2 Defining and categorizing collections

Don't worry about trying to define user groups, communities, organizations, or roles. Start figuring out some groupings. Some examples are anonymous visitors (potential customers), customers, community members, and specific groupings based on your web site. For example, if you're building a web site for do-it-yourselfers, you may come up with categories such as carpentry, plumbing, model rocketry, or even old computers.

At this point, you should have a good list of groupings. Now combine that list with your answers to the previous questions. Will any of the groups require pages? If so, you know which ones are communities or organizations. Are the groupings associated in any way? If so, how? You're beginning to identify a possible organization hierarchy.

Do some groupings cut across the entire portal (such as a bloggers group)? If so, that's a likely candidate for a user group, and you can begin thinking about whether these users should have page templates defined for them. Or it may be a good candidate for a community, if the grouping should have its own set of pages. When you've categorized your collections of users by organizations, communities, user groups, and roles, you can begin designing your content.

1.5.3 Designing content

Pages can be part of organizations or communities. By default, each can have public pages that everyone can see, as well as private pages that only authenticated members of the organization or community can see. Take each organization and community you've identified and determine the page hierarchy that will exist for it. This may even help you to further define your roles and user groups.

When you're finished with this process, you should have a nice, high-level design for your web site. You may have something very simple, like Liferay's default: one community called Guest for everyone to use. Or you may have something more complex. The point is, it's a start. From here, you can delve into the custom applications you need to write to make your site unique, as well as the customizations to Liferay that you need to make to satisfy all your requirements. That's what the rest of the book is about.

1.6 Summary

Liferay Portal is an ideal choice for building your web site. Using the unique constructs the platform gives you, you can design a site that can handle any situation you can throw at it. Liferay Portal also offers you an unbeatable platform for building web applications, as well as a ton of applications that are already implemented, in order to help jump-start the creation of your site.

In addition, Liferay Portal frees you from the limitations of the old Java portal standard. As an open source project, it enables you to be as lightweight or as heavyweight as you want to be. And because it provides a multitude of tools and utilities for increasing developer productivity, you can get your site done more quickly.

Liferay gives you a powerful paradigm for organizing users and getting them access to the content they want to see. You can use communities, organizations, roles, and user groups to make sure the right content gets to the right people and that restricted content is protected so only the proper users can view it.

Because Liferay is so easy to use, you can create complex web sites quickly. Because all the common applications you need to run a web site are included, it's a simple matter to pick the applications you need and drop them onto your pages. Because no further work is needed to integrate these applications, your time is freed to focus on the applications you need to build that are unique to your web site.

As you move further into this book, you'll learn how to customize Liferay to make it look the way you want it to look, act the way you want it to act, and host the applications you design and write. This will be an interesting journey, and I'm sure you'll find it as rewarding as I have. I hope you'll come along and take the red pill with me—it's going to be an exciting ride.

In the next chapter, you'll install Liferay Portal 6, unpack and configure the Plugins SDK, and dive into creating your first portlet application.

2 Getting started with the Liferay development platform

This chapter covers

- Installing a Liferay bundle and setting up a database
- Setting up the Plugins SDK
- Generating plugin projects
- Writing your first portlet

Liferay provides you with an extremely powerful development platform that allows you to do everything from provide your own portlet applications to customize the platform's core functionality. You probably have all kinds of ideas of what you want to do with your web site: what your users' first experience should be, how they will interact, and even mundane things like what the registration process will be like. You have the ability to define these features any way you want to with Liferay, but you need to understand where and how this is done before you begin implementing your site. This chapter will give you some direction as to where to start and how to proceed.

But first things first: you need to install Liferay and its development environment before you can begin developing anything on it. You'll spend the first part of the chapter installing Liferay and the Plugins SDK, and then you'll move on to your first projects.

Let's get to it!

2.1 Installing Liferay and the Plugins SDK

Liferay Portal is extremely easy to install. Installing the Plugins SDK takes a little longer. The process is pretty much the same on any operating system; I don't want to get into operating system wars here, although I do, of course, have a preference regarding what I use every day (doesn't everybody?). For the purpose of this book, I'll be operating system agnostic, as Liferay is, which benefits everybody.

The first thing you need to do before trying to install Liferay Portal is to make sure you have the Java SDK installed. This is the Java Development Kit (JDK), not the Java Runtime Environment (JRE). Why do you need the JDK? Because you'll be doing *development,* silly.

You need to do more than just install the JDK. On most—if not all—operating systems, the JDK install process doesn't set up one of the most important things for you: the `JAVA_HOME` environment variable. You'll have to do this yourself. In order to explain this, I need to define some rules for operating system agnosticism, which are designed to keep everyone happy. This means not everybody will be happy, of course, but I'm hoping you'll accept the trade of happiness for fairness:

- *Rule 1*—If something is done the same way in all operating systems, I'll explain it only once.
- *Rule 2*—File paths are denoted by forward slashes (/), because more operating systems use that format than anything else.
- *Rule 3*—Operating systems are presented in alphabetical order. This means (L)inux, (M)ac, and (U)NIX all beat (W)indows. This may make Windows users unhappy, but for fairness, see the next rule.
- *Rule 4*—Operating systems of the same family are presented together, unless some difference between them requires explanation (it usually doesn't). For this reason, I'll generally lump Linux, Mac, and UNIX together. Sorry guys, you get to go first, but I'm giving you a new name: *LUM.* (Why LUM? Well, I only had one vowel to work with, and LUM sounds better than MUL, UML stands for Unified Modeling Language, and LMU is unpronounceable.)

You'll perform this install in three easy steps. First you'll install the JDK, so you can get the Java runtime that underlies all the technology upon which you'll be working. Next, you'll install the Liferay/Tomcat bundle. Finally, you'll install Liferay's Software Development Kit, which is called the Plugins SDK.

2.1.1 *Installing the Java SDK*

You first need to install the JDK. Most LUM operating systems make this easy, as you can see in table 2.1. For other operating systems, download the JDK from Oracle and follow the installation instructions.

Table 2.1 JDK installation in LUM operating systems

Mac	Linux	UNIX and Windows
The JDK should be installed by default (that may change now that Apple has left maintenance of OS X's JDK to Oracle).	The JDK is available in your distribution's package manager. Liferay works with both the closed-source JDK and OpenJDK, so you're free to choose whichever one you want.	Download the JDK from Oracle: http://mng.bz/83Ct.

When you have the JDK installed, you need to set that pesky `JAVA_HOME` environment variable.

SETTING JAVA_HOME ON LUM

This is fairly easy for LUM users. First, you need to know where your JDK is installed. You edit a hidden file called `.profile` in your home directory and set the variable to that location. Here's a sample of what that might look like:

```
JAVA_HOME=/usr/lib/jvm/java-6-openjdk
export JAVA_HOME
```

If you're using a non-default shell such as csh or tsh, you won't need the second line, and you should precede the first line with `setenv`. Of course, if you're using csh or tsh, you probably already know that.

SETTING JAVA_HOME ON WINDOWS

On Windows, you need to navigate through the Control Panel to set environment variables:

- *Windows 7 / Vista*—Select Control Panel > System > Advanced Settings > Advanced tab > Environment Variables (think they hid it well enough?).
- *Windows XP*—Select Control Panel > System > Advanced tab > Environment Variables.

The resulting dialog box looks the same on all three versions of Windows (see figure 2.1).

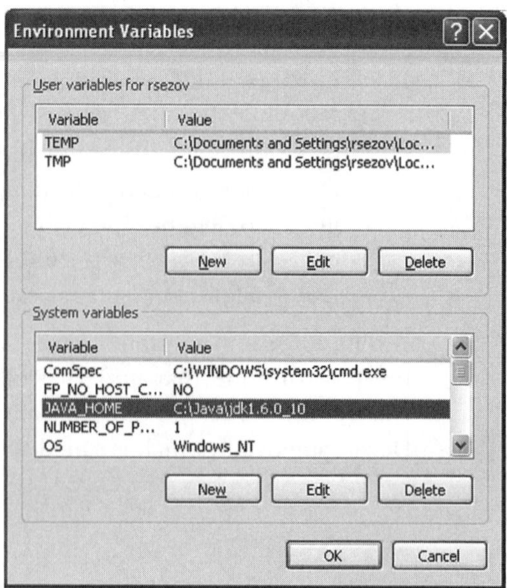

Figure 2.1 This dialog box sets environment variables on Windows operating systems.

Under System Variables, click New, set the `JAVA_HOME` variable to the location where you installed the JDK, and then click OK.

You now have a JDK installed. You can begin all kinds of development using Java, but of course you'll focus on Liferay here. Because of that, the next thing you need to do is install Liferay.

2.1.2 Installing a Liferay bundle

You've made it to the easy part: installing Liferay. You do this in two steps:

1. Unzip the archive.
2. Edit a text file.

Liferay Portal can be installed on a wide variety of application servers and comes bundled with a number of open source application servers. You can choose among GlassFish, JBoss, Jetty, JOnAS, Resin, and Tomcat, and you should use whichever bundle is right for your environment or organization. If you don't know which one to choose, I recommend using the Liferay-Tomcat 6.0 bundle, because Tomcat is small, fast, and takes up fewer resources than most other containers. But any supported container is fine—use the one that is best for your organization.

NOTE We'll use the Tomcat bundle throughout this book.

Before you copy or unzip anything anywhere, let me recommend a way of keeping your code organized. I always create a folder that I'll denote in this book as [Code Home]. Call this folder whatever you want, and put it wherever you want.

Organizing your code on Windows

I recommend that you create the [Code Home] folder in the root of your drive. Why? Because the default Windows file system, NTFS, limits the total number of characters that can make up a path. Although you can nest folders as deeply as you want, the entire path can consist of no more than 256 characters. This means if you put your code in a folder like C:\Documents and Settings\Administrator\Java, you've wasted 44 characters out of your total of 256. Because of Java's package-naming conventions, you can quickly create a path that is too deep for Windows to handle if you don't put your source code somewhere near the root of the drive (consider Liferay's package `com.liferay.portal.security.permission.comparator`, which is already inside the folder structure `portal-impl/src`, for example).

Create a folder called bundles inside [Code Home].

Download the latest Liferay-Tomcat bundle, and unzip it to [Code Home]/bundles. To start Tomcat, navigate to the [Code Home]/bundles/[bundle home]/tomcat-[version]/bin folder, and run the startup command.

On LUM, the command is as follows:

```
./startup.sh
```

Figure 2.2 This sample web site is included with a Liferay bundle. It showcases many of the things described in chapter 1, giving you a nice example of those elements (content management, forums, wiki, and more) working together to implement a single web site.

And on Windows, the command is

```
startup.bat
```

Liferay Portal will start, and your browser will automatically launch so you can view your portal. By default, open source versions of Liferay Portal ship with a sample welcome page and web site included for a fictional company called 7 Cogs, as you can see in figure 2.2. This is a great way to click around and see how an actual implementation works.

You could leave Liferay configured this way; but this isn't the most optimal configuration, because your portal is using an embedded database called HSQL to store its data. It's far better to use a real database. You should also make sure you start with a clean database, not one that contains a sample web site. In the next section you'll take a page from the administration side of things and connect your development server to a standalone, clean database.

2.2 A crash course in Liferay server administration

If you want to set up Liferay as a real server, you'll be best served by checking out Liferay's documentation. Because in this book you're only concerned with having a good development environment, you'll concentrate on connecting the Liferay bundle to a standalone database (hence, *crash course* instead of *full course*). You generally do this for stability reasons: HSQL is great for demos and stuff like that, but if you're going to start doing development, it's far better to use a standalone database. This configuration more closely mirrors a production configuration, and it provides your data with more stability because the database isn't running in the same process as Liferay. And when you're debugging, you may find it easier to use the data-querying tools your database vendor provides with the database.

Liferay also performs better when connected to a standalone database, because a database server is designed to have multiple connections to it at the same time rather than running in-process and queuing up requests. And finally, rather than inside the bundle, the data is stored with the database server, keeping it separate from your Liferay installation.

The first thing you need to do is to prepare your Liferay bundle for development. To do this, you'll remove the sample web site that ships with Liferay so you can start with a clean installation. When that's done, you'll be ready to connect Liferay to a database.

2.2.1 Removing the sample web site

To undeploy an application in the Liferay-Tomcat bundle, all you need to do is navigate to the folder where the applications are stored in Tomcat and delete the folder that contains the application.

NOTE If you're using Liferay Enterprise Edition, you can skip this step.

In a Liferay-Tomcat bundle, Tomcat is located in `[Liferay Home]/tomcat-[version number]`. Inside this folder is a folder called webapps, which is where Tomcat stores the applications that are installed. Go into this folder, and you'll see a list of folders containing Liferay and various plugins.

The folder you want to delete is called `sevencogs-hook`. Remove this folder by either deleting it or moving it to another location on your system. That's all you need to do to prevent the sample web site from being created when Liferay first starts. Make sure you do this any time you're setting up Liferay for development or as a real server, because you always want to start with a clean database. And speaking of databases, now that you've removed the sample web site, you're ready to connect Liferay to your MySQL database.

2.2.2 Setting up a database

Here's the heart of the crash course. What follows is the same procedure you would use to set up Liferay as a real server. The only difference is that you'll be doing everything locally on your machine, whereas in production you would likely have the database and the Liferay installation on separate machines.

Just as I had a recommendation for which bundle to use, I recommend that you use MySQL for this purpose, because it's small, free, and very fast. It's also easily obtained: on Linux, it's available in your package manager. If you're on Mac or Windows, it's easily downloaded and installed.

If you use a different database, there is no reason not to use it as long as you have the resources to run it. Liferay supports all the widely used databases in the industry today.

To install MySQL and its utilities, you need four components: MySQL Server, MySQL Query Browser, and MySQL Administrator. The first component is the server itself, which on Windows is installed as a service. The second component is a database browsing and querying tool, and the third is an administration utility that enables the end user to create databases and user IDs graphically. If you're running Windows or Mac, download these three components from MySQL's web site (www.mysql.com).

When you have a running MySQL server, you need to do two things: set the root password and create your database. By default, MySQL doesn't have an administrative (root) password set. You should definitely set one. To do this, drop to a command line and issue the following command:

```
mysqladmin -u root password NEWPASSWORD
```

Instead of `NEWPASSWORD`, type the password you want (such as `1337h4x0r`). Next, start the MySQL command-line utility via the following command:

```
mysql -u root -p
```

It displays some messages and then a MySQL prompt:

```
Welcome to the MySQL monitor.  Commands end with ; or \g.
Your MySQL connection id is 119
Server version: 5.1.37-1ubuntu5 (Ubuntu)

Type 'help;' or '\h' for help. Type '\c' to clear the current input statement.

mysql>
```

At the command prompt, type the following command:

```
create database lportal character set utf8;
```

MySQL should return the following message:

```
Query OK, 1 row affected (0.12 sec)
```

You'll be back at the MySQL prompt. Type `quit` and press Enter, and you return to your operating system's command prompt.

Linux Alert: MySQL should listen on the network

On some Linux distributions, MySQL is configured so that it won't listen on the network for connections. This is done for security reasons, but it prevents Java from being able to connect to MySQL via the JDBC driver.

To fix this, search for and open the my.cnf file (it's probably in `/etc`, `/etc/mysql`, or `/etc/sysconfig`). There are two ways in which this configuration may need to be changed. If you find a directive called skip-networking in `my.cnf`, comment it out by putting a hash mark (#) in front of it. Or if you find a bind-address directive that's configured to bind only to localhost (127.0.0.1), comment it out by putting a hash mark (#) in front of it. Save the file and then restart MySQL.

Liferay defines the folder it resides in as Liferay Home. The home folder is important to the operation of Liferay. It's the top-level folder that you extracted from the .zip file. Liferay creates certain resources that it needs in this folder, including some subfolders (`data`, `deploy`, and—if you're using Liferay Enterprise Edition—`license`). Next, you'll create a configuration file called portal-ext.properties that you can place here to change some of the Liferay configuration. You'll edit this file to connect Liferay to your database.

2.2.3 Connecting Liferay to the SQL database

To point your Liferay bundle to your database, create a file called `portal-ext.properties` in your Liferay Home folder. This file overrides default properties that come with Liferay. In this case, you'll override the default configuration that points Liferay to the embedded HSQL database.

To connect your installation of Liferay Portal to your database, add the appropriate template for your database to the newly created `portal-ext.properties` file. The template for MySQL is provided as an example here:

```
#
# MySQL
#
jdbc.default.driverClassName=com. mysql.jdbc.Driver
jdbc.default.url=jdbc: mysql://localhost/lportal?
[CA]useUnicode=true&characterEncoding=UTF-8&useFastDateParsing=false
jdbc.default.username=
jdbc.default.password=
```

Provide the username and password to the database as values for the `username` and `password` directives.

NOTE If you're using a different database, you'll find templates for the other databases in Liferay's documentation.

Save the file. You can now start your application server.

If you're JDBC savvy, you'll notice one thing is missing from these instructions: the JDBC driver for MySQL. Liferay includes the MySQL JDBC driver for convenience, so you don't have to worry about downloading it and making it available to your Liferay bundle: you'll find it in the Tomcat bundle in [Tomcat Home]/lib/ext/mysql.jar. If you're using a different database, copy your database's JDBC driver to this folder before starting Liferay.

> **NOTE** For a production machine, you'll also generally connect Liferay to a mail server so it can send mail notifications. Because on a developer machine it's likely that no mail server is running, this step isn't necessary.

Now you can move on to installing the Plugins SDK, which you'll use to create Liferay development projects.

2.3 Setting up the Plugins SDK

Building portlet and theme projects in the Plugins SDK requires that you have a utility from Apache called Ant installed on your machine. This utility is a scriptable build tool, and it's what the Plugins SDK uses to provide its IDE-agnosticism. After you install Ant, you'll be able to install the Plugins SDK.

2.3.1 Installing Ant

If you already have Ant installed, or if it's built into the IDE you'll be using (it's on every IDE I can think of), you can skip this section.

Otherwise, download the latest version of Ant from http://ant.apache.org, and uncompress the archive into an appropriate folder of your choosing.

Next, you need to set two more environment variables as you did for the Java SDK:

- `ANT_HOME` needs to point to the folder where you installed Ant.
- `ANT_OPTS` contains the proper memory settings for building projects.

After you set these variables, there's one more step, because you'll likely want to be able to run Ant from the command line—especially if you're the command-prompt-plus-text-editor type of developer. This step adds the Ant binary to your `PATH` so you can call it from anywhere on the command line. You can use the `ANT_HOME` environment variable as a quick way to add the binaries for Ant to your `PATH`.

Here are the steps in LUM:

1 Modify your .profile file. Assuming you installed Ant in /java, the file should look like this:

```
ANT_HOME=/java/apache-ant-1.8.2
ANT_OPTS="-Xms256M -Xmx512M"
PATH=$PATH:$ANT_HOME/bin
export ANT_HOME ANT_OPTS PATH
```

2 Log out, and log back in. The new settings will take effect.

And here are the steps in Windows:

1. Return to the Environment Variables dialog you used to set `JAVA_HOME`, shown earlier in figure 2.1.
2. Under System Variables, click New.
3. Set Variable Name to `ANT_HOME`.
4. Set Variable Value to the path where you installed Ant (such as `c:\java\apache-ant-1.8.2`).
5. Click OK.
6. Click New again.
7. Set Variable Name to `ANT_OPTS`.
8. Set Variable Value to `-Xms256M -Xmx512M`.
9. Click OK.
10. Click New again, and scroll down until you find the `PATH` environment variable. Select it, and click Edit.
11. Add `%ANT_HOME%\bin` to the end or beginning of the path.
12. Click OK, and then click OK again.

Now, on any operating system, open a command prompt, type ant, and press Enter. If Ant attempts to run and you get a "build file not found" error, you have correctly installed Ant. If not, check your environment variable settings and make sure they're pointing to the directory to which you unzipped Ant.

2.3.2 Installing the Plugins SDK

Now you're ready to install the Plugins SDK. This is even easier than installing Liferay:

1. Go to your [Code Home] folder.
2. You should already have a folder here called bundles, where you installed Liferay.
3. Download or otherwise obtain the Plugins SDK from Liferay (http://mng.bz/KM22).
4. Unzip the file to [Code Home]/plugins.

That's it! It's installed.

The Plugins SDK contains many subfolders. The three you'll be working in most are the portlets, themes, and hook folders. It's here that you'll place your portlet, theme, and hook plugin projects.

2.3.3 Configuring the Plugins SDK

Notice that the Plugins SDK contains a file called `build.properties`. This file contains settings related to where Liferay is installed and where your deployment folder will be. You shouldn't customize this file. Open `build.properties` in a text editor and at the top you'll see a message, "DO NOT EDIT THIS FILE," as shown in figure 2.3.

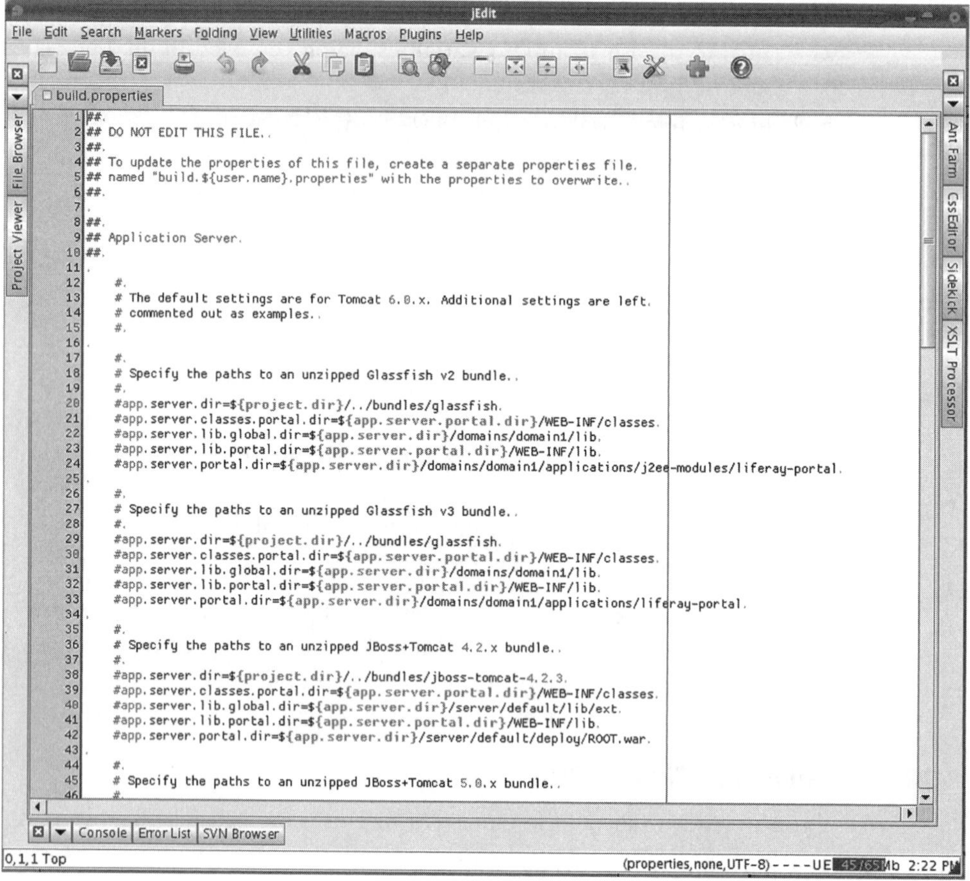

Figure 2.3 Don't edit the `build.properties` file that comes with the Plugins SDK. Override it with your own file, instead.

Instead of customizing `build.properties`, you can create your own file to override it. To do so, create a new file in the same folder called `build.[username].properties`, where [username] is your user ID on your machine. This is the ID you log in with every day. For example, if your user name is cooldude, create a file called `build.cooldude.properties`.

If you're using the default setup described so far, you won't have to do much to configure the Plugins SDK:

1. Open your build.[username].properties file.
2. Add the following line:

```
app.server.dir=[full path to Liferay bundle install]
```

   where `[full path to Liferay bundle install]` is the path to Tomcat in your Liferay bundle.

For example, a Liferay bundle extracts into a folder of its own. Inside that folder is a folder for Tomcat. Use the full path to Tomcat for this directive: this is the server directory. This tells the scripts in the Plugins SDK where everything else is relative to your Liferay install, because all paths (such as the deploy path) are defined relative to the server directory.

3 Save and close the file.

You're ready to begin creating projects.

2.3.4 Configuring a non-Tomcat application server

If you downloaded a Liferay bundle other than the Tomcat bundle, you'll need to customize the properties relating to your Liferay bundle. Copy the section for your application server of choice out of the `build.properties` file and paste that section into your build.[username].properties file, and then comment the section back in.

If you're not using a bundle but have installed Liferay manually on a proprietary application server, you'll have to customize the properties listed in table 2.2.

Table 2.2 Customizing build.properties for application servers

Property	Purpose
`app.server.dir`	Folder into which you installed your development version of Liferay. It's a best practice to put this in a folder called bundles next to the `plugins` folder. This is the default configuration.
`app.server.classes.portal.dir`	Folder containing the WEB-INF/classes folder in the Liferay installation.
`app.server.lib.global.dir`	Folder where .jars that should be on the global class path can be copied.
`app.server.lib.portal.dir`	Folder where the WEB-INF/lib folder in the Liferay installation can be found.
`app.server.portal.dir`	Folder where the Liferay installation can be found.
`java.compiler`	(If you use Eclipse as your development environment, you may find it convenient to modify this property.) Default value is the standard compiler that comes with Java, `modern`. You can also use the Eclipse compiler, ECJ. ECJ is an alternate Java compiler with fast performance that allows you also to replace code in memory at runtime (called *hot code replace*). If you set this option to use ECJ, the Ant script will install it for you by copying ecj.jar to your Ant folder. This may or may not work with the version of Ant that runs from within various IDEs.

After you save the file, you should have a directory structure that looks like this:

```
[Code Home]/bundles/[Liferay Bundle]
[Code Home]/plugins
```

You're now ready to begin developing for Liferay, because you've set up a Liferay bundle and connected a Plugins SDK to it. Congratulations!

Let's dive in and create a portlet plugin.

> **Ext plugin caveat**
>
> If you've been using Liferay's platform for a while, you may be considering using the Ext plugin for most, if not all, development. If I may give you a piece of advice for right now: don't. With Liferay 6 (and to some extent, 5.2), the Ext plugin is recommended only in a few of the rarest scenarios. For a more thorough discussion of this topic, see chapter 9.

2.4 Developing a portlet plugin

By now, you're probably saying something like, "Plugins, plugins plugins! All you can talk about is plugins! I have one simple question: what the heck is a plugin?!?" I hope that's all you're saying, and you're not following it with some variant of "$%&@!" Without any further ado, here's your answer: plugins are .war files.

Yes, that's all they are. If you have ever created a Java web application, you already know about 75% of what you need to know to write a portlet, theme, layout template, or hook. Plugins (portlets, themes, layout templates, hooks, and web modules) are how you add functionality to Liferay, and they have many benefits:

- Plugins can be composed of multiple smaller portlet and theme projects. This reduces the complexity of individual projects, allowing developers to more easily divide project functionality.
- Plugins are completely separate from the Liferay core. Portlet plugins written to the Java standard are deployable on any portlet container.
- Plugins can be hot deployed (that is, deployed while the server is running) and are available immediately. This prevents any server downtime for deployments.

Enough theory. Let's get down to using the Plugins SDK. In this section, you'll see how to use the Plugins SDK with a text editor and Ant. If you're an IDE user, please see appendix A for how to set up projects with Liferay IDE / Studio, Eclipse, or NetBeans.

The Plugins SDK is both a project generator and a location where your projects are stored. You'll create projects in the folders where they belong, and those folders will contain one or multiple projects of that type. You can then open the projects in an IDE or in a text editor to work on them.

If you check individual projects into a source code repository, you'll want to check them out into a fully configured Plugins SDK, because the Ant scripts in the projects depend on Ant scripts in the Plugins SDK for their functionality. Let's see how to create new projects.

2.4.1 Creating a portlet plugin: Hello World

Creating portlet plugins with the Plugins SDK is easy. As noted before, there is a portlets folder inside the Plugins SDK folder. This is where your portlet projects will reside. To create a new portlet, first decide what its name will be. You need both a project name (without spaces) and a display name (which can have spaces). When you've decided on your portlet's name, you're ready to create the project.

From the portlets folder, enter the following command in LUM

```
./create.sh <project name> "<portlet title>"
```

and this command in Windows:

```
create.bat <project name> "<portlet title>"
```

As a first exercise, let's create the classic example, which, of course, is Hello World. Create a portlet with the project folder name hello-world (-portlet will get added to the name automatically) and the portlet title Hello World.

Here's the LUM command:

```
./create.sh hello-world "Hello World"
```

And this is the Windows command:

```
create.bat hello-world "Hello World"
```

You should get a `BUILD SUCCESSFUL` message from Ant. There is now a new folder inside the portlets folder in your Plugins SDK.

This `hello-world-portlet` folder is your new portlet project. This is where you'll implement your own functionality.

At this point, if you wish, you can check the project or your entire Plugins SDK into a source code repository in order to share the project with others. And if you're the command-line-plus-text-editor type of developer, you can get to work right away.

Alternatively, you can open your newly created portlet project in your IDE of choice and work with it there. If you do this, you may need to make sure the project references some .jar files from your Liferay installation, or you may get compile errors. Because the Ant scripts in the Plugins SDK do this for you automatically, you don't get these errors when building with the Plugins SDK. Appendix A shows you how to do this specifically for Liferay IDE, Eclipse, and NetBeans, but this information applies to all IDEs. Of all of them, Liferay IDE makes this process easy and painless.

Regardless of what tool you've used, when you've implemented some functionality, you'll want to deploy the plugin in order to test it.

2.4.2 Deploying the Hello World plugin

You can deploy this portlet to Liferay right now if you want to, because it's already a Hello World portlet (how easy was that?). To deploy the portlet, go into its directory at the command prompt and type the following command (on all operating systems):

```
ant deploy
```

The portlet will be compiled and deployed to your running Liferay server (you do have Liferay Portal running, right?).

If you're watching the logs, you'll see status messages that look like this:

```
04:07:41,558 INFO  [AutoDeployDir:176] Processing hello-world-portlet-
     6.0.0.1.war
04:07:41,560 INFO  [PortletAutoDeployListener:81] Copying portlets for /home/
     me/code/bundles/deploy/hello-world-portlet-6.0.0.1.war
...
04:07:43,263 INFO  [PortletAutoDeployListener:91] Portlets for /home/me/code/
     bundles/deploy/hello-world-portlet-6.0.0.1.war copied successfully.
     Deployment will start in a few seconds.
04:07:44,827 INFO  [PortletHotDeployListener:250] Registering portlets for
     hello-world-portlet
04:07:46,729 INFO  [PluginPackageUtil:1391] Finished checking for available
     updates in 5092 ms
04:07:48,839 INFO  [PortletHotDeployListener:376] 1 portlet for hello-world-
     portlet is available for use
```

When you see the "available for use" message, your plugin is deployed and can be used immediately. This applies for all plugin types except the Ext plugin.

To add the plugin to a page, follow these steps:

1 Log in to Liferay Portal using the administrative credentials (user name: test@liferay.com; password: test).
2 From the Dockbar, select Add > More.
3 Your generated portlet project by default is placed in the Sample category (you'll see how to change this later).
4 Open the Sample category.
5 By default, portlets are generated as instanceable portlets, so your portlet appears with a green icon (see figure 2.4).

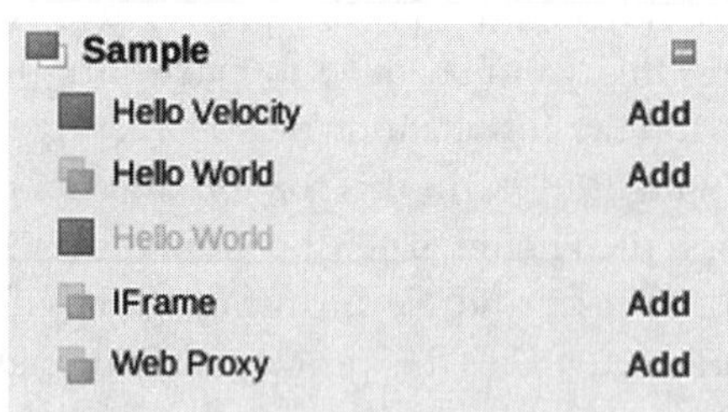

Figure 2.4 The Hello World portlet is deployed. Notice that two Hello World portlets are displayed, with different icons. The grayed-out one is already on the page you're browsing and is unavailable because it's non-instanceable.

6 Drag the portlet onto the page, as shown in figure 2.5.

Figure 2.5 The Hello World portlet. This definitely won't win any awards, but it was easy to create.

Obviously, it's easy to create a Hello World portlet: you didn't even have to write any code. So let's make your portlet do something.

2.5 Making Hello World into Hello You

Hello World examples are all over the internet, and they're used to introduce topics all the time. And maybe I'm just a rebel at heart, but I can't stand them. In my experience, Hello World examples aren't generally all that helpful, because they don't tend to introduce anything useful. So you'll try to add a little functionality using the Portlet API for your first example. You'll call this the Hello You portlet. This portlet will display a standard Hello message when it's first rendered in View mode.

The functionality you're going to add is in Edit mode. Users will enter their names (see figure 2.6), which will each be stored using the Portlet API as a portlet preference, similar to the way a Weather portlet developer would store a zip code in order to display the proper weather map. The portlet will then display each user's name in the Hello message when that user logs in (see figure 2.7).

Figure 2.6 The Hello You portlet lets the user use the portlet's Edit mode to enter a name and then uses that name when displaying its Hello message.

This example will introduce several features of the Portlet API:

- Portlet modes
- Portlet actions and how they're processed
- Portlet preferences

This discussion will provide a better foundation for building portlets than a simple Hello World portlet would provide. There's one additional thing I should mention: as I'm sure you've noticed, I've been throwing around some terms that relate to the Portlet API. If you need a short introduction to the Portlet API (on which the Liferay

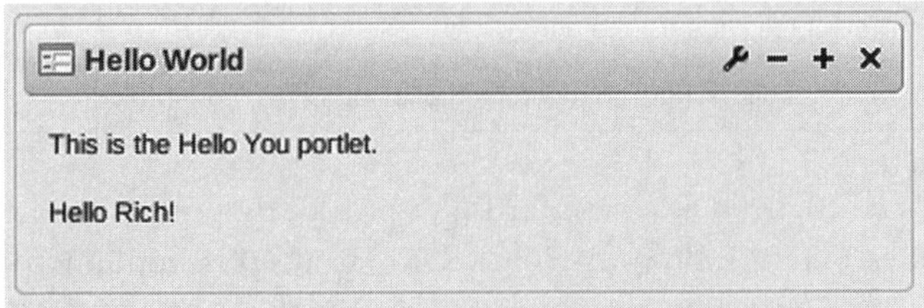

Figure 2.7 The user's name is saved as a portlet preference and is thereafter always displayed when the user logs in to the portal. Each preference is linked to the user who is logged in, so if somebody else logs in and sets a different name, that name will be displayed for that user. If you log in again, your name will be displayed. You get all this for free just by being on a portal platform.

development platform is based), you'll find one in appendix B. It should give you the basic foundation you'll need for this example and the rest of the book, which builds specifically on Liferay as a platform. If you're interested in exploring the Portlet API at a deeper level, I highly recommend Ashish Sarin's book *Portlets in Action* (Manning 2011).

Now, let's get to the portlet.

2.5.1 Anatomy of a portlet project

A portlet project is made up at least three components:

- Java source
- Configuration files
- Client-side files (*.jsp, *.css, *.js, graphics, and so on)

These files are stored in a standard directory structure that looks like figure 2.8. The example is a fully deployable portlet that can be deployed to your configured Liferay server by running the `deploy` Ant task. You did this in the previous chapter.

The various files and folders have different functions, listed in table 2.3.

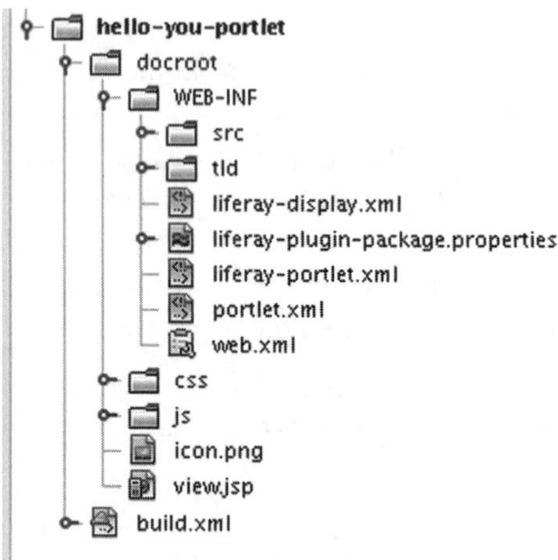

Figure 2.8 This is the folder structure of the Hello You portlet (or any portlet project, for that matter). As you can see, it's simple to follow, and there are places to put all your components.

Table 2.3 Folders of a portlet project

Folder	Description
docroot	The root directory of your application. As you can see in figure 2.2, it has several subdirectories.
WEB-INF	The standard WEB-INF folder for web modules. Because portlets are web modules too, you put your configuration files here. The directory contains several configuration files, which we'll go over separately.
WEB-INF/src	The source code for the portlet.
build.xml	The Ant build script you use to compile and deploy your project.

The default portlet is configured as a standard Java portlet that uses separate JSPs for its three portlet modes (View, Edit, and Help). Only view.jsp is implemented in the generated portlet; the code must be customized to enable the other modes. For Hello You, you'll only implement Edit mode.

In addition to the standard portlet configuration files, the Plugins SDK generates a project that contains some Liferay-specific configuration files (see table 2.4).

Table 2.4 Liferay-specific project configuration files

Configuration file	Purpose
liferay-display.xml	Describes for Liferay the category under which the portlet should appear in the Add > More dialog box.
liferay-portlet.xml	Describes optional Liferay-specific enhancements for Java portlets that are installed on a Liferay Portal server. For example, you can set whether a portlet is instanceable, which means you can place more than one instance on a page. The Document Type Definition (DTD) for this file explains all the possible settings.
liferay-plugin-package.properties	Describes the plugin to Liferay's hot deployer. One thing that can be configured in this file is dependency .jars. If a portlet plugin has dependencies on particular .jar files that come with Liferay, you can specify them in this file and the hot deployer will modify the .war file on deployment so that those .jars are copied from Liferay into the WEB-INF/lib folder of the .war file. This prevents you from having to include .jar files (such as Spring, Struts, and Hibernate) that are already used by Liferay.

Okay; enough lists of what it's possible to do. Let's put these files, directories, and code together to make something.

Open the Hello World project you created in the previous section; you're going to turn it into the Hello You portlet. To do this, you'll create your own portlet class, implement Edit mode in the portlet, and define your first portlet action.

2.5.2 Configuring Hello You

The first thing to look at is the portlet.xml file, which you'll find in the WEB-INF folder. This is the configuration file for the portlet. It contains a line that looks like this:

```
<portlet-class>com.liferay.util.bridges.mvc.MVCPortlet</portlet-class>
```

This defines what Java class implements the portlet. By default, projects are generated to use Liferay's `MVCPortlet`, which we'll get to later. It has certain benefits for the experienced developer, but it also abstracts much of the portlet life cycle from you, which you don't want to do just yet. You'll implement your own portlet class the way the portlet specification recommends so you can get familiar with the Portlet API first. When you understand the basic Portlet API, you'll be free later to move past it to `MVCPortlet` and other frameworks if you wish.

Follow these steps:

1 Because you aren't going to use `MVCPortlet`, you have to change this line to point to the portlet class you're going to create.

2 Modify the line so it looks like this:

```
<portlet-class>
   com.liferayinaction.portlet.HelloYouPortlet
</portlet-class>
```

3 You need to tell the portal that your portlet implements Edit mode as well as View mode (it assumes View mode; otherwise there would be no point to your portlet).

4 Change the `<supports>` tag in portlet.xml so it reads like this:

```
<supports>
    <mime-type>text/html</mime-type>
    <portlet-mode>view</portlet-mode>
    <portlet-mode>edit</portlet-mode>
</supports>
```

5 You may have noticed in portlet.xml another tag called `<init-param/>`. This tag, as you have probably figured out, defines initialization parameters that can be used in your portlet. The default project defines a parameter called view-jsp that defines the location of the JSP file that will be used to display the portlet in View mode. This parameter can thus be used in the portlet class to forward processing over to the view.jsp file in the project. This worked in the initial portlet because this functionality was implemented already in `MVCPortlet`; now that you're using your own portlet class, you'll have to implement it yourself.

6 Below the definition of your portlet class, add the additional initialization parameter under the existing one, like this:

```
<init-param>
     <name>edit-jsp</name>
     <value>/edit.jsp</value>
</init-param>
```

Imagine Darth Vader's voice: "All of your configuration is now complete."

You can now begin implementing the portlet's logic:

1 Create a package in your src folder called `com.liferayinaction.portlet`.
2 In this package, create a Java class called `HelloYouPortlet`.
3 This class should extend the `GenericPortlet` class, which is included with the Portlet API and is available in every portal implementation.

So far, your class should look like this:

```
package com.liferayinaction.portlet;

import javax.portlet.GenericPortlet;

public class HelloYouPortlet extends GenericPortlet {

}
```

You now have the basic structure in place. Next you'll implement the logic for the Hello You application.

2.5.3 Portlet initialization and implementing View mode

First you need to implement the Portlet API's init() method to pull the values from your initialization parameters into your portlet class. All you need to do is define two instance variables to hold these values and then implement the method:

```
protected String editJSP;
protected String viewJSP;

public void init()
    throws PortletException {

    editJSP = getInitParameter("edit-jsp");
    viewJSP = getInitParameter("view-jsp");
}
```

When you add this code, you'll also have to add the import `javax.portlet.PortletException`.

Easy, right? You get access to the `getInitParameter()` method because you're extending an existing class in the Portlet API. Anything that is in those initialization parameters is pulled into these variables.

Now you can implement the default view of your portlet. You do so by implementing a method called `doView()`. As you can imagine, there are similar methods for the other portlet modes, and you'll also be implementing `doEdit()`.

The functionality for this mode is simple: you want to retrieve a preference that may or may not have been stored for the logged-in user. If you don't find a preference, you'll print "Hello!" If you do find one, you'll print a message that includes the preference. For example, if the user's name is Mortimer Snerd, you'll print "Hello Mortimer Snerd!" The following listing shows the code.

Listing 2.1 The default view of your portlet

```
public void doView(
        RenderRequest renderRequest,
RenderResponse renderResponse)
    throws IOException, PortletException {

    PortletPreferences prefs = renderRequest.getPreferences();
    String username = (String) prefs.getValue("name", "no");
    if (username.equalsIgnoreCase("no")) {
        username = "";
    }
    renderRequest.setAttribute("userName", username);
    include(viewJSP, renderRequest, renderResponse);
}
```

src/com.liferayinaction.portlet/HelloYouPortlet.java

You also need to add the following four imports to the top of the class:

```
import java.io.IOException;
import javax.portlet.RenderRequest;
```

```
import javax.portlet.RenderResponse;
import javax.portlet.PortletPreferences;
```

In listing 2.1, you first grab `PortletPreferences` and check to see if the preference is there. The method for getting the preferences wants to know what the preference you're looking for is called as well as a value to return if it can't find the preference. You provide a name for the preference and no for the value to return if the preference isn't found. You could just as easily provide an empty string instead of the word *no*, but I think this is cooler because I couldn't have gotten away with the two extra bytes on my old Timex Sinclair 1000.

If you find a name, you store it as an attribute in the request. If not, you store an empty string. You then forward to the view.jsp file which was previously defined in your portlet.xml file.

Note that you're using some objects here that are similar to `HttpServletRequest` and `HttpServletResponse`, both of which you're likely familiar with. These are similar to their servlet counterparts in that you can set parameters and attributes, retrieve information about the portlet's environment, and more. In this case, you're retrieving an object called `PortletPreferences` from the portlet instance.

Just as you can in a servlet-based web application, you can forward request processing to a JSP from a portlet. And just as in a servlet-based web application, you have to chain a bunch of methods together in order to accomplish it. To make your code neater, you can create a convenience method called `include()`, shown in the next listing, that chains those methods together for you so all you have to do is call this single method (which has a nice, short name) to forward processing to a JSP.

Listing 2.2 Shortening code with an `include()` convenience method

```
protected void include(
        String path, RenderRequest renderRequest,
        RenderResponse renderResponse)
    throws IOException, PortletException {

    PortletRequestDispatcher portletRequestDispatcher =
        getPortletContext().getRequestDispatcher(path);

    if (portletRequestDispatcher == null) {
        _log.error(path + " is not a valid include");

    }
    else {
        portletRequestDispatcher.include(
            renderRequest, renderResponse);
    }
}
```

docroot/WEB-INF/src/com/liferayinaction/portlet/HelloYouPortlet.java

When you add this code, you also have to add the import `javax.portlet.PortletRequestDispatcher`.

Listing 2.2 includes a check to make sure the `PortletRequestDispatcher` you get out of the `PortletContext` isn't null. If it's null, you log that. To use this method, therefore, you also have to enable logging in your portlet.

Liferay ships with Apache's Commons Logging classes, which make it easy to add log entries from your portlets. You only need to add an instance variable to the class for the _log object:

```
private static Log _log = LogFactory.getLog(HelloYouPortlet.class);
```

You also need to add the following two imports to the top of your class:

```
import org.apache.commons.logging.Log;
import org.apache.commons.logging.LogFactory;
```

To complete the portlet's View mode, you have to implement the JSP to which you're forwarding, which is shown here in its entirety.

Listing 2.3 Implementing the JSP for View mode

```
<%@ taglib uri="http://java.sun.com/portlet" prefix="portlet" %>

<jsp:useBean id="userName" class="java.lang.String" scope="request" />

<portlet:defineObjects />

<p>This is the Hello You portlet.</p>
<p>Hello <%= userName %>!</p>
```

docroot/view.jsp

In the first line, you declare the portlet tag library. This again is part of the Portlet API and is a standard across all portals. The next line should look familiar: you pull a bean out of the request you made available in the `doView()` method of your portlet. There's no difference in how this is done versus doing it with a servlet. The tag in the third line comes from the portlet tag library, which you declared in the first line. The `defineObjects` tag registers several objects with the JSP that may be useful: `renderRequest`, `renderResponse`, and `portletConfig`.

About backward compatibility

The tag library declaration is the declaration for Portlet 1.0. This is done for backward compatibility, because you aren't using any features in this portlet that require Portlet 2.0. This portlet, therefore, can be deployed on any Portlet 1.0 container (such as Liferay 4.4.x) or any Portlet 2.0 container (such as Liferay 5.0 and above).

The Portlet API's `RenderRequest` and `RenderResponse` objects correspond to the `HttpServletRequest` and `HttpServletResponse` objects with which you may be familiar, and you've already used these in your portlet class. The `PortletConfig` object corresponds roughly with the `ServletConfig` object used in a servlet, in that it holds data about the portlet and its environment. Because you may need to use these objects in your JSP's display logic, these three variables are defined through the `defineObjects` tag; it's a good idea to always put this tag at the top of your JSPs. Even though you're not using `RenderRequest`, `RenderResponse`, or any of the other variables defined by this tag in this simple portlet, you're starting with a good habit of sticking the tag in there anyway.

Otherwise, the logic of this JSP is simple. You pull the bean you stored in the request and print a Hello message. If the bean has a value, that value is printed after the message; if not, nothing is printed.

View mode is complete. You can deploy the portlet as it is, and it will display the Hello message. Because you haven't implemented Edit mode yet, though, the portlet doesn't have any functionality; that's what you'll add next. In Edit mode, you'll have a form which users will submit. In order to create this form, you'll need to understand how URLs work in portals, because it's probably a departure from what you're used to on other platforms.

2.5.4 URLs in portals are different

Before we jump into the code for Edit mode, I need to tell you something about URLs in portlet applications. Most web developers are used to manipulating the URL directly. That isn't something you can do in a portlet application. In most cases, portlet URLs are linked with portlet actions that cause the portlet to do some processing. You define portlet actions using a special portlet URL object called an `ActionURL`. Because a portlet is a fragment of a page that is assembled at runtime by the portlet container, developers can't define their own URLs as they can in regular web applications. Instead, URLs must be created programmatically. This is a paradigm shift, but it's fairly easy to make the transition. It's important to know that the contents of URLs must be generated by the portal server at runtime. Why? So there are no conflicts between URLs generated by different portlets.

For example, consider a search portlet that sits on a page; this portlet can search for any uploaded content. Say another portlet is placed on that page by a user; it contains a list of customers and has a search box at the top.

If developers knew ahead of time that these portlets would be placed on the same page, they could make sure the URLs to the two search functions were different. But they didn't know ahead of time that a portal administrator would do this, and so both search URLs point to `/search` in the application's context. Can you see how there would be a conflict? Which application's search would be called?

For this reason, the Portlet API provides URL objects. Developers can create URL objects programmatically and even set parameters in them. This allows the portlet container to generate the URL strings at runtime, preventing any conflicts like the one mentioned.

Now that we've gotten that out of the way, you're free to get Edit mode done.

2.5.5 Implementing Edit mode

Because your implementation of Edit mode consists of a simple form that users fill out and submit, you need a URL for the submit button. You have to create one using the Portlet API, as the `doEdit()` method reflects as shown in the following listing. (To learn why, see the previous section.)

Listing 2.4 Implementing `doEdit()` in your portlet

```
public void doEdit(
        RenderRequest renderRequest, RenderResponse renderResponse)
    throws IOException, PortletException {

    renderResponse.setContentType("text/html");
    PortletURL addNameURL = renderResponse.createActionURL();
    addName.setParameter("addName", "addName");
    renderRequest.setAttribute("addNameURL", addNameURL.toString());
    include(editJSP, renderRequest, renderResponse);
}
```

docroot/WEB-INF/src/com/liferayinaction/portlet/HelloYouPortlet.java

When you add the code in listing 2.4, you also need to add the import `javax.portlet.PortletURL`. You create an `ActionURL` and added a parameter to it called `addName`. You then put the URL in the request object so it can be used in the JSP to which you'll be forwarding the processing.

More about backward compatibility

The first line of code in listing 2.4—which sets the content type—is only required in the 1.0 (JSR-168) version of the API. It doesn't hurt anything, so you can leave it in the method to maintain backward compatibility. But if you're using Portlet 2.0 (JSR-286), it's not necessary.

Let's implement the JSP for Edit mode next. Create a file in the docroot folder called edit.jsp. Remember that you earlier pointed to this file by using an initialization parameter in portlet.xml. The following listing shows the edit.jsp file.

Listing 2.5 JSP for Edit mode

```
<%@ taglib uri="http://java.sun.com/portlet" prefix="portlet" %>

<jsp:useBean class="java.lang.String" id="addNameURL" scope="request" />

<portlet:defineObjects />

<form
    id="<portlet:namespace />helloForm"
    action="<%= addNameURL %>"
    method="post">
```

```
    <table>
        <tr>
            <td>Name:</td>
            <td><input type="text" name="username"></td>
        </tr>
    </table>
    <input type="submit" id="nameButton" title="Add Name" value="Add Name">
</form>
```

docroot/edit.jsp

In this code, you first declare the tag library for the Portlet API as you did before. Then you make your URL available to the JSP by using the `useBean` tag to retrieve it from the request object and place it in a variable called `addNameUrl`.

After this is a simple HTML form. Notice that you use a portlet tag called `namespace` in front of the form name. You do so for reasons that are similar to why portlet URLs exist: you could have multiple forms with the same name on the page, and they would conflict with each other. By using this tag, you allow the portal server to prepend a unique string to the front of the form's name, thereby ensuring that no other portlet will contain a form with the same name as yours.

Note also that the form's action is set to the value of the action name parameter in the `ActionURL` you created in the portlet class and then retrieved as a bean in the JSP. This URL contains the parameter `addName`, which will be captured by the `processAction()` method when this form is submitted so that processing can be directed to the right place.

Speaking of `processAction()`, that is the only element missing from your portlet. This method is part of the standard Portlet API; it provides a place where portlet actions can be processed. A default implementation is provided with the API using annotations (see appendix C for further information), but you're going to override it for this portlet and provide your own implementation.

Portlet URLs can be one of two types: `RenderURL` or `ActionURL`. A `RenderURL` tells the portlet to render itself again. Whatever parameters have been defined for the portlet at that time take effect, and the portlet redraws itself. In contrast, an `ActionURL` immediately forwards processing to the `processAction()` method, where logic can be in place to determine which action has been taken by the user, and then the appropriate processing can occur. You'll implement your own version of this so that you can see how it works, and later you'll take advantage of other (better) implementations. Because you have only one action, the logic is pretty simple, as you can see in the next listing.

Listing 2.6 Processing a portlet action

```
String addName = actionRequest.getParameter("addName");
if (addName != null) {
    PortletPreferences prefs =
 actionRequest.getPreferences();
    prefs.setValue(
"name", actionRequest.getParameter("username"));
```

```
        prefs.store();
        actionResponse.setPortletMode(PortletMode.VIEW);
}
```

docroot/WEB-INF/src/com/liferayinaction/portlet/HelloYouPortlet.java

You also need to add the following two imports to the top of your class:

```
import javax.portlet.PortletPreferences;
import javax.portlet.PortletMode;
```

This code searches for an `addName` parameter in the portlet's `ActionRequest` object. You created this parameter earlier as part of an `ActionURL` in the `doEdit()` method, which you forwarded to edit.jsp and then used as the action for the form. Having the form's action point to this URL directs processing to the four lines of code in the `if` statement. In larger portlets, this `if` block would be longer (under this implementation), because there would be multiple actions whose names you'd have to check in order to determine which action needed to be performed.

The `username` parameter is found in the request, because it's a field on the form. The Portlet API is then accessed in order to store a preference for this particular user. The preference is called `name`, and you use whatever value was in the parameter. Yes, I know: you're not doing any field validation. Normally you would do that before storing anything, but I wanted to keep this example as simple as possible. This key/value pair is now stored for that portlet/user combination.

The last thing this code does is set the portlet mode back to View mode. When that is done, `doView()` is called, and the user sees the "Hello <name>" message.

To summarize: you now have all the processing for the portlet's Edit mode in place. The doEdit() method creates a URL with the action name parameter `addName`. Processing is then forwarded to the edit.jsp file, where this parameter is used as the action of a form. The form contains one field in which users type their name. When the form is submitted, the portlet's processAction method runs and retrieves the action's `name` parameter, which has the value `addName`. Checking for this value leads to code that stores the name the user submitted as a `PortletPreference`. To keep the example simple, you don't implement any validation on the data submitted.

So far, you've seen the code piecemeal, but it's sometimes easier to see how things work by looking at the whole thing. The following listing shows the entire portlet. I can only present an entire code example here at the beginning of the book, because it's fairly simple (of course, the source for the whole book is available online); look it over to make sure you understand the portlet's structure.

Listing 2.7 The complete Hello You portlet

```
package com.liferayinaction.portlet;

import java.io.IOException;

import javax.portlet.ActionRequest;
import javax.portlet.ActionResponse;
import javax.portlet.GenericPortlet;
```

```
import javax.portlet.PortletException;
import javax.portlet.PortletMode;
import javax.portlet.PortletPreferences;
import javax.portlet.PortletRequestDispatcher;
import javax.portlet.PortletURL;
import javax.portlet.RenderRequest;
import javax.portlet.RenderResponse;

import org.apache.commons.logging.Log;
import org.apache.commons.logging.LogFactory;

/**
 * The Hello You portlet, a simple example demonstrating
 * Portlet Modes, Portlet Actions, and Portlet Preferences.
 *
 * @author Rich Sezov
 *
 */
public class HelloYouPortlet extends GenericPortlet {

    public void init()
        throws PortletException {

        editJSP = getInitParameter("edit-jsp");
        viewJSP = getInitParameter("view-jsp");
    }


    public void doEdit(
            RenderRequest renderRequest,
RenderResponse renderResponse)
        throws IOException, PortletException {

        renderResponse.setContentType("text/html");
        PortletURL addNameURL = renderResponse.createActionURL();
        addName.setParameter("addName", "addName");
        renderRequest.setAttribute("addNameURL", addNameURL.toString());
        include(editJSP, renderRequest, renderResponse);
    }


    public void doView(
            RenderRequest renderRequest,
RenderResponse renderResponse)
        throws IOException, PortletException {

        PortletPreferences prefs = renderRequest.getPreferences();
        String username = (String) prefs.getValue("name", "no");
        if (username.equalsIgnoreCase("no")) {
            username = "";
        }
        renderRequest.setAttribute("userName", username);
        include(viewJSP, renderRequest, renderResponse);
    }

    public void processAction(
            ActionRequest actionRequest,
```

```
ActionResponse actionResponse)
        throws IOException, PortletException {

        String addName = actionRequest.getParameter("addName");
        if (addName != null) {
            PortletPreferences prefs = actionRequest.getPreferences();
            prefs.setValue(
"name", actionRequest.getParameter("username"));
            prefs.store();
            actionResponse.setPortletMode(PortletMode.VIEW);
        }
    }

    protected void include(
            String path, RenderRequest renderRequest,
            RenderResponse renderResponse)
        throws IOException, PortletException {

        PortletRequestDispatcher portletRequestDispatcher =
            getPortletContext().getRequestDispatcher(path);

        if (portletRequestDispatcher == null) {
            _log.error(path + " is not a valid include");
        }
        else {
            portletRequestDispatcher.include(
                renderRequest, renderResponse);
        }
    }

    protected String editJSP;
    protected String viewJSP;

    private static Log _log = LogFactory.getLog(HelloYouPortlet.class);

}
```

docroot/WEB-INF/src/com/liferayinaction/portlet/HelloYouPortlet.java

As you can see, not a lot of code is needed to implement this functionality. But in later chapters, you'll see how Liferay's platform helps you streamline things even more. For now, congratulations! You've completed writing your first portlet. Let's deploy and test it next.

2.6 Deploying and testing your portlet

When you generated this project with the Plugins SDK, it came with its own Ant script, which makes it easy to build and deploy the project. If your IDE supports Ant, you can deploy the project from within your IDE. If you're not using an IDE, you can run a simple command to deploy your project. Follow these steps:

Start your Liferay server. Again, if you're using an IDE and have followed the instructions from appendix A, you can do this from within your IDE. When Liferay has started, keep a window open to Liferay's console so you can watch the deployment take place.

Run the `deploy` task from the Ant build script. To do this from the command line (on any operating system), issue the following command from the project folder:

```
ant deploy
```

When you receive the `BUILD SUCCESSFUL` message, turn your attention to the Liferay console. You should see your portlet deploy right away.

Your new portlet is now indistinguishable from any other portlet deployed in Liferay. Go to http://localhost:8080, and log in using the administrative credentials:

User Name: test@liferay.com
Password: test

Now you're ready to test the portlet and see how it works:

1 Go to the Dockbar, and choose *Add > More*. You'll see many categories of portlets displayed. Open the Sample category; the Hello World portlet is listed there. Drag it off the list and drop it in the far-right column if it's not there already. If you deployed the portlet immediately after you generated it, it should already be there.
2 Your portlet is displayed. Close the Add > More dialog box by clicking the red X in its upper-right corner.

   The default message of "Hello!" is displayed in the portlet. This is the way it's supposed to function: you haven't set your portlet preference yet, so the portlet doesn't know your name.
3 To get to Edit mode, click the button in the portlet's title bar that has a wrench on it, and then click the Preferences link (Liferay Portal displays a portlet's Edit mode as a Preferences menu item). You're brought to the portlet's Edit mode, and edit.jsp is displayed.
4 Type your name, and click the Add Name button. Your portlet preference is stored, and because you changed the mode of the portlet back to View in the `processAction` method, the portlet redisplays itself in View mode. Because your portlet preference is now set, the portlet displays the name you entered.

You're probably asking yourself: why is my portlet in the Sample category, and how do I change it? And by the way, I made Hello World into Hello You; can I change the name? The answer to both questions is *yes*, and you'll do that next.

2.6.1 Changing the portlet's category and name

When you added the portlet, you had to select it from the Sample category in the Add > More dialog box. You also had to add the Hello World portlet, but now the portlet is called Hello You. The portlet is in a suboptimal category because the generated portlet project defaults to this category, and the portlet has the wrong name because you created Hello World early in the chapter. Let's see how to create your own category for your portlet—this is easy to do. At the same time, you'll rename the portlet Hello You. You can do these things by editing three XML files:

- portlet.xml
- liferay-portlet.xml
- liferay-display.xml

Remember: these three files are deployment descriptors for your portlet project. The portlet is declared and defined in portlet.xml, which is the descriptor defined by the standard. The other two files are Liferay-specific descriptors: liferay-portlet.xml extends portlet.xml with many extra settings specific to Liferay. You'll be using this file extensively as you proceed through the book. The other file, liferay-display.xml, is also specific to Liferay and is used to define where in the menu your portlet is displayed. You'll edit these three files next.

RENAMING THE PORTLET

First, let's change the name of the portlet. Open portlet.xml, which is in the WEB-INF folder. You need to change the name in two places in this file. The first takes effect at a system level, and the second takes effect for the portlet title.

Find these two lines in the file:

```
<portlet-name>hello-world</portlet-name>
<display-name>Hello World</display-name>
```

Change them so they read like this:

```
<portlet-name>hello-you</portlet-name>
<display-name>Hello You</display-name>
```

Next, find the `<portlet-info>` section of the file:

```
<portlet-info>
    <title>Hello World</title>
    <short-title>Hello World</short-title>
    <keywords>Hello World</keywords>
</portlet-info>
```

Change it so it reads like this:

```
<portlet-info>
    <title>Hello You</title>
    <short-title>Hello You</short-title>
    <keywords>Hello You</keywords>
</portlet-info>
```

Finally, open liferay-portlet.xml, which is in the same folder. Find the following line, which is in the `<portlet>` tag:

```
<portlet-name>hello-world</portlet-name>
```

Change it so it reads as follows:

```
<portlet-name>hello-you</portlet-name>
```

Upon the next deployment, the portlet will have the correct title. But don't deploy it yet—you still have to move it to another category.

CREATING A CUSTOM CATEGORY

In the same WEB-INF folder, you'll find a file called liferay-display.xml. This file controls the category under which your portlet appears in the Add > More dialog box. Open this file, and you'll see the following code:

```
<?xml version="1.0"?>
<!DOCTYPE display PUBLIC "-//Liferay//DTD Display 6.0.0//EN"
➥ "http://www.liferay.com/dtd/liferay-display_6_0_0.dtd">

<display>
    <category name="category.sample">
        <portlet id="hello-world" />
    </category>
</display>
```

Change the category name to something else, such as `My Portlets`:

```
<display>
    <category name="My Portlets">
        <portlet id="hello-you" />
    </category>
</display>
```

Now, deploy the portlet again. Refresh the page. You'll see that an interesting thing has happened to your portlet, as shown in figure 2.9.

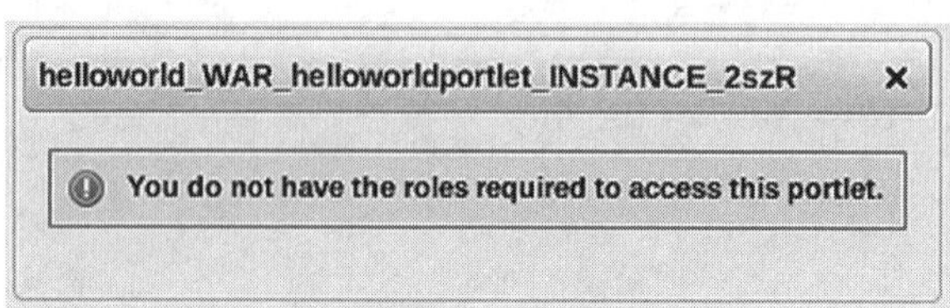

Figure 2.9 Aaarrgh! What happened to my portlet?!?

The portlet no longer exists.

2.6.2 Telling Liferay about a renamed portlet

You renamed your portlet Hello You, but Liferay thinks a Hello World portlet is on the page because, well, you put it there. Of course, now Liferay can't find the Hello World portlet, so it displays an error message. You need to remove the portlet from the page and add the newly renamed portlet to the page instead. Follow these steps:

1. To remove the portlet, click the X in the upper-right of the portlet window.
2. Select Add > More. The new category is displayed, and it includes your portlet (see figure 2.10).
3. Drag the portlet over to the page.

Figure 2.10 Your portlet is both renamed and in a custom category that you created.

4 When you do, notice what it says (see figure 2.11).

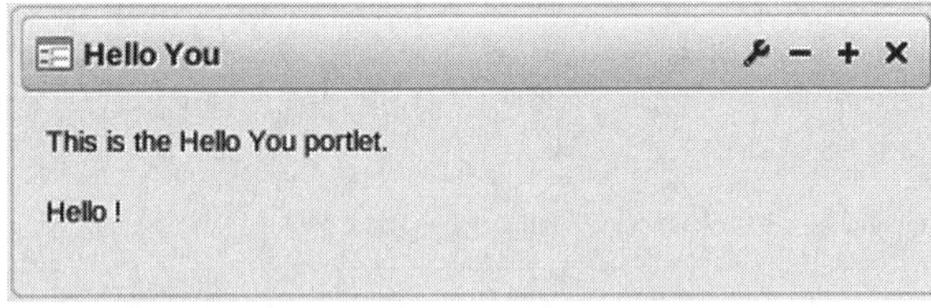

Figure 2.11 The Hello You portlet seems to have amnesia. What happened to your portlet preference?

The preference you stored earlier, when the portlet was named Hello World, was saved for that portlet. Now that you've renamed that portlet, it no longer exists. For all intents and purposes, even though the code is exactly the same, this is a new portlet according to Liferay, so Liferay treats it as such. The portlet's title bar also properly displays Hello You, because you configured it that way in the portlet.xml file.

Be aware that if you rename portlets after they've already been deployed and users have used them, you may have a bunch of orphaned preferences in your database—and unhappy users who have to reset them. That's one reason why the deployment descriptor includes both a portlet name and a display name. You can change the display name as many times as you want. But if you change the portlet name, the portal will think it's a different portlet.

2.7 Summary

The Plugins SDK provides a full development life cycle for all plugin types. You can generate projects, work on them, deploy them, and package them. Because plugins are simple .war files and the Plugins SDK uses Ant for all its operations, it's tool, application server, and operating system agnostic—you're free to use the tools of your choice to create Liferay development projects. I'm sure you'll enjoy using the Plugins SDK and that it will be a useful tool for you to create Liferay plugins.

In this chapter, you created a portlet according to the Java standard. You saw how a portlet is structured as well as the different configuration files that make up a portlet web module. You also saw how to deploy and test the portlet, as well as change which category it appears under in Liferay's Add > More menu. This portlet doesn't do much, but it serves as a good introduction to several highly used features of the Portlet API, such as portlet modes, portlet actions, and portlet preferences. You've so far used only Portlet 1.0 features in this portlet, so you can deploy it on containers that support either Portlet 1.0 (Liferay 4.4.x and below) or Portlet 2.0 (Liferay 5.0.x and above). The skills you've learned here will provide a good foundation for creating more complex portlet projects.

You'll focus next on projects more like those you might encounter every day. To do this, you'll begin building a site for a fictitious company. In that way, you'll be able to simulate the common challenges faced by developers and knock them out one by one.

Part 2

Writing applications on Liferay's platform

Now we get to the fun stuff. In part 2, you'll learn about using Liferay's platform and APIs to write portlets that do pretty much anything you want.

Chapter 3 starts with the data layer. You'll learn how to use Liferay's Service Builder tool to create tables, SQL, and the service layer from a single XML file. You'll also customize a generated DAO layer to create functional services.

In chapter 4, you'll use Alloy UI tag libraries to build an interactive, form-based application that allows users to interact with your data. This application will be fully internationalized and integrated with Liferay's permissions system.

Chapter 5 introduces Liferay themes, which let you customize the way Liferay looks so you can match your web site's design. You'll also learn about layout templates.

In chapter 6, you'll learn how to use Liferay's Social API to connect users. You can publish data from your applications as social activities and integrate Liferay applications with social networks like Facebook.

Collaboration is the focus of chapter 7. You'll learn how to use Liferay's assets, workflow, tags, categories, ratings, and discussions to create applications that foster collaboration.

When you've completed reading part 2, you'll be a seasoned Liferay application developer, ready to use Liferay's platform effectively to create modern, robust web applications.

3 A data-driven portlet made easy

This chapter covers

- Designing a portlet for database interaction
- Liferay's Service Builder code generator
- Architecting applications using DAOs and DTOs
- Defining relationships using Service Builder

For the rest of this book, we'll use a case study to illustrate the examples. You'll be building a site for a fictitious company. The example company is a combination of two things I love: fountain pens and technology. Normally, you wouldn't expect those to go together, but as you'll see, this may be possible (at least in theory).

If you're a business entrepreneur who wants to pursue this idea, you have my blessing. Just know that I had the idea first, so I'll be looking for my cut.

3.1 Introducing Inkwell: a case study

The purpose of using a case study as the unifying example site you'll be building is simple. This approach avoids abstract examples (like the ones in the preceding chapter) and lets you build real-world solutions like those you'll build for your own web site. This case study will help you apply concretely all the concepts we'll cover. We'll start with a data-driven portlet, which arguably is the most common type of application that developers work on every day. First let's look at some background information about the case study, and then we'll go over the design of your first portlet.

3.1.1 *Company profile: Inkwell*

Inkwell is a company dedicated to bringing back fountain-pen technology because it's better. In today's world of workers with desk jobs, repetitive-stress injury is a real danger. Couple that with the wide use of workstations that are ergonomically incorrect, and it can spell disaster.

Inkwell is bringing fountain-pen technology not only to the realm of physical pen and paper, but to the digital realm as well. Patented handwriting-recognition technology allows the information worker to write on a simple pad and paper, while all the time the words are being transcribed to a computer up to 200 feet away. And because fountain-pen technology is being used, repetitive-stress injury isn't a factor for data entry.

It's well known that modern pens cause hand injury due to the amount of pressure the user must exert to press down on the paper in order to place a mark on the page. With a fountain pen, only a slight amount of pressure is necessary, making the fountain pen an ideal choice for data entry.

Inkwell has many models of pens from which to choose, all updated with the latest technology. Some of these include the following:

- *USB data-entry pen*—These pens offer 512 MB to 10 GB of flash RAM.
- *PDA pen*—A screen is projected onto paper, and the user writes on it to enter data (see figure 3.1).
- *Pen-top*—An entire computer system consisting of a base model and a pen. This is a full-featured computer, and the pen can act as either a data-entry tool or a mouse.
- *Traditional fountain pen*—These pens are meant for everyday use.

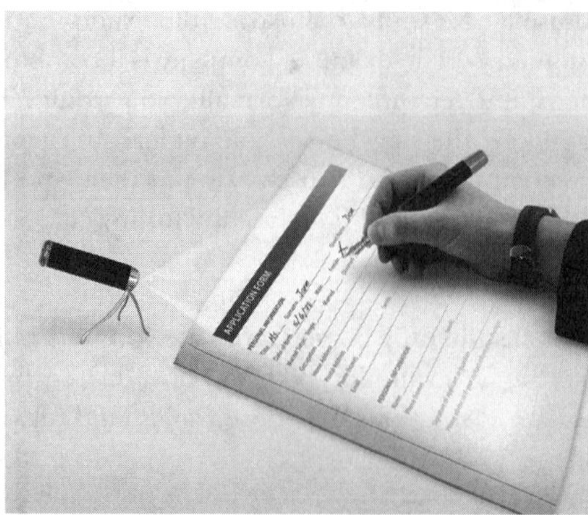

Figure 3.1 Inkwell's PDA pen product image. The company intends to use this image on the web site; currently it appears in paper brochures.

Now, you may be asking: aren't fountain pens messy? Not any more. Inkwell's patented leak-proof technology is backed by a five-year warranty, protecting users from leaks. And many of the company's technology pens don't use ink at all! You can feel safe knowing that there won't be a mess when you use Inkwell pens.

3.1.2 What Inkwell needs in a web site

Inkwell has several partnerships with various technology vendors. Rather than engineer new technology itself, Inkwell employs several teams of programmers and hardware engineers who handle technology integration with fountain pens. Each of the vendors has a special relationship with Inkwell, but they shouldn't need to know about each other. For this reason, Inkwell needs a secure extranet that can facilitate this relationship.

To enable its employees to better communicate, collaborate, and coordinate, Inkwell also needs a full-featured intranet that provides the communication and collaboration tools that users need. The intranet needs to allow for easy sharing of data, but its security model must also let Inkwell protect certain sensitive data so that only authorized persons can view it.

Inkwell also needs a robust internet site to facilitate marketing and support of the company's products and foster Inkwell's relationship with its community of users. To accomplish this, Inkwell has chosen Liferay Portal to handle its web-based activity. A single Liferay install will handle all three of its sites.

3.1.3 Inkwell's high-level portal design

The Inkwell web team went through the process outlined in chapter 1 to design the company's portal. At the end of the process, they had a design that they could express in the diagram shown in figure 3.2.

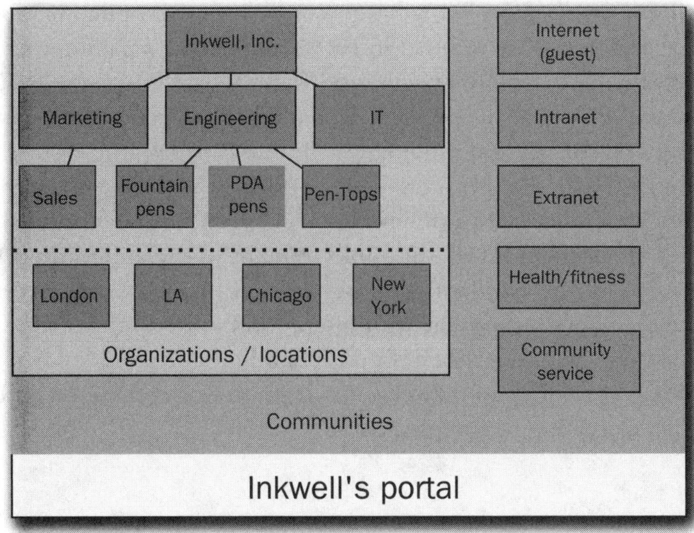

Figure 3.2 Inkwell's high-level portal design

This diagram represents the end state of Inkwell's portal project. We'll be looking at only the first phase of this project, which is a subset of the eventual full functionality. This first phase is designed to produce two outcomes:

- Take advantage of the low-hanging fruit, or functionality that can be implemented quickly that also provides core necessary features of the site. You'll do this by starting with the applications that form the site.
- Help the members of the development team get up to speed on the various features of the Liferay platform by first implementing site functionality that is less complicated and then moving to more complicated features toward the end of this phase and future phases of the project. You'll do this by moving on to Liferay customizations after you implement the applications.

Inkwell's organization chart will be mirrored using Liferay's organizations and locations (locations are leaf nodes in the hierarchical tree of organizations). Because of space considerations, not all organizations are depicted in the diagram. Corporate users will be registered in the portal as members of Inkwell, Inc., the organization for which they work (such as Sales, IT, or a product team), and the company's corporate location. Inkwell is headquartered in London, with small sales offices in New York, Los Angeles, and Hong Kong, so most of the employees are in the London location. Future locations are planned as the company grows.

Because both organizations and communities can have pages, this design allows individual organizations within the company to maintain the company's web pages on the company's intranet or the internet. For the first phase of this project, however, organizations won't have any pages of the company's own. Instead, an intranet community will be created for internal users to access.

3.1.4 Inkwell portal phase 1 requirements

The Inkwell portal will be a comprehensive web site covering all online needs of Inkwell, Inc. The current web site (developed in HTML with some separate web applications) no longer meets the company's needs, and Inkwell desires to have a site that's much more interactive and easier to manage. This will help the company to maintain better contact with its customers and will increase its ability to sell its products.

Additionally, Inkwell wishes to replace its intranet with something that is a bit more interactive and can be maintained by nondevelopers. Currently the corporate intranet consists of a home page done in HTML with links to many of the applications (hosted in separate environments and maintained by separate teams) that employees need. Inkwell will replace the main intranet site with Liferay and will over time migrate existing application functionality to the portal. End users will be responsible for maintaining the company's pages, freeing up Inkwell's web team to work on migrating existing applications and, later, creating new applications.

The following components of the Inkwell portal will be completed in phase 1:

- Internet-facing web site
- Intranet site
- Extranet site for partners

INKWELL INTERNET

Responsibility for creation of the internet site will be divided over two teams: a content-management team and a development team. The content-management team will be responsible for designing the pages and page layouts, as well as the content types, structures, and templates. Content will be created in collaboration with the Marketing department. The development team will be responsible for creating the applications (that is, portlets) that have been identified as in scope for phase 1.

INKWELL INTRANET

In the same manner as for the internet site, the content-management team will handle the management of the pages and site content on the intranet. The development team will handle the applications.

INKWELL EXTRANET

The extranet site will be a special community for interaction with Inkwell's suppliers and distributors. Currently, no applications are slated for phase 1 of the extranet. Liferay's Document Library portlet is sufficient to provide patches, fixes, and data sheets for companies with which Inkwell collaborates.

Your first task will be to work on Inkwell's internet site. The Inkwell development team has decided that the Product Registration portlet is the number-one priority.

3.2 Designing the Product Registration portlet

The lead developer on the team decided that the product registration application would be a good starting point for the development team to get their feet wet with Liferay. Providing this application early in the development phase of the project will also help the content-management team as they determine where on the site the application will be placed. Let's look at the design of this portlet so you can determine your first implementation steps.

3.2.1 A blueprint of the portlet

The team gathered the requirements from Marketing and came up with the design for the product registration form shown in figure 3.3. This design is based on the registration card that comes with products when customers purchase them.

When the team began the design process based on this form, they realized that many of the values on this form were already captured during Liferay's registration process. It was decided that the application will prefill the form with values from the

Inkwell Product Registration Form

First Name:
Last Name:
Street Address 1:
Street Address 2:
City:
State:
Zip:
Country:
Email Address:
Phone Number:
Date Purchased:
Date of Birth:
Gender: Male Female
How did you hear about this Inkwell product?

TV Advertisement
Radio Advertisement
TV News
Magazine Article
Retail Store
Friend/Family member
inkwell.com
Other web site
Trade Show
Home Shopping

Where did you purchase your Inkwell product?

Retail Store
TV Shopping Network
Gift
Catalog
Online Retailer
inkwell.com
Other

Product Serial Number:
Product Type:

Fountain Pen
PDA Pen
Pen Top

Figure 3.3 A design mockup of Inkwell's product registration form. This form appears on a business reply mail card that is shipped with all of Inkwell's products.

Liferay database if a user with an ID fills it out. Otherwise, the form will be blank. This prevents users from having to register on the site in order to register a product.

Additionally, every field that Liferay requires for user registration will be required on the form. This will allow the development team to add a check box to the form later, asking if the user wants to register on the site using this information. When the team is more familiar with the Liferay API, it's assumed that it will be a fairly easy process to register users who check this box.

The next step was to pass the form to the database group so they could complete the table design.

3.2.2 Designing the database tables

The form requirements were passed to the database analysts. They came up with the following table design.

The Product table shown in table 3.1 stores the types of products that can be registered. Employees of Inkwell will maintain the data stored here via an interface provided by the portlet application.

Table 3.1 Product table

Field name	Field type	Length	Description
productId	Integer	19	Unique key for each entry
productName	Varchar	75	Name of product
serialNumber	Varchar	75	Serial number mask of product

The Product Registration User table stores user data from the registration form (see table 3.2). The data can also be linked to a Liferay user account, as shown by having both a unique ID for this portlet and Liferay's user ID field stored here. This allows users to register products without becoming members of the site, and it allows users who are members to have their registration information linked with their accounts.

Table 3.2 Product Registration User table

Field name	Field type	Length	Description
regUserId	Integer	19	Unique key for each entry
userId	Integer	19	Liferay user ID, if applicable
firstName	Varchar	75	First Name
lastName	Varchar	75	Last Name
address1	Varchar	75	Address, first line
address2	Varchar	75	Address, second line
city	Varchar	75	City
state	Varchar	75	State
postalCode	Varchar	75	Postal code
country	Varchar	75	Country
email	Varchar	75	Email address
birthDate	DateTime		Birth date
gender	Integer	3	Gender

The Registration table stores the registration data and links it to a user ID from the Product Registration User table (see table 3.3). Because it's likely that one customer may purchase several different products, the registrations are stored in a separate table from the users. The Product Registration User table will only be used for those who decide *not* to obtain a portal user ID. The portal data will be considered to override data in the Product Registration User table.

Table 3.3 Registration table

Field name	Field type	Length	Description
regId	Integer	19	Unique key for each entry
regUserId	Integer	19	Registered User ID
datePurchased	DateTime		Date the product was purchased
howHear	Varchar	75	How did you hear about this product?
wherePurchase	Varchar	75	Where did you purchase your product?
serialNumber	Varchar	75	Product serial number
productType	Varchar	75	Product type

Now that you know what you need to build, let's get started building it.

3.2.3 *Defining portlet modes and generating the project*

The Product Registration application will contain two portlets. The administrative portlet will be completely hidden from regular users of the portal. Administrators will be able to use it in the Control Panel to add products for which users can register. These products will appear in the combo box on the form so users can pick them when registering their purchased products.

The registration portlet will display a Register button. If users click the button, they will be brought to a form like the mockup in figure 3.3. The users can fill out the form, and the data will be stored in the tables. After the data is stored, a message will be displayed to the users, thanking them for registering their products. This portlet will be placed on Inkwell's public site in an appropriate location for users to find.

The first thing you want to do, if you haven't already, is generate a new portlet project in the Plugins SDK. Use the following command on LUM:

```
./create.sh product-registration "Product Registration"
```

And use this command on Windows:

```
create.bat product-registration "Product Registration"
```

Import the project into your IDE of choice. You won't touch the portlet just yet. Instead, you'll go right to using Service Builder to generate persistence objects, and you'll implement the portlet when your database layer is complete.

3.3 *Generating DB code with Service Builder*

If you're an experienced developer, it's likely that you've dealt with a data-driven application before. Liferay ships with a tool called Service Builder that makes the creation of data-driven applications easy. I highly recommend that you use Service Builder when writing applications on Liferay's platform, because it will help get you going quickly. How? By generating a lot of the database plumbing code for you, so you can concentrate on your application's functionality.

We'll look first at the need that Service Builder responds to. Then you'll see how to configure and run Service Builder to create the layer of code that handles your database transactions.

3.3.1 Filling a definite need

In the old days, we used to roll our own JDBC code by getting a connection to the database and implementing methods that had SQL embedded in them. Of course, this approach was fraught with problems. Code maintenance was difficult, because developers had to map predefined SQL statements with application functions that tended to change frequently. Another issue was that applications became tightly coupled to the database layer, presenting challenges to the portability, stability, and maintainability of applications. Applications became susceptible to SQL injection attacks. Developers had to worry about opening and closing connections manually, managing transactions manually, and a slew of other things. Doing this well required a lot of knowledge about both databases and good programming practices.

Next, everyone tried container-managed Enterprise Java Beans (EJBs). Using these, developers could rely on the EJB container to manage connection pools, dynamically insert parameters, and more. Often, application server vendors supplied tools for generating these automatically, including the queries the application needed. The problem was that using these tools tied applications to a particular application server and a particular database against which you generated the EJBs—as well as to the tool that was used to generate the code. Additionally, developers found that EJBs were complex to write and carried too much overhead in memory and processing power. Another solution was needed, and again, it was open source to the rescue.

The Hibernate project took a different approach. In order to offer developers a simple API to access data from a database, Hibernate does what is called *object/relational mapping* (ORM). Using this paradigm, database tables are *mapped* to Java objects. This frees developers to work with the Java objects with which they're already familiar, and Hibernate takes care of persisting those objects to the database—any database that Hibernate supports. Your database code is now much more easily applied to multiple databases, allowing your application to be deployed on a wider variety of systems. This is sort of an oversimplified description of Hibernate—because it includes a lot more—but it should be sufficient for your needs. If you want to learn more about Hibernate, I strongly recommend you pick up *Java Persistence with Hibernate* (Manning, 2006).

Another technology that is sometimes used with Hibernate but is also useful for many other things is Spring. If you've ever heard of dependency injection (DI), then you've probably heard of Spring. And if you haven't heard of DI, it's a totally different way of thinking about how your application is organized. For example, all Java developers are familiar with this sort of thing:

```
MyObject something = new MyObject();
```

This is one of the first things you learn in a Java class: using a constructor to create a new instance of an object. You do this all the time without thinking about it, if you're writing Java code. But what if, before writing something like this, you first asked this question: Does the class I'm working on *depend* on a fully instantiated object of this type? In other words, when you create the instance of this object, do you have to then populate it with a bunch of stuff that you already have? If so, you'll like DI.

Interacting with a database manually requires that you juggle a bunch of objects that you set up once and then keep passing around: `Connection`, `DataSource`, `DriverManager`, and so on. Whenever you make a query, you need to pass around these objects (some of which wrap the others) in order to get something out of the database. Hibernate requires the same sort of things, but the objects are slightly different (`SessionFactory`, `DataSource`, `HibernateProperties`, and more). Wouldn't it be great if you could set up all this stuff once and then *inject* already instantiated versions of these objects into the classes that need them? Wouldn't it be great if you could automatically instantiate objects with known parameters and then inject those objects into other objects that need them? With Spring, you can. DI lets you define objects that depend on other objects, and Spring can inject instances of those needed objects automatically. All you need to do is configure an XML file that defines those dependencies. Using Spring, you can automatically inject a Hibernate session into the code that queries the database, saving you from having to get an instance of the session every time you want to ask the database for data. The combination of Spring and Hibernate is used all the time, because it makes developers' jobs a lot easier.

But let's go one step further. What if you could define a database table in an XML file and, from that definition, generate all the Hibernate configuration, all the Spring configuration, finder methods, the model layer, the SQL to create the table on all leading databases, and the entire Data Access Object (DAO) layer in one fell swoop? That's what Service Builder gives you. Figure 3.4 illustrates this.

This tool is an excellent database persistence code generator that makes it easy to define new tables and to manipulate the data through select, insert, update, and delete operations. It uses a combination of standard technologies that Java developers use every day—Hibernate and Spring—to do this. It's important to note that all of Liferay's internal database persistence is generated using this tool, so it's a proven tool that produces code that is suitable for enterprise deployments.

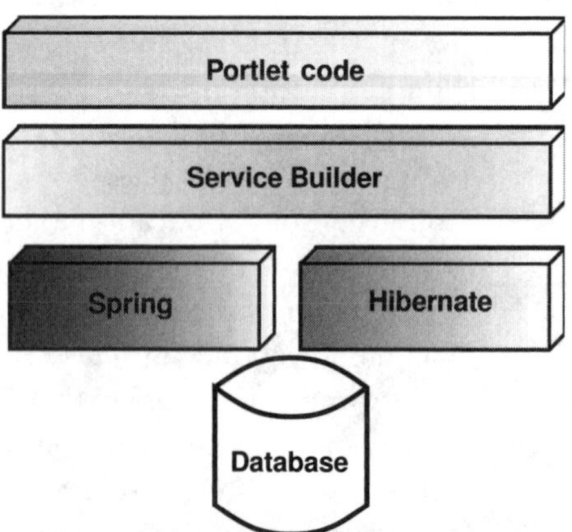

Figure 3.4 Service Builder is a tool that sits on top of Hibernate and Spring, automatically generating both configurations for you—along with the Java code necessary to persist your entities to the database.

If you're like me, I know what popped into your head immediately when I said "code generator." It was, "Oh, no. Code generators are bad." And then you began justifying that statement with many sound, accurate, and excellent arguments. Believe me, I agree with you. But Service Builder is different. You'll see why in more detail as the rest of the chapter unfolds, but let me reassure you—from one code generator hater to another—Service Builder is designed to *enable* you to write custom code, not prevent it. It takes care of the mundane stuff you hate writing anyway. *That* is a code generator I can get on board with, and I think you'll like it too.

You'll use Service Builder to generate the database tables that were defined earlier for Inkwell's Product Registration portlet, and then you'll use it for database persistence. To start, you have to create the one XML file that is the key to generating the rest of the code.

3.3.2 Creating the service.xml file

Create a file called service.xml in the WEB-INF folder of your project. This file will contain the table definitions. You'll populate this file with all the information Service Builder needs to generate the SQL to create the tables—for all the databases Liferay supports—as well as database persistence objects you can use in your Java code.

You'll start with the simplest of the tables: Product. Use the following code to define the table for Service Builder.

Listing 3.1 Defining a table using Service Builder

```
<?xml version="1.0" encoding="UTF-8" ?>
<!DOCTYPE service-builder PUBLIC
➥ "-//Liferay//DTD Service Builder 6.0.0//EN"
➥ "http://www.liferay.com/dtd/liferay-service-builder_6_0_0.dtd">

<service-builder package-path="com.inkwell.internet.productregistration">   ← Global Information (1)

  <author>Rich Sezov</author>

  <namespace>PR</namespace>

  <entity name="PRProduct" local-service="true" remote-service="false">   ← Define entity (2)

    <column name="productId" type="long" primary="true" />   ← Define columns (3)

    <column name="productName" type="String" />
    <column name="serialNumber" type="String" />

    <column name="companyId" type="long" />
    <column name="groupId" type="long" />

    <order by="asc">
      <order-column name="productName" />
    </order>

    <finder name="G_PN" return-type="Collection">   ← Define finder methods (4)
      <finder-column name="groupId" />
      <finder-column name="productName" />
    </finder>
```

```
    <finder name="GroupId" return-type="Collection">
      <finder-column name="groupId" />
    </finder>

    <finder name="CompanyId" return-type="Collection">
      <finder-column name="companyId" />
    </finder>

  </entity>

</service-builder>
```

docroot/WEB-INF/service.xml

This file is pretty easy to read, so we'll attack it section by section instead of line by line.

GLOBAL INFORMATION

You can define the Java package into which Service Builder generates the code that powers this database table ❶. Service Builder also generates Javadoc, and the name you place in the `Author` tags in ❶ winds up in the Javadoc as the author of the code. By default, tables you define with Service Builder go in the Liferay database. To set them off from the rest of Liferay's tables, you can prefix them with a namespace. This table, when created, will be called `PR_PRProduct` in the database.

DEFINING AN ENTITY

Now we get to the cool stuff. The database entity—here, a `PRProduct`—is defined using the `Entity` tag ❷. The two parameters in this tag define how you want Service Builder to generate the service that retrieves and saves these entities. You need to at least have a local service. But you can also have a *remote* service. This isn't an EJB; it's instead a web service, complete with a WSDL document describing it, so your service may participate as part of a Service Oriented Architecture (SOA).

DEFINING COLUMNS

All that's left is to define the columns ❸ and finder methods ❹. The first column is defined as a primary key in the database. Other fields you want to store come after this and are defined as `Strings`. You also define two foreign keys: `companyId` and a `groupId`. Notice that the DBA team didn't specify these two foreign key fields in the tables, but you add them anyway. You do this because the DBAs didn't know the internal workings of Liferay when they designed the table. These fields are internal to Liferay and are used for context purposes in non-instanceable portlets. `CompanyId` corresponds to the portal instance to which the user has navigated, and `groupId` corresponds to the community or organization to which the user has navigated. Because you'll use these field values as parameters in all your queries, the portlet will have different data in different portals, communities, and organizations. Quick test: from the information just stated, and without reading the next sentence, is our portlet an instanceable or non-instanceable portlet? It's a non-instanceable portlet, because we'll be using these fields to make sure that the portlet ties all data to the portal and to the community or organization upon which the portlet is placed.

Next you defined a default ordering of the entities when they're retrieved from the database. You can choose to have them returned in ascending or descending order. You aren't limited to one column; you can specify multiple columns, and the ordering will happen by priority in order of the columns.

DEFINING FINDER METHODS

The finder methods ❹ that retrieve the objects appear next. Specifying these finders means that Service Builder will automatically generate methods that retrieve objects from the database using the parameters you specify in the finder. For example, the first finder returns products by `groupId` and `productName`. Now that you've defined the table, it's time to run Service Builder.

3.3.3 Running Service Builder

Save the service.xml file, and then run the Ant task called `build-service`. Several files are generated, and the task completes with a BUILD SUCCESSFUL message. If you're using an IDE that compiles source files automatically (other than Liferay IDE, which has a convenient *Build Services* button), you'll notice that errors suddenly appeared in your project. Don't worry about this; it's easy to fix.

What has happened is that Service Builder generated several Java source files. Some of them are in your existing src folder. Others are in a new source folder called service that Service Builder also generated. This folder resides inside WEB-INF like the src folder. To fix the errors in the project, use your IDE's facility to add another source folder to the project so the classes in that folder are available to your IDE's error-checking facility. For example, to do this on Eclipse, right-click the project, select Properties, select Java Build Path, and from the Source tab, add the new service source folder. When you do that, the errors will go away. If you're using Liferay IDE, you don't need to do this.

Service Builder divides the source it generates into two layers: an interface layer and an implementation layer. The interface layer is generated in the aforementioned service folder. You'll never change anything in the interface layer manually; Service Builder always generates the code that is found there. The implementation layer is generated in your src folder and is initially skeleton code that allows you to implement the functionality you need.

You'll notice that there is also a new file in the root of your src folder called service.properties. This file was also generated by Service Builder. It contains properties that Service Builder needs at runtime in order to perform its functions. The most important of these properties is a list of Spring configuration files that were also generated.

Another new construct that was generated is a META-INF folder in the src folder. This folder contains all the Spring configuration files and Hibernate configuration.

This means Service Builder has taken care of all your database persistence configuration for you. If you've ever used Hibernate alone or in combination with Spring, you know there are multiple configuration files to juggle between the two. Service Builder automatically configures all that for you and provides static classes you can use to perform all your database persistence functions. It provides both a Data Access Object (DAO) layer and a Data Transfer Object (DTO) layer automatically. Your next step is to provide the functionality in your DTO to keep your portlet code from being dependent on anything having to do with SQL databases.

3.4 Creating a buffer to the persistence layer

Liferay's Service Builder encourages the proper layering of functionality within a portlet application. Generally, when building an application, it's a good practice to separate the various layers of the application: UI, model, persistence, and so on. This is sometimes called *separation of concerns.* By keeping the layers as separate as possible, you gain the ability to change the implementation of any one layer more easily if for some reason you find a better way to do it later.

To some, this must seem like some unnecessary work. But let me give you an example of why this is important, and then we'll go into how to implement it.

3.4.1 Why layering is important

Consider this example. Say you have a poorly designed application that consists of only two layers: your JSPs and your portlet class. You develop the application by creating action URLs in the JSPs that correspond to various methods within the portlet. These methods use JDBC to connect to a database and select, insert, update, and delete data. Your database, validation, and page navigation code is all in the portlet or the JSPs, resulting in large files with lots of logic in them. You test the portlet as well as you can, and it then gets deployed to production.

Within the first day of its use, a bug is found. Your application has a last name field, and a user tried to insert the last name *O'Bannon.* Because you coded all your database interaction manually, you forgot that sometimes you needed to escape out certain characters. In this case, the apostrophe (') in the name is causing your database insert to fail.

With the poor design you've used for your portlet, you'll now have to modify the `Insert` and `Update` methods of your portlet class and add code that checks the values your users insert for apostrophes. This is an example of a *tightly coupled* design: the database code is inside the portlet, so your implementation of code that communicates with the database is intertwined with the business and display logic. Because you were recently working on this portlet, you know where the problem is and can fix it and redeploy the application.

Users work with the application for several months before another bug is found. It seems that somewhere in the portlet, a database connection isn't being closed and is causing the database server to run out of connections.

Significant time has passed, and you're on another project—you don't remember exactly what you did when you wrote this one. You have to slog through mounds of spaghetti code in your one portlet class looking for the problem: database code that is mixed in with all kinds of other functionality, such as JavaScript functions, field-validation code, database-access code, and so on. It's become a hard-to-maintain mess. After hours of debugging, you finally find the condition where the database connection isn't being closed: it's part of a long block of if-then-else conditions, which includes field-validation logic, business logic, and persistence logic. It takes you almost an entire day to find a single problem because it's buried in a lot of code that should have been separated into different layers of code logic.

If you had properly layered your application so the UI code was in one place, the business logic was in another, and the persistence logic was in another, you'd have a much more maintainable project. You might decide that you could use something like Hibernate for database persistence, and you'd only have to replace a few classes in the one layer. Doing that would solve all your persistence problems, because Hibernate escapes characters and closes connections automatically. You might then go another step further and replace your home-grown application logic with an MVC framework like JavaServer Faces (JSF) or Struts. On each refactor, you could modify one layer of the application at a time. Let's see how to do that for the persistence layer.

3.4.2 Using two layers for persistence

While the previous section describes a simplistic example, it shows how important it is that Service Builder encourages proper separation of concerns. For database persistence, two of these layers are DAO and the DTO. These two layers can be written by developers manually, and often a lot of time is spent writing and debugging code in them. Service Builder generates both layers for you automatically (see figure 3.5).

The layer you'll work most in is the DTO layer. This layer talks to the service layer, which is automatically generated and allows you to work with objects that need to be persisted or have been retrieved from the database. These are the `-Impl` classes you've generated, and this is the reason why they were placed in the src folder with the rest of your portlet code. You'll call DAO layer methods that invoke methods in the persistence layer to do the actual persisting. These methods are generated from the `<finder>` tags you placed in the service.xml file.

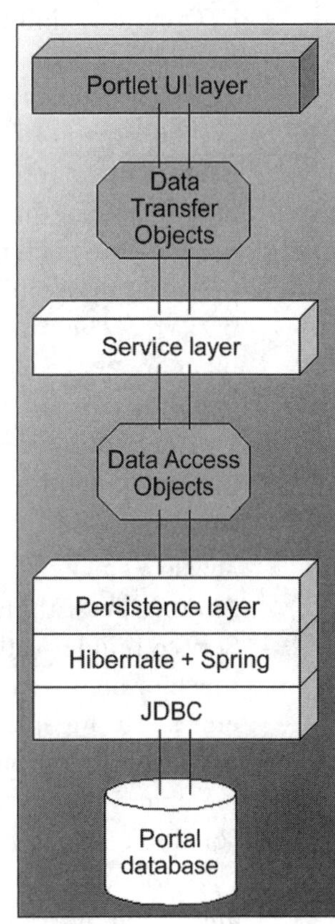

Figure 3.5 Service Builder generates for you everything from the portal UI layer down. You'll need to modify/customize some of this code, but you won't have to touch most of it. This significantly increases developer productivity.

Let's see how this works.

Although you haven't created it yet, the design calls for a form in the administrative portlet. This form lets users enter products that will appear in a drop-down selection box on the registration form in the registration portlet. Only two fields will come from this form (because the third is the primary key, which is generated): the name of the product and a serial-number mask that is set by the manufacturing department and can be used for field validation. How do you get the data the user entered into the database?

Remember, you're after the idea of *loose coupling*. This means you don't want to have any database-insertion code in your business logic. The business logic (when you get to it) will need to call a generic method that has nothing to do with the database. This is where the DTO layer comes in. It acts as a buffer between your business logic and your underlying database code. Service Builder generates both layers, leaving the DTO layer as a stub for you to implement as you wish.

3.4.3 Implementing the DTO layer

Presumably, you want a method that has two parameters in the method signature for your two values: the product name and the product's serial-number mask. Let's create it. Open the file PRProductLocalServiceImpl.java. You'll find it in a newly generated package called `com.inkwell.internet.productregistration.service.impl`. This class extends a generated class called `PRProductLocalServiceBaseImpl` (see figure 3.6). If you're using an IDE (such as Eclipse) that doesn't automatically recognize when another tool adds files, you may need to click the project name and press F5 to refresh the project to see this package. The first thing you'll implement in `PRProductLocalServiceImpl` is adding a product.

After you implement adding a product, implementing the other methods is simple.

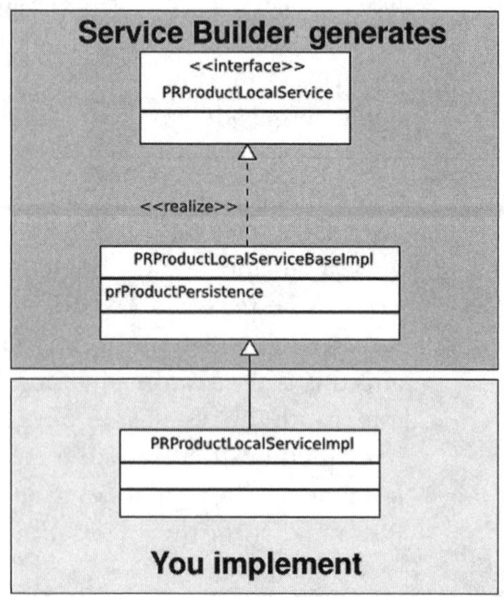

Figure 3.6 Service Builder generates both the DAO and DTO layers. Shown here is the DTO layer, which has an instance of the DAO layer (the `prProductPersistence` attribute) injected into it by Spring at runtime.

ADDING A PRODUCT

Another great thing about the design of Service Builder is that you never have to touch or modify any of the classes it generates. All the Spring dependency injection, the Hibernate session management, and the query logic stay in classes you don't have to edit. You add code in a class that extends the generated class, and if you add something that changes the interface/implementation contract, those changes are propagated up the chain so the contract is never broken. You'll see an example of this a bit later. For now, this file is an empty stub because you have yet to implement anything. The following listing implements the first method, which takes the values passed to it and calls the underlying database code to persist the data to the database.

Listing 3.2 Adding a product to the database

```
public PRProduct addProduct(PRProduct newProduct, long userId)
    throws SystemException, PortalException {

    PRProduct product = prProductPersistence.create(
        counterLocalService.increment(
            PRProduct.class.getName()));                    ❶ Create empty object

    resourceLocalService.addResources(
        newProduct.getCompanyId(),
 newProduct.getGroupId(), userId,
        PRProduct.class.getName(),
product.getPrimaryKey(), false,
        true, true);                                        ❷ Create permissions resources
    product.setProductName(newProduct.getProductName());
    product.setSerialNumber(newProduct.getSerialNumber());
    product.setCompanyId(newProduct.getCompanyId());
    product.setGroupId(newProduct.getGroupId());

    return prProductPersistence.update(product, false);
}
```

docroot/WEB-INF/src/com/inkwell/internet/productregistration/service/impl/PRProductLocalServiceImpl.java

The first thing you do ❶ in this method is create a new `PRProduct` object. `PRProduct` is the interface (inherited from `PRProductModel`), and `PRProductImpl` (which extends `PRProductModelImpl`) is the implementation. Note that all you have to do is specify the interface here, because a factory design pattern creates the object for you, using the `prProductPersistence` object that will be injected into this class by Spring. The interface and implementation of this object were both generated automatically by Service Builder, and the fields within the object map directly to the fields in the `PRProduct` table that was defined. In order to obtain a new instance of this object, you call a `create` method that was also generated by Service Builder.

Because Liferay is database-agnostic, by default it doesn't use any database-specific means of generating primary keys for databases it manages. Additionally, some databases don't support auto-incrementing primary keys. To account for this, Liferay provides its own utility for generating primary keys when you need to generate database-agnostic code. Because this is Liferay's practice, and it has proven to perform well in many large implementations of Liferay, we'll follow suit here. Note that Service Builder does allow you to use your database's facility for generating primary keys if you wish; all of the options available are documented in the DTD for the service.xml file, and this DTD can be found in the definitions folder in Liferay's source code.

Because the `create` method that was generated requires a primary key, you need to call Liferay's `Counter` utility to generate this. Here's the cool thing about how this is done: the `Counter` is automatically injected into the class you're working on. Why? Because if you're doing work with databases and Service Builder, you're very likely to need to use the `Counter` to create new objects that will be persisted.

You next make a call to `resourceLocalService` to persist resources ❷. Resources are used in Liferay to define permissions on the objects that are persisted. We'll get to the rest of this later; for now, it's important to note that you need to save resources with your entities.

Also remember that you added companyId and groupId fields to your tables in order to make your portlet a non-instanceable portlet; and also to enable you to later implement Liferay's permissions system. These two variables track the portal instance and the community/organization, respectively. For example, say a user adds your portlet to a page in the Guest community of the default portal instance. Users then begin adding products to the database. Because you've added the company ID and the croup ID to the product entities, users can add your portlet to another community, organization, or portal instance, and the set of records returned will be different, based on the company ID and group ID. Your finder methods filter the records being returned by company ID and group ID.

This is how Liferay allows you to place, for example, a Message Boards portlet in two different communities, and have completely different content in them. You'll do the same thing as you write your portlet.

When you have your object, it's a simple matter to set the proper values in the object and then persist it to the database. You then return the object you've created back to the layer that called this method in the first place.

You aren't finished yet. Remember when I said a couple of pages ago that changes to the interface/implementation contract are propagated up the chain automatically by Service Builder? You were just working in an implementation class that extends a `-BaseImpl` class. All the methods generated by Service Builder have entries in their interfaces and implementations in their `-BaseImpl` class. If developers wish to add more, they're added where you added yours: in the `-LocalServiceImpl` class.

Because you've added a new method to a class that implements an interface, there is no method stub in the interface for the method you just created. To continue without errors, you need to run Service Builder again. This, as you've seen before, can be done by running the `build-service` Ant task. When you run the task, Service Builder will regenerate the interface, which is called `PRProductLocalService`, to include a stub for the method you created in the implementation class.

This is generally the point where people scratch their heads and say, "Isn't this backward? Aren't you supposed to define the interface first and then write the implementation?"

In a sense, yes, that is correct. But remember that you're working with a code generator, and it's that code generator's job to make things easier for you as a developer.

By using Service Builder, you define the interface first, as much as you can do so up front. You did this in one step when you defined your database table in service.xml. Service Builder generated the interface as well as the default implementation—as best as it could guess what you needed. That's what went in PRProductLocalService-BaseImpl.java. If you need further customization—and you generally do—you can add your own methods. These need to be added to a class that is free of the code generator, so your changes aren't overwritten. PRProductLocalServiceImpl.java is provided as a DTO layer, which allows you to add any methods you may need.

You'll generally only need to make customizations in one class: `-LocalService-Impl`. In some cases, you may need to make customizations in `-Impl` classes in the `model.impl` package, but we'll cover that later. For now, the only thing you need to worry about is the `-LocalServiceImpl` class.

Now that you're done with adding products, let's try deleting products.

DELETING PRODUCTS

Because you can create products now, why not try deleting them? If you think about how you might want to delete products, there are two ways:

- You have a `PRProduct` object already, and you want to delete it.
- You have a `PRProduct`'s primary key, and you want to delete it using that without having to retrieve the whole `PRProduct`.

To make things easier for you in the controller layer, you'll overload the `delete` method by creating versions of it that can handle both cases:

```
public void deleteProduct(long productId)
    throws NoSuchProductException, SystemException, PortalException {

    PRProduct product =
 prProductPersistence.findByPrimaryKey(productId);
    deleteProduct(product);
}

public void deleteProduct(PRProduct product)
    throws PortalException, SystemException {

    resourceLocalService.deleteResource(
        product.getCompanyId(), PRProduct.class.getName(),
        ResourceConstants.SCOPE_INDIVIDUAL, product.getPrimaryKey());
    prProductPersistence.remove(product);
}
```

This code enables you to delete a `PRProduct` using its primary key or the `PRProduct` object. If you're using the primary key, you first retrieve the `PRProduct` object and then call `deleteProduct` on it. Note that you delete the resource as well as the product; doing so keeps Liferay's permissions tables free of dead data that might otherwise be left there taking up space. When you're finished modifying the `-Impl` class, run Service Builder again using `ant build-service`. As before, doing so will add your new methods to the interface.

The only thing remaining to do is to query the database for the products you've entered. Presumably, users will want to view them and/or edit them.

QUERYING THE DATABASE

Just like adding and deleting, getting products out of the database is easy. You probably remember that you had Service Builder generate a finder that queries the database for products by the `GroupId`. You always want to query by groupId because the portlet is non-instanceable. You implement this in the DTO layer as follows:

```
public List<PRProduct> getAllProducts(long groupId)
    throws SystemException {

    List<PRProduct> products =
        prProductPersistence.findByGroupId(groupId);
    return products;
}
```

This code returns a `List` of `PRProducts` that can be used in the UI layer to display products for viewing or editing purposes. And as you can see, whatever calls this method (it will be your portlet class) doesn't need to know anything about JDBC or databases. It's requesting a `List`. This frees you to do something like swap out Service Builder for something else without ever touching your portlet code.

You started with Product because it was a simple, standalone table. Now that you see how easy it is to use Service Builder, we can move on to looking at tables with relationships.

3.5 Service Builder in action

You created the PRProduct table first for a reason: it's a simple table that has no relationships to any other tables (except the implied relationships with Liferay's Resource and Counter tables). The other two tables that Inkwell's DBAs defined do have a relationship: there can be one-to-many registrations per registered user. Let's see how you define those two entities and their relationship to each other. When you've done that, you'll see how to share services across applications. Then we'll go into the implementation of adding related entities to the database.

3.5.1 Defining table relationships

The following listing sets up the relationship between `PRUser` and `PRRegistration` in the service.xml file.

Listing 3.3 Remaining entities in service.xml

```
<entity name="PRUser" local-service="true" remote-service="false">

  <column name="prUserId" type="long" primary="true" />     <-- (1) Primary key of User

  <column name="firstName" type="String" />

  <column name="lastName" type="String" />
```

```
<column name="address1" type="String" />

<column name="address2" type="String" />

<column name="city" type="String" />

<column name="state" type="String" />

<column name="postalCode" type="String" />

<column name="country" type="String" />

<column name="phoneNumber" type="String" />

<column name="email" type="String" />

<column name="birthDate" type="Date" />

<column name="male" type="boolean" />

<column name="userId" type="long" />

<column name="companyId" type="long" />

<column name="groupId" type="long" />

<column                                          <-- ❷ Foreign key relationship
  name="userRegistrations"
  type="Collection"
  entity="PRRegistration"
  mapping-key="prUserId" />

<order by="asc">

  <order-column name="lastName" case-sensitive="false" />

</order>

<finder name="G_LN" return-type="Collection">

  <finder-column name="groupId" />
  <finder-column name="lastName" />

</finder>

<finder name="G_E" return-type="Collection">

  <finder-column name="groupId" />
  <finder-column name="email" />

</finder>

<finder name="G_U" return-type="Collection">

  <finder-column name="groupId" />
  <finder-column name="userId" />
```

```
  </finder>

</entity>

<entity name="PRRegistration"
  local-service="true"
  remote-service="false">

  <column name="registrationId" type="long" primary="true" />

  <column name="prUserId" type="long" />                    <-- 3 Foreign key for User

  <column name="datePurchased" type="Date" />

  <column name="howHear" type="String" />

  <column name="wherePurchased" type="String" />

  <column name="serialNumber" type="String" />

  <column name="productId" type="long" />

  <column name="companyId" type="long" />

  <column name="groupId" type="long" />

  <finder name="GroupId" return-type="Collection">

    <finder-column name="groupId" />

  </finder>

  <finder name="G_RU" return-type="Collection">

    <finder-column name="groupId" />
    <finder-column name="prUserId" />

  </finder>

  <finder name="G_DP" return-type="Collection">

    <finder-column name="groupId" />
    <finder-column name="datePurchased" />

  </finder>

  <finder name="G_SN" return-type="Collection">

    <finder-column name="groupId" />
    <finder-column name="serialNumber" />

  </finder>

</entity>
```

docroot/WEB-INF/service.xml

In examining this code, you'll find there isn't much you haven't already seen. There is only one new concept here: relationships.

If you recall from the beginning of the chapter, Inkwell's database analysts defined a relationship between a registered user and a particular product registration. This is a one-to many-relationship: it's hoped that most customers will be repeat customers, and will own many Inkwell products.

To reflect this in the data, there is a separate `PRUser` table and a separate `PRRegistration` table, with a relationship between them defined by the `prUserId` column ❶. You define that relationship in the `PRUser` table by using the code in ❷ and in the `PRRegistration` table in ❸. This does two things:

- Service Builder creates a Spring configuration that injects the `PRRegistration` persistence objects into the `PRUser` DTO classes, so all the operations on `PRRegistration` objects are available.
- Service Builder generates a `getRegistrations()` method in the `PRUser` objects that let you seamlessly pull all registrations that belong to that user into a `List`.

You won't use the latter query in this portlet, but it would be useful in another application that could be written for the marketing teams to use, to see how much repeat business Inkwell is getting. That brings up another point: Service Builder classes can be shared.

3.5.2 *Sharing services*

If you're building a larger web site in which several plugins need access to the same services, you can make those services available to the plugins pretty easily. One way would be to put all the plugins in the same .war file, as in appendix D with the Inter-portlet Communication (IPC) portlets. Another way—and one that keeps projects from being monolithic—is to make the services available on the classpath of your other projects.

Service Builder makes your services available in a convenient .jar file that is generated and placed in the WEB-INF/lib folder of your project. You can easily put this .jar file in another .war file or on the global classpath of your application server. Doing so has the effect of making the services in that .jar file available to other plugins that may need to access those services. If you do this, be sure to remove the .jar file from your project's WEB-INF/lib folder to ensure that your application uses the classes from the global classpath.

Inkwell obviously needs these services for the Product Registration portlet, which will be placed on the company's public web site. But the company is also likely to need these services for an internal reporting portlet that can be used by the marketing and support teams. Because Service Builder makes it easy to share services by packaging them separately, this will be no problem for the development team to implement. All they have to do is take the .jar file from this project and put it on the global classpath of the company's application server.

But, of course, you're not done yet implementing services, so the development team can't give away that .jar file yet. You need to add to the DTO layer the methods that add to the database registered users and registrations that go with them.

3.5.3 Adding registered users and their products

Next, you implement the methods you need in the DTO layer to add registered users.

Listing 3.4 Maintaining registered users

```
public PRUser addPRUser(PRUser user, long userId)
    throws SystemException, PortalException {

    PRUser prUser =
      prUserPersistence.create(
        counterLocalService.increment(
          PRUser.class.getName()));                 <-- Creates empty entity

    resourceLocalService.addResources(
        prUser.getCompanyId(), prUser.getGroupId(),
        PRUser.class.getName(), false);              <-- Adds resources

    prUser.setAddress1(user.getAddress1());
    prUser.setAddress2(user.getAddress2());
    prUser.setBirthDate(user.getBirthDate());
    prUser.setCity(user.getCity());
    prUser.setCompanyId(user.getCompanyId());
    prUser.setCountry(user.getCountry());
    prUser.setEmail(user.getEmail());
    prUser.setFirstName(user.getFirstName());
    prUser.setGroupId(user.getGroupId());
    prUser.setLastName(user.getLastName());
    prUser.setMale(user.getMale());
    prUser.setPhoneNumber(user.getPhoneNumber());
    prUser.setPostalCode(user.getPostalCode());
    prUser.setState(user.getState());

    prUser.setUserId(userId);


    return prUserPersistence.update(prUser, false);  <-- Adds filled entity to database

}
```

docroot/WEB-INF/src/com/inkwell/internet/productregistration/service/impl/PRUserLocalServiceImpl.java

You implement only an add method here, because this portlet is designed for end users to add their registrations to the database through the web site, rather than submit postcards by mail. For that reason, you don't need to implement anything but add functionality.

Next, you add the DTO methods for your registration objects, as shown in the following listing.

Listing 3.5 Adding registrations

```
public PRRegistration addRegistration(PRRegistration reg)
    throws SystemException, PortalException {              <-- Add registration

    PRRegistration registration =
        prRegistrationPersistence.create(

           counterLocalService.increment(
PRRegistration.class.getName()));

    resourceLocalService.addResources(
        registration.getCompanyId(),
        registration.getGroupId(),
        PRRegistration.class.getName(),
false);

    registration.setCompanyId(reg.getCompanyId());
    registration.setDatePurchased(reg.getDatePurchased());
    registration.setGroupId(reg.getGroupId());
    registration.setHowHear(reg.getHowHear());
    registration.setProductId(reg.getProductId());
    registration.setPrUserId(reg.getPrUserId());
    registration.setSerialNumber(reg.getSerialNumber());
    registration.setWherePurchased(reg.getWherePurchased());

    return prRegistrationPersistence.update(registration, false);
}

public List<PRRegistration> getAllRegistrations(long groupId)
    throws SystemException {                               <-- Get all registrations by groupID

    List<PRRegistration>registrations =
        prRegistrationPersistence.findByGroupId(groupId);
    return registrations;

}
```

docroot/WEB-INF/src/com/inkwell/internet/productregistration/service/impl/PRRegistrationLocalServiceImpl.java

As you can see, in addition to the method for adding registrations, you provide a method for getting all the registrations by groupId out of the database as an example. If the team writing the reporting portlet for marketing requires more services, it will be easy to add them to this class. You'll implement a rudimentary "view registrations" screen in the meantime while the requirements are being gathered for that other portlet.

This is all the database interaction that the Product Registration portlet needs. From here, we'll move on to the portlet layer of the application in the next chapter.

3.6 Summary

After looking at the Inkwell development team's design for the Product Registration portlet, you saw that you could jump-start development by using Liferay's code generator for database persistence, which is called Service Builder. This utility (which ships as part of Liferay) creates code and SQL for accessing database from within portlets. Because it uses Spring and Hibernate to implement this functionality, it isn't much different from what developers already do manually—with the important exception that it does much of this grunt work automatically, freeing time for developers to implement the company's business logic.

Service Builder makes it easy to generate an entire persistence layer of an application. Using well-known design patterns such as DAO and DTO, it not only implements a consistent design but also helps developers to do so. Finders are automatically generated that allow developers to access data as Java objects. Additionally, you saw that Service Builder has no problem with table relationships or with sharing services among several applications.

You'll use Service Builder for the rest of this book, so you should know that this chapter only scratches the surface of what Service Builder can do. Later, you'll see that you can do pretty much anything you want to do—including custom SQL—with Service Builder. For now, you have an application to finish, so you'll continue with the Product Registration portlet in the next chapter.

4 MVC the Liferay way

This chapter covers

- The MVC design pattern
- Liferay's implementation of MVC: `MVCPortlet`
- Control panel portlets
- Liferay JSP patterns and objects, including `ThemeDisplay`
- Tag libraries such as the search container and AlloyUI Taglibs
- Internationalization in Liferay
- Liferay permissions

I hope you didn't have a visceral reaction to the first three letters in the chapter title. If you did, I certainly can understand why. MVC (which stands for Model-View-Controller) is probably one of the most overused buzzwords (if you can call an abbreviation a buzzword) you'll see. Framework after framework has been released, all claiming to implement MVC in one way or another. At the time of this writing, the Wikipedia article on MVC lists a total of 17 MVC frameworks for Java alone. They seem to keep multiplying like some kind of virus.

With that in mind, what in the world is Liferay thinking by having its *own* MVC framework? The answer to this question becomes apparent when you see the framework. Many of the MVC frameworks that are available can be heavy, with somewhat of a learning curve. They have configuration files that point to various parts of the application, and these files need to be kept in sync with the Java code they point to. Liferay's MVC doesn't have any of that. It's much simpler to use than the other frameworks: there's no configuration file like struts-config.xml or faces-config.xml to worry about. And it's a simple extension of the `GenericPortlet` class you've already seen. For that reason, I like to use it. But if you're still balking at the idea of another MVC framework, try thinking of it this way: you're getting into Liferay now, so you might as well become familiar with `MVCPortlet`, because if you need to look at any of Liferay's portlets, you'll see it anyway. And you may find that you like it once you start using it.

You'll continue working with the Product Registration portlet that you started in the last chapter. In that chapter, you used Service Builder to create the database persistence layer, or service layer, of your application. Now that the all foundational code is finished, you can concentrate on the layers of your application that interact with your users. These layers form the Model, the View, and the Controller.

4.1 Using Model-View-Controller

By using this pattern, you separate your concerns into various layers of the application, just as you did with Data Transfer Objects (DTOs) and Data Access Objects (DAOs) in your service layer. If you've been developing Java-based web applications for a while, you're probably familiar with some of the MVC frameworks that are available. The same concepts apply here, but as you'll see, they're implemented in a way that is a bit easier to use. Let's look at the various components of the MVC design pattern and see how they're implemented.

- *Model*—The model layer of the application holds the data of the application and contains any business rules for manipulating that data. Your `PRProduct` object with its fields containing values for the name and serial number is part of your model and was generated by Service Builder. Any logic that would change those values based on certain rules would also be part of the model layer.
- *View*—The view layer of the application contains all the logic for displaying the data to the user. Handling fields, check boxes, and other form elements, as well as hiding or showing data, are functions provided by the view layer. You'll create JSPs that will handle the view layer, and you'll see some tools that Liferay provides that makes this easy.
- *Controller*—The controller layer acts as a traffic director. It passes data back and forth to and from the model and view layers, providing a separation of concerns. The controller, for example, might be responsible for determining which action a user has clicked and directing processing to the proper function to update the model. Generally, the model and view speak only to the controller, with the exception that the view may use objects from the model for display purposes (such as iterating over a List to populate a table).

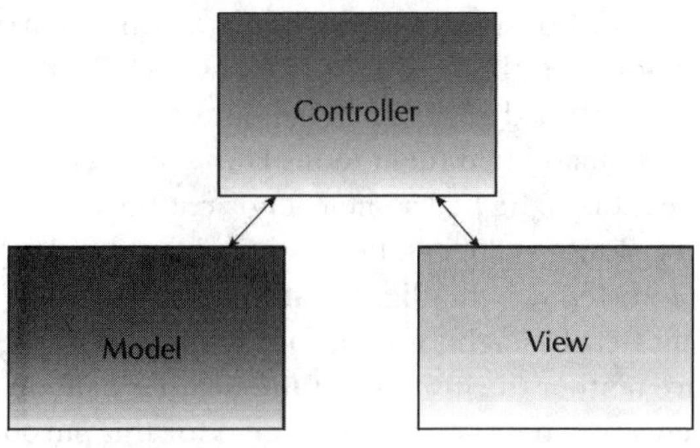

Figure 4.1 The MVC design pattern provides an easy way to structure your web application by separating concerns into easily digestible components.

These three layers are pictured in figure 4.1.

How would you implement this design pattern in a portlet? The model layer is generated for you by Service Builder from your table design. I stated earlier that your JSPs will be your view layer. That leaves the portlet class as your controller. As you'll see, this design will provide a good implementation of the MVC design pattern, allowing you to separate your concerns in a way that is maintainable and straightforward.

Liferay has subclassed `GenericPortlet` to provide functionality that makes it easy to create MVC applications using portlets. This subclass is called `MVCPortlet`, and it enhances the way portlets handle actions and page management. All of Liferay's portlet plugins are based on `MVCPortlet` instead of `GenericPortlet`, because it's a much better option.

What's different? Well, `MVCPortlet` is a lot easier to use. You won't have to worry about page management anymore; you get it for free. Liferay's `MVCPortlet` provides a simple means for page management. If you want to determine what JSP to display, all you need to do is point a render parameter called `jspPage` to the location of the JSP, and that's the page that will be displayed to the user. This functionality does several things for you:

- You don't have to worry about `doView()`, `doEdit()`, or any other `do` method.
- Your portlet class doesn't need to implement any portlet-specific APIs.
- Your portlet class is simple: all it contains is action methods.
- If you wish, you can use any piece of the standard portlet API that you want: `MVCPortlet` is subclassed from `GenericPortlet`, so feel free to override any functionality for your own purposes.

One of the other things this project will have is a portlet in Liferay's Control Panel as an alternative to Edit mode for administrative functions.

4.1.1 Edit mode? What Edit mode?

One of the things Liferay has learned with regard to portlets is that some things that are part of the portlet standard don't necessarily work well in real-world use. Portlet modes are one example. Sometimes the inventors of a thing envision a particular use for that thing, but when it gets in the hands of the general populace, uses are found that the inventors never dreamed of. Consider the case of Lawn Chair Larry. Larry always dreamed of flying, but poor eyesight kept him from serving in the United States Air Force. Undaunted, he purchased 45 weather balloons from an Army-Navy surplus store, filled them with helium, and tied them to his lawn chair. Thinking he'd float leisurely to a height of 30 feet or so, he had some friends cut the cord that kept him tied down. Instead of floating slowly to 30 feet, he shot to a height of 16,000 feet, scared himself half to death, interfered with flight traffic into and out of LAX, knocked out the power to a Long Beach neighborhood for 20 minutes, and got himself arrested.[1] The point? I'm sure neither the inventor of the weather balloon nor the inventor of the lawn chair ever envisioned someone using them for this purpose.

Similarly (and I say that with tongue firmly planted in cheek), the inventors of the portlet envisioned a single use for portlets: a web desktop environment for large enterprises. The design doesn't provide enough flexibility for the wild, wild west of custom designed web sites whose designers don't want to be locked into the boxy, window-like interface that was the original design for a portlet. Minimize, maximize, and close buttons are for desktop operating systems, not the web. And portlet modes haven't been used very much. I have yet to see someone implement Help mode in a portlet. Why? Because there are much better ways to implement a help system in an application than by using Help mode.

Edit mode can be confusing from an end user point of view. It's not intuitive to click an icon in the portlet window title bar to enter another mode from which you can control various portlet settings. And of course, if you use Edit mode, you're locked into that boxy design for your web site, because you have to provide a title bar so the icon can reside there.

Liferay has the unique position of being used for internet-based web sites as often as it's used internally for large enterprises. For that reason, a slightly different (and I think better) paradigm is used: the Control Panel.

Instead of providing an Edit mode for your portlet where you can control settings, you can implement a separate portlet for those settings and embed it in Liferay's Control Panel. Doing so puts all settings and options in one place, rather than having them scattered around your web site. It also frees your site designers to come up with whatever they want, because they're not bound to the window paradigm espoused by the portlet standard. Rather than use Edit mode to control the settings for your Product Registration portlet, you'll create a separate portlet in the same application and embed it in the Control Panel.

There are benefits to this approach for the developer too. Rather than having one big portlet that does everything, you can implement your application as several smaller, more tightly focused portlets. This not only makes the code easier to follow but also gives your end users freedom to arrange the application on the page any way they like.

---

1 http://darwinawards.com/stupid/stupid1998-11.html

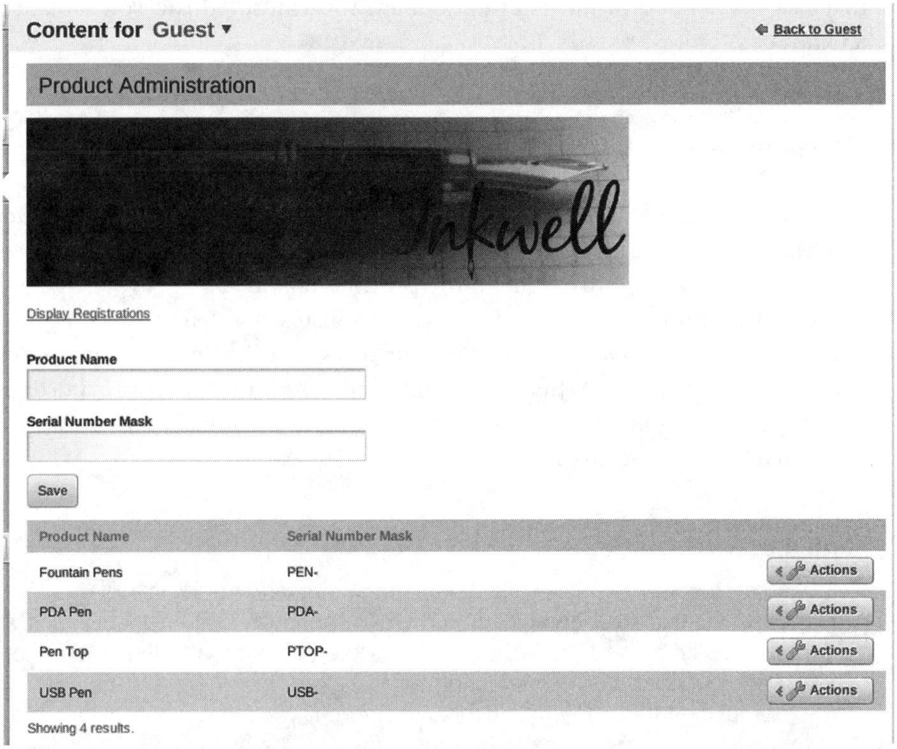

Figure 4.2 The Product Admin portlet allows portal administrators to add products that the Product Registration portlet displays in a selection box. This enables end users to choose from a list which product they wish to register, to enable their one-year warranty protection.

Your first task, therefore, will be to create the administrative portlet for the Control Panel, shown in figure 4.2.

Before you get started, let's take a quick look at how Liferay does MVC. You'll see that it's a welcome simplification of many of the concepts you've no doubt encountered before.

4.1.2 MVC according to Liferay

When you first create a portlet in the Plugins SDK, you've already seen that no portlet class is generated—yet if you deploy the portlet, you get the equivalent of Hello World functionality. First question: how does the portlet do that?

If you look at the portlet.xml that is generated with your project, you'll see that the portlet class is defined as `com.liferay.util.bridges.mvc.MVCPortlet`. This class is based on the `GenericPortlet` class you've already been working with, but it contains enhancements. `MVCPortlet` can do all page management for you. It does so by providing a default view, which is defined as an `init` parameter for each portlet mode. Because portlets default to View mode—and aren't required to implement any other mode—this portlet automatically directs to a JSP file called view.jsp, because that's what's defined in the `init` parameter. You can see this if you look at the portlet.xml file:

```
<init-param>
   <name>view-jsp</name>
   <value>/view.jsp</value>
</init-param>
```

By generating the project, you have a portlet that works (although it doesn't do much), but it doesn't have a portlet class. To do anything interesting, you need to create a portlet class, as you've done in the previous chapters.

What you'll do now is extend `MVCPortlet` instead of `GenericPortlet` so you can take advantage of its page-management features and thus make your portlet smaller and easier to work with. When you're finished, you'll find that your portlet contains nothing but action methods. All page management is controlled through the mechanisms that `MVCPortlet` gives you.

> **An alternative pattern**
>
> Some developers like to use the default implementation of `MVCPortlet` and implement their applications completely with JSPs. Although this obviously goes against the MVC design pattern, it's a way of doing development that will be more familiar to those who cut their teeth on scripting languages for the web, such as PHP. None of the examples in this book follow this pattern, but you'll be able to glean enough information from the examples to do it this way if you wish.

The first thing you need to do is configure some deployment descriptors to reflect the two portlets you'll have.

4.2 Configuring the portlet project

To make your life easier, you'll set things up in a way that lets you reuse some configuration going forward. You haven't had to worry much about this yet, because you've only concentrated on the persistence layer so far. But when you first created the project, the Plugins SDK generated a project containing a single portlet with the same name as the project, which you called `product-registration`. This is a good guess on the Plugins SDK's part, but it isn't exactly what you want. Because you'll be having a Product Registration portlet, you'll keep that configuration, and you'll add a new portlet for the Product Admin portlet. You can do this by modifying the deployment descriptors for your project and adding a section for the other portlet you'll need. The nice thing about this is that you can have two portlets (or more) in one project, which enables you to share common code easily.

Because you're sharing common code in Java, you may as well do the same for your JSP files. I'll also show you a pattern Liferay uses in JSP files to share common imports and objects on the page.

4.2.1 Defining portlets in your deployment descriptors

Open the portlet.xml file, and add the following portlet configuration below the portlet that is already there.

Listing 4.1 Adding the Product Admin portlet

```
<portlet>
  <portlet-name>product-admin</portlet-name>
  <display-name>Product Administration</display-name>
  <portlet-class>
    com.inkwell.internet.productregistration.registration.
    ➥ portlet.ProductAdminPortlet
  </portlet-class>
  <init-param>
    <name>view-jsp</name>
    <value>/admin/view.jsp</value>                    ❶ Moves JSP to admin folder
  </init-param>
  <init-param>
    <name>add-process-action-success-action</name>    ❷ Disables Liferay status messages
    <value>false</value>
  </init-param>
  <expiration-cache>0</expiration-cache>
  <supports>
    <mime-type>text/html</mime-type>
  </supports>
  <resource-bundle>content.Language</resource-bundle> ❸ Create multilingual portlet
  <portlet-info>
    <title>Product Administration</title>
    <short-title>Product Administration</short-title>
    <keywords>Product Administration</keywords>
  </portlet-info>
  <security-role-ref>
    <role-name>administrator</role-name>
  </security-role-ref>
  <security-role-ref>
    <role-name>guest</role-name>
  </security-role-ref>
  <security-role-ref>
    <role-name>power-user</role-name>
  </security-role-ref>
  <security-role-ref>
    <role-name>user</role-name>
  </security-role-ref>
</portlet>
```

docroot/WEB-INF/portlet.xml

When you've added this portlet, go ahead and create the admin folder under the docroot folder of the project, because ❶ tells `MVCPortlet` that your JSP for View mode is in this folder. If you've used Liferay before, you've probably noticed that when you save anything in the built-in portlets, a green status message is displayed, saying that it was saved successfully. `MVCPortlet` by default does this automatically after every portlet action. Because you don't want it to do this every time, you can use the initialization parameter ❷ to turn off that functionality. You'll also be creating a multilingual portlet, so you need a language bundle ❸.

The next file you need to edit is liferay-portlet.xml. As you'll remember, this file is the Liferay-specific deployment descriptor. You need some custom settings for the administration portlet, as follows.

Listing 4.2 Configuring the admin portlet for the Control Panel

```
<portlet>
  <portlet-name>product-admin</portlet-name>
  <icon>/icon.png</icon>
  <control-panel-entry-category>content</control-panel-entry-category>
  <control-panel-entry-weight>1.5</control-panel-entry-weight>
  <header-portlet-css>/css/product-admin.css</header-portlet-css>
  <header-portlet-javascript>/js/test.js</header-portlet-javascript>
</portlet>
```

docroot/WEB-INF/liferay-portlet.xml

To put your portlet in the Control Panel, you need only tell Liferay you want to do that via its deployment descriptor. You add the portlet to the Content area of the control panel and specify a weight that determines where it appears in the list.

The Control Panel is divided into four areas, each of which has a particular purpose:

- *Personal*—Used for administration items that the logged-in user needs to access, such as My Account.
- *Content*—Used to administer any type of content in the portal. In this chapter you'll define Inkwell's products as content, so you'll add the portlet to this section.
- *Portal*—Contains administrative tools that affect the portal globally.
- *Server*—Contains administrative tools that affect the entire Liferay installation.

Your configuration places the portlet in the *content* section of the Control panel.

The Control Panel looks a bit different from the rest of the portal, but now you know it's populated entirely with portlets! You already have the basic knowledge for adding anything you want to the Control Panel.

Defining the weight this way makes sense when you understand that the weights for the default items range from 1.0 to 11.0. By making the weight for your portlet 1.5, you're making sure it appears second in the list.

Last, you have one final configuration file: liferay-display.xml. This is how you configure the way the portlets appear in the Add > More menu:

```
<?xml version="1.0"?>
<!DOCTYPE display PUBLIC "-//Liferay//DTD Display 6.0.0//EN"
➥ "http://www.liferay.com/dtd/liferay-display_6_0_0.dtd">

<display>
  <category name="Inkwell Internet">
    <portlet id="product-registration" />
  </category>
```

```
  <category name="category.hidden">
    <portlet id="product-admin" />
  </category>

</display>
```

As you can see, you're creating a category to hold Inkwell's portlets destined for its internet site. You also have another category, `category.hidden`. Any portlets in this category are prevented from appearing in the Add > More menu, so you put the administrative portlet there. Because it appears in the Control Panel, you don't want users to also be able to place it on pages.

You've now finished configuring your portlet project and can move on to implementing it.

4.2.2 Having one location for JSP dependencies

If you've ever looked into Liferay's source code, you've probably seen that it doesn't follow a pattern that many organizations have tried to get to over the years. That pattern is the artificial separation between site designers and site programmers. The vision for this is simple: site designers understand tags and styling; programmers understand code. Therefore, JSPs should be as free of code as possible so as not to confuse the site designers. Many products have been architected to support this idea.

Liferay goes in a different direction and mixes code with tags. I know some people will have a visceral reaction to this. My goal isn't necessarily to evangelize one way over the other (that is up to individual developers, who should do things the way they're most comfortable doing them) but instead to let you know before you get into the code that I'm well aware that I'm not doing things the way many others do them. My goal is to show you the Liferay way of doing things, because that will enable you to understand Liferay's code better—and you may decide you like it. If you don't, you're always free to use another framework such as Struts or ICEfaces for your portlets. Although I was a bit puzzled by Liferay's code at first, I eventually came on board with Liferay's philosophy. If you think about your experience, rather than what all the articles will tell you, this division between designers and programmers doesn't exist in most cases. And if it does, the designers don't understand *any* code, including markup and CSS. They tend to deliver graphics files that front-end developers chop up and turn into pages.

With that said, because there will be some Java code in your JSPs, you'll need to manage the imported classes and tag libraries. A pattern that Liferay uses to make this easier is to throw all imports, tag library declarations, and variable initializations in one file called init.jsp. Every other JSP that is created imports init.jsp so it can take advantage of those declarations (see figure 4.3).

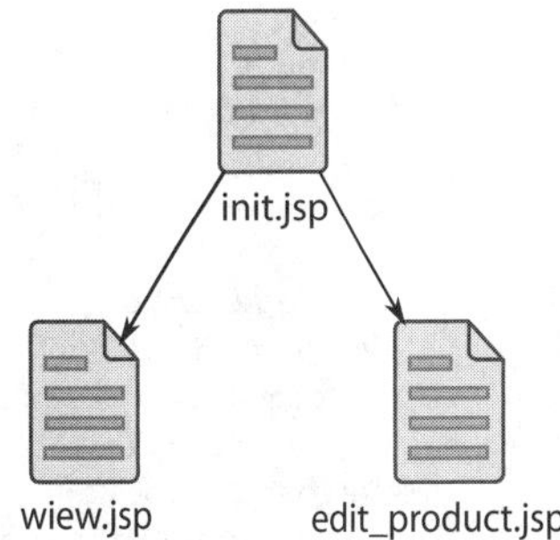

Figure 4.3 Every JSP file in the project includes init.jsp so that all initialization and configuration can be done in one easy-to-maintain file.

The completed init.jsp appears in listing 4.3. Obviously, if you were writing this portlet from scratch, you'd add imports and initialization code as needed. I have the advantage of being able to give you the completed file for the whole project, with everything you'll use already in it.

Listing 4.3 Putting initialization code in one place

```
<%@ taglib
➥ uri="http://java.sun.com/portlet_2_0" prefix="portlet" %>      Tag library declarations
<%@ taglib
➥ uri="http://java.sun.com/jstl/core_rt" prefix="c" %>
<%@ taglib
uri="http://liferay.com/tld/aui" prefix="aui" %>
➥ <%@ taglib
uri="http://liferay.com/tld/portlet" prefix="liferay-portlet" %>
<%@ taglib
➥ uri="http://liferay.com/tld/security"
➥ prefix="liferay-security" %>
<%@ taglib
➥ uri="http://liferay.com/tld/theme" prefix="liferay-theme" %>
<%@ taglib
➥ uri="http://liferay.com/tld/ui" prefix="liferay-ui" %>
<%@ taglib
➥ uri="http://liferay.com/tld/util" prefix="liferay-util" %>

<%@ page import="java.util.List" %>                          Import statements
<%@ page import="java.util.Calendar" %>
<%@ page import="java.util.Collections" %>
<%@ page import="com.liferay.portal.kernel.util.HtmlUtil" %>
<%@ page import="com.liferay.portal.kernel.util.ParamUtil" %>
<%@ page import="com.liferay.portal.kernel.util.CalendarFactoryUtil" %>
<%@ page import="com.liferay.portal.kernel.dao.search.ResultRow" %>
<%@ page import="com.liferay.portal.kernel.dao.search.SearchEntry" %>

<%@ page import="com.liferay.portal.kernel.exception.SystemException" %>
<%@ page import="com.liferay.portal.kernel.util.WebKeys" %>
<%@ page import="com.liferay.portal.security.permission.ActionKeys" %>
<%@ page import="com.liferay.portal.kernel.util.ListUtil" %>
<%@ page
➥ import="com.liferay.portal.service.permission.PortalPermissionUtil" %>
<%@ page
➥ import="com.liferay.portal.service.permission.PortletPermissionUtil"
➥ %>
<%@ page
➥ import="com.inkwell.internet.productregistration.model.PRProduct" %>
<%@ page
➥ import="com.inkwell.internet.productregistration.model.PRRegistration"
➥ %>
<%@ page import="com.inkwell.internet.productregistration.model.PRUser" %>
<%@ page import=
➥ "com.inkwell.internet.productregistration.registration.portlet.
ActionUtil" %>
<%@ page import="com.inkwell.internet.productregistration.service.
➥ PRProductLocalServiceUtil" %>
```

```
<%@ page import="
➥ com.inkwell.internet.productregistration.service.
➥ PRRegistrationLocalServiceUtil" %>
<%@ page import="javax.portlet.PortletURL" %>

<portlet:defineObjects />                      <-- Initializes portlet taglibs

<liferay-theme:defineObjects />                <-- Initializes Liferay taglibs
```

docroot/init.jsp

As you can see, this JSP is fairly simple: it declares the tag libraries you'll be using in this portlet application, imports the classes you'll need in your scriptlets, and then initializes any tag libraries that need initializing. What makes this nice is that because you'll be using all this stuff in the rest of your JSPs, you don't have to bother reimporting classes or reinitializing tag libraries in every JSP. You can add this at the top of any JSP you create:

```
<%@include file="/init.jsp" %>
```

The last tag in this file is Liferay-specific. This tag, like the Portlet API's similarly used tag, makes available to the page several variables you're likely to need. These variables are shown in table 4.1.

Table 4.1 Liferay objects in JSPs

Object	Description
`account`	The user's `Account` object. This object maps to the Account table in the Liferay database.
`colorScheme`	An object representing the current color scheme in the theme that is being rendered by the portal.
`company`	The current `Company` object. This represents the portal instance on which the user is currently navigating.
`contact`	The user's `Contact` object. This object maps to the Contact table in the Liferay database.
`layout`	The page to which the user has currently navigated.
`layoutTypePortlet`	This object can be used to programmatically add or remove portlets from a page.
`locale`	The current user's locale, as defined by Java.
`permissionChecker`	An object that can determine–given a particular resource–whether the current user has a particular permission for that resource.
`plid`	A portal layout ID. This is a unique identifier for any page that exists in the portal, across all portal instances.
`portletDisplay`	An object that gives the programmer access to many attributes of the current portlet, including the portlet name, the portlet mode, the ID of the column on the layout in which it resides, and more.

Table 4.1 Liferay objects in JSPs *(continued)*

Object	Description
`realUser`	When an administrator is impersonating a user, this variable tracks the administrator's `User` object.
`scopeGroupId`	By default, contains the groupId for the community or organization in which this portlet resides. If the `scopeable` attribute is set to true, this may contain a unique scope identifier for custom scopes, such as the page scope that was introduced in Liferay Portal 5.2, if the portlet has been configured to use a custom scope.
`theme`	An object representing the current theme that is being rendered by the portal.
`themeDisplay`	A runtime object that contains many useful items, such as the logged-in user, the layout, logo information, paths, and much more.
`timeZone`	The current user's time zone, as defined by Java.
`user`	The `User` object representing the current user.

Because you've added this initialization tag to init.jsp, these objects are available on all your pages.

You have one place where all initialization stuff is maintained, and all your JSPs can benefit from it. Now you're ready to add functionality, and the first thing you'll create is a form that lets users add products.

4.3 Creating a form with AlloyUI taglibs

As you've seen, `MVCPortlet` uses an initialization parameter to forward processing to a JSP for the user to view. Your first step will be to make this JSP display what you want to show to the user. If you refer back to figure 4.2, you can see that you want to show the user a form that allows them to quickly add products. On that form, you'll display a table of products that have already been added and that users can view, edit, or delete.

To create the form, you'll use another Liferay tool: AlloyUI tag libraries. The form you're creating is small, so you won't necessarily see the benefits of using AlloyUI taglibs just yet; but suffice to say you'll be glad you're getting an introduction, because it will make your life a lot easier later in the chapter.

But first, what is AlloyUI?

4.3.1 Getting started with AlloyUI tag libraries

AlloyUI is an *interface metaframework*. Okay, that probably sounded like gobbledegook, but bear with me for a second. Web site front ends are created using a combination of three technologies: HTML, CSS, and JavaScript (see figure 4.4), right? These three technologies together form the user experience for any site. HTML provides the overall structure of the document served up by the site, including its content. CSS provides the visual layer: how the document is presented visually to the user. It depends on a well-defined structure from the HTML in order to do this. JavaScript provides the

Figure 4.4 AlloyUI unifies three components, HTML, CSS, and JavaScript, in one easy-to-use metaframework.

interactive elements of any web page. If something moves, changes, or can be dragged, dropped, resized, or removed, JavaScript is enabling that for the end user.

AlloyUI was designed because user interface developers tend to have to solve the same kinds of problems over and over. Rather than continuing that cycle, you can use AlloyUI to solve common problems across the spectrum of HTML, CSS, and JavaScript. It combines the best of existing solutions under one consistent API, which makes it easier to use than trolling the internet to find a cookbook recipe for a common problem you know someone has already solved. Been there, done that, don't want to do it anymore.

One important way AlloyUI does this is by generating the proper markup for you. To do this, it has two types of components: a tag library and a JavaScript API. This chapter is concerned with the tag libraries, which are incredibly helpful for building web forms. In chapter 5, we'll look at some of AlloyUI's JavaScript functions.

Let's start gently with AlloyUI. You have a simple form that hardly needs it, but you'll use AlloyUI to build the form because it's a best practice when coding on Liferay's platform. This form is shown in the following listing.

Listing 4.4 An AlloyUI form

```
<portlet:actionURL name="addProduct" var="addProductURL"/>

<aui:form action="<%= addProductURL.toString() %>" method="post">

  <aui:fieldset>

    <aui:input name="productName" size="45" />

    <aui:input name="productSerial" size="45" />

    <aui:button-row>

      <aui:button type="submit" />

    </aui:button-row>
```

```
  </aui:fieldset>

</aui:form>
```

docroot/admin/view.jsp

Because this is a portlet, you have to let Liferay create the URL for submitting the form, which you can then use in the `action` attribute of the form declaration. You're using AlloyUI tags here, which you declared in init.jsp. The form is simple, with just the two fields you need to add products. You should recognize these fields from the Service Builder configuration you used in the last chapter to generate database tables and Java code for accessing them.

Liferay's `MVCPortlet` class enhances the `GenericPortlet` class in one important way: naming a method with the same name as the action URL's name causes the portlet to execute that method if that URL is clicked. To enable your form, all you have to do is create a method in your portlet class called `addProduct`, and that method will be executed. Let's look at that in the next listing.

Listing 4.5 Adding products

```
public void addProduct(ActionRequest request, ActionResponse response)
    throws Exception {

    ThemeDisplay themeDisplay =
        (ThemeDisplay) request.getAttribute(WebKeys.THEME_DISPLAY);
    PRProduct product = ActionUtil.productFromRequest(request);     <-- Convenience method
    ArrayList<String> errors = new ArrayList<String>();

    if (ProdRegValidator.validateProduct(product, errors)) {    <-- Validate input
        PRProductLocalServiceUtil.addProduct(
          product,themeDisplay.getUserId());                  <-- Call service layer
        SessionMessages.add(request, "product-saved-successfully");

    }
    else {
       SessionErrors.add(request, "fields-required");

    }

}
```

docroot/WEB-INF/src/com/inkwell/internet/productregistration/portlet/ProductAdminPortlet.java

I don't know about you, but I like to keep my methods short and sweet. Rather than having tons of logic embedded in a method, I'll offload some of it to another class—particularly if I can use it again somewhere else. You can see two examples in this code. First, you call a method in `ActionUtil` that can retrieve a `PRProduct` object out of the form the user submits. Because it's likely you'll want to pull `PRProducts` from the request over and over, this method is placed in a class that can be shared by both portlets. Next, you call a method in `ProdRegValidator`. This class contains code that validates the input from the user-submitted form. Again, because you'll likely reuse these validation routines, they're in a class that can be used by both portlets. We'll go over the validator later, because that class uses Liferay's `Validator` class to perform the actual validations.

Next, I want to highlight the use of the service layer you created in the previous chapter. If the values on the form pass validation, you need to save them to the database. You can do this easily, because all of your services are available via static methods in a `-LocalServiceUtil` class. In this case, you're using `PRProductLocalServiceUtil`, because you're saving `PRProduct` entities.

You now have basic functionality for saving product records from a web form to a database. Let's take a closer look at some features that provide an underlying infrastructure for implementing this functionality.

4.3.2 Providing feedback and messages

You probably noticed that some vital information was missing from the form in listing 4.4. Generally, when you have a field on a form, you also have a label for that field, as shown in figure 4.5.

Product Name

Figure 4.5 A field and a label. If you had just a field, users would have no idea what to type. This is common sense, but the code in listing 4.4 doesn't reflect the fact that you have a label. Or does it?

But your code looks like this:

```
<aui:input name="productName" size="45" />
```

Where is the text that prints the words *Product Name* for the field label? Back when you were configuring the portlet.xml file, you included a line of code for a resource bundle. To refresh your memory, here's the line:

```
<resource-bundle>content.Language</resource-bundle>
```

The text comes from there. This file allows you not only to put all your form messages in one place, but also to support multiple languages for your portlet application.

Create a folder called content in your src folder, and create a file called Language.properties there. The file for this project has the following contents.

Listing 4.6 Supporting multiple languages with Language.properties

```
Product=Product
com.inkwell.internet.productregistration.model.PRProduct=Product
model.resource.com.inkwell.internet.productregistration.model.PRProduct=
➥ Product

product-saved-successfully=Product Saved Successfully       <- Product form messages
productDeleted=The product has been deleted successfully.
product-name=Product Name
product-serial=Serial Number Mask
productUpdated=The product was updated successfully.
```

```
there-are-no-products=There are no products yet to display.

error-deleting=There has been an error deleting this product.   ◁ Product form errors
error-updating=There has been an error updating this product.
fields-required=Please fill out all fields
product-name-required=Product Name is required
serial-number-prefix-required=Please enter the serial number prefix

add-registration=Register a New Inkwell Product   ◁ Registration form fields
address1=Street Address 1
address2=Street Address 2
catalog=Catalog
city=City
country=Country
birth-date=Date of Birth
date-purchased=Date Purchased
email-address=Email Address
first-name=First Name
friend-family-member=Friend / Family Member
gender=Gender
gift=Gift
home-shopping=Home Shopping
how-hear=How did you hear about this Inkwell product?
inkwell.com=inkwell.com
last-name=Last Name
magazine-article=Magazine Article
online-retailer=Online Retailer
other-web-site=Other Web Site
other=Other
phone-number=Phone Number
please-choose=Please Choose
postal-code=Zip
product-serial-number=Product Serial Number
product-type=Product Type
radio-advertisement=Radio Advertisement
registration-saved-successfully=Registration Saved Successfully
retail-store=Retail Store
state=State
thank-you-message=Thank you for registering your product with us!
trade-show=Trade Show
tv-advertisement=TV Advertisement
tv-news=TV News
tv-shopping-network=TV Shopping Network
where-purchase=Where did you purchase this Inkwell product?

address-required=Address Required   ◁ Registration form errors
birthdate-required=Birth Date Required
date-purchased-required=Please enter the date you purchased the product
email-required=Please enter your email address
enter-valid-date=Enter A Valid Date
error-saving-registration=Error Saving Registration
firstname-required=First Name Required
gender-required=Gender Required
howhear-required=Please tell us how you heard about our product
```

```
lastname-required=Last Name Required
missing-company-id=Missing Company ID
missing-group-id=Missing Group ID
phone-number-required=Phone Number Required
product-type-required=Please enter the type of product you purchased
serial-number-required=Serial Number Required
where-purchased-required=Please tell us where you purchased the product

display-registrations=Display Registrations                  <-- View messages
there-are-no-registrations=There are no registrations
```

docroot/WEB-INF/src/content/Language.properties

You use the one file for the messages both portlets will need. This is part of the power of AlloyUI form tags. If you have a tag that specifies a field in the format `fieldName`, the tag will search the resource bundle for a matching language property in the format `field-name` and use that property value as the label for the field.

There's more, of course. There are two lines of code in the `addProduct` method that I didn't mention before, but about which you may have been curious. If you're successful in adding a product to the database, you add a key to an object called `SessionMessages`. If you aren't successful, you add a key to an object called `SessionErrors`. These keys correspond to messages in the Language.properties file. The key you add to `SessionMessages` is `product-saved-successfully`, whose matching value is the English text *Product Saved Successfully*. Similarly, you add a key for an error message to `SessionErrors`. Liferay makes these objects available to any JSP it's serving, and it has tag libraries that can take advantage of the fact that these objects are available. You can make these messages appear to your users by adding the following lines above the form in view.jsp:

```
<liferay-ui:success key="productSaved"
➥ message="product-saved-successfully" />
<liferay-ui:success key="productDeleted" message="productDeleted" />
<liferay-ui:success key="productUpdated" message="productUpdated" />
<liferay-ui:error key="fields-required" message="fields-required" />
<liferay-ui:error key="error-deleting" message="error-deleting" />
<liferay-ui:error key="error-updating" message="error-updating" />
```

If any of these messages appear in `SessionMessages` or `SessionErrors`, the tags activate and the messages from the Language.properties file are displayed to the user. If the messages aren't in `SessionMessages` or `SessionErrors`, nothing appears on the page. If you've used Liferay for any amount of time, you've seen these messages. An example is shown in figure 4.6.

Figure 4.6 When you save a product, this message appears to show that everything's okay and the action the user took was successful. This message is taken out of the Language.properties file and displayed properly to the user.

And of course, there's even more. You can make these messages appear in the user's language.

4.3.3 Translating messages to multiple languages

You can provide alternate translations for your message keys. Normally, you do this by creating companion files to Language.properties that have two-letter language codes appended to them. For example, if you wanted to provide message keys in Spanish, you could create a file called Language_es.properties, and the application would automatically pick up the values in that file if the end user has `es` (the language code for Spanish, which is *Español* natively) as his or her default locale.

This approach is generally a lot of work, because you have to get someone to translate your messages and place those translations in a file for each language you want to support. But what if you could generate a translation automatically? Liferay lets you do just that.

Open the build.xml file that you've been using to deploy your project. Notice that it's pretty small, because all of its functionality is derived from other Ant scripts stored in the Plugins SDK. Insert the following Ant task just below the `<import>` tag:

```
<target name="build-lang">
  <antcall target="build-lang-cmd">
    <param name="lang.dir" value="docroot/WEB-INF/src/content" />
    <param name="lang.file" value="Language" />
  </antcall>
</target>
```

Save the file, and then run the Ant target you just created, using the following command on all OSs:

```
ant build-lang
```

You'll see messages like the following, among others:

```
Translating en_it Product Name
Translating en_it Serial Number Mask
Translating en_ja Product Name
Translating en_ja Serial Number Mask
Translating en_ko Product Name
Translating en_ko Serial Number Mask
Translating en_pt Product Name
Translating en_pt Serial Number Mask
Translating en_es Product Name
Translating en_es Serial Number Mask
```

When the task completes, look at your content folder. It should now contain files for many languages.

> **NOTE** If you're using Liferay IDE or Liferay Developer Studio, you don't need to create this Ant task, because this functionality is built into the product. You can right-click the project (or the build file) and then select Liferay > Build Languages to run this task.

What just happened? The Plugins SDK contains Ant targets that use an online service to translate all the keys in your file to multiple languages. By providing the Ant task you created, you give those Ant targets the parameters they need to do their work: namely, the folder where your Language.properties file exists and the name of the file. Then, you were able to use the service to generate the language files you now see in that folder.

> **NOTE** You may run into a problem with the service blocking your IP because you've called it too much, especially if you have a lot of keys. Don't worry; the block only lasts for about five minutes. If you run the script again, it will pick up where it left off, and eventually, you'll get everything translated.

Because this is an automated translation service, sometimes the translations it provides aren't optimal. But they certainly serve as a good starting point and are better than nothing. If you're targeting your application for a specific audience in a specific language, you should send the generated translation file to someone who can go over the translation and make sure it's correct before you release it. If you don't have a resource who can do that, at least you have a basic translation file you can use. If you want to provide a translation yourself, you can provide to your translator the file with the .native extension appended to it. Liferay generates this file by default as well; it overrides the automatic translations. Have your translator put his or her translations in this file, and then copy it back to the content folder; those translations will then be used in place of the generated ones.

Another nice thing about the way languages work in Liferay is that the language files from the portal are inherited by the portlets. This means you don't have to redefine common actions (such as `Save` and `Cancel`) that are already used by the portal: you can use them in your portlets as is. Your portlets inherit the translations of these common labels that are provided by Liferay.

If you have Liferay's source, you can find Liferay's Language.properties file in the Liferay source code in portal-impl/src/content.

There's one more thing about this form that we haven't gone over: field validation. Yes, Liferay has tools for that too.

4.3.4 Validating user-submitted forms

Liferay includes a utility that can perform field validation. Rather than writing something yourself or using a framework, you can use Liferay's utility to easily validate the data your users enter. Often this utility is much easier to use than what comes with a particular framework—especially if you're learning the framework for the first time. It can be used for any portlet, whether you're using a framework or not.

Liferay's utility is the `com.liferay.portalkernel.util.Validator` class. You create a separate `Validator` class for your portlet that contains validation logic for all the objects you want to persist to the database. You've already seen this class in use in the addProduct method. The following listing contains the method you call to validate the product coming from the form.

Listing 4.7 Validating fields from a form

```
public static boolean validateProduct(PRProduct product, List errors) {

    boolean valid = true;

    if (Validator.isNull(product.getProductName())) {
        errors.add("product-name-required");
        valid = false;
    }

    if (Validator.isNull(product.getSerialNumber())) {
        errors.add("serial-number-prefix-required");
        valid = false;
    }

    if (Validator.isNull(product.getCompanyId())) {
        errors.add("missing-company-id");
        valid = false;
    }

    if (Validator.isNull(product.getGroupId())) {
        errors.add("missing-group-id");
        valid = false;
    }

    return valid;
}
```

docroot/WEB-INF/src/com/inkwell/internet/productregistration/portlet/ProdRegValidator.java

As you can see, this is pretty basic. Obviously, you could implement better validation here, because all you're checking for is a value. Liferay's `Validator` class has many useful methods, such as `isPhoneNumber()`, `isEmailAddress()`, and so on. If any field fails validation, you set the boolean to `false`, and you also add a key from your Language.properties file to the `List` object called `errors`. This is the `SessionErrors` object you saw earlier, and because you've put the `liferay-ui` tags that display these messages on your form, any messages coming from the `Validator` class are displayed to the user.

If you were to submit your form without filling out any of the fields, it would look like figure 4.7.

The presence of messages in `SessionErrors` triggers the first message; the second message is the one you want to display to the user. You can have an individual message for every field, as you'll see when you get to the more complicated form for registering a product. Your page isn't complete yet. You still need a way to display the data you're entering so you can view and edit it. For that, you'll use another helpful utility from Liferay: the search container.

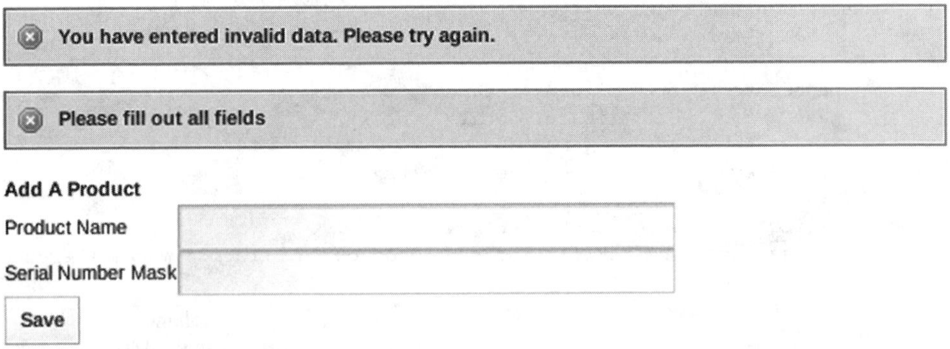

You have entered invalid data. Please try again.

Please fill out all fields

Add A Product

Product Name

Serial Number Mask

Save

Figure 4.7 Error messages look different from regular messages, and should immediately "pop" to the user.

4.3.5 *Displaying data with the search container*

Search Container is a class that works in conjunction with Liferay's UI tag libraries to provide a user interface wrapper around lists of objects. Whenever you create a data-driven application like this one, naturally you'll be working with lists of objects. In this case, you're working with lists of `PRProducts`. You could conceivably create a way to manually iterate through `PRProducts` in a table and then create another table for `PRRegistrations`, and so on. But Liferay solves this problem through the search container. It wraps your list of objects (the type of object doesn't matter) and automatically provides features such as pagination (for very large lists) and table formatting (using the tag libraries that go with it). Because of this, it contains attributes such as column headers, rows, and cursor positions.

Search Container is powerful but easy to use. Let's see how to display and edit data using this component.

4.3.6 *Using the search container to present your data*

Let's jump right into the code so you can see how this works. Place the following code directly under the form in view.jsp.

Listing 4.8 Using the search container to show data

```
<liferay-ui:search-container
    emptyResultsMessage="there-are-no-products"

    delta="5">

  <liferay-ui:search-container-results>
  <%
  List<PRProduct> tempResults = ActionUtil.getProducts(renderRequest);

  results = ListUtil.subList(
      tempResults, searchContainer.getStart(),
```

Display works from these values

```
searchContainer.getEnd());
  total = tempResults.size();

  pageContext.setAttribute("results", results);
  pageContext.setAttribute("total", total);
  %>
  </liferay-ui:search-container-results>

  <liferay-ui:search-container-row
    className="com.inkwell.internet.productregistration.model.PRProduct"
    keyProperty="productId"
    modelVar="product">                                    <-- Columns to display

    <liferay-ui:search-container-column-text
        name="product-name"
        property="productName"
 />
    <liferay-ui:search-container-column-text
        name="product-serial"
        property="serialNumber"
 />
    <liferay-ui:search-container-column-jsp
        path="/admin/admin_actions.jsp"
        align="right"
 />

  </liferay-ui:search-container-row>

  <liferay-ui:search-iterator />

</liferay-ui:search-container>
```

docroot/admin/view.jsp

The first thing you see is the initialization of the search container. You set an empty results message from `Language.properties` and set the delta for pagination to a pretty low number, because you're not envisioning many products in this search container. You get the results from the `ActionUtil` class, which calls the service layer you generated in chapter 3 to retrieve the products you need from the database. When you've calculated the total and the delta, you set these attributes in the `pageContext` so the search container can iterate over them.

After you get to the rows to be displayed, all you need to tell the search container is the name of the bean it's displaying, the property of the primary key, and the name of the variable to represent your model. From there, you can list the columns by their names (from Language.properties) and the property from the model bean.

Note the last column: it contains another JSP that defines the actions for each row. This JSP defines the Actions button that appears on every row of the search container table, allowing users to perform certain actions on `PRProducts`. Figure 4.8 shows this button.

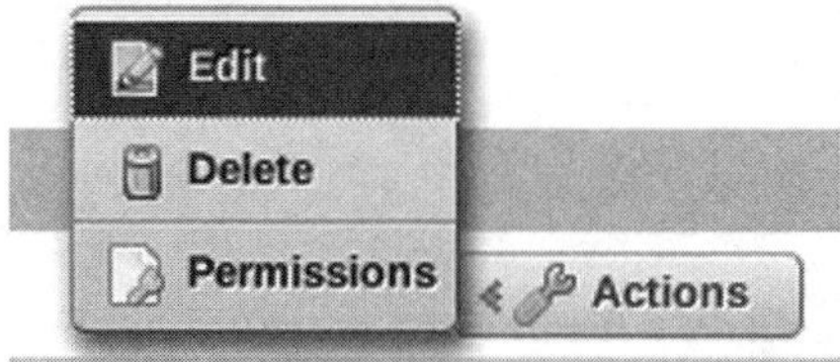

Figure 4.8 At the end of every row, an Actions button appears. When users click this button, they can perform three actions on each record: edit it, delete it, or set permissions on it.

The Actions button is implemented in another JSP, `admin_actions.jsp`.

Listing 4.9 Adding actions to the search container

```
<%@include file="/init.jsp" %>

<%
ResultRow row =
 (ResultRow) request.getAttribute(
    WebKeys.SEARCH_CONTAINER_RESULT_ROW);
PRProduct myProduct = (PRProduct) row.getObject();       <- Gets object from row
long groupId = themeDisplay.getLayout().getGroupId();
String name = PRProduct.class.getName();
String primKey = String.valueOf(myProduct.getPrimaryKey());
%>

<liferay-ui:icon-menu>

  <c:if test="<%= permissionChecker.hasPermission(groupId, name, primKey,
 ActionKeys.UPDATE) %>">
    <portlet:actionURL name="editProduct" var="editURL">
      <portlet:param name="resourcePrimKey" value="<%= primKey %>" />
    </portlet:actionURL>

    <liferay-ui:icon image="edit" message="Edit" url="
<%= editURL.toString() %>" />
  </c:if>

  <c:if test="<%= permissionChecker.hasPermission(groupId, name, primKey,
  ➥ ActionKeys.DELETE) %>">
    <portlet:actionURL name="deleteProduct" var="deleteURL">
      <portlet:param name="resourcePrimKey" value="<%= primKey %>" />
    </portlet:actionURL>

    <liferay-ui:icon-delete url="<%= deleteURL.toString() %>" />   <- Delete is different
  </c:if>

  <c:if test="<%= permissionChecker.hasPermission(groupId, name, primKey,
  ➥ ActionKeys.PERMISSIONS) %>">
    <liferay-security:permissionsURL
        modelResource="<%= PRProduct.class.getName() %>"
        modelResourceDescription="<%= myProduct.getProductName() %>"
        resourcePrimKey="<%= primKey %>"
        var="permissionsURL"
 />
```

```
    <liferay-ui:icon image="permissions"
    ➥ url="<%= permissionsURL.toString() %>" />
  </c:if>
</liferay-ui:icon-menu>
```

docroot/admin/admin_actions.jsp

As the search container loops through records, certain attributes of that container are available in the request, such as the current row in the loop. For each row, you can retrieve the `PRProduct` object and pull information about it that you need in order to implement the Actions button functionality.

For example, the database code operates from primary key values. The view layer therefore needs to provide a primary key to the action method so that the `PRProduct` to be operated on can be found in the database. You use the list of `PRProduct` objects that are wrapped in the search container to retrieve these keys, and then you define the key that is found as a parameter on each action URL you generate. In this file you're defining the action URLs that you'll use to call functionality for specific `PRProduct` objects. These URLs are then used in Liferay tags that assemble the Actions button with its links that fly out when the button is clicked.

Note that you haven't used any JavaScript or CSS to generate this; it's automatically generated by the tag library. This makes the tag library convenient to use, and your code looks clean. Additionally, the delete action uses a slightly different tag:

```
<liferay-ui:icon-delete url="<%= deleteURL.toString() %>" />
```

Because you never want to delete something without asking the user, "Are you sure?" the `icon-delete` tag automatically generates a JavaScript-based dialog that pops up and asks that question, allowing users to cancel if they clicked it by mistake.

Pretty cool, eh?

Now that you've got things working in the front end, you need to make sure those actions have functionality behind them.

4.3.7 Editing and deleting data

By now, you're probably getting the idea that the amount of code you have to write in Liferay's `MVCPortlet` for these kinds of applications is drastically reduced compared to what you might be used to. When a user clicks the Edit button in the search container, the `editProduct` portlet action runs. Because the action URL contained in a parameter the primary key of the record you want to edit, you can use that to retrieve the entity for editing:

```
public void editProduct(ActionRequest request, ActionResponse response)
    throws Exception {

    long productKey = ParamUtil.getLong(request, "resourcePrimKey");

    if (Validator.isNotNull productKey)) {
        PRProduct product =
            PRProductLocalServiceUtil.getPRProduct(productKey);
```

```
        request.setAttribute("product", product);
        response.setRenderParameter("jspPage", editProductJSP);

    }

}
```

Of course, you validate the key to make sure it has a value before you pass it on in your processing logic. Then you grab the `PRPRoduct` from the database and put it in the request so you can display it on a form for editing. This form will be almost the same form used for adding products; in fact, it could be the same form if you wanted it to be. But I'd like to point out one more thing before you get to the form: the last line of the previous code. Because you've defined the location of the edit form in the portlet's instance variable `editProductJSP`, you can point the page-management render parameter, `jspPage`, to the page where you want the user directed when this action completes. The following listing shows that form.

Listing 4.10 Editing a product

```
<%@include file="/init.jsp" %>

<%
PRProduct product = (PRProduct) request.getAttribute("product");
%>

<portlet:renderURL var="cancelURL">
  <portlet:param name="jspPage" value="/admin/view.jsp" />
</portlet:renderURL>

<portlet:actionURL name="updateProduct" var="updateProductURL" />

<h2>Edit A Product</h2>

<aui:form
   name="fm" action="<%= updateProductURL.toString() %>"
   method="post">

  <aui:fieldset>

    <aui:input
        name="resourcePrimKey"
        value="<%= product.getProductId() %>"
        type="hidden" />

    <aui:input
        name="productName"
        value="<%= product.getProductName() %>"
        size="45" />
    <aui:input
        name="productSerial"
        value="<%= product.getSerialNumber() %>"
        size="45" />

    <aui:button-row>
```

Cancel button is render URL

Submit button is action URL

```
        <aui:button type="submit"/>
        <aui:button
            type="cancel"
            value="Cancel"
            onClick="<%= cancelURL.toString() %>"
        />

      </aui:button-row>

    </aui:fieldset>

  </aui:form>
```

docroot/admin/edit_product.jsp

As you can see, you use the `jspPage` functionality again in the form to let the Cancel button know where to send the users if they decide editing this product isn't what they want to do. The action URL points to another action that updates the product. Can you see how much easier it is to manage page flow with `MVCPortlet`? The only place you have to look for where the users are directed next is the natural place: the view layer.

Because the `update` method is so similar to the `add` method, there's no point in outlining it here (although, of course, you can see it by downloading the source code for this chapter). The same goes for the `delete` method. Let's instead get to something more interesting. You've seen it sprinkled throughout the earlier code, but we haven't touched on it yet: permissions.

4.3.8 Protecting data with Liferay permissions

Liferay Portal has a robust permissions system that allows you to implement just about any security model you can think of. This system has been designed so that developers who write portlets to be deployed on Liferay can make the same use of the permissions system as the portlets that ship with Liferay. This means you can implement security all the way down to the object level of your code.

You can now implement security in a portlet to enable administrators to set permissions so that only the users they want can add products. Doing so is surprisingly easy, particularly if you're already familiar with conditionally displaying HTML fragments to users. You'll implement that part of it using JavaServer Pages Standard Tag Library (JSTL) for this example.

To configure your portlet to use Liferay permissions, you don't have to write any code. The only code you'll ever write with regard to permissions is simple `if` statements to check permissions. You enable permissions in a portlet by creating two files: portlet.properties and a permissions XML file.

4.3.9 Pointing to the permissions configuration

In the source folder of your project, create portlet.properties with the following content:

```
resource.actions.configs=resource-actions/default.xml
```

Save the file. This properties file is automatically read by Liferay and contains directives that configure the portlet or override settings from portal.properties.

The previous directive tells Liferay that the configuration file for the permissions system is in a folder called resource-actions and the file name is default.xml.

4.3.10 Configuring Liferay permissions

Create the resource-actions folder in your src folder, and create the default.xml file in this folder. The following listing shows the file's contents.

Listing 4.11 Defining Liferay permissions

```
<?xml version="1.0" encoding="UTF-8"?>

<resource-action-mapping>                                   ❶ Portlet resource actions

  <portlet-resource>
    <portlet-name>product-admin</portlet-name>
    <permissions>
       <supports>
         <action-key>ADD_PRODUCT</action-key>
         <action-key>VIEW</action-key>
       </supports>
       <community-defaults>
         <action-key>VIEW</action-key>
       </community-defaults>
       <guest-defaults>
         <action-key>VIEW</action-key>
       </guest-defaults>

       <guest-unsupported>
         <action-key>ADD_PRODUCT</action-key>
       </guest-unsupported>

    </permissions>
  </portlet-resource>                                       ❷ Model resource actions

  <model-resource>
    <model-name>
      com.inkwell.internet.productregistration.model.PRProduct
    </model-name>
    <portlet-ref>
      <portlet-name>product-admin</portlet-name>
    </portlet-ref>
    <permissions>

      <supports>
        <action-key>DELETE</action-key>
        <action-key>PERMISSIONS</action-key>
        <action-key>UPDATE</action-key>
        <action-key>VIEW</action-key>
      </supports>
      <community-defaults>
        <action-key>VIEW</action-key>
```

```
    </community-defaults>
    <guest-defaults>
      <action-key>VIEW</action-key>
    </guest-defaults>
    <guest-unsupported>
      <action-key>UPDATE</action-key>
    </guest-unsupported>
  </permissions>
</model-resource>

<model-resource>
  <model-name>
    com.inkwell.internet.productregistration.model.PRUser
  </model-name>
  <portlet-ref>
    <portlet-name>product-registration</portlet-name>
  </portlet-ref>
  <permissions>
    <supports>
      <action-key>DELETE</action-key>
      <action-key>PERMISSIONS</action-key>
      <action-key>UPDATE</action-key>
      <action-key>VIEW</action-key>
    </supports>
    <community-defaults>
      <action-key>VIEW</action-key>
    </community-defaults>
    <guest-defaults>
      <action-key>VIEW</action-key>
    </guest-defaults>
    <guest-unsupported>
      <action-key>UPDATE</action-key>
    </guest-unsupported>
  </permissions>
</model-resource>

<model-resource>
  <model-name>
    com.inkwell.internet.productregistration.model.PRRegistration
  </model-name>
  <portlet-ref>
    <portlet-name>product-registration</portlet-name>
  </portlet-ref>
  <permissions>
    <supports>
      <action-key>DELETE</action-key>
      <action-key>PERMISSIONS</action-key>
      <action-key>UPDATE</action-key>
      <action-key>VIEW</action-key>
    </supports>
    <community-defaults>
      <action-key>VIEW</action-key>
    </community-defaults>
    <guest-defaults>
      <action-key>VIEW</action-key>
```

```
      </guest-defaults>
      <guest-unsupported>
        <action-key>UPDATE</action-key>
      </guest-unsupported>
    </permissions>
  </model-resource>
</resource-action-mapping>
```

docroot/WEB-INF/src/resource-actions/default.xml

Notice that there are two sections to this file: a section defining a *portlet resource* and a section defining a *model resource.*

DEFINING THE PORTLET RESOURCE

The portlet resource section ❶ defines all the actions the portlet supports. Two of the defaults are `configuration` and `view`. The `configuration` action is the standard Liferay configuration screen, to which users can navigate by clicking the Configuration button in the window title of a portlet. You don't have it here because your portlet is in the Control Panel and doesn't need a configuration screen.

The other default action you've added is `view`. This action lets users view the portlet. Without this action, no one would be able to view the portlet, which wouldn't make any sense.

The third action isn't a default action, but one you've defined as functionality for this portlet: `add product`. By defining this action, you're saying that you want to choose which users can add products and which users can't.

These actions are portlet actions, because they belong to the portlet itself. The portlet is the authority for whether `PRProducts` (and `PRRegistrations`) can be created, edited, or viewed. Therefore the `add product` action is a portlet action. If you wanted to set permissions for this action in Liferay, you could do so by creating a role and then defining permissions for it.

DEFINING THE MODEL RESOURCE

The resources in ❷ are the objects you've created that are stored in the database. You've been providing the functionality for creating, editing, and deleting `PRProducts`. If you want to wrap Liferay's permissions system around the objects that have been created, you need to define those permissions in this file as model resource permissions.

To define the permissions for a resource, specify the fully qualified class name for the object and then define what actions may be performed on instances of that object. `Delete`, `update`, and `view` are actions you may want to grant permission to do, and those functions have already been created. You're adding a new action—`permissions`—which is a user's ability to grant or take away permissions to do other actions. The nice thing about this is that *no coding has to be done to enable this.* You need to provide a link to Liferay's permissions system—which will be covered next—and this functionality will be added to your portlet. Figure 4.9 shows what happens when that link is in place: your entities can be permissioned in exactly the same way as any other entity in Liferay.

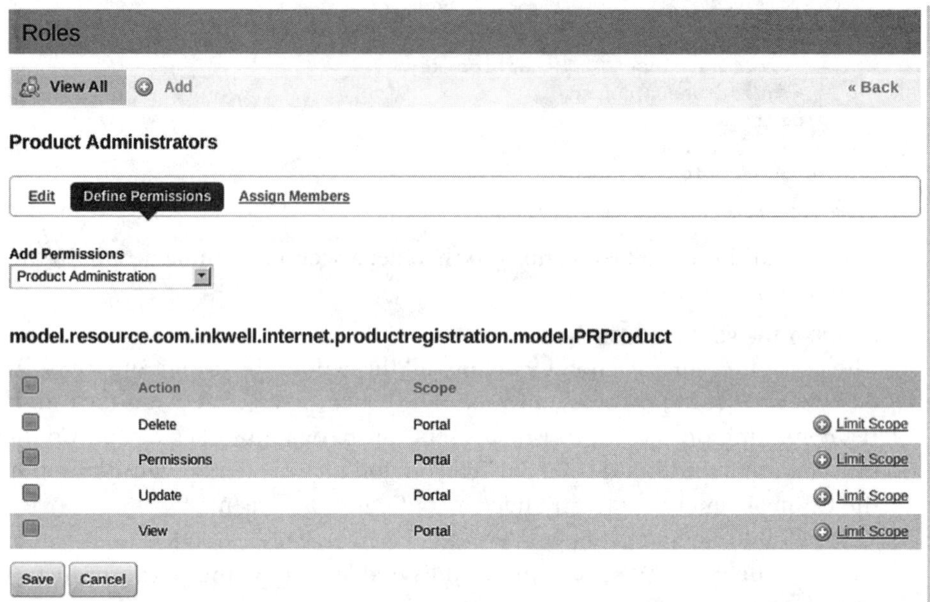

Figure 4.9 Any model resource you define can have permissions configured for it in Liferay. Here, you've created a role called Product Administrators. You can grant that role permission to delete, to define permissions, to update, or to view `PRProducts`.

In both the portlet resources and model resources sections of the file, you can define default permissions for guests or the community/organization in which the portlet is located. For portlet resources, you've given everyone the View permission by default and have made sure that for guests, the Add Product permission is unsupported. For model resources, you've given everyone permission to view `PRProduct` records (otherwise, users who aren't registered wouldn't be able to register their products online, because they wouldn't be able to pick them from a list) and have prevented guests from being able to update a product.

All these permissions can be overridden by administrators through the permissions system. These are the permissions that will be set by default when the portlet is added to a page.

Believe it or not, we've now covered all of the APIs that Liferay gives you for easily creating data-driven portlets. But you're not through yet: you'll probably need to do some more advanced things that I haven't shown you yet in the Product Registration portlet. Let's look at the registration form to hit those areas.

4.4 Generating different field types with AlloyUI taglibs

If you recall, the registration form has more than just text fields on it. Users are asked to pick from lists and fill out a couple of date fields. Anyone who has written data-driven applications knows that giving users a text field for these kinds of things leads

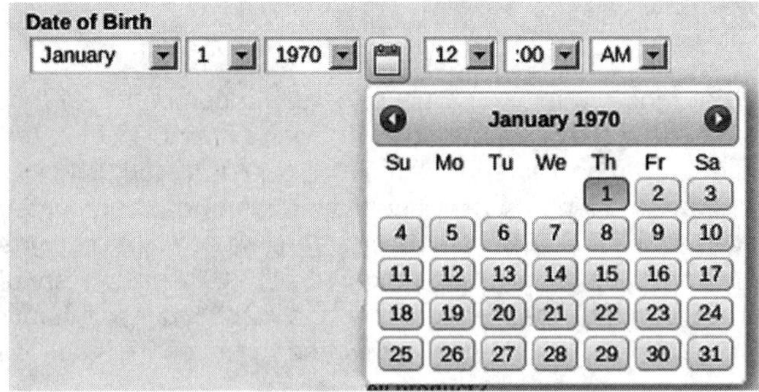

Figure 4.10 AlloyUI tag libraries make it easy to generate date pickers. No JavaScript required.

to inconsistent data. Dates can be entered in any number of ways, and users will likely never type things exactly the way you want them to. This means you need to provide ways to enter this data that both preserve the integrity of the data and are easy.

In this section, you'll create a date-picker control and a select box.

4.4.1 Generating date pickers

With AlloyUI taglibs, you can generate a date field that looks like figure 4.10.

You can generate this great date picker automatically by crafting the field as shown next.

Listing 4.12 Date picker without JavaScript

```
<liferay-ui:error
    key="birthdate-required"
    message="date-of-birth-required" />

<%
Calendar dob = CalendarFactoryUtil.getCalendar();
dob.setTime(regUser.getBirthDate());
%>                                          Initialize Calendar object

<aui:input
    name="birthDate"
    model="<%= PRUser.class %>"
    bean="<%= regUser %>"                   Tag contains model, bean, value
    value="<%= dob %>" />
```

docroot/registration/view_add_registration.jsp

Obviously, the date picker can't be created without JavaScript, so it may be an exaggeration to say it was. But *you* don't have to write any of it. By using the tag, the same JavaScript that Liferay wrote to provide date pickers for its own portlets is used to provide your date picker.

There's one thing missing, though. Notice that you're working with a date field, and the date in figure 4.10 is from 1970. This is so it's clear that users should pick a date in the *past*, not a recent date.

Why 1970?

Studies have shown that most people don't have the same perception of time that occurred before their birth that they have for time afterward. It's not as real to them. According to UNIX, time started on Thursday, January 1, 1970. Although it can represent time before that, that time isn't as real, because it has to be represented as a negative number. Why? Because UNIX (and most operating systems) represents time as "the number of seconds *since* midnight on January 1, 1970." This system of time works well, but it has some problems; for example, the Y2K38 bug will happen on Tuesday, January 19, 2038 when the integer that's used to represent time rolls over to a negative value.

Why did I pick 1970 for the example? Convenience. It's somewhere in the middle of the time range when people who are using this application were born. Plus you get geek cred for using January 1, 1970.

To make the tag display just a date, you have to give it *model hints*. This is the developer's equivalent of pulling Liferay aside and whispering in its ear, "Hey, I want you to display the field *this* way." You do so using a file that was generated when Service Builder created Java classes to manipulate your data. Open the file portlet-model-hints.xml, which you'll find in the META-INF folder of your src folder. Scroll down in the file until you find the field for birth date, and replace it with the following code:

```
<field name="birthDate" type="Date">
  <hint name="year-range-delta">70</hint>
  <hint name="year-range-future">false</hint>
  <hint name="show-time">false</hint>
</field>
```

This tells the tag that for this field, you want a date range of 70 years, and you want to disable the user's ability to select dates that are in the future. And because it's a birth date, you don't want to show the time attributes on the field. This makes the data entry appropriate for a birth date field.

Later in the form, you have a Date Purchased field. For this field, all you need to do is turn off showing the time.

The form uses another field type we haven't covered: a select box.

4.4.2 Selecting data with AlloyUI taglibs

When users select the product for which they're registering, you populate that selection field with values from the database (see the Product Type field in figure 4.11). This is a simple matter of using the AlloyUI tag for a select field along with some Java code that retrieves the data, as shown in the following listing.

Listing 4.13 Filling an AlloyUI option tag

```
<%
List<PRProduct> products =
    PRProductLocalServiceUtil.getAllProducts(themeDisplay.getScopeGroupId());
```

```
%>

<aui:select name="productType">
  <aui:option value="-1">
    <liferay-ui:message key="please-choose" />
  </aui:option>

  <%
  for (PRProduct product : products) {
  %>
  <aui:option
 value="<%= product.getProductId() %>">
    <%= product.getProductName() %>
  </aui:option>
  <%
  }
  %>

</aui:select>
```

docroot/registration/view_add_registration.jsp

You get the primary key as the value of the select, and you get the name of the product for display to the user. This populates the selection box, and AlloyUI takes care of the formatting. As you can see, AlloyUI tags do a lot in terms of providing both functionality and a consistent look and feel for your forms. You don't have to mess with CSS or JavaScript by default, and if you do want a custom look and feel for your fields and buttons, you can do so in one place by styling them in a theme (see chapter 5).

The completed form contains multiple field types, all generated using AlloyUI tag libraries (see figure 4.11).

I can't say this enough: use the AlloyUI tag libraries for forms. They're an incredible help and time saver, and they can make your forms a lot nicer with little effort.

Now that you've written the entire portlet, let's look at the portlet class as a whole to see the benefits of using Liferay's `MVCPortlet`.

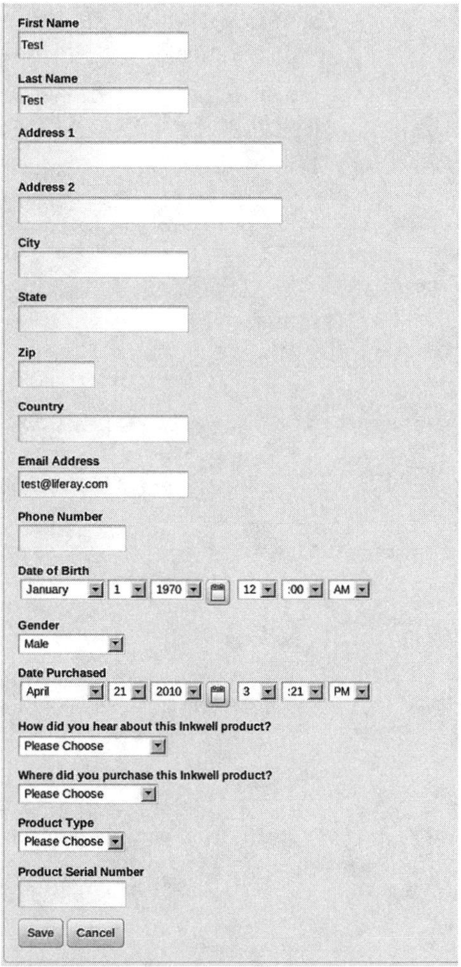

Figure 4.11 No HTML, CSS, or JavaScript was used to develop this form. Every element was created by AlloyUI tag libraries, which generate standard HTML and widgets to assist the user in filling out the form.

4.5 Using Liferay's MVC makes your portlets simpler

The great thing about Liferay's MVC framework is how it makes portlet classes simpler. You don't have to write page-management or page-flow code; `MVCPortlet` handles that for you. To demonstrate, the following listing shows the entire Product Registration portlet class.

Listing 4.14 Product Registration portlet class

```
public void addRegistration(
    ActionRequest request, ActionResponse response) {      ❶ User clicks Register button

    ThemeDisplay themeDisplay = (ThemeDisplay) request.getAttribute(
        WebKeys.THEME_DISPLAY);

    PRRegistration registration = new PRRegistrationImpl();
    PRUser prUser = new PRUserImpl();

    if (themeDisplay.isSignedIn()) {
        User user = themeDisplay.getUser();
        List<Address> addresses = Collections.EMPTY_LIST;
        Address homeAddr = null;

        try {
            addresses =
                AddressLocalServiceUtil.getAddresses(
                    user.getCompanyId(),
                    User.class.getName(),
                    user.getUserId());
        }
        catch (SystemException ex) {

        }

        if (addresses.size() > 0) {
            homeAddr = addresses.get(0);
        }

        prUser.setFirstName(user.getFirstName());
        prUser.setLastName(user.getLastName());
        prUser.setEmail(user.getEmailAddress());

        try {
            prUser.setBirthDate(user.getBirthday());
            boolean male = user.getMale();
            if (male) {
                prUser.setGender("male");
            }
            else {
                prUser.setGender("female");
            }
            prUser.setMale(male);
        }
        catch (PortalException e) {
            prUser.setBirthDate(new Date());
        }
```

```
        catch (SystemException e) {
            prUser.setMale(true);
        }

        if (homeAddr != null) {
            prUser.setAddress1(homeAddr.getStreet1());
            prUser.setAddress2(homeAddr.getStreet2());
            prUser.setCity(homeAddr.getCity());
            prUser.setPostalCode(homeAddr.getZip());
            prUser.setCountry(homeAddr.getCountry().toString());
        }

        registration.setDatePurchased(new Date());
    }
    else {


        registration.setDatePurchased(new Date());

        Calendar dob = CalendarFactoryUtil.getCalendar();
        dob.set(Calendar.YEAR, 1970);
        prUser.setBirthDate(dob.getTime());
        prUser.setGender("");

    }


    request.setAttribute("regUser", prUser);
    request.setAttribute("registration", registration);
    response.setRenderParameter("jspPage", viewAddRegistrationJSP);
}

public void registerProduct(
        ActionRequest request, ActionResponse response)
throws Exception {
    PRUser regUser = ActionUtil.prUserFromRequest(request);
    PRRegistration registration =
        ActionUtil.prRegistrationFromRequest(request);
    ArrayList<String> errors = new ArrayList<String>();
    ThemeDisplay themeDisplay =
        (ThemeDisplay)request.getAttribute(WebKeys.THEME_DISPLAY);

    long userId = themeDisplay.getUserId();

    User liferayUser = UserLocalServiceUtil.getUser(userId);

    boolean userValid = ProdRegValidator.validateUser(regUser, errors);
    boolean regValid =
        ProdRegValidator.validateRegistration(registration, errors);

    if (userValid && regValid) {

        PRUser user = null;

        if (liferayUser.isDefaultUser()) {
            userId = 0;
            user = PRUserLocalServiceUtil.addPRUser(regUser, userId);
```

2 User clicks Submit button

```
        }
        else {

            user =
                PRUserLocalServiceUtil.getPRUser(
                    themeDisplay.getScopeGroupId(), userId);

            if (user == null) {
                regUser.setUserId(userId);
                user =
                    PRUserLocalServiceUtil.addPRUser(
regUser, userId);

            }

        }

        registration.setPrUserId(user.getPrUserId());

        PRRegistrationLocalServiceUtil.addRegistration(registration);
        SessionMessages.add(request,
"registration-saved-successfully");
        response.setRenderParameter("jspPage", viewThankYouJSP);
    }
    else {
        for (String error : errors) {
            SessionErrors.add(request, error);
        }
        SessionErrors.add(request, "error-saving-registration");
        response.setRenderParameter("jspPage", viewAddRegistrationJSP);
        request.setAttribute("regUser", regUser);
        request.setAttribute("registration", registration);
    }

}
```

docroot/WEB-INF/src/com/inkwell/internet/productregistration/portlet/ProductRegistrationPortlet.java

Note that to save space (as I'll do for the rest of the book), I've removed ancillary elements like import statements, Javadoc, comments, and package declarations. The important point is this: the entire portlet class has been reduced to only two methods, and both of them are the result of actions the user performs. The first is when users click the Register button to display the form ❶, and the second is when users click the Submit button to submit the registration ❷. The Product Administration portlet is the same: it consists only of action methods that users trigger by clicking something. The full source code for this project is available as a downloadable companion to this book; if you want to check it out in more detail, please do so.

4.6 Summary

Liferay's MVC framework speeds up the development of portlets. Portlet classes are reduced to only action methods, because the framework handles the page management logic through a simple render parameter called `jspPage`. Because Liferay's MVC portlet is extended from the Portlet API's class, you can still use the full API of the portlet standard.

In addition to the MVC portlet itself, Liferay offers a wide range of utilities to assist the developer. The `Validator` class assists you in performing field validation for forms. AlloyUI tag libraries help you create good-looking, dynamic forms complete with CSS styling and autogenerated JavaScript widgets. Data tables are easy with the search container. Liferay also provides a way to automatically translate language bundles so they can support multiple languages easily. And finally, Liferay permissions are easy to integrate into any application by configuring those permissions in an XML file, which Liferay then reads in order to integrate its full permissions UI with your application.

We've covered a lot in this chapter, but I hope you're still with me and that you can see some of the power of Liferay's development platform. Next, we'll turn to another plugin type: themes. These let you completely control the way Liferay looks.

5 Designing your site with themes and layout templates

This chapter covers

- Creating theme and layout template projects
- The structure of Liferay's styles and layouts
- Alloy UI and JavaScript in themes
- Theme features, such as color schemes, conditional settings, and more

At one time, I was put in charge of the development standards for a particular web development platform at a Fortune 500 company. I'd just joined the company. A lot of applications on the company's intranet were written on this platform, and pretty much every one of them looked different. Management had a goal to try to unify the user interfaces of all of these applications so end users would approach something familiar whenever they had to use one of these applications.

I got to work. This was one of the first tasks I was assigned at my new position, and I wanted to do a good job and make a good impression. I began by looking at what all these applications needed to have in common: a way to link back to the intranet's home page, a consistent way to access their functions, and so on. I came up with a 100-pixel space at the top of every page that was the common "header" for all applications. The logo for the app went on the left; the logo for the intranet was on the right, and a drop-down menu system implemented in JavaScript went underneath.

Implementing this header for new applications was easy—it was a simple matter of getting management's approval on the design, after which it became a standard that everybody had to follow. Implementing it for older applications was a bit more difficult. The company's web apps were on three different software platforms, each of which held both new and legacy applications. To retrofit this common standard to all of them proved to be more complicated than I'd expected (but in my defense, my original task was only to apply the standard to the platform for which I was responsible).

As is usual in big companies, we brought in a new platform a year later that made the entire project moot. That platform happened to be a portal, and over the course of the next few years, as more applications went into the portal, the portal's inherent theming capabilities ensured that every application had a consistent look and feel. The best part for me was that the user interface possibilities were standardized by the portal's framework. That's the way portals work, and it's powerful.

Liferay themes allow developers and designers to completely customize the look and feel of Liferay Portal. They've been designed to integrate nicely with the web technologies you already know: HTML, Cascading Style Sheets (CSS), and JavaScript. As a theme developer, you won't need to know the ins and outs of Java. Instead, Liferay makes many variables available using the Velocity and FreeMarker templating languages. Both of these are easy-to-use languages that integrate with HTML in a similar manner to PHP; PHP developers should find it comfortable to work with either one.

When you've designed a theme, you can implement any number of layout templates. These enable you to provide custom page layouts into which your portlets can be placed. Although Liferay ships with many layout templates included, many times when working with a particularly complex page design, only a custom layout will do.

In this chapter, you'll learn the components of Liferay themes so you can use your artistic and design skills to make your site look—well, any way you want it to look. We'll go over the components of a theme and show how they can be customized to create your own look and feel. You'll also learn how to create layout templates to go with your themes that let you place portlets anywhere you want. Let's start with a couple of examples.

5.1 Understanding themes and their structure

Believe me when I say you can make Liferay look like *anything*. Don't believe me (after all the time we've spent together)? Okay. Before I get into the details of themes, I'll show you two web sites that run on Liferay but that couldn't be more different; nor could they be targeted to more different audiences.

Figure 5.1 You can find this site at www.sesamestreet.org. Targeted to children, the site won the first Emmy award, called New Approaches, for digital media. Can you tell it's running Liferay? No, I didn't think so.

The first is the web site for Sesame Street. Behold figure 5.1.

Obviously, the Sesame Street web site is geared for children. Using large fonts, minimal text, lots of colors, and running video, this site is easy for small children to navigate. If you don't believe that, I have a six-year-old daughter who would be glad to speak to you.

On to the next example, shown in figure 5.2.

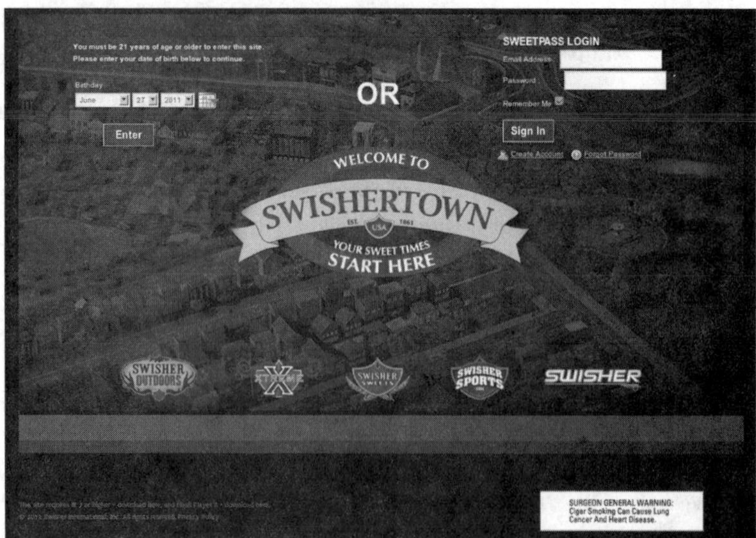

Figure 5.2 You can find this site at www.swisher.com. It's obviously *not* targeted at small children, as the Surgeon General's warning should make clear. This site also has a user community and includes "Swisher Sweethearts," which must be a kind of candy or something.

Ah, tobacco. Whether you smoke it, chew it, or stick it between your gums, you aren't going to be giving it to your kids. This site isn't for children, even though sometimes a cigar is just a cigar. But the important thing is, there's no way you can tell that this site is running on Liferay Portal. And it obviously has a completely different look than Sesame Street does, because it caters to a completely different audience.

The reason I wanted to show you these sites is simple: if *they* can do it, *you* can do it too. The goal of this chapter is to give you what you need to write your own themes, making your web site look however you want it to look, to target your particular audience.

5.1.1 *Generating a theme project*

Themes are plugins and are therefore hot-deployable just like portlet plugins. You can use the Plugins SDK (see chapter 2) to package a theme into a .war file just like a portlet, and this .war file can then be deployed to Liferay in the same manner you deploy a portlet.

Liferay makes writing themes as straightforward as possible. If you have experience in coding HTML, CSS, and JavaScript, you should be right at home with Liferay themes. Here's a warning up front about this chapter: as in the previous chapters, which assumed knowledge of Java web applications, here I'm assuming knowledge of HTML, CSS, and JavaScript. If you don't have familiarity with these technologies, there are many great books on the subject, including John Resig's *Secrets of the JavaScript Ninja* (Manning, 2011) and David Flanagan's *JavaScript: The Definitive Guide* (O'Reilly, 2011).

But before we get into all that complicated stuff, let's look at the structure of a theme.

5.1.2 *Deconstructing a theme*

Let's jump in and look at the directory structure of a theme using Inkwell as an example. You create a new theme in exactly the same way you create a portlet. The Inkwell developers want to create a theme called Inkwell Internet. This is how they do it in LUM

```
./create.sh inkwell-internet "Inkwell Internet"
```

and on Windows:

```
create.bat inkwell-internet "Inkwell Internet"
```

This creates your new theme project, which has a surprisingly small and simple directory structure (see figure 5.3).

Figure 5.3 The structure of a newly generated theme. You can see that it doesn't contain any code, but you can deploy it and get a copy of the default theme. What gives?

As you can see, initially there isn't much in a theme project. To build your theme, we need to look at how theming works in Liferay.

If you look inside Liferay's .war file or into the webapps folder of a Tomcat installation that contains Liferay, you'll find that Liferay contains a few themes bundled in by default. Two of these are important and form the basis of all other themes:

- *_unstyled*—This theme contains all the default Velocity templates and image files necessary for a full theme, but it's *unstyled* in the sense that no CSS styling is applied to the layout. The CSS files are there, but only the descriptors are in the file—no style information is added for any of them.
- *_styled*—This theme contains nothing but CSS styling (and a screenshot image of the theme) that applies a basic look and feel. Liferay's default theme, called *Classic*, is an extension of the _styled theme.

When you create a new theme, you concentrate on the *differences* between the designated parent theme (specified as a property in the build.xml file for the theme) and your theme. That is why the _diffs folder is there, and that is where you'll put your theme code. You can use the _unstyled theme as a template for your own theme, mirroring the directory structure that you find there under the _diffs folder.

To get started, create the following folders under _diffs:

- css
- images
- js
- templates

Examine the code in the _unstyled theme and decide if you need to change the markup. For example, the default page contains a `div` for a top banner that pulls in the logo that was uploaded to Liferay. Perhaps you want your theme to randomly choose a different banner for each page visit, and none of the banners will use the uploaded logo. In this case, you need to modify portal_normal.vm and change the markup to support the functionality you want. You also likely need to add some JavaScript functions in the js folder to implement the banner switch. Note that your markup goes in the templates folder under _diffs.

Now that you know where everything goes, it's important to understand how you can use the three components of a theme, which we'll look at next.

5.2 Understanding theme markup, CSS, and JavaScript

In this section, we'll take a closer look at the markup (HTML/Velocity/FreeMarker), the styling (CSS), and the scripting (JavaScript) that go into a theme. A lot of this look and feel stuff is more art than science, so I'll go the route of showing you the Liferay-specific things you need to know about themes rather than delving deeply into markup, CSS, and JavaScript. If you're a site designer, you probably already have all sorts of designs and scripts that you use on your sites. The rest of this chapter should help you apply those to your Liferay-powered web sites. We'll start with the easy stuff: markup.

5.2.1 How markup works in a theme

The purpose of each of the markup files that make up a default theme is described in table 5.1. If you need to customize any of the standard components on a Liferay Portal page, you create your own implementation of that particular file in the _diffs folder. And of course, you can use `includes` to break up the logic more than Liferay has if you wish.

Table 5.1 Default theme markup files

File	Purpose
init_custom.vm	Allows you to add custom Velocity variables.
init.vm	In conjunction with VelocityVariables.java in Liferay, sets many Velocity variables that correspond to Liferay Java objects.
navigation.vm	Implements the page navigation within the theme.
portal_normal.vm	The overall template for all pages the theme implements. This file includes the other files.
portal_pop_up.vm	The overall template for any portlets that use the Liferay pop-up custom window state.
portlet.vm	The template for portlet windows within the theme.

The global page markup is handled by portal_normal.vm. This page defines several layers of the page where page elements reside. Figure 5.4 shows the structure of the default Liferay page.

These elements are styled via CSS using styles that have been predefined in the parent theme. Of course, you're free to add your own styles as well. The Banner section is the top of the page; in the default theme, it includes the Liferay logo at top left, the Sign In link on the right, and the navigation menu underneath. The Content section contains the breadcrumbs as well as the layout template (which is another plugin type; you'll see this in section 5.6).

These elements of markup can be styled as you see fit. Next, you'll see how to use the styles provided and where to put your custom styles.

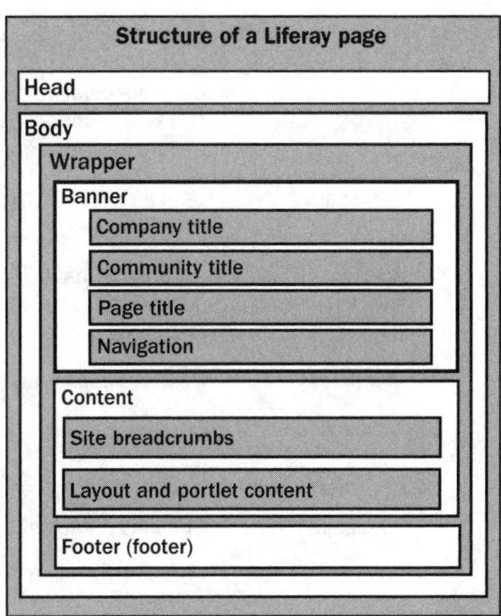

Figure 5.4 The default structure of a Liferay page. This figure shows the elements that can be styled via CSS. You may decide to include all of them, some of them, or only the portlet content elements in your theme.

5.2.2 Using CSS in themes

The default theme contains multiple .css files that handle every aspect of Liferay's UI and are divided in order to keep styling for similar components in the same place. When you create a theme, start your modifications with the global elements, such as the banner or the navigation menu. After that, you can move on to things in the Content section, like the tabs inside portlets.

For this reason, a best practice is to create a single file in the _diffs/css folder called custom.css. This file will contain all of the styles you want to implement that will override the default styles provided by Liferay. Because this file is processed last by the browser (due to the order of the import statements in main.css), all styles in this file are guaranteed to take precedence over any of the styles provided by default in Liferay. Any of the styles in multiple files can be overridden in custom.css; this file contains only the styles you need to modify from the default implementation. That way, your theme still works as you add customizations to it, because the default styles stay in place until you override them.

Table 5.2 describes the organization of the styles within Liferay's various .css files.

Table 5.2 Default theme CSS files and their purposes

File	Purpose
application.css	Contains default styling having to do with components of applications. This includes the tabs, expandable trees, dialog overlays, and the results grid (that is, search container). Much of the markup for these styles is created by Liferay's tag libraries.
base.css	Contains default styling for standard HTML tags, such as paragraphs, headings, tables, and more. This file also contains styling for some Liferay-specific page elements, such as errors, warnings, tooltips, the loading animation, and more.
dockbar.css	Contains default styling for the Dockbar, which floats at the top of the page when a user is logged in.
custom.css	A blank file that is loaded last. As a best practice, theme developers should put their custom styles here to override default styles provided by Liferay in the other theme CSS files.
forms.css	Contains default styling for all form elements.
layout.css	Contains default styling used by layout templates.
main.css	Contains no styling, but imports the rest of the files.
navigation.css	Contains default styling for the main navigation elements.
portlet.css	Contains default styling for the portlet windows.

You can override any style in any of the files in custom.css. Table 5.2 should help you to find a particular style that you may need to override. You can section off your custom.css file with comments and place related styles together to help you keep the styles organized. You can also separate your styles with `includes` as Liferay does in main.css.

When you've got the styling down, you may want to provide dynamic functionality using JavaScript. Next we'll look at where and how you can plug JavaScript functions into your theme.

5.2.3 Using JavaScript in themes

JavaScript goes inside a js folder in your _diffs folder. Liferay provides a default file that contains no implementation but that defines three events (see listing 5.1).

Listing 5.1 Liferay JavaScript events

```
AUI().ready(
    function() {

    }
);
Liferay.Portlet.ready(
    function(portletId, node) {

    }
);
Liferay.on(
    'allPortletsReady',
    function() {

    }
);
```

docroot/_diffs/js/main.js

Each of these events fires at a certain point when the page loads. The first fires when the HTML is delivered to the browser, sans portlets that are loaded dynamically. The second is executed for each portlet when it loads. The third runs when all the HTML has been loaded and all the portlets have been initialized.

In addition to theme-wide JavaScript, there is also support for page-specific JavaScript. When end users create a page using Liferay's GUI, the Page Settings form provides three separate placeholders for JavaScript that you can insert anywhere in your theme. Use the following in your theme markup to include the code from these settings:

```
$layout.getTypeSettingsProperties().getProperty("javascript-1")
$layout.getTypeSettingsProperties().getProperty("javascript-2")
$layout.getTypeSettingsProperties().getProperty("javascript-3")
```

The content of the JavaScript settings fields are stored in the database as Java properties. This means each field can have only one line of text. For multiline scripts, the newlines should be escaped using \, just as in a normal .properties file. For these reasons, the default themes provided by Liferay don't use this feature, because it's kind of a pain in the butt to use. I'm just letting you know it exists in case you want to use it.

We looked at Alloy UI in the last chapter from the perspective of its tag libraries. Let's next take a closer look at Alloy UI as a JavaScript library, because you may want to use it in your themes.

5.3 Reaping the benefits of Alloy UI

Alloy UI is a user interface web application framework. In other words, it's a set of pre-built components that you can use to build user interfaces in web applications. Underlying Alloy UI is the Yahoo! User Interface library (YUI), which is a well-known JavaScript library developed by Yahoo!, Inc. Alloy UI solves common problems faced by developers across the spectrum of HTML, CSS, and JavaScript, and it does so by combining the best of existing solutions under one consistent API that is easy to use.

You can use Alloy UI's components instead of hacking together your own markup, figuring out how to style it properly with CSS, and then coding up your own dynamic behavior with JavaScript. Alloy UI gives all of that to you.

First, its components use tags proposed in HTML 5 and are implemented with common markup patterns that work. That means you don't have to experiment with your markup until you come up with something usable. For non-front-end people, Alloy UI provides tag libraries that generate this—you've already seen this in the Product Registration portlet in chapter 4, when you used these tag libraries to generate forms.

Second, Alloy UI provides styling using CSS3 for layouts and forms, and its widgets gracefully degrade for browsers that don't support all CSS3 modules. This means that no matter which browser your end users are using, they will see the best possible result that their browser can render.

Third, Alloy UI's components are fully JavaScript enabled, complete with their own documented APIs. The JavaScript is based on YUI 3, which is a well known, widely used JavaScript library. This means the JavaScript is distributed across the spectrum of browsers and environments and therefore is well tested and robust. But this doesn't make the page heavy; instead, Alloy UI's JavaScript has built-in lazy loading, which means components don't load until they're needed. If you have a portlet on a page using one of Alloy UI's components, but the user is interacting with another portlet, Liferay doesn't have to waste time assembling all the portlet resources the user isn't using—instead, those resources load only when the user begins interacting with that portlet.

What does this mean practically to you? A lot. Two things come to mind right away: you get components, and you get good design.

5.3.1 You get components

A major benefit of using Alloy UI is its components. These are working pieces of code that already solve the problems you're probably trying to work out. You can use them in your themes and in your portlets to provide the best possible interface for your users. Figure 5.5 shows some of the components available with Alloy UI.

Here's a list of some of the kinds of components Alloy UI gives you:

- Autocomplete
- Charts
- Calendars
- Data grids
- Tabs

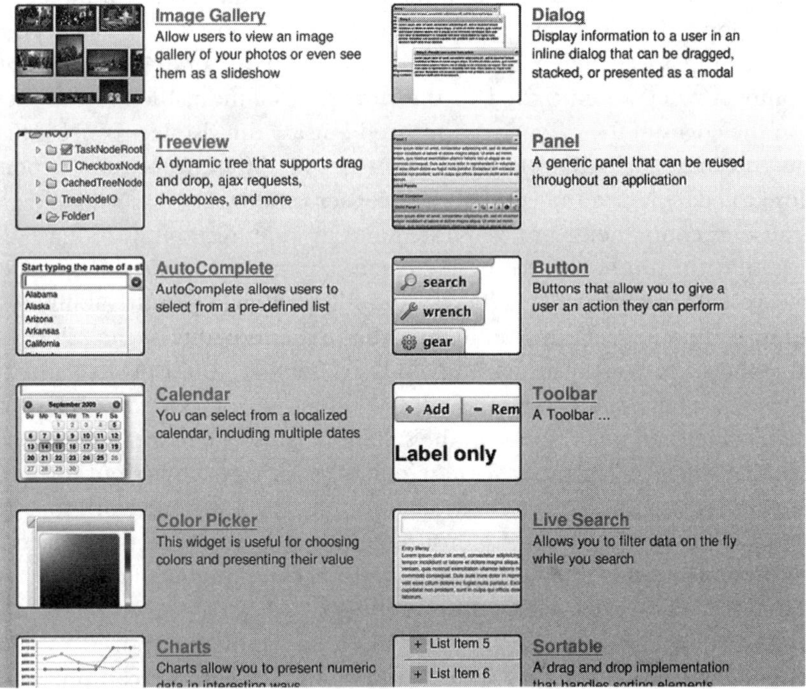

Figure 5.5 A few of the growing list of components available for Alloy UI. I had to cut off the image somewhere, but check http:// alloy.liferay.com for a complete, current list.

- Menus
- Paginator
- Trees
- Toolbars
- Slider
- Panels, dialogs, and overlays
- Ajax History management

As you can see, there are plenty of components you can use that will enable you to be more effective in your development projects. There's one more benefit I want to highlight: Alloy UI design.

5.3.2 You get good design

I can't tell you how many times I've written an application, deployed it, and then found that when used in the real world, either it didn't perform to expectations or the user did something I didn't foresee that completely borked the system.

If you've ever had to figure out why something was slow, or if you've ever asked a user, "Why'd you click that?!?" then you probably know what I mean. This can be a rude awakening for developers (like me), who sometimes assume everyone else's machine is configured the same way as theirs. For example, I once implemented a calendar that popped up different events when the user moused over dates. I completed the feature, and users began to test. Immediately it became apparent that if your screen and browser weren't sized to the proper resolution, the pop-ups (especially those on the edges of the calendar) appeared outside the visible area. Needless to say, I had to add some logic that placed the pop-up in a different location depending on how close the date was to the edge of the browser window.

Because its components are well-tested and in wide use, you won't have this problem with Alloy UI. You're not writing these components from scratch, so you won't run into unforeseen user interface glitches. And Alloy UI gives you the ability to add features to its components easily. You inherit all the functionality of the Alloy UI component and then add your own methods to that. Because you'll probably be adding a small piece of functionality to a preexisting, well-tested component, it's less likely that you'll add something that'll mess up the system or cause a performance issue.

If you use Alloy UI's forms or form tag libraries, you get consistent forms throughout your site. If you use Alloy UI's layouts, you get a great framework for organizing your content on the page and a consistent way to manipulate the objects on your pages, if that is necessary. Regardless, you get rich components that are well designed and well tested that you can use on your web site.

Like YUI, Alloy UI can be used as a generic JavaScript library outside of Liferay. An entire book could probably be written on Alloy UI alone, so we can only scratch the surface here. Liferay also has custom JavaScript that is based on Alloy UI; let's look at that in more detail.

5.3.3 Using Liferay custom JavaScript

Liferay includes a lot of custom JavaScript (much of it dependent on Alloy UI) that can help you to create a dynamic, modern web site. You'll find that a lot of the common things you want to do are already covered by Liferay's included JavaScript functions, so you don't have to reinvent the wheel. These are all properly namespaced, so even if you don't wish to use Liferay's implementations of certain pieces of functionality, you're free to write your own.

Note also that if you're a Java developer, many of the tag libraries you'll use implement their functionality using Alloy UI's JavaScript. You've seen an example of this with the `<aui:input />` tag you used as a date picker in the Product Registration portlet (see chapter 4). This is an incredible time saver, because you don't have to spend hours developing highly functional web widgets in JavaScript: Liferay has already done it for you.

The exhaustive list of what JavaScript functionality is available can be found in Liferay's source under portal-web/html/js/liferay. What follows is a list of some common things web developers may want to do:

- `Liferay.AutoFields`—Contains functions for forms that have fields that repeat. A well-known example can be found in Google's Gmail: when a user wants to attach a file, initially only one field is available. If the user wants to attach another file, there is a link stating Attach Another File that the user can click. When the user does so, another file browser is created, allowing the user to attach another file to the message. Users can duplicate the field as many times as they want to attach as many files as they want. Liferay includes similar functionality that is used in places such as the CMS, where users can create repeatable fields. Using this class, you can implement this feature as well.

- `Liferay.ColorPicker`—Creates an inline dialog that allows users to pick a color that is already being displayed and have that color's hexadecimal value inserted into a field.
- `Liferay.Language`—Allows you to get the values of language keys by using JavaScript instead of by using the tag library. It defines a single method, `get()`, which requires the key. In themes, you can get the global Liferay Portal keys; in portlets, you can get both Liferay Portal keys and custom keys you've created for your portlet.
- `Liferay.Notice`—Controls the notification area that appears at the top of the screen. You may have seen it if you've let your session time out: Liferay displays a countdown, and if it reaches zero, you're automatically logged out. You can use this area for your own notifications. Because Liferay uses this notification area, you shouldn't use it a lot, or you may run into instances where you accidentally cover up a notification that Liferay is trying to display to the user.
- `Liferay.Panel`—A basic container for content. If you place your markup inside a panel, that panel can then be manipulated by the functions in this class (that is, it can be collapsed and certain events can be sent to it).
- `Liferay.Upload`—The widget used by the Document Library portlet to upload files.
- `Liferay.Util`—Contains many utility methods for working with document elements, especially form elements. For example, there are methods for dealing with check boxes (such as `checkAll()`), for enabling and disabling elements, for escaping HTML so it can be inserted into a database, for focusing fields, and much more. You'll be more likely to use these in portlets than in a theme.

The question becomes, how do you use this cool stuff? Let's look at some code that uses JSP to call Liferay JavaScript objects:

```
<aui:script use="liferay-autofields,liferay-notice,liferay-upload">
   new Liferay.Upload();
   new Liferay.AutoFields();
   new Liferay.Notice();
</aui:script>
```

Notice that, similar to a Java `import` statement, you have to declare what you're going to use first. This is because the modules aren't initialized right away; they're lazy-loaded. This speeds up the rendering of the page.

This same thing can also be done via JavaScript. This code uses JavaScript to call Liferay JavaScript objects:

```
AUI().use('liferay-autofields', 'liferay-notice', 'liferay-upload',
   function(A){
     new Liferay.Upload();
     new Liferay.AutoFields();
     new Liferay.Notice();
   });
```

As you can see, it's done in a similar way. The `AUI()` object is the global Alloy UI object, and it's used to do the initialization. The one exception to this initialization process is the `Liferay.Util` class. You don't have to explicitly initialize that class in order to use it; it's available by default on every page.

Suffice it to say that Alloy UI gives you a lot, and I hope this information is enough to get you started using it. As I've stated, an entire book could be written on Alloy UI, but we only have space to sprinkle it throughout *Liferay in Action.*

Next, you'll see how to configure a theme by using the liferay-look-and-feel.xml configuration file.

5.4 The liferay-look-and-feel.xml file

You can do all sorts of advanced things with themes by creating a liferay-look-and-feel.xml file according to the DTD found in the portal source of the version of Liferay on which you're building your site. It's possible, for example, to limit who can use a particular theme, use a different markup language, provide various color schemes, and more. Let's look at how you do some of these things in themes.

5.4.1 Limiting themes by company

You can limit the use of a particular theme to a company, community, or organization. This can become useful, for example, for corporate sites that want to enforce a particular look and feel.

This is done via includes and excludes. Consider the following configuration:

```
<company-limit>
   <company-includes>
      <company-id>liferay.com</company-id>
      <company-id>yoursite.com</company-id>
   </company-includes>

   <company-excludes>
      <company-id>mysite.com</company-id>
   </company-excludes>
<company-limit>
```

With this configuration, company IDs liferay.com and yoursite.com are allowed to use the theme, but mysite.com isn't. The same configuration can be done for communities and organizations using the `<group-limit>` tags defined in the DTD.

Inkwell might want to make two different themes: one for the external site and one for the internal site. Using company includes and excludes, you could easily

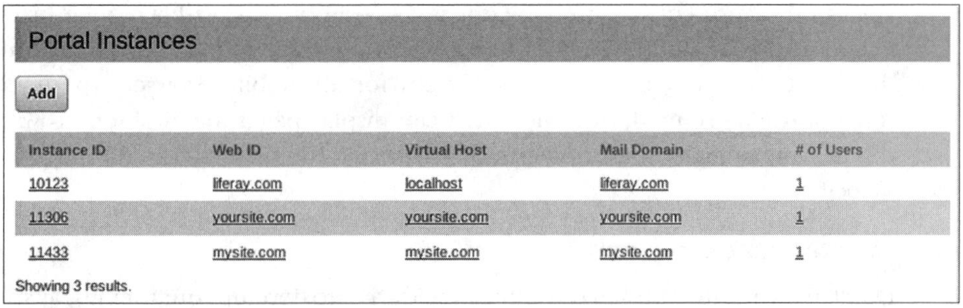

Portal Instances

Add

Instance ID	Web ID	Virtual Host	Mail Domain	# of Users
10123	liferay.com	localhost	liferay.com	1
11306	yoursite.com	yoursite.com	yoursite.com	1
11433	mysite.com	mysite.com	mysite.com	1

Showing 3 results.

Figure 5.6 Creating new portal instances is easy in Liferay's Control Panel. Each portal instance acts as though it's a completely separate installation of Liferay Portal, with a different set of users, communities, organizations, user groups, and more.

make it so that site administrators can choose the right theme when adding new pages. You can have several different themes installed, but allow only certain themes that contain the proper branding to be used in particular areas of the portal. Company IDs are created in the Control Panel when you create a new portal instance. Select Server > Portal Instance to create a new one (see figure 5.6).

Click the Add button to create another instance. The number of portal instances you can create is limited only by the traffic coming to your server hardware.

5.4.2 *Modifying the default paths*

The default paths within the theme (specified in section 5.1) are just that: defaults. You can modify the paths to your markup, your images, your CSS, or your JavaScript by specifying the appropriate settings in liferay-look-and-feel.xml. You can define paths for any of the elements of the theme, from the root path to the paths to templates, images, JavaScript, or CSS.

For example, if I wanted to change the path to the images in my theme, I could add this code to my liferay-look-and-feel.xml file:

```
<images-path>
   ${root-path}/resources/images
</images-path>
```

You can do this if for some reason you don't like the organization of the files as Liferay has them. To me, Liferay's organization of the theme works just fine. The cooler part of this is that you can refer to paths programmatically in your theme code, using Velocity variables.

For example, Liferay's Browser Sniffer utility is available in themes via the `$browserSniffer` variable. This allows you to write something like this in your theme:

```
#if ($browserSniffer.isMobile())
    #parse ("$full_template_path/mobile_portal_normal.vm")
#else
    #parse ("$full_template_path/desktop_portal_normal.vm")
#end
```

You can then present your web site one way to users visiting with a regular browser and a different, more lightweight way to users visiting with a mobile device. Of course, just the `isMobile` check may not be sufficient for all mobile browsers (particularly for some of the more modern devices that can display pages like desktop browsers), but this is a way to make your themes more dynamic. It only scratches the surface of what Velocity can do.

5.4.3 The <template-extension> tag

Don't like Velocity? You can use JSP or FreeMarker to develop your themes, by specifying

```
<template-extension>jsp</template-extension>
```

or

```
<template-extension>ftl</template-extension>
```

> **NOTE** In addition, Liferay's content management system (CMS) can use Velocity, XSL, or FreeMarker to define templates for content display. You may have XSL experts in your organization who love using that language, and that's fine—you should use it for web content. But if it doesn't matter, and you need to learn one of the templating languages, you may as well use Velocity or FreeMarker; learning either of these templating languages for web content also gives you the knowledge to work with them in themes.

Historically, Liferay themes were implemented first with JSPs and then with Velocity. FreeMarker was added for Liferay 6, because of customer demand and also because Service Builder's code-generation templates are implemented with FreeMarker. All are equally supported, so you should use whichever technology makes you the most productive. Velocity is the default and is likely to remain so, but JSPs and FreeMarker are just as good for developing themes. And it's likely in the future that Liferay will support other technologies for building themes.

5.4.4 Conditional settings

Themes can define individual settings. Using settings enables you to programmatically access the settings in your theme template and then take action based on the settings you've defined.

Settings are key/value pairs and can be defined in the liferay-look-and-feel.xml using the following syntax:

```
<settings>
  <setting key="my-setting" value="my-value" />
</settings>
```

After defining a setting, you can access it in your theme code fairly easily using this method:

```
$theme.getSetting("my-setting")
```

For example, some web sites have a large banner at the top that prominently displays the site's logo and some navigation, allowing users new to the site to become familiar with the navigation. As a user delves deeper into the site, the content becomes more important than the huge banner, and it may be wiser to shrink the site logo and navigation on these pages.

You can do this the hard way by creating two themes that are exactly the same except for the header and then applying the two different themes on the appropriate pages. Of course, now you've got to manage two different themes and fix bugs in both of them. But if you use theme settings, you can instead create only one theme and use a setting to choose the appropriate header.

Let's look at an example. In the liferay-look-and-feel.xml file, create two different entries that refer to the same theme but have a different value for the `header-type` setting, as shown in the following listing.

Listing 5.2 Theme settings

```
<theme id="corporate1" name="Corporate 1">
  <root-path>/html/themes/corporate</root-path>
  <templates-path>${root-path}/templates</templates-path>
  <images-path>${root-path}/images</images-path>
  <template-extension>vm</template-extension>
  <settings>
    <setting key="header-type" value="detailed" />        <-- Detailed header
  </settings>
  <color-scheme id="01" name="Blue">
    <css-class>blue</css-class>
    <color-scheme-images-path>
      ${images-path}/color_schemes/${css-class}
    </color-scheme-images-path>
  </color-scheme>
  ...
</theme>
<theme id="corporate2" name="Corporate 2">
  <root-path>/html/themes/corporate</root-path>
  <templates-path>${root-path}/templates</templates-path>
  <images-path>${root-path}/images</images-path>
  <template-extension>vm</template-extension>
  <settings>
    <setting key="header-type" value="brief" />           <-- Brief header
  </settings>
  <color-scheme id="01" name="Blue">
    <css-class>blue</css-class>
    <color-scheme-images-path>
      ${images-path}/color_schemes/${css-class}
    </color-scheme-images-path>
  </color-scheme>
  ...
</theme>
```

docroot/WEB-INF/liferay-look-and-feel.xml

In the portal_normal.vm template, use the following code:

```
#if ($theme.getSetting("header-type") == "detailed")
   #parse("$full_templates_path/header_detailed.vm")
#else
   #parse("$full_templates_path/header_brief.vm")
#end
```

When this theme is deployed to Liferay, it will display to the user as two different themes. When your content managers are setting up the pages for your web site, all they need to do is choose the detailed theme for the top-level pages and the brief theme for the pages that are deeper in the site. You as the theme developer only need to maintain the one theme to enable your users to use both.

5.4.5 Theme security and roles

You can limit which themes are available based on roles defined in your portal. For example, if a portal installation serves both an intranet and an outward-facing internet site, you may want to make it so that only the managers of the external site can choose the theme for the external site. Other users can only choose internal themes that are available to them. You can use this instead of limiting themes by company (see section 5.4.1) if you need to limit a theme's use *within* a particular portal instance. For example, you may have a community that houses your main web site, and you may have another community that's set aside for something like photographs. Using roles, you can make sure the administrators of the photograph community have to use the theme you've built for them and can't choose the theme for the main site.

By default, no role names are set, so anyone with access to the Manage Pages function for a community or organization can use your theme. To limit theme usage to specific roles defined in the portal, use the following code in your liferay-look-and-feel.xml file:

```
<roles>
  <role-name>Internet Admins</role-name>
  <role-name>Admins</role-name>
</roles>
```

This limits the usage of this particular theme to users who have either the Internet Admins or the Admins role.

5.4.6 Color schemes

Liferay themes support different *color schemes.* You can define a theme that has an overall style but that can present itself in several different ways. You can achieve this by knowing that the body element has special CSS classes for each of the different color schemes. The most dramatic way to use this capability is to change all text colors, border colors, and background colors—hence the name *color scheme* (see figure 5.7).

In the css folder, create a folder called color_schemes. In that folder, place a .css file for each of your color schemes. For example, if you have two color schemes—one

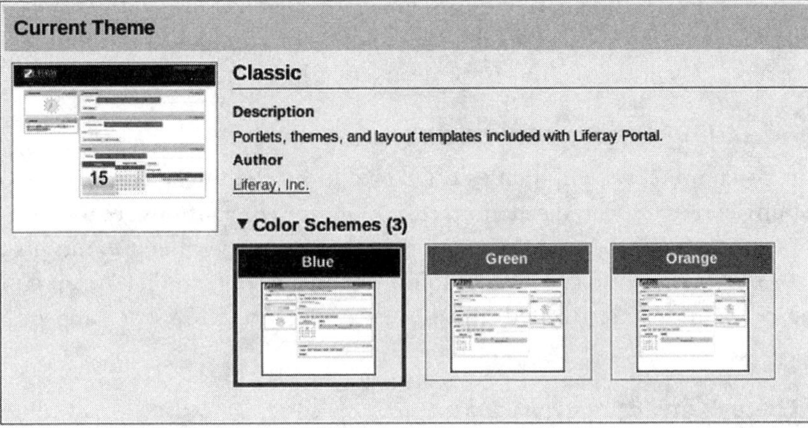

Figure 5.7 Color schemes can be added to themes to give your users more options without changing the entire structure of the theme.

for green and one for blue—in your theme, you can implement green.css as the default and specify blue as an alternative color scheme.

In your custom.css file, import the color schemes you'll need:

```
@import url(color_schemes/blue.css);
@import url(color_schemes/green.css);
```

When defining styles, use prefixes for the color schemes. For example, in blue.css, prefix your CSS styles like this:

```
.blue a {color: #2E3DFF;}
.blue h1 (border-bottom: 1px solid #2E3DFF;}
```

And in green.css, prefix your CSS styles like this:

```
.green a {color: #06C;}
.green h1 (border-bottom: 1px solid #06C;}
```

To enable Liferay to recognize your color schemes, modify liferay-look-and-feel.xml to define the class name prefixes you used in your CSS styles:

```
<theme id="a_cool_theme" name="A Cool Theme">
  <color-scheme id="01" name="Blue">
    <css-class>blue</css-class>
    <color-scheme-images-path>
      ${images-path}/color_schemes/${css-class}
    </color-scheme-images-path>
  </color-scheme>
  <color-scheme id="02" name="Green">
    <css-class>green</css-class>
  </color-scheme>
  <color-scheme id="03" name="Orange">
    <css-class>orange</css-class>
  </color-scheme>
</theme>
```

When you deploy the theme, Liferay will make it available as usual. But when you select the theme for your pages, you'll get a choice of color schemes to go along with it.

Let's next look at the styling conventions used in Liferay themes.

5.5 Understanding theme conventions

As with any complex system, themes use conventions that make reading the code and performing certain repeated functions easier. Theme conventions are used throughout Liferay's code; I'll list them in this section so that if you ever need to modify a Liferay theme or make your code conform to Liferay's conventions, you'll have an easier time.

The conventions are divided into two categories: one for styles and one for CSS coding.

5.5.1 Using Liferay's styling conventions

It would be beyond the scope of this book to go over CSS and styling in general, but I can give you an introduction to Liferay's styling conventions so you can see how they're generally organized.

Liferay's various styles are divided into several CSS files that group the styles under relevant categories. Additionally, you can use some global styles to apply browser- or OS-specific styling to themes. This, of course, enables you to easily support your look and feel on multiple browsers on multiple OSs using multiple rendering engines to render the same page.

The first group covers browsers and browser engines. On page load, Liferay adds browser selectors to the HTML element using simple JavaScript. As such, a convention in Liferay is to use these CSS selectors to style for specific browsers (see table 5.3).

Table 5.3 Selectors for rendering engines

CSS selector	Description
.gecko	Refers to the Gecko rendering engine used by Mozilla Firefox and its variants
.webkit	Refers to the WebKit rendering engine used by Safari, Google Chrome, Konqueror, and others

Because multiple browsers use the two engines, you can cover them all by using the selectors in table 5.3. Sometimes, though, you need to target a specific browser version, and Liferay provides selectors for that too. These are shown in table 5.4.

Table 5.4 Selectors for browsers

CSS selector	Description
.aol	The browser embedded within the America Online client.
.camino	A Mac-based browser that uses the Mozilla Gecko rendering engine.

Table 5.4 Selectors for browsers *(continued)*

CSS selector	Description
.firefox	Mozilla Firefox, one of the most popular browsers in use today. Uses the Mozilla Gecko rendering engine.
.flock	A browser that focuses on support for social networks, based on the Mozilla Gecko rendering engine.
.icab	A shareware browser for Mac-based systems.
.konqueror	The default browser on the Linux-based KDE desktop. This browser originated WebKit and is still WebKit-based.
.mozilla	A catch-all for Mozilla-based browsers.
.ie	Microsoft Internet Explorer, one of the most popular browsers in use today, and the default on Windows systems.
.netscape	The Netscape browser. Recent versions are based on the Mozilla Gecko rendering engine.
.opera	A browser used on both the desktop and many mobile devices, as well as the Nintendo Wii.
.safari	The default browser on Mac-based systems. Safari is based on the WebKit rendering engine.
.browser	A catch-all for all other browsers.

If, for example, you need to create a style for a specific browser and version, you can use the following code:

```
.ie6 a { }
```

This style will take effect for the anchor tag only for users who visit your site on Internet Explorer version 6.

You can also combine the selectors. This becomes useful when you want to target users of specific browser and OS combinations. Because several of the browsers are cross-platform, you may want to style something for particular users. For example, if you want to target Firefox users who are running on Microsoft Windows, you can use the following code:

```
.firefox .win #hidden-message {
     visibility: visible;
}
```

Not only that, but you can also have styles specific to color schemes:

```
.firefox .blue #hidden-message {
     visibility: hidden;
}
```

In a similar fashion, you can style elements for certain operating systems. As with browsers and rendering engines, you use the CSS selector to show one thing for users of one OS and something different for users of another OS (see table 5.5).

Table 5.5 Selectors for operating systems

CSS selector	Description
.win	Microsoft Windows OSs
.mac	Apple Macintosh OSs
.linux	Linux OSs
.iphone	iPhone OS
.sun	Sun Solaris OSs
.os	A catch-all for other OSs

Using these CSS selectors, theme developers can create styles that apply just to these rendering engines, browsers, or operating systems. The nice thing is that you can enforce a consistent look and feel regardless of browser. Your users will—regardless of their browser choice—have the same experience using your site. Liferay makes this easy to do.

I hope you can see that the convention of using these selectors makes handling multiple browsers a lot easier. It frees you from having to deal with the contortions of other, less elegant means of detecting and styling.

5.5.2 Using Liferay's CSS coding conventions

Liferay adheres to certain code conventions when providing CSS. These are designed to make the code easy to read. If your organization already has code conventions for CSS, they may be similar to Liferay's.

> **NOTE** If you wish to contribute changes to Liferay's CSS, you'll need to follow these conventions when you submit your code. See appendix D for further details about contributing to the Liferay open source project.

The conventions are as follows outside of selector bodies:

- Group selectors under the common element that they style using comment tags.
- Keep global selectors toward the top and more specific selectors toward the bottom.
- Keep only one end line between all selectors and comments.

And these are the conventions inside selector bodies:

- Insert only one space between the selector name and the opening bracket (`{`).
- If you're using multiple selectors for the same body of declarations, separate selectors with a comma and one end line.

- All declarations should be indented by one tab.
- Keep all declarations in alphabetical order within the declaration body.
- For each declaration, be sure to put one space between the property and the value, after the colon.
- Colors should only be specified by using their hexadecimal value.
- Use all caps for hexadecimal values, and condense to three digits whenever possible.
- For the `background` property, make sure there is no space between the `url` attribute and the opening parenthesis.
- No quotes are required when using `url()` or for font names, unless you're using fonts that aren't browser-safe.
- Insert spaces after commas between font names. Doing so enhances readability.
- When using URLs, always use a relative address instead of an absolute one.
- Condense all padding, margin, and border values whenever possible, leaving out measurement units on `0` values (`px`, `pt`, `em`, `%`, and so on).
- Comments are used only to head and divide each section of the code appropriately. Comments without any content below them aren't necessary.
- Use shorthand properties where applicable.

Now that you've seen how you can take your design skills to the max with Liferay themes, let's look at something easy: layout templates.

5.6 Designing a page with layout templates

Layout templates are ways of choosing how your portlets are arranged on a page. They make up the body of your page—the large area where you drag and drop your portlets to create your pages. Liferay Portal comes with several built-in layout templates, but if you have a complex page layout (especially for your home page), you may wish to create a custom layout template.

In this section, I'll walk you through the process of creating, implementing, and deploying a simple layout template.

Layout templates are the easiest plugins to create. They comprise only a few files with simple table or `<div>`-based containers into which portlets can be dropped, as well as a thumbnail image of what the layout looks like. This thumbnail is displayed when the end user clicks Page Template from the Dock menu to choose a layout for the current page.

5.6.1 Creating layout template projects

Creating a layout template project is similar to creating portlet and theme projects. There is a layouttpl folder inside the plugins SDK where all new layout template projects reside. To create a new layout template project, you run a command in this folder similar to the one you use to create a new portlet or theme. For LUM, type

```
./create.sh <project name> "<layout template title>"
```

And for Windows, type

```
create.bat <project name> "<layout template title>"
```

For example, to create a layout template with the project folder three-columns-II and the theme title Three Columns-II, type

```
./create.sh three-columns-II "Three Columns-II"
```

On Windows, type

```
create.bat three-columns-II "Three Columns-II"
```

This command creates a blank layout template project in your layouttpl folder.

Now that you've created a layout template, let's see what the project looks like.

5.6.2 *Anatomy of a layout template*

Layout template projects are simple. Say, for example, that you want the Three Columns layout template you just created to display left and right columns that take up 20% of the available space and a middle column that takes up 60%. This is a common site layout, but surprisingly, Liferay doesn't ship with it (although it does have a template with the aforementioned three evenly spaced columns).

To separate this template from the one that ships with Liferay, call it Three Columns II, because it will be the newer, slicker sequel. You now have a new project with the layout shown in figure 5.8.

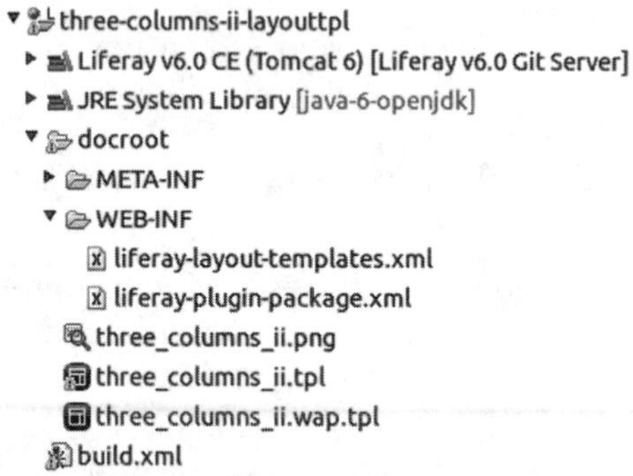

The next step is to open the three_columns_ii.tpl file and create the three-column template. This file is for regular web browsers; Liferay will automatically detect the client being used to connect to the site and serve up the appropriate template. For instance, if the client is a phone, Liferay will serve the three_columns_ii.wap.tpl file.

```
three-columns-ii-layouttpl
  Liferay v6.0 CE (Tomcat 6) [Liferay v6.0 Git Server]
  JRE System Library [java-6-openjdk]
  docroot
    META-INF
    WEB-INF
      liferay-layout-templates.xml
      liferay-plugin-package.xml
    three_columns_ii.png
    three_columns_ii.tpl
    three_columns_ii.wap.tpl
  build.xml
```

Figure 5.8 Layout templates are perhaps the simplest of Liferay plugins. They contain only a few files and are easy to configure.

Open the three_columns_ii.tpl file in your text editor of choice. You'll see that by default, it's blank. In future versions of the Plugins SDK, there may be a commented-out template to help you get started; but right now all you get is a blank file. To implement the layout, use the code in the following listing.

Listing 5.3 A three-column layout template

```
<div class="three_columns_ii" id="main-content" role="main">
  <div class="portlet-layout">
    <div class="aui-w20 portlet-column portlet-column-first" id="column-1">
      $processor.processColumn("column-1",
      ➥ "portlet-column-content portlet-column-content-first")
```

```
    </div>
    <div class="aui-w60 portlet-column" id="column-2">
      $processor.processColumn("column-2", "portlet-column-content")
    </div>
    <div class="aui-w20 portlet-column portlet-column-last" id="column-3">
      $processor.processColumn("column-3",
      ➥ "portlet-column-content portlet-column-content-last")
    </div>
  </div>
</div>
```

docroot/three_columns_ii.tpl

Note that each table cell has a CSS class associated with it, as well as an ID. These may be customized by modifying the theme you're using to display the layout.

For the WAP version (an unfortunate naming convention that's used now in Liferay to refer to mobile development—it will be changed soon) of the file, you use simpler syntax:

```
<table>
  <tr>
    <td>
      $processor.processColumn("column-1")
    </td>
    <td>
      $processor.processColumn("column-2")
    </td>
    <td>
      $processor.processColumn("column-3")
    </td>
  </tr>
</table>
```

WAP doesn't have the benefit of CSS, so you have to settle for three evenly spaced columns.

The other file you need to customize is three_columns_ii.png. The default file in the project is a blank layout template preview. You have to customize it in an image-manipulation program such as GNU Image Manipulation Program (affectionately known as *the GIMP*; www.gimp.org) or Adobe Photoshop. This file can be modified so it looks like your layout. This should make it blend in somewhat with the other layout template preview icons.

When you've customized the icon, all that is left is to deploy the layout template—the various configuration files have already been generated by the Ant scripts in the Plugins SDK. A layout template is deployed in exactly the same way as any other plugin, by using the `ant deploy` task.

I've done my best to give you guidance for your own site designs. Because this isn't a book on design or on front-end technologies, I've tried to balance giving you the information you need and avoiding a discussion on technologies that Liferay uses (like CSS and JavaScript) but that aren't the subject of this book. Now, let's look at how Inkwell used this information to implement a theme.

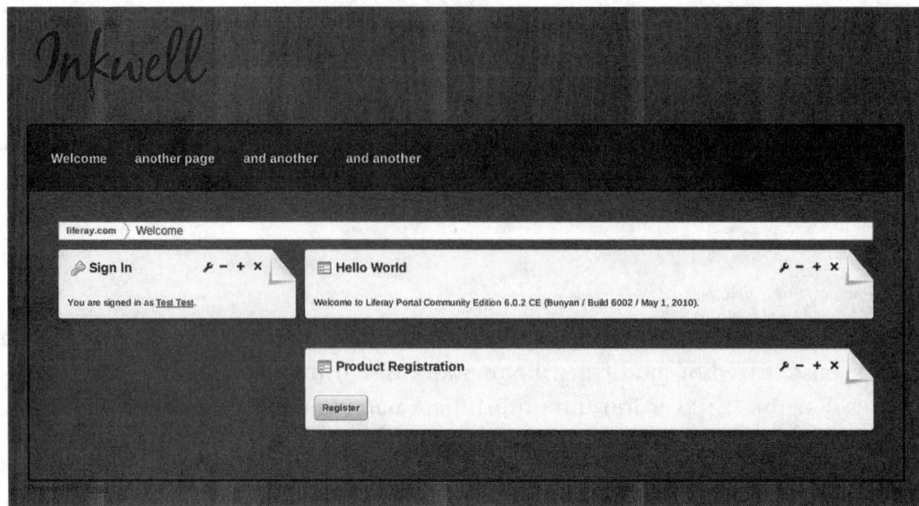

Figure 5.9 The Inkwell theme features a wood-grain desktop surface, a leather blotter, and various pages lying on the blotter. Of course, you know those pages are really portlets, don't you?

5.7 Inkwell implementation

The design team at Inkwell created a theme for the internet that they thought would appeal to customers. Because Inkwell is a company that successfully mixes digital technology with the real-world, analog feel of fountain pens, it was thought that the web site should reflect that.

The designers set out to design a web site that would mimic the experience many of their customers have of writing with Inkwell products on a desk (see figure 5.9).

The design team chose to implement the desk by using a tiled background image of wood grain. Superimposed on this is the navigation menu and the content section of the page, both of which have different tiled background images depicting a blotter of sorts. Portlet windows also have backgrounds that contrast nicely with the blotter. This design works well to simulate a desk with paper on it. All of these styles are contained in one custom.css file; if you didn't have to include one small piece of global JavaScript (see chapter 8) in the theme, this would be the only file (other than the images) you'd have to customize in order to achieve this look and feel.

The Inkwell web site is starting to take form. Using existing HTML, JavaScript, and CSS skills, the design team was able to create this theme quickly, using tools they were already comfortable using. When the content creators begin creating content for the site, it will really begin to shape up.

5.8 Summary

This chapter introduced you to the world of creating themes for Liferay Portal. You've learned how to create theme projects in the Plugins SDK and have seen what the overall structure of a theme looks like.

Themes are based on differences from a base that is provided by Liferay; this enables you to keep your themes small and light and rely on the baseline that Liferay provides. From there, you learned how Liferay's CSS files are organized and where you can find the styles you need to override in custom.css.

Next, you learned how and where to implement your own JavaScript functions in your themes. Alloy UI plays a prominent role in the JavaScript that is available in Liferay, not only for themes but also for portlets. You were also introduced to some of the JavaScript that is provided by Liferay in addition to Alloy UI. This allows you to take advantage of functionality that is provided out of the box and, more important, is maintained by the Liferay development team.

You explored the ins and outs of the liferay-look-and-feel.xml file, which lets you provide many features in your theme including security, settings, color schemes, and more. You also learned how Liferay provides an easy way to style theme elements so that your theme can be supported by all browsers.

Finally, you saw how simple it is to create layout templates, enabling you to arrange portlet applications on pages in any way that suits you. Coupled with a theme, you get the flexibility to present content and applications however you've designed them.

All of this can be brought together to implement a look and feel that makes Liferay appear to be anything. Inkwell's design team used this information plus Liferay's CSS style conventions to implement a look and feel that is appropriate for their business.

Armed with the information from this chapter, you should be able to create beautiful themes for Liferay. We'll move from here into some of Liferay's specific APIs, starting with its API for social networking.

6 Making your site social

This chapter covers

- Integrating your Liferay-based site with social networks
- Liferay's social networking plugin
- Using Liferay's Social API to connect users
- Checking for social relationships
- Publishing activities from your applications

Unless you've been hiding under a rock for the past several years, you've probably heard the term *social networking*. Web sites like Facebook and MySpace have made the term almost ubiquitous, and now we have a craze on our hands similar to the general internet craze of the '90s. It used to be that you met and interacted with different people on different web sites, primarily using discussion forums to talk about topics of common interest. Nowadays, social networking brings that idea to a whole new level, allowing users to put more of their activities online and to grant others permission to see what's going on in their lives.

My first high school reunion was, uh, before the advent of social networking. It was pretty much as reunions are described in countless movies, TV shows, and novels—except, of course, for its size. Although I grew up in a Jersey shore town (no jokes, please) that is ostensibly larger than the small town of Superman's upbringing, my reunion wasn't as big as the one in Smallville depicted in *Superman 3*. We didn't rent out a big hall in a hotel, a restaurant, or even a fire station. No, we had our reunion in a bar. Did I get to see some people I hadn't seen since high school? Yes. Was it my whole class? Not by a long shot. Today people get so spread out that there's little chance that, once they get disconnected, they'll find each other again.

That is, until the advent of Facebook.

I'm obviously older (not *that* much older) than the original Facebook generation, which I define as those who were able to access Facebook back when it required a university email account. I resisted joining Facebook for a while, because, in my infinite wisdom, it was something "those kids" used. I certainly wasn't going to find anybody I knew on there—except, of course, for the people younger than me who were telling me I should join.

Boy, was I wrong.

People I never thought would be on Facebook were there. Heck, people I wasn't sure knew how to use the internet were there. And far more people I knew from high school were on Facebook than were at the reunion. I could see what they were doing, contact them and talk to them directly, see pictures of them and their kids, and become somewhat of a participant in their lives again. And they could do the same with me. I had to admit it: that was pretty cool. That's the power of social networking.

For these reasons, social networking has become popular, and all kinds of web sites are building social features into their previously unsocial experience. If you're building your site on Liferay, you'll be happy to know that Liferay contains an API for building social web sites. This API is tried and tested and is in use today, powering sites that connect users for everything from exercise-routine accountability to making friends with one another's pets. Let's take a deeper dive into this concept and see what it entails.

6.1 Social networking: why is it important?

There are all kinds of social networking sites that are used for different purposes. Sites like Facebook and MySpace are general-purpose social networking sites—anybody can get an account and start posting stuff to share. Other sites have a more focused purpose. For example, LinkedIn is meant to help maintain work relationships you've built over the course of your career. You won't be posting family pictures there, but you might post your resumé and current activities, and you certainly might want to keep connected to current and former colleagues in order to take advantage of opportunities to work together again.

The same features power all these varying purposes. And this list of features can be used to expand your reach, by using your connections. This translates into a more positive user experience, because users are presented with the connections they have and the information they want. You're about to see how that works in more detail.

6.1.1 Allowing users to connect with each other

Quick: picture someone you haven't seen or talked to in five years. What's the first thing you might want to know about what's happened to this person in the intervening time? It depends on your relationship, doesn't it? If you had a professional relationship with the person, you might wonder if he or she is still working in the same place or in the same position. If you were friends with the person, you might wonder what he or she is up to and who he or she is hanging out with now.

Regardless of the reason, people connect with each other all the time in real life. Social networking tries to mirror that in the online world. This becomes especially useful when people are separated by distance or life patterns (for example, they may not work at the same physical location anymore).

Allowing users to connect with each other on your web site will make your site more popular with your users. When users connect and interact online, they're in control. If users are in control, they're far more likely to participate. Users participate because of the relationships they have with other people online. If they can be free to pursue those relationships on *your* site, they will keep coming back. To misquote James Carville, "It's the relationships, stupid."[1]

Liferay has a social networking API you can use to let your users make connections with each other. When those connections are made, you can use the API to check whether connections exist, query a list of connections, and a lot more. We'll go through examples of using this API as the rest of the chapter unfolds.

First, we'll look at how you can increase participation on your site by connecting it to other social networks.

6.1.2 Expanding your reach beyond your own site

If you've used Facebook, chances are you've played at least one game on the site. Although I don't frequent the games, I have to confess I played one or two before the novelty wore off.[2] Did you know that the games on Facebook aren't hosted on Facebook? Instead, they're served from their own servers by the entities that created them. Many of these entities operate their own sites that allow you to play the games directly; it's just that Facebook gives them a visibility they wouldn't have if they didn't make their games available there. Because of that visibility, more people play the games.

Liferay Portal allows you to serve your Liferay-based application on Facebook, as a Google Gadget, on Netvibes, or on any other web site. You don't have to do anything extra to make this happen. In fact, you can add the Product Registration portlet you wrote in chapter 3 and 4 to any external web site. To do so, click the Configuration button to see options for Facebook or any other site, as shown in figure 6.1.

---

1 http://mng.bz/R2dO

2 It didn't take long to realize that a lot of Facebook games are nothing but derivatives of Cow Clicker: www.bogost.com/games/cow_clicker.shtml

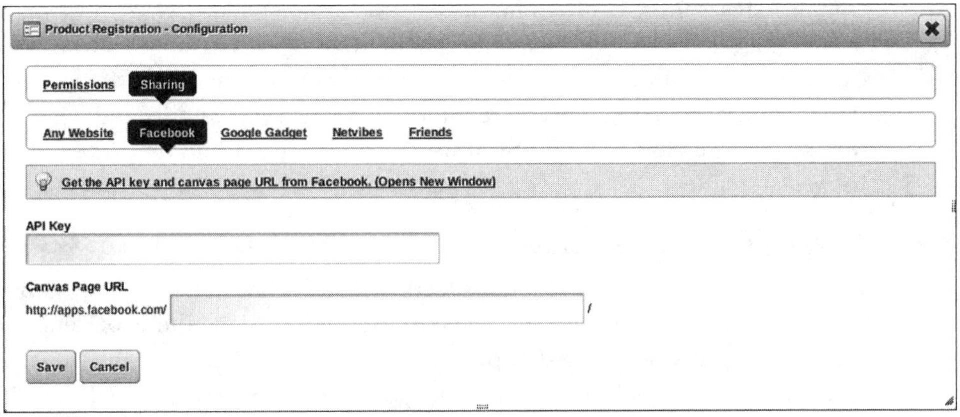

Figure 6.1 You can add your Liferay-based applications to other social networking sites, such as Facebook. You can also let friends share your application. Who knows? Maybe your application can become viral!

There's nothing stopping you from writing an awesome role-playing game on Liferay, serving it up on Facebook, and making millions. Nothing, of course, except your own ingenuity. This brings me to my next point: social networking gives users a more positive experience by bringing together their many interests.

6.1.3 *Creating a dynamic, more positive user experience*

Way back, I used browser bookmarks extensively. I'd find a site, realize I wanted to visit it again, and bookmark it. I spent a lot of time organizing my bookmarks into folders because I had so many and I was afraid I wouldn't be able to find a particular site again. Over time, I used bookmarks less and less, to the point that I still have a highly organized folder structure of bookmarks to sites that mostly don't exist anymore. I tend to visit only a few sites repeatedly, and rarely do I come across something I'd like to bookmark for later.

What's the point of all this? The point is that aggregation is key on the web in the twenty-first century. We tend to visit fewer individual sites because the sites we do visit aggregate so much content that we don't have to go all over the place to find what we're looking for. We get to that content because of social-networking features that are built into these sites.

It's ridiculously easy to upload and share videos on Facebook or YouTube. Additionally, those sites have the bandwidth to serve up those videos optimally so people can view them without a lot of buffering and stuttering. If I come across an interesting blog post or news article, I can post a link to it on my Twitter feed if I want to share it. Because I am sharing these links via social networking, anyone connected to me can see them. And I have things set up so I can post simultaneously to Twitter, Facebook, and LinkedIn if I want to. That's better than spamming all my friends via email.

All of this is to say that social networking creates a more positive user experience than the siloed applications we used to have. It's much easier to upload your own content, share links, and communicate using social-networking tools than it is by using separate applications like email, static web sites, and single-purpose web applications. Social networking combines that into one dynamic experience. And Liferay Portal is an engine that can power it all. Now that you understand what social networking is and what you can use it for, let's get started building those features into Inkwell's web site.

6.2 Installing Liferay's social networking portlets

Liferay by default contains all you need to build a social-networking web site from the ground up. You can use the social API to build exactly the experience you want. But Liferay has also created a default implementation (using this API) of several social-networking applications that tend to be common across social sites. If you use these, you'll get a jump start on your site, and you can concentrate on the features you need to build. Of course, if you don't like the way Liferay has implemented things using its API, you can provide your own implementation, because everything is done with plugins.

If you don't already have the Social Networking portlet plugin installed (it comes packaged by default if you use Liferay Community Edition), choose Plugins Installation > Install More Portlets from the Control Panel. When the plugin is installed, the Social category of the Add > More menu displays additional portlets, as you can see in figure 6.2.

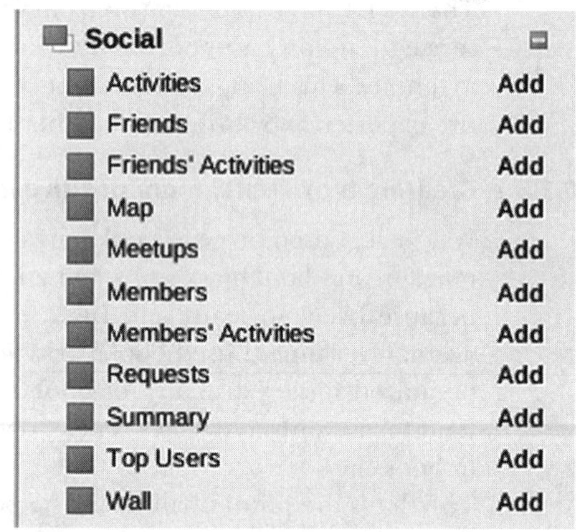

Figure 6.2 Liferay provides many social portlets you can use as a starting point to get your social-networking site running.

Before you start putting these portlets on pages, let's take a step back and see what they do. That way, you can make the best assessment you can of how Inkwell may want to use them.

6.3 Understanding Liferay's social features

As already stated, Liferay Portal contains an API specifically designed for building social web sites. This API enables you to implement the following features:

- Relating with others
- Publishing activities
- Determining an online presence (in the case of the Chat portlet)

These functions can power a host of features, as you're about to see.

6.3.1 Relating with others

Friends, connections, buddies—whatever you want to call them, social networking is powered by relationships. Those relationships are defined as connections between people. Liferay calls these *social relations*, and the methods in the API reflect that terminology. This means you'll see methods with names like `addRelation`, `isRelatable`, and such.

Liferay goes further than providing the API; the Summary portlet implements this API to create those social relations in ways you would expect. Although you may want to implement your own version of this portlet, you've got a great starting point in the Summary portlet, as you'll see in a bit.

Once you've established relationships with people, the next step in social networking is to keep up with their activities.

6.3.2 Publishing activities

I'm sure you remember that back in chapter 1, I showed you a little thing called the Activities portlet. This portlet is a one-stop shop for your activities. In that example, you saw how adding a wiki portlet to a page generates an activity, because whenever you add a wiki to a page, the default wiki article is created at the same time.

The wiki is an internal portlet that comes with Liferay. But this doesn't mean you can't publish activities in your portlets too. You'll see how to do this when you enable the Product Registration portlet for social networking. If a user with an account registers a product, you'll make it an activity that is displayed in the Activities portlet.

Activities are important, but they're only visible to those who are socially related. Users become related by responding to social requests.

6.3.3 Sending social requests

Liferay's social API allows users to send other users social requests. The social-networking portlets implement this in the Summary portlet and the Requests portlet. One way to do this right out of the box is to put the Summary portlet on users' public profile pages, where other users can see it (see figure 6.3).

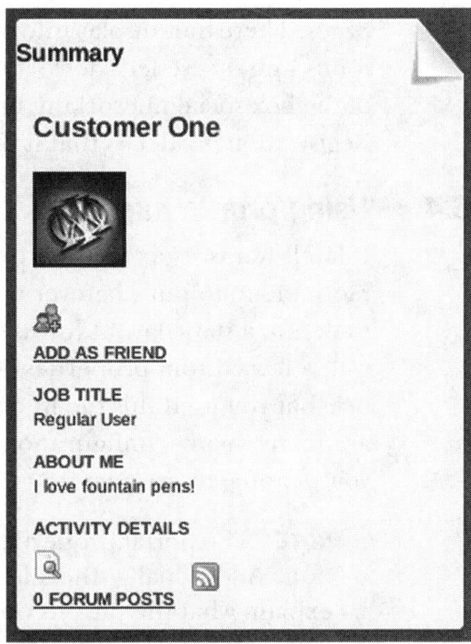

Figure 6.3 If you place the Summary portlet on a user's public profile page, it displays a link labeled Add as Friend. To Liferay, this is a social relation, so you can label it anything you like. For example, if you were doing a site for fantasy role-playing gamers, you might label the link Add as Fellow Warrior.

You don't have to use Liferay's Summary portlet; it just happens to already include a

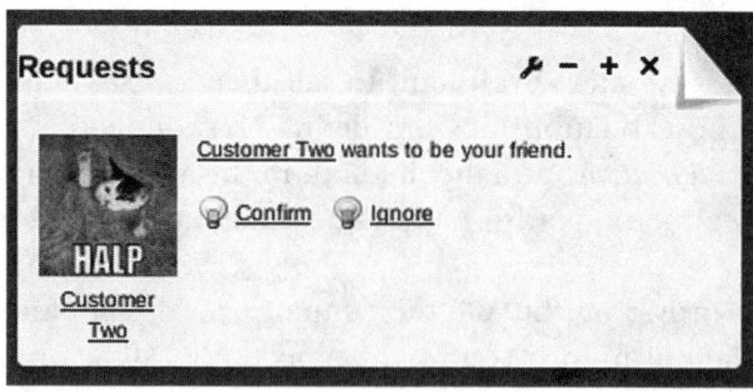

Figure 6.4 The Requests portlet shows a list of those who have requested to be a social relation. You can see their profile pictures and links to their profiles, and you can either confirm the request or ignore it.

user interface for adding a social relation. You can implement any portlet you like and use Liferay's social API the same way the Summary portlet does. But let's continue with how relation request/relation acceptance flows, so you can get a high-level understanding of how it works before you dive in to the low level. Clicking the Add as Friend link sends a social request to that user, and the user can then choose whether to confirm that the requestee is somebody it's worth having as a social relation.

Social requests are captured by the Requests portlet, which ships by default in Liferay. When you place it on a page, if the user has no requests, it's invisible. When a user has a request, the portlet displays that request, as you can see in figure 6.4.

Obviously, these social portlets are designed to be placed on users' individual profile pages. There they display information appropriate for that user. Inkwell wants to do this for its web site, so let's delve into the configuration for Inkwell's site. You'll get the out-of-the-box social networking up and running first, and then you'll modify the Product Registration portlet so that it displays activities whenever a user registers a product.

6.4 Using profile pages

Inkwell wants users to have profile pages, but it doesn't want users using the Add > More menu to put whatever portlets they want on those pages. Instead, Inkwell wants to define a static layout for users' pages that the users can't modify. This is easy to do with a few custom properties added to the portal-ext.properties file. You may remember that you used this file in chapter 2 to connect Liferay to a MySQL database. There are many, many configuration options for Liferay that you can put in this file, and you're going to use a few to control how users' profile pages work.

NOTE The portal.properties file is fully documented in Liferay's documentation. Additionally, the file is self-documented: many comments in the file explain what the various options do.

Everything you put in portal-ext.properties overrides the default in Liferay's portal.properties file. In this case, you're interested in the following properties:

```
layout.user.private.layouts.enabled=true
layout.user.private.layouts.modifiable=false

layout.user.public.layouts.enabled=true
layout.user.public.layouts.modifiable=false
```

The first two properties control *private layouts*, which are the user's private pages. The second two properties control *public layouts*, which are the user's public pages. You're making sure the layouts are enabled, and you're making them unmodifiable. This keeps users from being able to add portlets or move them around on their pages.

Next, you need to provide defaults for users' profile pages. Inkwell management has determined that the public pages should have a two-column, 30/70 layout. The first column (the thinner one) should contain the Summary and Search portlets, and the second column should contain the Activities and Wall portlets. The private pages will contain the defaults as set up by Liferay, except that the Requests portlet will be added to the top of the left column and the Friends' activities will be added to the top of the right column. You can configure this through properties as well. In order to do this, you need to be able to identify a portlet, so you can tell Liferay where specific portlets should go.

6.4.1 Identifying a portlet

Like secret agents, portlets in Liferay are identified by a code number, not a name. You didn't adhere to this convention when you created portlets in earlier chapters because frankly, it's confusing. Let me show you what I mean.

You identified the Product Registration portlet like this in the portlet.xml file:

```
<portlet>
    <portlet-name>product-registration</portlet-name>
    <display-name>Product Registration</display-name>
    ...
</portlet>
```

Makes sense, right? The portlet is given a name without a space, and the display name (what appears in the portlet window) looks the way a human would want to read it.

If you look at the way this is configured in the portlets that ship with Liferay, you see something else entirely in Liferay's portlet-custom.xml file:

```
<portlet>
    <portlet-name>121</portlet-name>
    <display-name>Requests</display-name>
    ...
</portlet>
```

As you can see, the portlet is given a code number for a name, but its display name is a human-readable name telling you that this is the Requests portlet. I don't know about you, but I can translate *Requests* to *requests* in my head to come up with a given portlet's name, but I'll never be able to translate *Requests* to *121.* I'll always have to go look up the number in the portlet-custom.xml file.

Portlets that are parts of plugins are also identified by their portlet names; and yes, Liferay numbers them too. And the numbers overlap. For example, the Summary portlet is defined in the plugin's portlet.xml file like this:

```
<portlet>
    <portlet-name>1</portlet-name>
    <display-name>Summary</display-name>
```

```
...
</portlet>
```

Why am I going over this? Because to define certain portlets to be on users' profile pages by default, you need to be able to refer to them by their root portlet IDs. When you do this for a portlet that ships with Liferay, the root portlet ID is the portlet name, which Liferay defines as a number. When you do this for a portlet that is in a separate WAR file (that is, a plugin), the root portlet ID is its name with *_WAR_[name of war]* appended to it. You'll set this up next.

6.4.2 Defining content for public and private pages

When you know which portlets you want to be on users' pages by default, you use properties to set up this configuration. Because Liferay provides defaults for this, you override what Liferay ships with by placing these properties in your portal-ext.properties file:

```
default.user.public.layout.column-1=1_WAR_socialnetworkingportlet,3
default.user.public.layout.column-2=116,3_WAR_socialnetworkingportlet

default.user.private.layout.column-1=121,2,23,11
default.user.private.layout.column-2=4_WAR_socialnetworkingportlet,29,8
```

As you can see, you set up the public pages so they look as described here by placing portlet IDs in the columns in which they belong.

When you do this for public pages, you get the result you wanted, shown in figure 6.5. Similarly, you configure users' private pages so they contain the portlets you want, using similar properties. Notice that you use the convention outlined earlier: for portlets that ship with Liferay, you use their numbers. For portlets contained in the social-networking plugin, you use the number plus the suffix. Table 6.1 provides a map of what you've done in the configuration in the previous snippet. If the names were human-readable (which unfortunately isn't practical for Liferay,

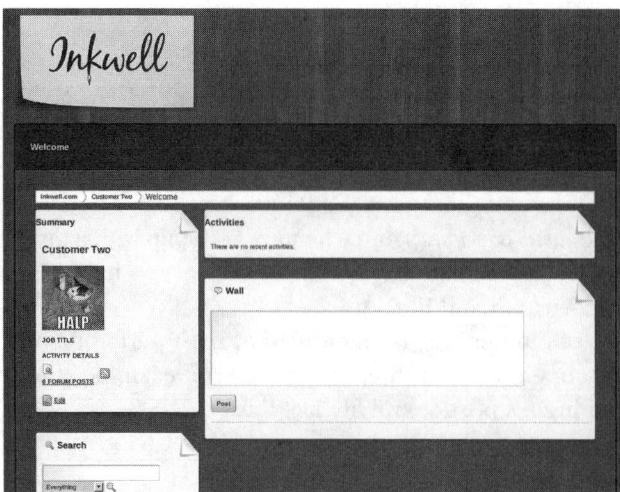

Figure 6.5 Users' public pages contain the Summary, Activities, and Wall portlets, and they're placed right where you wanted them. The Search portlet is there by default, and you've left it there because it'll likely be useful.

given the need for backward compatibility and due to display names evolving over time to match user expectations of portlet functions), you wouldn't need table 6.1.

Table 6.1 Map of portlet numbers to human-readable names

Portlet number	Portlet display name
2	My Account
3	Search
8	Calendar
11	Directory
23	Dictionary
29	My Communities
116	Activities
121	Requests
1_WAR_socialnetworkingportlet	Summary
3_WAR_socialnetworkingportlet	Wall
4_WAR_socialnetworkingportlet	Friends' Activities

You could have done the same thing with the Product Registration portlet, but that portlet isn't one you'd want on users' profile pages. If you needed to do this, though, the portlet's ID would be productregistration_WAR_productregistrationportlet. The Product Admin portlet would be productadmin_WAR_productregistrationportlet.

The result for the private pages is shown in figure 6.6.

Figure 6.6 Users' private pages, in addition to the defaults provided by Liferay (which you've left in place), contain the Requests portlet and the Friends' Activities portlet. You can see that Customer Two has sent a social-relation request to Customer One.

As you can see, using Liferay's out-of-the-box social-networking features is easy. The product provides the tools you need to set up social networking in a generic way. Your next task will be to integrate your own applications with your budding social network.

6.5 Friends, Romans, and countrymen: they're all social relations

You may have noticed in figure 6.6 that the Requests portlet says "Customer Two wants to be your friend." This comes out of the Language.properties file in the portal, not from the portlet itself. Remember: internally, Liferay calls this concept a social relation, in order to keep the concept as generic as possible and to let *you* decide what you want to call these things in your own social network. They can be friends, Romans, countrymen, connections, relatives, coworkers, or whatever.

When we go over hooks in chapter 8, you'll see how to customize the Language.properties file in the portal so the Requests portlet displays whatever you want it to. If you want your social relations to be "homeys," so be it. But I need to mention one last important factor about social networking before you delve deeper into the code: security.

6.5.1 Social relations aren't security

It's important to note that social relationships aren't security. Yes, portlets can be written to display or not display their contents based on whether the viewing user has a social relationship with the user who owns the portlet, as you can see with the Wall portlet in figure 6.7. But social relationships aren't built into the security framework of Liferay, and so they don't inherit any of the platform's role-based security and permission-checking features.

In short, if you want to protect the contents of a portlet based on whether the current user has a social relation with another user, you'll need to make a separate check. The Wall portlet does this, and any portlets you write that take advantage of Liferay's social API will need to do the same. Let's see how the Wall portlet does this so you can get a feel for it.

6.5.2 Coding for relationships

Social portlets that display data specific to a particular user are designed to be placed on users' profile pages. Rather than use `PermissionChecker` to determine whether

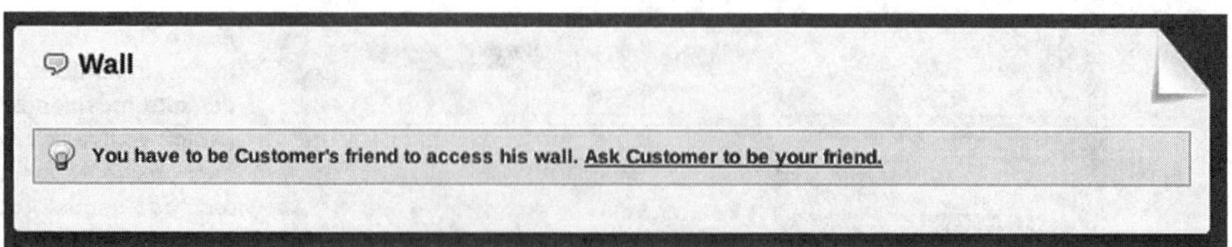

Figure 6.7 The Wall portlet specifically checks to see if the current user `hasRelation` with the user whose profile is being viewed. If the user doesn't have a social relation, the Wall portlet won't display its contents. This is a different check than the permissions check you saw in chapter 4.

certain data should be displayed (as you did in chapter 4), you'll check a couple of other things:

- Is the portlet placed on a user's profile page?
- Does the user viewing the portlet have a social relationship with the user on whose page the portlet has been placed?

Checking whether a portlet is on a user's page or a community/organization's page is fairly simple using the `scopeGroupId`. You may remember this from chapter 4: you can get it from Liferay's `themeDisplay` object, and it denotes an entry in the Group table. Each entry in the Group table contains information about the type and primary key of the Java object that represents that group; from there it's possible to retrieve the original object. In this case, you're on a user's public page, so the original object is a user. The following listing shows how the Wall portlet does it.

Listing 6.1 Checking the group type

```
Group group = GroupLocalServiceUtil.getGroup(scopeGroupId);      Get group

Organization organization = null;
User user2 = null;
                                                                  Check type
if (group.isOrganization()) {
    organization =
        OrganizationLocalServiceUtil.getOrganization(group.getClassPK());
}
else if (group.isUser()) {
    user2 = UserLocalServiceUtil.getUserById(group.getClassPK());
}
```

Combined code from social-networking-portlet/docroot/init.jsp, social-networking-portlet/docroot/wall/view.jsp

This code checks to see whether the current group—which is retrieved using the `scopeGroupId` found on the current page—is a user's group or is an organization. If the group is a user's group, you need to retrieve that user, because a little later you'll check to see if the current user has a social relation with the user who owns this page.

Next, the Wall portlet uses a small block of code to make sure the portlet itself has been placed on a user's profile page:

```
<c:choose>
  <c:when test="<%= user2 == null %>">
    <div class="portlet-msg-error">
      <liferay-ui:message key=
        "this-application-will-only-function-when-placed-on-a-user-page
" />
    </div>
  </c:when>
  <c:otherwise>
    <%@ include file="/wall/view_wall.jspf" %>
  </c:otherwise>
</c:choose>
```

You know you're on a user's profile page if the `user2` variable was populated in the previous code block. Here, all you have to do is check to see if it has a value. If it has a value, you include the JSP fragment that displays the wall. If it doesn't have a value, you show a message from the Language.properties file telling users to place this portlet on a user's profile page.

Here comes the fun part. When it's time to display the wall, you need to make sure the user attempting to view the wall has a social relation to the user on whose profile the wall resides. And these social relations can be of different types, which allows you to support a wide variety of relationships, both bidirectional and unidirectional. We'll get to that in a moment; right now, let's look at what the social relationship check looks like:

```
<c:choose>
  <c:when test="<%= themeDisplay.isSignedIn() &&
      ((user.getUserId() == user2.getUserId()) ||
        SocialRelationLocalServiceUtil.hasRelation(
              user.getUserId(), user2.getUserId(),
              SocialRelationConstants.TYPE_BI_FRIEND)
      ) %>">

[logic for displaying the wall goes here]

  </when>
</choose>
```

You have several checks in one line. You check for the following:

- Is the user signed in?
- Is the user viewing his / her own profile? Or...
- Does the user viewing the profile have a social relation with the user who owns the profile?

Notice the social relation check: it includes as part of the check a social relation *type*. In this case, you're checking for a type of *friend* that is *bidirectional*. That's the definition of a friend, right? If you're my friend, I must be your friend; otherwise the friendship doesn't exist. This is only one of the types of social relationships available in the API, and it gives you options you may not have considered. For example, consider the possibility of *another* Wall portlet—this one coded to check for the unidirectional relationship type between parent and child. This way, content uploaded by users can be targeted to people with the appropriate relationships.

For example, you might want to create a portlet for uploading photos. This portlet would use the back-end API of Liferay's Image Gallery for photo storage. But on the front-end, you could filter photo folders by the type of social relationship users have. Some pictures would be appropriate for co-workers. Other pictures would be appropriate for family. All the default relationship types are defined in a file called SocialRelationConstants.java in the Liferay source. The types are

- `TYPE_BI_COWORKER`
- `TYPE_BI_FRIEND`

- TYPE_BI_ROMANTIC_PARTNER
- TYPE_BI_SIBLING
- TYPE_BI_SPOUSE
- TYPE_UNI_CHILD
- TYPE_UNI_PARENT

If you look at the request that was sent in the Summary portlet, you'll see the following code:

```
SocialRequestLocalServiceUtil.addRequest(
    themeDisplay.getUserId(), 0, User.class.getName(),
    themeDisplay.getUserId(), FriendsRequestKeys.ADD_FRIEND,
    StringPool.BLANK, user.getUserId());
```

That `FriendsRequestKeys.ADD_FRIEND` variable maps to the type of social relationship that is being requested. This variable is defined in `FriendsRequestKeys` in the `social-networking-portlet` project, and its value is 1. But if you look at the types defined in Liferay's SocialRelationConstants.java file, you'll see that 1 is `TYPE_BI_COWORKER`. Although the Summary portlet and the Requests portlet are communicating to users that they're making a "friend" request, the actual request is a co-worker request.

Why is this? Because the portlets in the `social-networking-portlet` project were originally designed specifically for use on Liferay's web site. On Liferay's web site, Liferay employees are made "friends" with each other automatically—and now you know that the relation type is co-worker. Unlike some of the other portlets available in Liferay's repository, these are provided as examples of using the Social API, not necessarily as drop-in functionality like the Mail portlet or the Chat portlet. But think of the possibilities: you can write a portlet that allows users to request all different types of social relationships. When your users organize themselves into these relationships, you can provide all sorts of social functionality based on these relationships.

Now that you understand how social relationships are created, you need to figure out what to do with them. Users perform *activities* on your web site, don't they? Next, we'll turn to how to publish activities to those with whom you have a social relationship, and you'll do this specifically for Inkwell's web site.

6.6 Implementing social activities in your portlets

You wrote a portlet for Inkwell in chapters 3 and 4 that allows customers to register products that they purchase on the web site. This portlet is a perfect candidate for social networking, because the act of registering a product can be made easily into a social networking activity. In a nutshell, here's what you need to do:

- Modify the service layer so it adds an activity when it adds a registration.
- Create an object called a `SocialActivityInterpreter` in the portlet project to help the Activities portlet display your custom activity.

Cosmetically, this won't change the Product Registration portlet. But if Inkwell wants to use the social-networking features of Liferay for the company's web site, then whenever

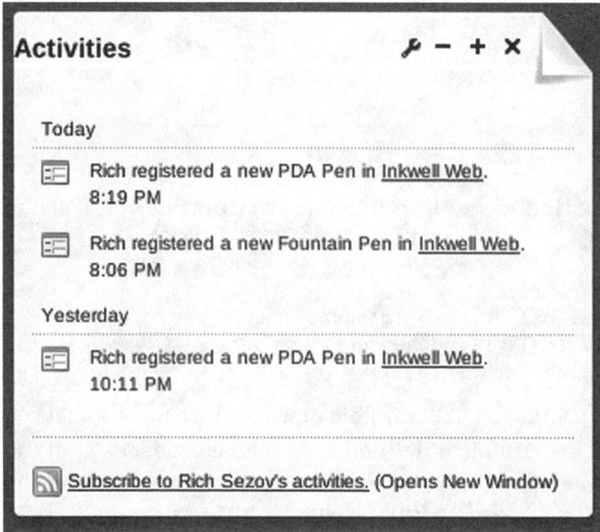

Figure 6.8 The Activities portlet can show any number of activities that are possible in your web site. If you've written games portlets, activities in those games can be published here. Users can even subscribe to an RSS feed of individual users' activities and read them offline.

a user registers a new product, the Activities portlet (which could be placed on users' profile pages) will display something like figure 6.8.

Notice also in the figure that the Activities portlet displays the icon for the portlet that published the activity. What you see tells you that yes, it's important to customize the portlet icon, and that maybe you should get your designers on that task, pronto.

> **NOTE** There's a known bug in Liferay 6.0 CE GA3 and the first release of Liferay 6.0 EE that prevents messages from a portlet plugin's Language.properties file from appearing in the Activities portlet. Instead, what appears is the key. To get around this bug, place your key/value pairs in a file called Language-ext.properties in your Liferay install's WEB-INF/classes/content folder. This bug is fixed in later versions of the product.

The code in the next section gives you the pattern that Liferay uses for its own portlets that publish social activities. I'm telling you this because it may seem overly modularized for our example's simple use case. The benefit is that you can immediately pick apart what Liferay is doing when examining its code, *and* you'll have a great model for more complicated portlets that publish lots of activities, such as those games I keep mentioning.

6.6.1 Adding an activity in the service layer

The first step is to add the activity when you're saving your entity, similar to the way you add a resource to use Liferay's permissions system. You want, of course, to do this in as efficient a manner as possible; thus you have to think about the transaction, because you're introducing another database call. Service Builder makes it easy to wrap all your database calls in a single transaction. You took advantage of this fact when you made the call to add the permissions resources to the database at the same time you added your entities, but the configuration for that transaction was built in to Service Builder. This time, you'll have to configure it yourself. Fortunately, doing so is easy—it's only two lines of configuration in service.xml:

```
<entity name="PRRegistration" local-service="true" remote-service="false">
.
.
.
  <reference package-path="com.liferay.portlet.social"
      entity="SocialActivity" />

  <reference package-path="com.liferay.portal" entity="User" />

</entity>
```

You can reference any package that contains Service Builder entities, and Service Builder takes care of the Spring/Hibernate configuration file wiring for you. What happens under the hood is the same thing that happens with resources and the counter, except this time you're defining that entities are injected. You do this through *references.*

By defining a reference in your entity, you cause Service Builder to generate a Spring configuration that injects an implementation of the entity you've referenced (see figure 6.9). In plain terms, this means there will be an instance variable of the referenced service in your implementation class.

Why do you do this? Wouldn't it be easier to use the generated static `-Util` class that Liferay provides for its services? If you were working up in the portlet layer, the answer would be yes. Because you're down in the service layer, the answer is no. The reason this is the case has to do with transactions.

Pretend that you (or if this is too painful, a friend) have purchased a cheap hosting plan for your MySQL database. You've connected Liferay, running on a different system, to this database. Unbeknown to you, the database hosting service is so cheap because the servers consist of racks of white-box machines running in somebody's basement. There's no backup battery, generator, or even surge protection. To top it

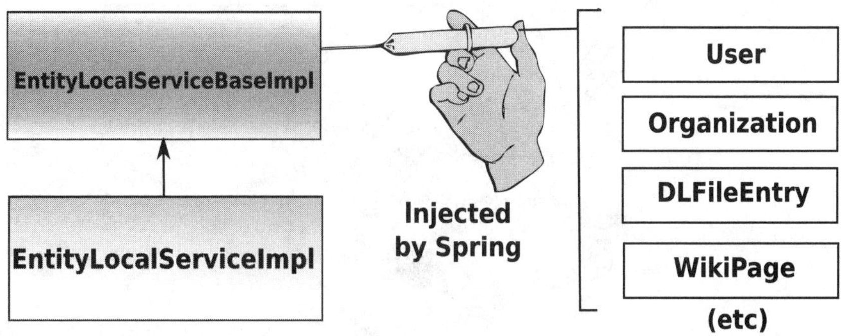

Figure 6.9 You can inject any Service Builder service into your service by providing a reference in service.xml. The injection occurs in the base class, which your implementation class inherits, so you don't have to touch anything in your code to make this happen.

off, the network connection is provided by a residential cable service. If you want your data backed up, well, back it up yourself.

Obviously, this situation is untenable and needs to be set right. No one should be able to get away with taking advantage of people in order to make huge profits on such a badly implemented service. Additionally, I'm sure the cable company doesn't take an especially kind view of this sort of thing. Because I believe in justice (and I'm the one making up this story), say a thunderstorm to end all thunderstorms comes, and with a single, blazing flash of light and high-decibel boom, it puts this particularly nefarious scheme to a fiery end.

Unfortunately, at the same time this was happening, your Liferay-based web site was chugging along, saving data to the database in multiple tables. If you have a call like this, a best practice is to create a reference from one service to the other and use the injected service. The Service Builder–generated Spring configurations tell Spring to propagate the transaction in your original service call to the new service call, and the entire operation becomes a single transaction that can be rolled back if the service or network is disrupted. Figure 6.10 shows how this works.

Of course, if your entire data center is disintegrated in a blinding explosion, this won't help you much. Suppose that in the explosion, the hard drive containing your

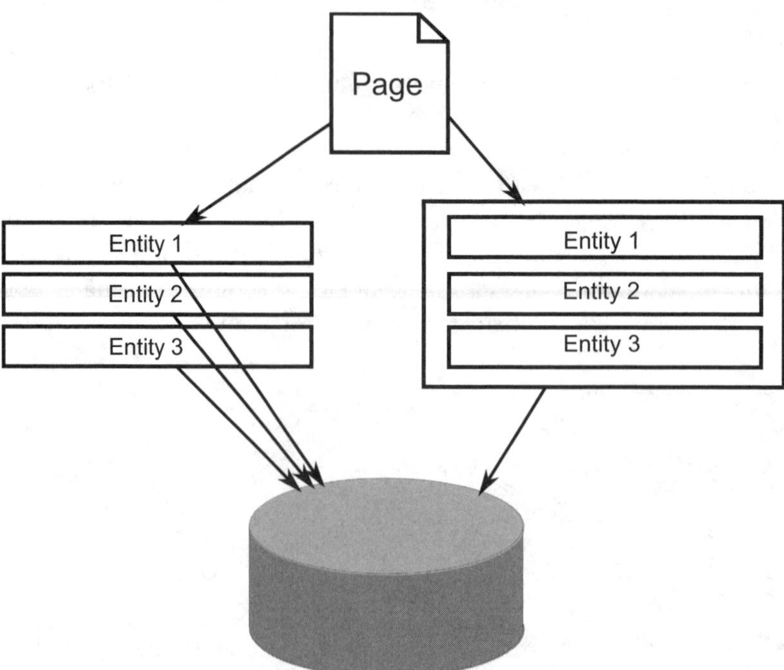

Figure 6.10 If data coming from the same web page is saved to the database as three different entities, it's best to group the entire operation in one transaction. That way, if there is an interruption in service, you don't wind up with corrupted or orphaned data in your database.

(or your friend's) database is miraculously blown clear of the data center, gets tangled in a bunch of helium balloons that were accidentally released at a child's birthday party, and lands gently on your porch. When you pick up the hard drive and access its data, if you've used references in Service Builder, you'll find that no part of the transaction that was in the process of being saved was committed, and your database is clean. If you made separate calls to separate services, you'll find that you now have orphans in your tables.

In any case, I highly recommend that you (or your friend) back up that data immediately and find a better database-hosting service.

Now that you've injected both the `SocialActivity` service and the `User` service into your `PRRegistration` service, you can use them to make a call to add the activity when a registration is added to the database. You put this code in the `PRRegistrationLocalServiceImpl` class.

Listing 6.2 Adding social activities

```
public PRRegistration addRegistration(PRRegistration reg)
    throws SystemException, PortalException {

    PRRegistration registration =
        prRegistrationPersistence.create(
            counterLocalService.increment(
                PRRegistration.class.getName()));

    registration.setCompanyId(reg.getCompanyId());
    registration.setDatePurchased(reg.getDatePurchased());
    registration.setGroupId(reg.getGroupId());
    registration.setHowHear(reg.getHowHear());
    registration.setProductId(reg.getProductId());
    registration.setPrUserId(reg.getPrUserId());
    registration.setSerialNumber(reg.getSerialNumber());
    registration.setWherePurchased(reg.getWherePurchased());

    resourceLocalService.addResources(
        registration.getCompanyId(), registration.getGroupId(),
        PRRegistration.class.getName(), false);

    PRUser prUser =
prUserPersistence.findByPrimaryKey(
        registration.getPrUserId());

    User user = userPersistence.fetchByPrimaryKey(prUser.getUserId());   <- Get user from PRUser

    if (user != null) {

        socialActivityLocalService.addActivity(
            user.getUserId(), reg.getGroupId(),
            PRRegistration.class.getName(),
            registration.getPrimaryKey(),
            ProductActivityKeys.ADD_REGISTRATION,
            StringPool.BLANK, 0);               <- Add social activity
    }
```

```
    return prRegistrationPersistence.update(registration, false);
}
```

docroot/WEB-INF/src/com/inkwell/internet/productregistration/service/impl/PRRegistrationLocalServiceImpl.java

Adding a social activity obviously requires a user ID. And because you coded the Product Registration Portlet to be able to accept registrations from anybody—whether they were logged in or not—you have to check to see if you have a Liferay user ID mapped to the user information you saved with the registration. You can only add an activity if you have a mapped portal user who was logged in saving the registration.

You'll probably also notice that while you add an activity, you make a call to another class called `ProductActivityKeys`. This class holds nothing but the list of possible activities for this portlet. It's overkill for this portlet because it has only one type of activity, but I wanted to give you an example of the pattern Liferay uses. All this line of code does is add an entry in Liferay's SocialActivity table for this activity, for this company, for this group, for the logged-in user, and for the class you've specified.

It's obvious that if we've added a call to add the activity, we need to add a call to delete the activity as well, so I won't bore you with the details of that—it's in the source code for the book. Next, we'll look at how to make the Activities portlet interpret your activity correctly so that it displays what you want.

6.6.2 Giving the Activities portlet an interpretation of a custom activity

The Activities portlet is kind of a strange bird. When it's placed on a page, it looks around to try to figure out where it is, and then it displays activities based on where it finds itself. For this reason, you need to handle one of two conditions: whether the Activities portlet is in the same community/organization in which the activity occurred, or whether it's in a different community/organization.

For example, many Liferay social-networking implementations place the Activities portlet on users' profile pages. If a user performs an activity in another community, the Activities portlet displays a message like

Some Dude did this thing in Community X.

The words *Community X* are a link to that community. This lets anyone browsing a social relation's profile hit the public pages of that community in order to look at the content and decide whether to join that community.

If the Activities portlet is in the same community in which the activity occurred, it displays a message like

Some Dude did this thing.

For this reason, you have to create not one but two keys in the Language.properties file for your activity message:

```
activity-product-registration-add-registration-in={0} registered a new {1}
➥ in {2}.
activity-product-registration-add-registration={0} registered a new {1}.
```

As you can see, you've got an `in` property and a (for lack of a better term) "not in" property, complete with tokens that represent what will be placed there.

The next thing you need to do is create an interpreter class, as shown in the next listing.

Listing 6.3 Interpreting activities

```
public String[] getClassNames() {                    ❶ Entities to interpret

    return _CLASS_NAMES;
}

@Override
protected SocialActivityFeedEntry doInterpret(
        SocialActivity activity, ThemeDisplay themeDisplay)
    throws Exception {                               ❷ Overridden from parent class

    PermissionChecker permissionChecker =
        themeDisplay.getPermissionChecker();

    PRRegistration registration =
        PRRegistrationLocalServiceUtil.getPRRegistration(
            activity.getClassPK());

    if (!permissionChecker.hasPermission(
            registration.getGroupId(), PRRegistration.class.getName(),
            registration.getPrimaryKey(), ActionKeys.VIEW)) {

        return null;                   ❸ Returns null if private
    }
                                                     ❹ Activities have link, key, title, body
    String link = StringPool.BLANK;

    String key = "activity-product-registration-add-registration";

    PRProduct product =
 PRProductLocalServiceUtil.getPRProduct(
        registration.getProductId());

    String title = getTitle(
        activity, key, product.getProductName(), link, themeDisplay);

    String body = StringPool.BLANK;

    return new SocialActivityFeedEntry(link, title, body);
}

protected String getTitle(
    SocialActivity activity, String key, String content, String link,
    themeDisplay themeDisplay) {                              ❺ il8n of activity

    String userName = getUserName(activity.getUserId(),themeDisplay);

    String text = HtmlUtil.escape(cleanContent(content));
```

```
        if (Validator.isNotNull(link)) {
            text = wrapLink(link, text);
        }

        String groupName = StringPool.BLANK;

        if (activity.getGroupId() != themeDisplay.getScopeGroupId()) {
            groupName = getGroupName(activity.getGroupId(),themeDisplay);
        }

        String pattern = key;

        if (Validator.isNotNull(groupName)) {
            pattern += "-in";
        }

        return themeDisplay.translate(
            pattern, new Object[] {userName, text, groupName});
    }

    private static final String[]_CLASS_NAMES = new String[] {
        PRRegistration.class.getName()
    };
```

docroot/WEB-INF/src/com/inkwell/internet/productregistration/social/RegistrationActivityInterpreter.java

Every `SocialActivityInterpreter` needs a list of class names for which this interpreter is responsible ❶. This way, you can use `doInterpret()` to check for class names with an `if` statement and then have separate methods for interpreting each type of activity. Because you're interpreting only one class, you can use `doInterpret()` directly. You're overriding from a parent base class, rather than implementing the interface directly ❷. This gives you access to some helpful methods (used in `getTitle()`) that you otherwise wouldn't have. Next, ❸ you check to make sure the current user has permission to view the entity for which an activity has been published. If you can't view the entity, you shouldn't be able to view the activity either.

Next come the contents of the activity ❹. Activities have various properties: a link to the activity, the key from Language.properties that should be used, and a title and body that can be displayed. Because this is a registration, you're not using a link (which would provide a link to that user's personal registration information) or a body; but as you can see, they're handled similarly to the title, and code in `getTitle()` handles a link if you have one. If you're interested, you can look at how Liferay's Message Boards portlet publishes an activity with a link to the relevant message boards post. You'll need to know how to do friendly URLs, which are introduced in chapter 10.

Finally, the `getTitle()` method uses Liferay's internationalization API to pick the proper translation of the key and populate it with the data from the activity ❺. Notice the code that checks to see if the community in the activity matches the community the user is currently browsing. If they don't match, you pull the `in` key and then make the call to translate it. The translator wants the pattern (the value from the key) and the values to insert in place of the tokens. You pass in these values as the name of the user, the name of the product (which could have been displayed as a link), and the community where this activity took place. The `doInterpret()` method then returns a fully interpreted `SocialActivityFeedEntry` that the Activities portlet can display.

That's all there is to publishing an activity. As you can see, activities are simple but powerful. They give developers a common interface to publish to social relations what users are doing across the entire portal installation. You can use them to great effect to provide a dynamic experience for your users.

6.7 Summary

Liferay Portal is a great platform for social web sites. Not only does it integrate nicely with other social sites such as Facebook, but it also provides a comprehensive API that lets you build your own social web site. This API provides everything you need to manage different types of social relationships, query for those relationships, allow sharing of information between users who have relationships, and more.

You can also integrate your own Liferay portlet applications with the social API to provide users with a running list of all the activities their friends are performing on your site. Whether your site contains games, collaboration, or any other type of application, you can publish that application's activities so all your users' networks can see them. Liferay Portal gives you an entire social platform on which to build your site.

There is, of course, more. Next, we'll look at the collaboration tools Liferay offers. Combining these with the social API gives you an unmatched platform for creating interactive web sites.

7 Enabling user collaboration

This chapter covers

- Assets, and why they're important
- Workflow-enabling your applications
- Empowering users to tag and categorize your data
- Integrating Liferay's commenting and rating systems
- Custom SQL in Service Builder

Way back before the turn of the century (isn't it cool to be able to say that?), I used to do development on a proprietary collaboration engine whose name you may recognize: Lotus Notes/Domino. In fact, I think it was due to that experience that I picked up my first Manning book, *Domino Development with Java* (Anthony Patton, 2000). I've been doing collaboration for a long time, and it's amazing to think about what can happen in a decade's time.

But back to my story. At that time, when we were first exploring all the ways to help people make use of internet technologies to streamline their work, we had to use software that was proprietary and, well, expensive. But the principles used back then are pretty much the same things—although not as AJAXy-slick—we see today:

replace email and file shares with collaborative tools and online discussions. This keeps all the metadata (comments, rankings, approvals, and more) with the *actual* data that is the subject of this collaboration. If you don't do this, that important metadata is scattered in multiple email accounts and file systems and is likely to get lost. The first collaborative systems were designed to capture all this together in one place, but that one place happened to be a single vendor's proprietary system. That meant you had to purchase both a server to store the data and multiple clients to access it.

It was a closed (and expensive) system, but it worked very well.

Then things started to change. As the web transformed from a place to store static, electronic documents to a place where applications generated pages dynamically (enabling the creation of applications like shopping carts, forums, and pretty much anything else that could be imagined), a lot of these collaborative features began to pop up in nonproprietary, web-based systems. And all of a sudden, people like me who were writing collaborative software on proprietary platforms were asked to "webify" it, because those platforms were moving toward the web. This way, desktops didn't have to be loaded with client software for proprietary platforms; instead, a browser could become the *über* client for them all.

My first "webification" project was called a Virtual Team Room. Another developer had already created the application for the proprietary client, and my job was to take this application and make it work in a browser.[1] The Virtual Team Room was designed to be a generic application for team collaboration. It included a list of team members, a forum for discussion, a document library for sharing documents, and more.

Sound familiar?

Now, of course, we're out of that proprietary world and into the open world of the web, where we can match and exceed the collaboration features of those rich, proprietary clients of years ago. What have we gained? Well, for one thing, we now have choice. You can run whatever operating system and whatever browser you want and successfully access the same application. We've also lowered the barriers to entry. You don't have to purchase an expensive client/server system to implement the application you want; instead, you can download Liferay for free, and you get great collaboration features that previously were only available to those who could pony up the cash.

The focus of this chapter is how you can implement these features in your own applications. We'll look together at workflow-enabling, tagging and categorizing data, and adding discussions and ratings to applications. When we've finished with that, you'll enhance your Service Builder skills by adding a custom, SQL-based query so that you can sort entities by their ratings. Building on the skills you've already learned, you'll take advantage of the collaboration APIs that Liferay provides.

You've only built the Product Registration portlet so far, and that's not an application that contains content on which users would be collaborating. Starting with this chapter, you'll write another application that will allow Inkwell's community of users to participate in a project of their own: a slogan contest.

---

[1] The totally awesome Netscape Navigator 4.5.1, to be precise.

7.1 Building a collaborative app: a slogan contest

Inkwell has decided to run a contest to see if a member of its community can come up with a new slogan for the company's products. The winner of the contest will receive one each of every product Inkwell makes, and the runners-up will also receive various prizes. Inkwell will run this contest by taking advantage of Liferay's collaboration features. These features are a perfect fit for what the company wants to do.

The design team came up with the design you see in figures 7.1 and 7.2. Figure 7.1 shows the default view of the application: it displays slogans that have been entered by users for the contest in order of ranking by how other users have rated the slogans. This feature will be powered by Liferay's built-in ranking engine. After users enter slogans, other users will be able to comment on them. This will be powered by Liferay's built-in messaging engine.

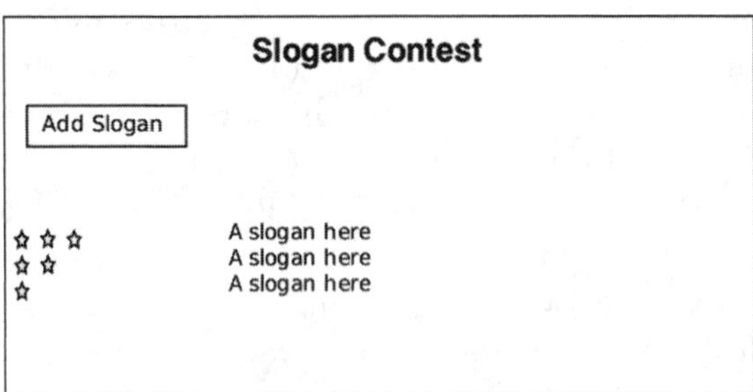

Figure 7.1 Slogans appear in a list sorted by their ranking. Logged-in users can add new slogans, but they won't appear until they've gone through the approval process, which is powered by Liferay's workflow engine.

You can probably see some problems with this plan, right? Allowing users to post anything they want as a slogan might lead to some, uh, inappropriate slogans. Because Inkwell doesn't want bad or abusive language cluttering up its web site, this application will be integrated with Liferay's workflow. Only slogans that go through the approval process will show up on the web site where they can be ranked. The rest will be discarded. In this way, Inkwell employees can vet the slogans as they're submitted.

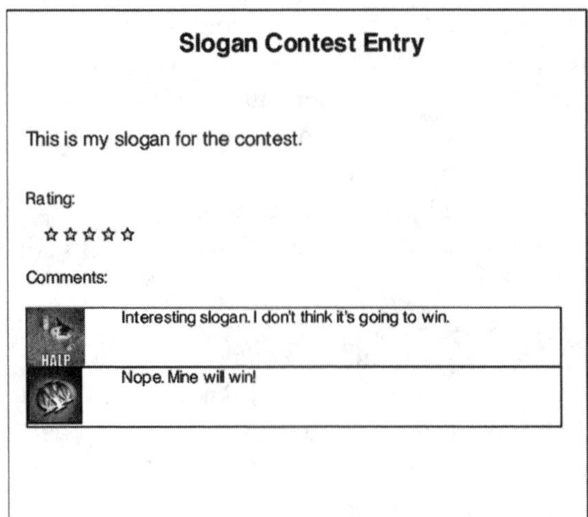

Figure 7.2 After slogans are entered and approved, they can be ranked by users and discussed. These are features provided by Liferay, not things you'll have to write yourself.

Now that you've got your design, let's get started building the application. Although you'll be using some technologies this book has already covered (Service Builder, `MVCPortlet`, and Alloy UI Forms), I'll spare you some suffering by not rehashing stuff you already know. Instead, I'll point out the new things so you can see how these features work in concert with what you've already learned.

As in previous chapters, we'll start with the back end of the application.

7.2 Adding assets to your applications

For this example, the back end is a Service Builder configuration file. Although this application is much simpler than the Product Registration portlet (because it has only one table), you should notice some differences right away in the following listing.

Listing 7.1 Service Builder with workflow configuration

```
<?xml version="1.0" encoding="UTF-8"?>
<!DOCTYPE service-builder PUBLIC "-//Liferay//DTD Service Builder
➥ 6.0.0//EN" "http://www.liferay.com
➥ /dtd/liferay-service-builder_6_0_0.dtd">
<service-builder package-path="com.inkwell.internet.slogan">
  <author>Rich Sezov</author>
  <namespace>Slogan</namespace>

  <entity name="Slogan"
      uuid="true" local-service="true" remote-service="false">     ❶ UUID

    <column name="sloganId" type="long" primary="true" />
    <column name="sloganDate" type="Date" />
    <column name="sloganText" type="String" />
    <column name="status" type="int" />                 ❷ Status fields
    <column name="statusByUserId" type="long" />           for workflow
    <column name="statusByUserName" type="String" />
    <column name="statusDate" type="Date" />

    <column name="companyId" type="long" />
    <column name="groupId" type="long" />
    <column name="userId" type="long" />

    <order>
      <order-column name="sloganId" order-by="asc" />
      <order-column name="sloganDate" order-by="desc" />
    </order>

    <finder name="GroupId" return-type="Collection">
      <finder-column name="groupId" />
    </finder>

    <finder name="CompanyId" return-type="Collection">
      <finder-column name="companyId" />
    </finder>

    <finder name="SloganText" return-type="Collection">
      <finder-column name="sloganText" />
    </finder>
```

```
    <finder name="G_S" return-type="Collection">
      <finder-column name="groupId" />
      <finder-column name="status" />
    </finder>

    <reference package-path="com.liferay.portal" entity="User" />
    <reference package-path="com.liferay.portlet.asset"
        entity="AssetEntry" />                                  <-- 3 Reference assets
    <reference package-path="com.liferay.portlet.ratings"
        entity="RatingsStats" />                        <-- 4 Reference ratings

  </entity>

</service-builder>
```

docroot/WEB-INF/service.xml

A UUID ❶ is a Universally Unique Identifier, and it's used by Liferay to make sure any entity can be identified regardless of the system in which it exists. Liferay uses these for things like importing and exporting content as LAR files, and you need it because some of the APIs you'll be using require the UUID in the method call.

Some new fields ❷ are necessary in order to implement Liferay's workflow in the application. It's important to note that you're one logical level up from the actual implementation of workflow. As of this writing, Liferay supports Kaleo (its own workflow engine), jBPM, and Activiti through various plugins. No matter which workflow engine you've installed, if you use Liferay's workflow API, which you'll see later in the chapter, your application will support it. Your first step is to add these fields to your entity.

Finally, ❸ and ❹ reference two different Liferay entities: assets and ratings. Assets allow built-in Liferay services to access attributes of your entities. You'll give Liferay's asset framework all the information it needs to interpret your entity properly and show the data you want it to show, in case users want to publish your data in something generic like Liferay's Asset Publisher. Assets are also used by Liferay's workflow framework. Ratings are scores attached to assets. You'll allow users to rate the slogans using from one to five stars.

Now that you've got your Service Builder configuration, you can generate the back-end code. As usual, you do this by running `ant build-service` from the project.

Your next task, as before, is to implement the back-end methods. Let's look at how workflow affects the code for these methods.

7.2.1 Adding assets with entities

As you perform this next task, you should begin to see a pattern. Do you remember the `SocialActivityInterpreter` that you created in the last chapter? Its function was to *interpret* a social activity for the calling class. It did this by returning certain pieces of information that the calling class needed in order to display a message to the user (a `String` containing the message, the user who performed the activity, and such). This enabled the Activities portlet to display messages that *you* generated.

Assets do almost the same thing and follow the same pattern. Let's look at the code to see how this works. The first thing you need to do is modify the `SloganLocalServiceImpl` class to support assets.

Listing 7.2 Adding an entity with assets

```
public Slogan addSlogan(Slogan newSlogan, long userId,
        ServiceContext serviceContext)                    ❶ Requires ServiceContext
    throws SystemException, PortalException {

    Slogan slogan =
 sloganPersistence.create(
        counterLocalService.increment(
Slogan.class.getName()));

    slogan.setCompanyId(newSlogan.getCompanyId());
    slogan.setGroupId(newSlogan.getGroupId());
    slogan.setUserId(serviceContext.getUserId());
    slogan.setSloganDate(newSlogan.getSloganDate());
    slogan.setSloganText(newSlogan.getSloganText());
    slogan.setStatus(WorkflowConstants.STATUS_DRAFT);

    sloganPersistence.update(slogan, false);

    resourceLocalService.addResources(
        newSlogan.getCompanyId(), newSlogan.getGroupId(), userId,
        Slogan.class.getName(), slogan.getPrimaryKey(), false,
        true, true);

    assetEntryLocalService.updateEntry(                   ❷ Registers asset
        userId, slogan.getGroupId(), Slogan.class.getName(),
        slogan.getSloganId(), serviceContext.getAssetCategoryIds(),
        serviceContext.getAssetTagNames());

    return slogan;
}
```

docroot/WEB-INF/src/com/inkwell/internet/slogan/service/impl/SloganLocalServiceImpl.java

As you can see, something else is new. The method requires something called a `ServiceContext` ❶ This is a handy object that was created by Liferay's engineers as a way to simplify method signatures in the API. Some of Liferay's method calls require a lot of parameters. As an example, look at this one, which comes from Liferay's `UserLocalServiceUtil` class and is used to add a user:

```
public User addUser(
    long creatorUserId, long companyId, boolean autoPassword,
    String password1, String password2, boolean autoScreenName,
    String screenName, String emailAddress, long facebookId,
    String openId, Locale locale, String firstName, String middleName,
    String lastName, int prefixId, int suffixId, boolean male,
    int birthdayMonth, int birthdayDay, int birthdayYear,
    String jobTitle, long[] groupIds, long[] organizationIds,
    long[] roleIds, long[] userGroupIds, boolean sendEmail,
    ServiceContext serviceContext)
```

That's a pretty long method signature. But it's nothing compared to what it used to be *before* adding `ServiceContext` to it. As Liferay exposed more and more APIs to developers, it became obvious that many APIs needed a lot of the same context variables. Why not place all that context information into a single object that can be passed into other methods? This not only simplifies the method call but also provides a convenient way of retrieving all the context information you need from one place. For the remainder of this book, you'll be using `ServiceContext` all over the place. Table 7.1 shows its attributes.

Table 7.1 `ServiceContext` attributes

Attribute	Purpose
`addCommunityPermissions`	A flag that indicates that default community permissions should be applied to the resource being manipulated (if there is one). When using the `<liferay-ui:input-permissions>` tag, this value is prepopulated into the `ServiceContext`.
`addGuestPermissions`	A flag that indicates that default Guest permissions should be applied to the resource being manipulated (if there is one). When using the `<liferay-ui:input-permissions>` tag, this value is prepopulated into the `ServiceContext`.
`assetCategoryIds`	An array of `assetCategoryIds` that should be added to the asset entry being manipulated (if there is one). When using `<aui:input name="categories" type="assetCategories" />`, these are prepopulated into the `ServiceContext`.
`assetTagNames`	An array of `assetTagNames` that should be added to the asset entry being manipulated (if there is one). When using `<aui:input name="tags" type="assetTags" />`, these are prepopulated into the `ServiceContext`.
`attributes`	An arbitrary number of serializable attributes that are passed along with the `ServiceContext` during its lifetime. By default, all request parameters are automatically added.
`command`	The value of the `Constants.CMD` parameter used in most Liferay forms for internal portlets.
`communityPermissions`	An array that contains the specific community permissions that should be applied to the resource being manipulated (if there is one). When using the `<liferay-ui:input-permissions>` tag, this array is prepopulated into the `ServiceContext` with the choices made by the user.
`companyId`	The `companyId` of the current portal instance. This is a legacy variable name that is used to denote which portal instance the user is logged into. A portal instance used to be called a company and has been renamed in the UI, but not the back end.

Table 7.1 `ServiceContext` attributes *(continued)*

Attribute	Purpose
`createDate`	The date used to indicate creation time when creating a new entity.
`expandoBridgeAttributes`	An arbitrary number of attributes that is applied to a given entity when it's persisted (if those are defined for the entity). If using the `<liferay-ui:custom-attribute>` or `<liferay-ui:custom-attribute-list>` tag, these values are prepopulated into the `ServiceContext` with user input. You'll see how this works in the next chapter.
`guestPermissions`	An array that contains the specific Guest permissions that should be applied to the resource being manipulated (if there is one). When using the `<liferay-ui:input-permissions>` tag, this array is prepopulated into the `ServiceContext` with the choices made by the user.
`languageId`	The current user `Locale` as a `String`.
`layoutFullURL`	The complete URL of the current page (if a page context can be determined at the time).
`layoutURL`	A relative URL of the current page (if a page context can be determined at the time).
`modifiedDate`	The date used to indicate the modification time when updating an existing entity.
`pathMain`	The main context path of the portal, concatenated with `/c`.
`portalURL`	The URL, including protocol and domain (and port if nondefault) of the portal (relative to company instance and any virtual host).
`portletPreferencesIds`	The `PortletPreferencesIds` of the current portlet (if currently within a portlet), which can be used to look up the portlet preferences of the current portlet.
`scopeGroupId`	The id of the `Group` corresponding to the current data scope.
`userDisplayURL`	The complete URL of the current user's profile page (typically the first public user page).
`plid`	The id of the current page.
`workflowAction`	The action to be taken by the workflow (if there is one).
`userId`	The id of the current user.
`uuid`	Used to correlate entities across systems or scopes. It signifies that two entities of the same type having different primary keys, but having the same `uuid`, have the same origin and thus are the same entity. This value is used when creating or updating entities that may have originated elsewhere but for which you want to retain the correlation.

In listing 7.2, ❷ is the call to update the asset (in this case, it adds the asset). As you can see, it's similar to adding a `Resource`, which you're already doing to implement permissions. And as with `Resources`, you have to delete `Assets` at the same time you delete your entity, as is evidenced by the delete method:

```
public void deleteSlogan (Slogan slogan)
    throws SystemException, PortalException {

    long companyId = slogan.getCompanyId();

    resourceLocalService.deleteResource(
        companyId, Slogan.class.getName(),
        ResourceConstants.SCOPE_INDIVIDUAL, slogan.getPrimaryKey());

    assetEntryLocalService.deleteEntry(
        Slogan.class.getName(), slogan.getSloganId());

    sloganPersistence.remove(slogan);
}
```

Simple, right? But you're not finished yet. Remember: you're following pretty much the same pattern you saw in chapter 6 with activities, which means you'll be declaring an interpreter in liferay-portlet.xml that can convert your entity into something more generic. This interpreter is an `AssetRendererFactory` that can generate generic entries for any portlet that queries for assets (in this case, the Asset Publisher portlet). Let's do that next.

7.2.2 Using asset renderers to publish your data

When Liferay's Asset Publisher portlet finds assets it's configured to publish, it needs to be able to display something about those assets to the user. Because an asset can be anything—and in this case, it's a slogan—the type of asset can't be foreseen, and so there needs to be a translation layer that can convert an entity you know about into a format that the asset publisher understands. Hence, the asset renderer.

An asset renderer is generated by an asset renderer *factory*, and the factory is registered with the portlet in the liferay-portlet.xml deployment descriptor. This again, is the same place you registered your social activity interpreter in the last chapter, so this pattern should be starting to become familiar to you (and if it isn't, don't worry: you'll see it again). This file is shown next.

Listing 7.3 liferay-portlet.xml

```
<?xml version="1.0"?>
<!DOCTYPE liferay-portlet-app PUBLIC
➥ "-//Liferay//DTD Portlet Application 6.0.0//EN"
➥ "http://www.liferay.com/dtd/liferay-portlet-app_6_0_0.dtd">

<liferay-portlet-app>
```

```
  <portlet>
    <portlet-name>slogan-contest</portlet-name>
    <icon>/icon.png</icon>
    <asset-renderer-factory>
com.inkwell.internet.slogan.asset.SloganAssetRendererFactory
    </asset-renderer-factory>
    <instanceable>false</instanceable>
    <header-portlet-css>/css/portlet.css</header-portlet-css>
    <footer-portlet-javascript>
        /js/javascript.js
    </footer-portlet-javascript>
    <css-class-wrapper>slogancontest-portlet</css-class-wrapper>
  </portlet>
  <role-mapper>
    <role-name>administrator</role-name>
    <role-link>Administrator</role-link>
  </role-mapper>
  <role-mapper>
    <role-name>guest</role-name>
    <role-link>Guest</role-link>
  </role-mapper>
  <role-mapper>
    <role-name>power-user</role-name>
    <role-link>Power User</role-link>
  </role-mapper>
  <role-mapper>
    <role-name>user</role-name>
    <role-link>User</role-link>
  </role-mapper>
</liferay-portlet-app>
```

❶ **Specify instantiating class**

docroot/WEB-INF/liferay-portlet.xml

The asset renderer factory declaration ❶, just under the portlet icon declaration, specifies the class to use that can instantiate asset renderers for entities in this portlet. The factory is simple, as is shown in the next listing.

Listing 7.4 Asset renderer factory

```
public AssetRenderer getAssetRenderer(long classPK, int type)
    throws PortalException, SystemException {

    Slogan slogan = SloganLocalServiceUtil.getSlogan(classPK);

    return new SloganAssetRenderer(slogan);
}
```

docroot/WEB-INF/src/com/inkwell/internet/slogan/asset/SloganAssetRendererFactory.java

The factory code calls the constructor for the asset renderer, giving it the primary key of the slogan you want to render as an asset. The `type` field isn't used in this portlet; you would use it if you had multiple different kinds of assets in your portlet that you wanted to render. In this case, you might return a different asset renderer based on the type of asset that is being requested.

Because the real work is being done in the asset renderer itself, let's look at that next.

Listing 7.5 Rendering an asset

```
public SloganAssetRenderer(Slogan slogan) {

    _slogan = slogan;

}

public long getClassPK() {

    return _slogan.getSloganId();
}

public long getGroupId() {

    return _slogan.getGroupId();
}

public String getSummary() {                          ❶ Convert entity data to asset

    return _slogan.getSloganText();
}

public String getTitle() {                            ❷ Title for entry

    return "Slogan Contest Entry";
}


public long getUserId() {

    return _slogan.getUserId();
}


public String getUuid() {

     return _slogan.getUuid();
}

public String render(
        RenderRequest request,
 RenderResponse response,
        String template)
    throws Exception {
                                                      ❸ JSP to render asset
    if (template.equals(TEMPLATE_FULL_CONTENT)) {
        request.setAttribute(WebKeys.SLOGAN_ENTRY, _slogan);

        return "/html/" + template + ".jsp";
    }
```

```
    else {
        return null;
    }
}
```

docroot/WEB-INF/src/com/inkwell/internet/slogan/asset/SloganAssetRenderer.java

What's going on here is a simple conversion process. Specific data from your entity is converted to an asset entry, which has a title and a summary ❶ ❷. Both of these are `Strings`. Because you know everything there is to know about the entity, you can write whatever code is necessary to convert properties from the entity into these two `Strings`. In this case, the code is simple: you return the full slogan for the summary, and you return the text "Slogan Contest Entry" for the title.

The Render method ❸ is doing a bit more. In the Asset Publisher, you can see a list of assets in the portlet window. When slogans are displayed, the Asset Publisher calls ❶ and ❷, which show users two things: that this is a slogan contest entry, and the full content of the slogan. If they want to click the slogan entry to see the full view of the slogan, you need to implement the view logic in your JSP. The render method tells Liferay where to find this JSP: in the html directory of the portlet plugin. The name comes from a constant that is defined in the superclass: `TEMPLATE_FULL_CONTENT = "full_content"`, so you'll name the JSP full_content.jsp.

We'll get to the JSP later, because it includes some cool stuff we need to go over when we get to the view layer. For now, just know that you need to implement a JSP that can display the content of your entity.

What you've got now is code that allows you to publish your data in a generic way throughout the portal, using the Asset Publisher portlet. If you were to configure an Asset Publisher portlet to display only slogans, it would look something like figure 7.3.

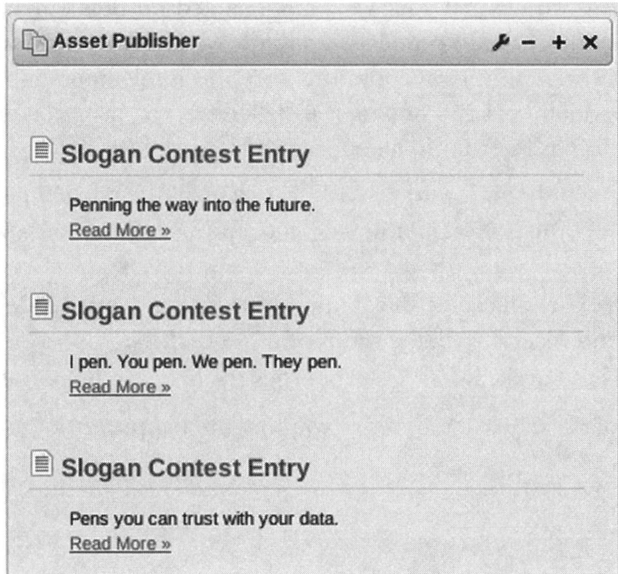

Figure 7.3 You've made your application portal-wide. Although you need to implement a few more things in order to increase the relevancy of the data returned, your entities can now be published across the portal by Asset Publisher.

Clicking the Read More link in the portlet causes Asset Publisher to render the slogan using the JSP defined in the `render()` method of your asset renderer. I'm not going to show you that until later (of course, nothing prevents you from flipping a few pages and sneaking a peek)—you'll be implementing tagging, categorizing, and comments in this page, so it'll require some explanation. For now, we can move on to another of your requirements: workflow.

7.3 Running your data through a workflow

If you've been reading this chapter nonstop until now, I recommend taking a break. Go outside, let the sun shine on your face, come back in, hit the bathroom, and maybe grab something to drink. This is an extended discussion of workflow, so it's best to approach it fresh. Ready? Here we go.

Liferay 6 is the first version to implement a workflow service that can be used throughout the product. What's cool about Liferay's workflow is that it has many pluggable implementations. By default, Liferay CE ships with the Kaleo workflow engine. This is the workflow engine that Liferay provides, and it's new as of this release. Improving all the time, Kaleo has been designed to hit the most common workflow use cases. It's likely that you'll be well served by Kaleo, and it's easy to use.

But if your workflow requirements are more complex, there are other workflow plugins you can use. As of this writing, JBoss's jBPM (www.jboss.org/jbpm) and Activiti (www.activiti.org) are both supported as Liferay plugins: you can grab them from the repository and install them just like any other plugin. You can have only one workflow plugin installed at a time, so be sure to pick the one that will serve you best. But there's one important benefit to using Liferay's workflow API, regardless of which workflow implementation you use: you code to the API, and the underlying implementation doesn't matter. This means that your workflow-enabled portlets will work with any of the workflow engines Liferay supports, and you won't have to do anything extra. Because Liferay's workflow API sits above the workflow implementations, developers aren't affected by which workflow engine is installed.

You need to do four things in order to be effective with workflow:

1. You need to understand how it works, so I'll show you all the moving parts.
2. You'll modify the existing service in the Slogan Contest portlet to support workflow.
3. You'll create a workflow handler that knows how to hand off entities to the workflow system and receive back the status of those entities.
4. We'll look at a way to handle language properties that need to be portal wide.

But let's not get ahead of ourselves: let me show you first the big picture of how workflow works.

7.3.1 *Understanding the flow of Liferay workflow*

Implementing workflow in your applications is easy; but it helps first to get a big picture idea of how it works, because the implementation pattern works in a somewhat roundabout fashion. Figure 7.4 attempts to illustrate how workflow is called in a Liferay application.

The first thing you do is to add a call to the `startWorkflowInstance()` method of `WorkflowHandlerRegistryUtil` in your `-LocalServiceImpl` class ❶. You do this in exactly the same manner in which you call the `Resource` service to persist resources, the `AssetEntry` service to persist assets, and the `SocialActivity` service to persist social activities.

The nice thing about the `startWorkflowInstance()` method is that it automatically detects whether workflow is installed and/or enabled for your entity type. You don't have to do any checking for that yourself; you as a developer assume that workflow is enabled. If it isn't, the status of your entities is automatically set to the approved status.

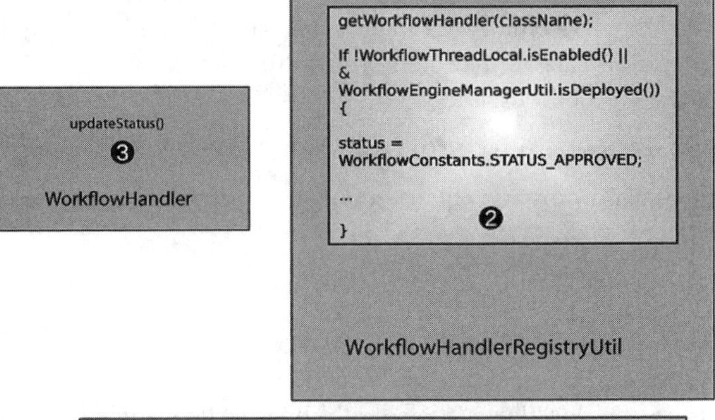

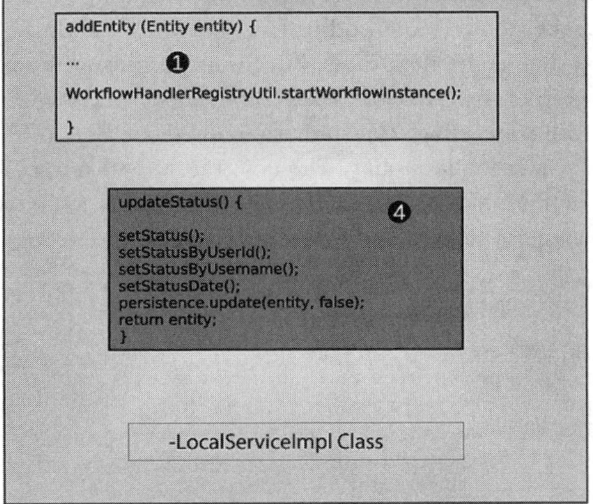

Figure 7.4 Workflow is called through a combination of your service and a specialized `WorkflowHandler` class that you create for your entity.

Next, after the workflow instance is started, an instance of the `WorkflowHandler` class for your application is created ❷, and `updateStatus()` is called on that instance ❸. This method contains any logic you need for updating the status of your entity in the workflow engine. Generally, though, the pattern within Liferay's code is to delegate this logic to a method with the same name in the service layer ❹. Why? Because you'll need to resave the entity after the status changes, and that should be done in the service layer.

Now that you understand how all this will work, let's implement it.

7.3.2 Workflow-enabling your services

Workflow is kicked off from the service layer when you add an entity to the database. You first hard-code the status as a draft, and then the Liferay workflow engine handles determining whether workflow is enabled and updates the status accordingly. If your users don't have workflow enabled, you don't have to worry: nothing about your application functionally changes. The only thing you have to add is a call to start the workflow instance. You can do this any time before you return the entity. If you refer to listing 7.2 (which is the service implementation that saves an entity to the database), you can add the workflow calls to that method. You first set the status of the entity to *draft* at the end of the set methods:

```
slogan.setStatus(WorkflowConstants.STATUS_DRAFT);
```

Next, you start the workflow instance before the `return slogan` line at the end of the method:

```
WorkflowHandlerRegistryUtil.startWorkflowInstance(
     slogan.getCompanyId(), slogan.getGroupId(), userId,
     Slogan.class.getName(), slogan.getPrimaryKey(), slogan,
     serviceContext);
```

This method registers the workflow instance with the workflow engine, if it's installed, and it calls the `updateStatus()` method in your `WorkflowHandler` class for the first time. (We'll look at that as the next topic, but I want to finish the service layer first.) Remember how I said earlier that the `WorkflowHandler`'s `updateStatus()` method delegates most of the processing to a similarly named method in the service layer? Let's see what that processing looks like. The next (and final) thing you need to do to the service implementation class is to add `updateStatus()` to the service layer, as shown in the following listing.

Listing 7.6 Updating an entity's status and storing the result

```
public Slogan updateStatus(
        long userId, long resourcePrimKey, int status,
        ServiceContext serviceContext)
    throws PortalException, SystemException {

    User user = userLocalService.getUser(userId);
    Slogan slogan = getSlogan(resourcePrimKey);
```

```
    slogan.setStatus(status);                               <-- ❶ Set workflow fields
    slogan.setStatusByUserId(userId);
    slogan.setStatusByUserName(user.getFullName());
    slogan.setStatusDate(serviceContext.getModifiedDate());

    sloganPersistence.update(slogan, false);

    if (status == WorkflowConstants.STATUS_APPROVED) {

        assetEntryLocalService.updateVisible(
            Slogan.class.getName(), resourcePrimKey, true);
    }                                                           ❷ Set visibility
    else {

        assetEntryLocalService.updateVisible(
            Slogan.class.getName(), resourcePrimKey, false);
    }

    return slogan;
}
```

docroot/WEB-INF/src/com/inkwell/internet/slogan/service/impl/SloganLocalServiceImpl.java

Notice that you didn't set these workflow status fields when you added the entity; instead, you set them as part of the workflow call (which happens anyway when you add the entity, because you call `startWorkflowInstance()` during the add). You could just as easily have set them in the `WorkflowHandler`'s `updateStatus()` method, but it's better to delegate to the service layer. Why? Because of something I found out the hard way when I was learning: workflow won't re-persist your entity—you have to do it. And where does persistence code get called? In the service layer. Here is where you update all the fields in your entity that have to do with workflow; then you save it. Note that you also update the visibility of the asset, so anything that's not approved is invisible to Asset Publisher. Otherwise, your tag queries in that portlet would show all the slogans, regardless of whether they had been approved, and you certainly don't want that. If Inkwell's management got sued because of objectionable material on the site, the prospect of holding on to a job there would be rather dim.

What about this `WorkflowHandler` I keep mentioning? That's the next thing you'll implement. If you can believe it, after you've done that, you'll have completely implemented workflow in your portlet.

7.3.3 Handily handling workflow

This will be easy to set up, because you've seen this particular pattern *twice*. As with social activities and assets, you declare `WorkflowHandler` in liferay-portlet.xml in order to tell Liferay about it. You do so with a single declaration, which you can place right under the one you already have for the asset renderer:

```
<workflow-handler>
    com.inkwell.internet.slogan.workflow.SloganWorkflowHandler
</workflow-handler>
```

When you've declared your workflow handler, you're free to implement it, which you can see in the next listing (minus the `import` statements).

Listing 7.7 A workflow handler for slogans

```
public String getClassName() {

    return CLASS_NAME;
}

public String getType(Locale locale) {                    ❶ LanguageUtil API

    return LanguageUtil.get(locale, "model.resource." + CLASS_NAME);

}

public Object updateStatus(int status,
        Map<String, Serializable> workflowContext)
    throws PortalException, SystemException {

    long userId = GetterUtil.getLong(                     ❷ Getter Util
        workflowContext.get(
WorkflowConstants.CONTEXT_USER_ID));

    long resourcePrimKey = GetterUtil.getLong(
        workflowContext.get(
WorkflowConstants.CONTEXT_ENTRY_CLASS_PK));

    ServiceContext serviceContext =
        (ServiceContext) workflowContext.get("serviceContext");

    return SloganLocalServiceUtil.updateStatus(           ❸ Call service layer
        userId, resourcePrimKey, status, serviceContext);
}

public static final String CLASS_NAME = Slogan.class.getName();   ❹ Liferay code style
```

docroot/WEB-INF/src/com/inkwell/internet/slogan/workflow/SloganWorkflowHandler.java

There are a few things in this code that I definitely want to point out. First, ❶ shows a use of Liferay's `LanguageUtil` API. You haven't used this in the Java code yet, but you have used tags (such as `<liferay-ui:error />` and `<liferay-ui:message />`) that call the same code. This call returns the message that's associated with the text *model.resource.* concatenated with the name of the class for which this `WorkflowHandler` was designed. If you need to grab a message from your language resource bundle anywhere in your code, you can get at it this way.

I used Liferay's `GetterUtil` in ❷ to show another utility class provided by the platform. This class makes it easy to get values of certain types without having to call parsers, `SimpleDateFormatters`, or anything of the sort. Here, you're getting some variables (the user ID and the primary key of the entity that's being—for lack of a better word—workflown) out of the `WorkflowContext`, which, as you can see, is a simple `Map` object.

At the end of the `updateStatus` method ❸, you call the one from the service layer, using all the variables you've been able to retrieve out of the context. This sets the fields in the entity and saves it, as you have already seen. And finally, I included ❹ almost as a humorous aside. Liferay's coding style is a bit, uh, different than what most Java coders use, and this is just an example of it. Instance variables of the class go at the bottom. I'm mentioning it (and following the Liferay convention) because if you go through Liferay's code, you're going to see it all over the place, so you may as well get used to it. I'm *still* getting used to it.

You're about finished, but there's one thing you haven't done: add those `model.resource` language properties to your content/Language.properties file. And there's a good reason why: these *are* language properties, but they're different language properties, and you're not going to add them to that file. Let me explain what I mean.

7.3.4 Portal-wide language properties

You've already used language properties for internationalization, and they work well. But there's one thing to remember about them, and it goes back to the design of Java EE. Because different web applications are isolated in their own classloaders, Liferay can't see the language properties of plugins that are registered with it, because Liferay and the plugin are in two different classloaders. The `model.resource` properties you're defining don't appear anywhere *in* the Slogan Contest portlet; instead, these properties (actually, any property prefixed with `model.resource`) appear in the portal, in various configuration screens like the one shown in figure 7.5. This means the

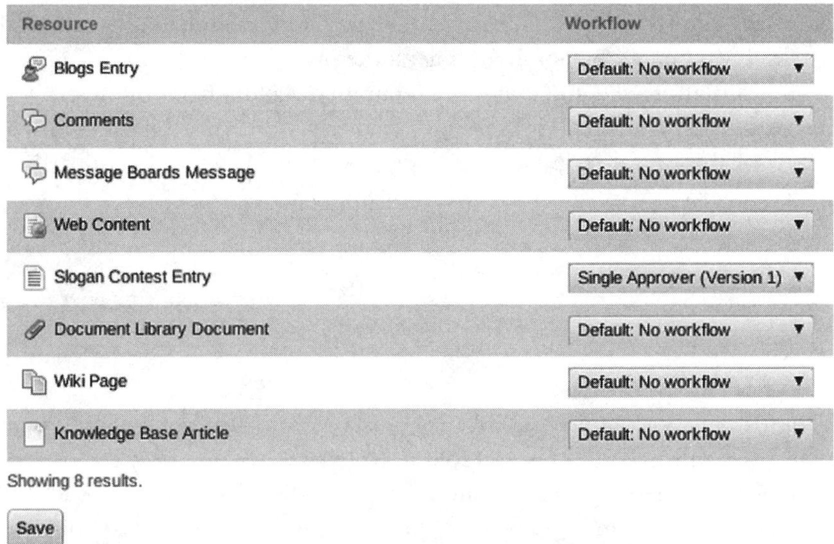

Figure 7.5 When configuring workflow for the portlet, you want your entity displayed properly. Liferay somehow must be able to read a properties file from your application that exists in a separate classloader. The text *Slogan Contest Entry*, without the global language properties hook, would display *model.resource.com.inkwell.internet.slogan.model.Slogan*.

portal *must* be able to read the properties from the language resource bundle in the portlet if this is going to look right, no matter what the Java EE spec says. Fortunately, Liferay gives you a way to do just that: hooks.

Consider this a small preview of the next chapter. You'll use a hook for your `model.resource` properties. This will get them into Liferay's classloader so the portal can look them up. It also shows that you can include both a hook and a portlet plugin in the *same* project, which is pretty cool all by itself.

To define your hook, you create a file called liferay-hook.xml in the WEB-INF folder of your project. The hook configuration is simple:

```
<?xml version="1.0"?>

<!DOCTYPE hook PUBLIC "-//Liferay//DTD Hook 6.0.0//EN"
➥ "http://www.liferay.com/dtd/liferay-hook_6_0_0.dtd">

<hook>
  <language-properties>
      content-portal/Language_en.properties
  </language-properties>

  <language-properties>
      content-portal/Language_ar.properties
  </language-properties>

...

</hook>
```

I placed an ellipsis in the code to show that you include every translation you have—I'm saving paper by not including all the ones I generated. Notice also that you place the translations in a file that's in a separate directory from the rest of your translations. You don't need to hook *all* of your translations into Liferay—only the ones that parts of the portal core need to know about. In order to do this, you also add another target to the Ant script for this project:

```
<target name="build-portal-lang">
  <antcall target="build-lang-cmd">
    <param name="lang.dir" value="docroot/WEB-INF/src/content-portal" />
    <param name="lang.file" value="Language" />
  </antcall>
</target>
```

Running this `ant` task builds out all the translations for the Language.properties file that you place in the content-portal folder. Note that because only the portal and not your application needs to know about these properties, you don't have to declare the bundle as a resource bundle in your portlet.xml file. In fact, if you do this, the file will no longer validate.

That's all there is to making certain language properties available to the portal itself. It's a best practice to set them up separately this way, because you avoid mixing the ones you need to be portal-wide with your local properties, and you add only the properties the portal needs to display. This prevents the portal from having to load more properties in its own classloader than necessary, which saves on both memory and processing. When you deploy the plugin now, Liferay will recognize that it's both a portlet and a hook, and you'll be able to use the capabilities of both.

At this point, workflow is working in your portlet. You should be able to activate workflow for slogans in the *workflow configuration* section of Liferay's Control Panel, as shown in figure 7.5. After it's activated, if a slogan is submitted, the slogan won't go right up on the web site; instead, it will show up in the My Workflow Tasks section of the Control Panel for anyone in the role who can approve this type of workflow (see figure 7.6).

Liferay's documentation

Using workflows, creating workflows, and defining the roles that go with them is covered in Liferay's *Portal Administrator's Guide* for Liferay 6.0, and *Using Liferay Portal* for Liferay 6.1. Definitely check out those books to see how to create workflows with any number of approvers. You'll also see how to use the workflow applications that appear in the Control Panel.

You can click any of the slogans to review it, or you can choose Actions > Assign to Me to take on the responsibility of approving or rejecting the slogan. If you click one of the slogans shown in figure 7.6, you'll get something that looks like figure 7.7.

When you click the Assign to Me action, you get the ability to add a comment. Then the available actions change to Approve, Reject, Assign To (which lets you assign it to someone else), and Update Due Date.

▾ Assigned to Me

There are no pending tasks assigned to you.

▾ Assigned to My Roles

Task	Asset Title	Asset Type	Last Activity Date	Due Date	
Review	Slogan Contest Entry	Slogan Contest Entry	12/13/10 10:31 PM	Never	Actions
Review	Slogan Contest Entry	Slogan Contest Entry	12/13/10 10:32 PM	Never	Actions
Review	Slogan Contest Entry	Slogan Contest Entry	12/13/10 10:32 PM	Never	Actions
Review	Slogan Contest Entry	Slogan Contest Entry	12/13/10 10:32 PM	Never	Actions
Review	Slogan Contest Entry	Slogan Contest Entry	12/13/10 10:33 PM	Never	Actions

Showing 5 results.

Figure 7.6 Slogans that have been submitted won't show up immediately in the Slogan Contest portlet after you enable workflow for it. Instead, they appear in My Workflow Tasks for anyone in the role who can approve slogans. The workflow definition defines these roles.

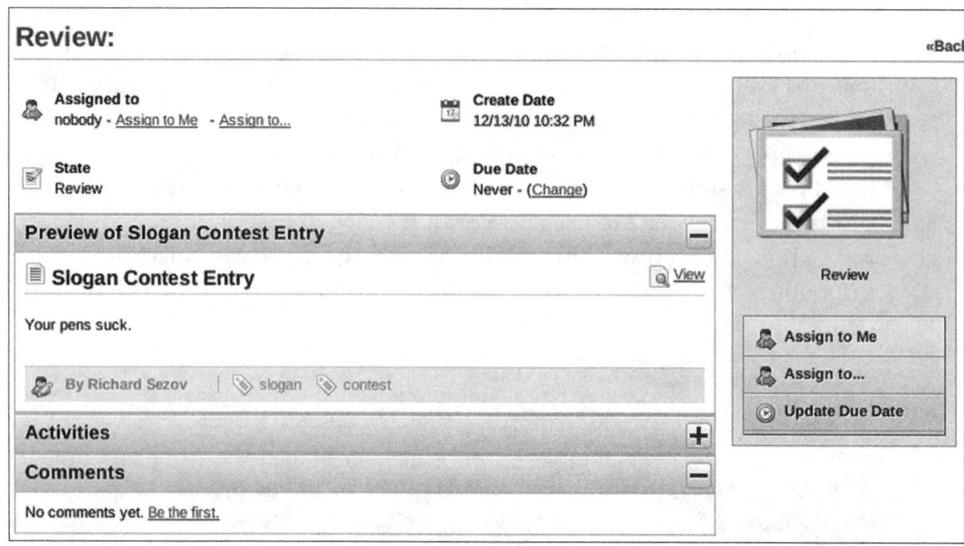

Figure 7.7 Clicking a slogan lets you look at the entry before you assign yourself the responsibility to approve or reject it. This one is probably a slogan you would want to reject, which is the purpose of workflow-enabling the slogan contest.

After slogans are approved, they appear in the Slogan Contest portlet. Next, we'll look at how you can enable interactivity for your slogans.

7.4 Tagging and categorizing content

Whenever you have content going into a portal, it helps people to find that content if you tag or categorize it. If you've played around with Liferay at all, you've probably noticed that many of its applications allow you to tag and/or categorize the content you're creating. If you write a blog entry, you can tag that entry based on the content of the entry or with meta information such as *rant, review,* or *recommendation.* You can do the same thing in message boards, wikis, Web Content Display, and more.

Notice that I said you can both *tag* and *categorize* content. Tagging generally happens inline, while you're creating the content. But when and how does categorizing happen? And what's the difference between the two?

7.4.1 Choosing between tags and categories

The difference makes a lot of sense when you think about it. Categories are predefined structures into which content can fit. Think of them like a table of contents or an outline: the categories are defined generally *before* the content is created. If you're building something like a catalog of different types of music, you might start with some high-level categories, like Classical, Jazz, and Rock. Then you'd define subcategories for each one, such as Baroque and Romantic for classical, and Metal and Progressive for rock (I don't know anything about jazz, so I won't venture to subcategorize it—I know, this is painful for some of you to hear, and I apologize; I will broaden my horizons some day). Then, as you're loading content, you can put your content in these previously structured categories. This is sometimes called a *taxonomy*. Categories are created in the Control Panel by those with administrative access, who are creating large amounts of content that needs to be organized.

Tags are similar, but they lack the structure of categories. Tags are generally created by users, although any users—including administrators—can tag content. Think of categories as being like a table of contents, and think of tags as being like an index: a flat list of topics that is applied to content either at its creation or after the fact. if you've browsed the categories of your content and have chosen Rock > Metal > Yngwie Malmsteen, you might find this particular artist tagged with adjectives like *guitarist*, *classical*, and *self-indulgence*. Although these descriptions don't rise to the rank of being browsable categories, they do further describe this particular artist, and who knows? Someone may be searching for music similar to that.

Tags are sometimes described as a *folksonomy*, because—well, they're created by the regular folks. Sometimes they can be humorous. Recently I was browsing a news site that had the headline, "Facebook is down"; somebody had given that story the tag *andnothingofvaluewaslost*.

Now that you know what tags and categories are, how do you enable them in your portlets? That's what's next.

7.4.2 A tag for tags and a tag for categories

There's a popular catchphrase in current usage in the smartphone world: "There's an app for that." With Liferay, you can modify this slightly and say that in many cases, when it comes to adding functionality that the platform gives you, there's a tag for that.

You've already done most of the work to make tags and categories work. Remember all that stuff at the beginning of the chapter about assets? That's all the back-end effort you need to make to get tags and categories working, because they operate off of Liferay's asset framework. All you need to worry about is the front end.

As with your Product Registration portlet, you have a JSP for editing slogans that was given the incredibly imaginative name edit_slogan.jsp. This JSP works on the same principles you learned in chapter 4, so I won't bore you with repetition. I do want to show you a section of it, though, which you'll find in the next listing.

Listing 7.8 Find the tags and categories

```
<aui:fieldset>

  <aui:model-context bean="<%= slogan %>" model="<%= Slogan.class %>" />

  <c:if test="<%= slogan != null %>">
    <aui:workflow-status id="<%= String.valueOf(resourcePrimKey) %>"
     status="<%= status %>" />
  </c:if>

  <aui:input name="sloganId" type="hidden" />
```

```
<h1>Slogan Contest Entry</h1>

<liferay-ui:error
    key="slogan-required"
    message="slogan-required" />

<aui:input name="sloganText" first="true" autoFocus="true" size="45" />

<aui:input name="categories" type="assetCategories" />      <-- Categories

<aui:input name="tags" type="assetTags" />      <-- Tags

<aui:button-row>

  <aui:button type="submit" />

  <aui:button
      type="cancel"
      value="Cancel"
      onClick="<%=cancelURL %>"
  />


</aui:button-row>

</aui:fieldset>
```

docroot/html/edit_slogan.jsp

Wow. Can it be that easy? Yes it can, my friend, yes it can. After you've implemented assets, you can place these two tags in your form, and you get the interface shown in figure 7.8.

Figure 7.8 Clicking Select under Categories gives you a view of your nicely categorized list, and you can mark off whatever categories are appropriate for this content. You can type tags into the field, add them from a pop-up, select existing tags, or ask Liferay to suggest some for you.

As you can see, Liferay's design includes an easy integration of its own tagging and categorizing engine with your applications. The only thing it requires is an implementation of assets with your entity, which *is* a best practice, so you should be doing it anyway. When you've got assets, tags, and categories going, you make it easier to get content to your users. One way of doing this is with Liferay's Asset Publisher. Liferay's documentation shows how you can use Asset Publisher to dynamically select content based on tags and categories and make it available to your users. For now, though, we'll move on to some other ways you can get users to interact with your content.

7.5 Adding discussions and ratings

Online interaction is what builds communities on the web. If your users can't interact with each other on your site, they probably won't find the site interesting after long. Liferay makes it easy to add discussions after you've implemented the asset framework for your entities. Liferay also makes it easy for users to *rate* your entities, either with a thumbs up / thumbs down, or by giving an entity from one to five stars. Ratings are pretty much as easy to implement as tags and categories: there's a tag for that.

You need to make a slight architectural change in your portlet in order to support this functionality. Users who are commenting on or rating entities shouldn't be *editing* those entities, should they? This means you can't use the same JSP for editing and viewing, as you did for the Product Registration portlet. You'll create a view_slogan.jsp that displays a slogan and also allows users to comment on and/or rate it. You can see this JSP in the following listing.

Listing 7.9 Discussions and ratings

```
<%@include file="/html/init.jsp"%>

<portlet:renderURL windowState="normal" var="backURL">
  <portlet:param name="jspPage" value="/html/view.jsp" />
</portlet:renderURL>

<liferay-ui:header backURL="<%= backURL %>" title="Slogan Contest Entry" />

<%
Slogan slogan = (Slogan) request.getAttribute(WebKeys.SLOGAN_ENTRY);

%>

<h1><%= slogan.getSloganText() %></h1>

<liferay-ui: ratings className="<%= Slogan.class.getName() %>"
    classPK="<%= slogan.getSloganId() %>" type="stars" />        ❶ Ratings

<liferay-ui:panel-container extended="<%= false %>"
    id="sloganCommentsPanelContainer" persistState="<%= true %>">

  <liferay-ui:panel collapsible="<%= true %>" extended="<%= true %>"
      id="sloganCommentsPanel" persistState="<%= true %>"
      title='<%= LanguageUtil.get(pageContext, "comments") %>'>

    <portlet:actionURL
        name="invokeTaglibDiscussion"
        var="discussionURL" />

    <liferay-ui:discussion className="<%= Slogan.class.getName() %>"
        classPK="<%= slogan.getSloganId() %>"
```

```
        formAction="<%= discussionURL %>" formName="fm2"
        ratingsEnabled="<%= true %>" redirect="<%= currentURL %>"
        subject="<%= slogan.getSloganText() %>"
        userId="<%= slogan.getUserId() %>" />                  <-- 2 Discussion

  </liferay-ui:panel>

</liferay-ui:panel-container>
```

docroot/html/view_slogan.jsp

Again, with two simple tags, you can create a powerful, dynamic experience for your users. The `ratings` tag needs the entity's primary key and its class name ❶. You can set the type to either `thumbs` or `stars`. Additionally, if you choose `stars`, you can set an attribute called `numberOfStars` in case you want to increase or reduce the granularity of your ratings system.

The `discussion` tag is similarly simple ❷. It needs much of the same data as the `ratings` tag, but also requires a few more pieces of information. It needs an `ActionURL` that points to an action that is built into `MVCPortlet`, called `invokeTaglibDiscussion`. This is what implements the discussion processing, and it's a feature you don't get for free if you're not using Liferay's `MVCPortlet`. You're also enabling ratings on the discussion, so users can meta-moderate the discussion. If somebody posts spam, users can vote it down. If somebody posts something useful, they can vote it up. You also set a redirect URL that points back to the page you're currently viewing. This way, users see their posts as soon as they create them.

Remember that full_content.jsp file you created in order to show slogans in Asset Publisher? There's nothing stopping you from adding these tags to that JSP; users can then rate and comment on slogans from inside Asset Publisher. This makes it possible for you to publish slogans on a page *and* let your users interact with them without even using the Slogan Contest portlet. And here's the kicker: the code for full_content.jsp is the same as the code for view_slogan.jsp. No further explanation about it is necessary—you already know everything about it that you need to know.

That's all there is to discussions and ratings. But cool as they are, as you can see, they're pretty much built in to Liferay. Because this is Liferay *in Action*, let's go a step further and use the ratings in a way that is *not* built in. Let's show users all the slogans in order by their rating, so the best slogans come to the top of the list. In order to do that, you'll have to add a custom query of your own, because this functionality isn't built in to Service Builder.

7.6 Creating custom queries using SQL

Way back in chapter 3, I made the somewhat incredible statement that Service Builder—a code generator, you remember—doesn't limit you if you want to do something specific (not generated), and I meant it. If you need to do some manual queries in your application, Service Builder will happily step out of the way and let you do your query. To show you how this is done, you'll do a join.

7.6.1 Crafting your query

This takes me back to the old days of doing development, before I used Liferay as a platform. When I used to do this, I'd fire up a client to the database, craft my query until I got it just right, and then parameterize it for the code. I did exactly this to come up with the query you'll use for your join. And because Service Builder is based on Hibernate, you can use the Liferay-wrapped versions of the Hibernate objects to send your custom query right into Hibernate, where it can get executed and returned.

In order to make your query readable by Service Builder, you have to wrap it in an XML file that identifies the query. This file serves as your master query file, and you can put as many custom queries in it as you want. This file, by convention, is called default.xml, and it resides in a folder called custom-sql in the same location as your source. Let's look at this file.

Listing 7.10 A query that does a join of slogans and ratings

```
<?xml version="1.0" encoding="UTF-8"?>

<custom-sql>

  <sql
     id="com.inkwell.internet.slogan.service.persistence.
     ➥ SloganFinder.findByRatingsStats">

    <![CDATA[
        SELECT
            RatingsStats.averageScore AS averageScore,
            Slogan_Slogan.sloganId AS sloganId,
            Slogan_Slogan.sloganText AS sloganText
        FROM
            RatingsStats, Slogan_Slogan
        WHERE
            (Slogan_Slogan.groupId = ?) AND
            (Slogan_Slogan.status = ?) AND
            (RatingsStats.classNameId = ?) AND
            (Slogan_Slogan.sloganId = RatingsStats.classPK)
        ORDER BY
            RatingsStats.averageScore
        DESC
    ]]>
  </sql>

</custom-sql>
```

docroot/WEB-INF/src/custom-sql/default.xml

This query searches against the cross-product of slogans and ratings, making sure you retrieve only the slogans and ratings that belong to the current community and that are approved in the workflow. You make sure you put the result in descending order by the average score, which Liferay conveniently calculates and stores in the database; this is why you're querying the RatingsStats table instead of the RatingsEntry table. If you've done this sort of thing before, you'll recognize that the question marks in the query denote parameters that are inserted at runtime.

Next, you need to hook up this query with your service so you can start using it.

7.6.2 Making your own finder

When you generated your service (see listing 7.1), you defined several finders that Service Builder conveniently created for you. Your custom query is a finder too; it's just that you have to implement it yourself, because you're doing something that Service Builder can't do by itself. I want to reiterate something about Service Builder that I mentioned in chapter 3: it works backward from what we've been taught about Java. Instead of creating an interface and then an implementation, you create the implementation, and then Service Builder *generates* the interface. This will be no different. As you create a finder, you have to assume you're implementing an interface that will be generated when you run Service Builder.

This tends to wreak havoc on IDEs, which complain endlessly that they can't find the interface you're implementing. That's okay. When you're working on these, create the method stubs you'll need and then run Service Builder. It'll generate an interface, and all those compilation errors will go away. Then you can go about adding implementation to the stubs.

The finder you want to create, minus the `import` statements, appears in the following listing.

Listing 7.11 A custom finder

```
public class SloganFinderImpl extends BasePersistenceImpl<Slogan>
    implements SloganFinder {

    public static String FIND_BY_RATINGSSTATS =
        SloganFinder.class.getName() + ".findByRatingsStats";    ❶ SQL identifier

    public List<Slogan> findByRatingsStats(
            long groupId,
int status, int start, int end)
throws SystemException {

        long classNameId =
 PortalUtil.getClassNameId(
            "com.inkwell.internet.slogan.model.Slogan");    ❷ From Liferay DB

        Session session = null;

        try {
            session = openSession();

            String sql = CustomSQLUtil.get(FIND_BY_RATINGSSTATS);    ❸ SQL lookup

            SQLQuery q = session.createSQLQuery(sql);

            q.addScalar("averageScore", Type.DOUBLE);
            q.addScalar("sloganId", Type.LONG);
            q.addScalar("sloganText", Type.STRING);
```

```
            QueryPos qPos = QueryPos.getInstance(q);

            qPos.add(groupId);
            qPos.add(status);
            qPos.add(classNameId);

            List<Object[]> ratedSlogans =
                (List<Object[]>) QueryUtil.list(
                    q, getDialect(), start, end);

            List<Slogan> slogans = assembleSlogans(ratedSlogans);

            return slogans;
        }
        catch (Exception e) {
            throw new SystemException(e);
        }
        finally {
            closeSession(session);
        }
    }

    private List<Slogan> assembleSlogans(List<Object[]> ratedSlogans) {

        List<Slogan> slogans = new ArrayList();

        for (Object[] ratedSlogan: ratedSlogans) {
            SloganImpl slogan = new SloganImpl();

            slogan.setAverageScore((Double) ratedSlogan[0]);
            slogan.setSloganId((Long) ratedSlogan[1]);
            slogan.setSloganText((String) ratedSlogan[2]);

            slogans.add(slogan);

        }

        return slogans;

    }

}
```

Create objects ❹

docroot/WEB-INF/src/com/inkwell/internet/slogan/service/persistence/SloganFinderImpl.java

The first thing you see in this code ❶ is that you create an instance variable that contains the identifier of the piece of SQL you want to use from your default.xml file. Because this file (and this finder) can contain any number of queries, you have to determine which one you want, even though in this case you have only one. I used `PortalUtil`, which is a cornucopia of convenience methods, in ❷ to get the `classNameId` of your entity. Every Service Builder-generated entity registered with Liferay gets an ID for use with shared services. Ratings are one of those shared services. Because ratings can be attached to anything, they need a way of identifying what they're attached to, so that the proper rating appears next to the proper entity. Because you're querying just for ratings that are attached to slogans, you need to pass the `classNameId` of the `Slogan` class to your query.

`CustomSQLUtil` looks up the proper query from your default.xml file ❸, using the identifier defined in ❶. Everything else that happens in this method is standard Hibernate: adding scalars, sticking variables into the proper SQL parameters, and finally doing the query. It's beyond the scope of this book to go too deeply into this process; for further information, please see *Java Persistence with Hibernate* by Christian Bauer and Gavin King, also from Manning Publications (2006). A convenience method appears in ❹. It takes the results of your query and assembles a list of `Slogan` objects containing those results, so the search container can display them. You'd think this might be a performance hit, but because you're grabbing only 20 records at a time (due to the `start` and `end` variables), it's not.

There's one thing in this method that you might be wondering about:

```
slogan.setAverageScore((Double) rated Slogan[0]);
```

Where did that field come from? It's not declared in service.xml, so Service Builder couldn't have generated it, right? Yes, you're right. Remember: any `-Impl` class generated by Service Builder is free for you to customize. You've already added methods to the implementation classes in the service layer to expose functionality to your portlet layer; you can do the same thing with the implementation classes in the model layer too.

You have a situation here where you have a value which is actually stored in another table, and was retrieved as the result of a JOIN. Since you need a way of displaying that value (in the form of a rating) to the user, you need to get it into your model. The way you do that is to customize `SloganImpl` and add an `averageScore` field to it, complete with a `getter` and a `setter`. Then you can store any values not normally associated with that entity in the entity itself.

You have one more piece of the puzzle to put in place: now that you've got this great class that can query your database, how do you call it? Simple: from the existing service. All you need to do is add the following tiny method to `SloganLocalServiceImpl`:

```
public List<Slogan> getSlogans(
   long groupId, int status,
   int start, int end)
 throws SystemException {

    List<Slogan> slogans =
        sloganFinder.findByRatingsStats(groupId, status, start, end);

    return slogans;
}
```

After implementing this, run Service Builder again. It will pick up the change to the `-Impl` class and generate all the interfaces for your services. You can now call your custom query in the exact same manner you'd call one that was generated by Service Builder. Next, you'll do just that.

7.6.3 Displaying custom columns in a search container

You're almost finished: your entities go through workflow and can be categorized and tagged, commented on, and rated. Next you need to make it so they can be displayed according to their ratings, so that those in charge of running the contest can see which slogans are the most popular. You already have a query that returns the slogans in the proper order; all you need to do now is display them properly, according to the number of stars. As before, you'll use a search container; but this time, you'll display the rating in the form of stars so it's easy to see at a glance the most popular slogans.

You set up the search container in listing 7.12 exactly the way you did before but add some logic of your own to the first column.

Listing 7.12 Search container with a custom column

```
<liferay-ui:search-container
➥ emptyResultsMessage="there-are-no-slogans"
➥ delta="20" iteratorURL="<%=iteratorURL %>">
  <liferay-ui:search-container-results>

  <%

  results = ActionUtil.getSlogans(
      renderRequest,
 searchContainer.getStart(), searchContainer.getEnd());
  total = ActionUtil.getSlogansCount(renderRequest);

  pageContext.setAttribute("results", results);
  pageContext.setAttribute("total", total);
  %>
  </liferay-ui:search-container-results>

  <liferay-ui:search-container-row
      className="com.inkwell.internet.slogan.model.Slogan"
      keyProperty="sloganId"
      modelVar="slogan">

    <portlet:renderURL windowState="maximized" var="rowURL">          ❶
      <portlet:param name="jspPage" value="/html/view_slogan.jsp" />
      <portlet:param                                               URL for
          name="resourcePrimKey"                         view_slogans.jsp
          value="<%= String.valueOf(slogan.getSloganId()) %>" />
      <portlet:param name="redirect" value="<%= currentURL %>" />
    </portlet:renderURL>

    <liferay-ui:search-container-column-text name="rating">  ❷ Custom column
      <liferay-ui:ratings-score
          score="<%= slogan.getAverageScore() %>" />
    </liferay-ui:search-container-column-text>
    <liferay-ui:search-container-column-text
        href="<%= rowURL %>"
        name="slogan-text"                           ❸ Clickable column
        property="sloganText"
    />
    <liferay-ui:search-container-column-jsp
        path="/html/slogan_actions.jsp"
        align="right"
    />
```

```
    </liferay-ui:search-container-row>

    <liferay-ui:search-iterator />

</liferay-ui:search-container>
```

docroot/html/view.jsp

As you can see, it's pretty easy to customize a search container to have columns with any information or layout you want. First you need a render URL that maximizes the page and passes in the primary key of the slogan for that row ❶. This allows the target JSP (view_slogan.jsp) to display that slogan, along with the comments and ratings you've already seen. The custom column that displays the ratings is ❷. You declare the column and then implement the display logic as code directly in the column. Then you use another Liferay tag to display the slogan's rating as a rate of from one to five stars. Finally, you use the URL you created earlier in ❸ in the only column in which you have text: the slogan itself. This gives users a link to click that brings them to the page where they can rate slogans and/or discuss them.

This code gives you the user interface shown in figure 7.9.

Notice that figure 7.9 has two tabs: By Rating and By Date. That's another technique used in Liferay portlets to make it easy to switch functions inside an application. You can see how that works by looking at the code, because it's fairly straightforward. You've accomplished a lot already!

7.7 Summary

We've covered a lot of ground in this chapter. We started with the prerequisite: assets. If you want to use any of the collaborative features of Liferay, you need to asset-enable your entities, because it's a framework that powers a whole host of things. The first of these is workflow, and you saw that Liferay has an API that allows you to support workflow regardless of which particular workflow engine is installed. You used workflow to implement a simple approval system that allows Inkwell administrators to prescreen slogans before they wind up on the web site.

After this, you saw how you can enable tags and categories for your own entities, so that your content can be queried for by other portlets such as Asset Publisher. This

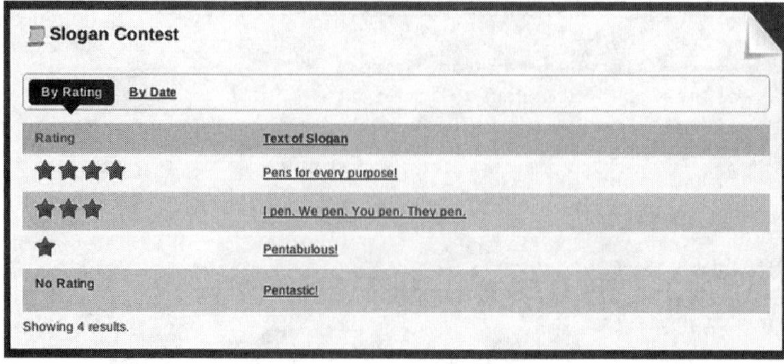

Figure 7.9 Your custom query and custom search container column let you display slogans according to how users are rating them, in real time.

gives you the power to publish content that is the most relevant to your users. When we finished with that, we looked at comments and ratings. These are incredibly easy to implement once your entities are asset-enabled, because all you have to add is the proper tag to your JSPs, and Liferay does the rest.

Finally, you created a custom SQL query that enabled you to show users slogans according to how users were ranking them. Service Builder didn't get in the way of doing this; rather, it provided consistency by allowing you to call your custom query in exactly the same way you've been calling generated queries. And the search container was easily able to accommodate a custom column to display ratings by the number of stars they scored.

Each of these things by itself is powerful, and together they showcase the ease with which you can implement great things on Liferay's platform.

With this, we've come to the end of part 2. You should be well equipped to create great applications on Liferay's platform. From here, we move on to customizing Liferay, starting with hooks. We touched on hooks a little in this chapter; next, we'll look at them in depth, and you'll see how you can customize even Liferay's core functionality.

Part 3

Customizing Liferay

The final part of this book shows you how to take Liferay's existing, built-in functionality and customize it to do whatever you want. Liferay is built for customization, and you'll see how easy and extensible it is as you go through these chapters.

Chapter 8 covers hooks, which are Liferay plugins that give you access to existing Liferay extension points. By the end of the chapter, you'll have modified Liferay's Shopping portlet and given it a completely new user interface.

Liferay extension doesn't stop there. Chapter 9 shows you how to extend Liferay not from existing extension points, but *anywhere*, using Ext plugins. We'll also go over some best practices showing you how to approach a Liferay development project.

Finally, chapter 10 goes through a plethora of Liferay APIs. You'll learn how to use friendly URLs, how to organize larger applications, and how to access other databases. You'll find out what Liferay's message bus can be used for and how to schedule jobs, as well as how to use indexing and search in Liferay.

By the time you've finished with the book, you'll be well equipped to use the Liferay platform to build your site.

8 Hooks

This chapter covers

- Hooks, and why they're necessary
- Hooking into Liferay properties
- Hooking into Liferay JSPs
- Hooking into services
- Customizing a Liferay portlet with a hook

Open source is making great headway in the business world today, but some organizations are still wary of it, and they have their reasons. One of the reasons is the maintenance problems you run into if you customize open source software with stuff that's meant for your own organization but isn't applicable to the project as a whole. Now you've got an issue: you have to maintain this customization through every new release of the open source software yourself. This means you probably have to understand the open source project at a much deeper level than you've been prepared for, and you need to be ready at each release to keep track of where your customizations go in order to reintroduce them into the base project.

Let's take a concrete example, and we'll keep it simple. Say there's an open source image gallery application that you like and want to use, but you have to integrate it with some custom software written by your development team. The custom software is responsible for keeping track of employee ID cards and is the gatekeeper for other systems. When a user is created in the custom system, it gets propagated out to other systems—including the image gallery—and the image gallery can be used to browse not only employee mug shots for the ID cards, but also galleries that employees create. To integrate the image gallery with this system, you customized the code in the image gallery's security module so it will create a user ID in the image gallery for every user who gets an ID card in the other system.

Now say that some security problem is found with the image gallery, and the developers of the open source project produce another release to fix the issue. Of course, because the problem is with the security module, you now have to figure out how to integrate your custom code with the new code—and it may not be easy. It's possible that the fix for the security flaw impacts the customization you made. Now you have to find a way to code around the new security implementation or continue using software that has a security flaw.

Liferay hooks are designed to solve exactly this problem. With a hook, you can deploy your customization without touching Liferay's source code. This provides a level of separation between your customizations and the Liferay core, giving you freedom to upgrade whenever you want. You won't have to worry about trying to maintain customized versions of any of Liferay's source files and then trying to integrate those customizations back into an upgraded version of Liferay. Instead, you can take advantage of the fact that Liferay is built to be easily customized.

Did you know...

Liferay hooks are the newest type of plugin that Liferay Portal supports. They were introduced late in the development cycle for Liferay Portal 5.1.x, and are now the preferred way to customize Liferay.

As with portlets, layout templates, and themes, hooks are created using the Plugins SDK and are used for multiple scenarios. Let's take a closer look at hooks so you can see what they're useful for, and then we'll jump in and start customizing Liferay.

8.1 What is a hook?

What are hooks? Aptly named, they're pieces of code that are designed to hook into Liferay and take over certain pieces of functionality. They allow you as a developer to override parts of core Liferay with your own implementation.

Liferay Portal has had functionality like this for a long time. The Ext plugin (formerly the Ext environment) was designed for exactly the same use case: overriding and customizing Liferay itself. The first question usually asked when experienced Liferay developers are presented with hooks is, why? Why did we need another way to customize Liferay? Isn't the Ext plugin enough? Are you purposefully trying to confuse me?!?

8.1.1 An easier customization paradigm

The Ext plugin was always positioned as an easier way to customize Liferay than modifying the Liferay source code, and it is. It keeps your custom code separate from the portal, so there is a clear delineation as to where Liferay's code leaves off and your code picks up. Customers have used the Ext environment to do many amazing (and unexpected) things with Liferay. But this doesn't come without a cost in complexity.

Because the Ext plugin gives the developer complete access to the internals of Liferay Portal, custom code becomes tightly coupled to particular implementations of functionality within Liferay, and these implementations often change from version to version—or even point release to point release. This has caused developers unnecessary headaches, as whenever upgrade time came around, very often they would encounter a lot of changes within the Liferay code base: method signature changes, package refactoring, class renaming, and so on.

Additionally, Ext can be hard to work with, particularly for a team of developers. It's a large, monolithic environment that can't be deployed piecemeal and isn't easily divided into subprojects. If multiple developers are working on different pieces of functionality, everybody has to wait until all pieces are relatively stable before doing a deploy to test.

To relieve the pressure on developers, a different paradigm was needed, a paradigm which allowed for customization against a stable API that was guaranteed not to change between versions—and if it needed to change, functionality would be deprecated appropriately so that developers would have a chance to update their code on a schedule that was more conducive to their projects. The new paradigm needed to be smaller and more nimble, with the ability to cobble together multiple deployable assets to build out the whole feature set. Hence, hook plugins were born.

8.1.2 Hook basics

Hook plugins are hot-deployable, just like portlets, layout templates, and themes, so you can add them to and remove them from your portal at will. You can divide functionality into multiple hooks written by multiple developers, allowing for a more dynamic development environment. And hooks are written to Liferay's public API, which is properly deprecated when it changes. As you can see, hooks were designed to overcome many of the limitations of using Ext.

Even though hook plugins have advantages over Ext, the Ext plugin also has some advantages over hooks. Using Ext, you can customize anything in Liferay, because you're working in the same class loader as the portal. Hooks are in the plugin class loader, so it doesn't have access to all those core classes; thus the Liferay engineering team has had to choose the extension points that are available. In other words, you can't customize as much with hook plugins as you can with the Ext plugin; but the list of what you *can* customize grows with each release of the portal as Liferay receives feedback from users.

> **Favor hooks over EXT plugins**
>
> How do you go about choosing which to use? Simple: use hooks wherever you can. They're much easier to write, to deploy and undeploy, and to maintain. If you run into something that can't be customized with a hook, then use the Ext plugin. See chapter 9 for further information about Ext plugins.

Let's get started with hooks by creating one.

8.1.3 Creating a hook

You can create a hook in exactly the same manner in which you create portlets or themes. Go to the hooks folder in your Plugins SDK, and in LUM, type

```
./create.sh my-hook "My Hook"
```

In Windows, it would be

```
create.bat my-hook "My Hook"
```

Easy, right? And wonderfully consistent.

I must mention one caveat now. Usually, the next step for a developer is to import the project into an IDE, and I don't want to discourage you from doing this. But I've never met an IDE that likes customizing Liferay's JSPs in a hook. Why? Well, because a hook is one project, and the portal (if you have the source) is another project. If you have a JSP with dependencies from an included JSP in another project (as Liferay does often with its pattern of using init.jsp for imports), the IDE doesn't know where to find the included file. Because of this, it can't compile or validate the file. What you wind up with is a file full of red Xs and little squigglies underneath all the objects that the IDE doesn't understand.

For that reason, when writing hooks, I use a text editor (jEdit is my current favorite all-purpose text editor). It's much simpler that way. Of course, you should use whatever tools you're most comfortable using.

Now that you have a hook project, let's look at what hooks can do.

8.2 What hooks can customize

Hooks are designed to customize four main features within the portal:

- Portal properties
- Language properties
- JSP files
- Services

In this section, we'll take each feature one by one. In order to create any customization, you first have to create a configuration file called liferay-hook.xml and place this file in the WEB-INF folder of your hook project in your Plugins SDK. The following code creates a skeleton of liferay-hook.xml:

```
<?xml version="1.0" encoding="UTF-8"?>
<!DOCTYPE hook PUBLIC "-//Liferay//DTD Hook 6.0.0//EN"
➥ "http://www.liferay.com/dtd/liferay-hook_6_0_0.dtd">

<hook>
</hook>
```

Once you've got this file skeleton set up, you're ready to tell Liferay what it is that you want to customize. We'll start with the simplest customization.

8.2.1 *Customizing portal properties*

Hooks can override portal properties in the same way in which you override them via the portal-ext.properties file. Not all properties can be overridden, but the properties that can are listed in the DTD for the liferay-hook.xml file for the version of Liferay you're running. You'll find this DTD in the definitions folder of the portal source for your version of Liferay.

Let's take a simple property and customize it. As you probably know, the first time users log into Liferay Portal, they're presented with a "terms of use" page. Users must agree to the terms of use in order to continue. This feature is controlled by a property in Liferay's default portal.properties file that looks like this:

```
terms.of.use.required=true
```

You can configure a hook to turn off this feature by changing the property from true to false. This is extremely easy to do and requires no code. First, you configure your hook to override properties by editing liferay-hook.xml to look like this:

```
<?xml version="1.0" encoding="UTF-8"?>
<!DOCTYPE hook PUBLIC "-//Liferay//DTD Hook 6.0.0//EN"
➥ "http://www.liferay.com/dtd/liferay-hook_6_0_0.dtd">

<hook>
  <portal-properties>portal.properties</portal-properties>
</hook>
```

As you can see, you have defined a file called portal.properties in the hook where your overridden properties will be placed. This file must be on the classpath of the project, so the best place to put it is in the src folder. All you need to do to override the property is put in the file the key/value pair you want to override:

```
terms.of.use.required=false
```

Save and close the file, and deploy your hook in the same manner in which you deploy other plugins:

```
ant deploy
```

Your hook will be deployed, and this property will now be overridden—dynamically. New users won't need to accept the terms of service, and you won't need to restart your portal for this to take effect. By the same token, if you wanted to revert this property back to the default behavior, all you would need to do is undeploy the hook, and the portal would immediately revert without the need for a restart.

See? Hooks are easy. Let's now try something a little more complex.

8.2.2 Customizing portal event properties

Some properties in Liferay aren't meant to have a single value. Instead, they're a list of multiple values. In this case, any values you specify in a hook don't override the list defined in the portal, but rather are appended to that list.

For example, you can append a value to the `application.startup.events` property in your hook. That property defines a list of classes that will run when the portal starts. You can implement the classes in the src folder of your hook project and then deploy the hook to Liferay. Your actions will then fire when Liferay Portal starts in addition to the list of actions that are specified in the default Liferay installation.

Events fire *actions*, which is where you place your code. There are as of this writing three different kinds of actions you can implement:

- `SimpleAction`—This kind of action is simple because it doesn't rely on any prior communication between Liferay and a user. Because you're adding an event that fires on Liferay's startup, this is the kind of action you'll use in this example.
- `Action`—This kind of action relies on the `HttpServletRequest` and `HttpServletResponse` objects. For this reason, it's not appropriate for a startup event, but you might want to use it for a user event, such as `login.events.pre` or `login.events.post`.
- `SessionAction`—This kind of action relies on the `HttpSession` object. It's not used in Liferay but is available for you to use.

As I said, events fire actions. When you extend an action class, you put the functionality in a `run()` method that you must override. Here's a simple example of how to define the class:

```
package com.liferay.test.hook.events;

import com.liferay.portal.kernel.events.ActionException;
import com.liferay.portal.kernel.events.SimpleAction;

public class StartupAction extends SimpleAction {

    public void run(String[] ids) throws ActionException {    <-- (1) companyId array
        System.out.println("### StartupAction");
    }

}
```

The `String` array of IDs (1) are company IDs. This value is populated when the event is fired by the portal, and it isn't something you'll need to populate yourself. Events are fired once for each portal instance that's been defined, which is tracked by company ID.

Beyond event properties, there are other kinds of properties that you can customize.

8.2.3 Customizing listener properties

Hooks also support overriding the `value.object.listener.*` properties. This is a powerful feature of hooks, allowing you to add your own custom listeners for any model class in Liferay.

For example, say you want to trigger the sending of an email whenever a new blog entry is created. You first, as you've already done, define the portal.properties file in liferay-hook.xml so that you can override the appropriate value object listener property for the class to which you want to attach a listener. Then you define your listener on the property in the portal.properties file:

```
value.object. listener.com.liferay.portlet.blogs.model.BlogsEntry=
➥ com.inkwell.liferay.portlet.blogs.NewBlogEntryListener
```

When you've defined the listener, all you need to do is implement it. All model listeners must implement the `com.liferay.portal.model.ModelListener` interface, and a base implementation is provided in the `com.liferay.portal.model.BaseModelListener` class. You'll find that you have a class that contains the following:

```
public void onAfterCreate(BaseModel arg0) throws ModelListenerException {
    BlogsEntry entry = (BlogsEntry)arg0;

    /* Code for sending an email goes here */

}
```

There are a lot of events in the listener where you can add custom code. The previous example listens to the `onAfterCreate` event, but you can also listen for these events:

- `onBeforeCreate`
- `onAfterRemove`
- `onBeforeRemove`
- `onBeforeUpdate`
- `onAfterUpdate`

This allows you to do pretty much whatever you want in response to any event in the lifecycle of an entity—including, of course, your own Service Builder–generated entities.

There's one other type of property that I want to make sure you know is available.

8.2.4 Customizing language properties

In a similar fashion to portal properties, you can override Liferay's language resource bundles by using a hook. The syntax in liferay-hook.xml is as simple as the previous examples:

```
<?xml version="1.0" encoding="UTF-8"?>
<!DOCTYPE hook PUBLIC "-//Liferay//DTD Hook 6.0.0//EN" "http://
     www.liferay.com/dtd/liferay-hook_6_0_0.dtd">

<hook>
  <language-properties>
      content/Language_en.properties
```

```
  </language-properties>
</hook>
```

Note that you can add as many language bundles as you like in order to override as many different languages as you wish. Your changes will overlay the values from the portal, meaning that anything you override gets overridden, but you don't have to override everything. For example, say for whatever reason you don't like the word *Save.* This word is used in the language bundles throughout Liferay for saving message board posts, blog posts, documents, and pretty much everything else. If you wanted to change this word to *Store,* all you have to do is define a language properties file and then change the value for that key. The language file would have this in it:

```
save=Store
```

Deploy your hook, and everywhere Liferay uses the value of the `save` key, it will display the word *Store* instead of *Save.*

Let's go beyond properties and look at some more interesting things we can customize.

8.2.5 Customizing JSP files

Hooks allow you to replace any of Liferay's JSP files with your own implementation. Again, this was once only possible to do with Ext. This enables you to modify what is rendered by the JSP files of Liferay's core portlets. If, for example, you don't like the way Liferay's Document Library presents itself, you can modify its JSPs with a hook and include styling in your theme to go along with the modifications. And again, if you undeploy your hook, Liferay will revert back to its default behavior without the need to restart.

Let's look at how to configure a hook for custom JSPs. All you need to do is tell Liferay in the liferay-hook.xml file where the custom JSPs are:

```
<?xml version="1.0" encoding="UTF-8"?>
<!DOCTYPE hook PUBLIC "-//Liferay//DTD Hook 6.0.0//EN"
➥ "http://www.liferay.com/dtd/liferay-hook_6_0_0.dtd">

<hook>

  <custom-jsp-dir>/META-INF/custom_jsps</custom-jsp-dir>

</hook>
```

Under the META-INF/custom_jsps folder, you create the same folder structure Liferay Portal uses to store its JSP files. For example, if you want to customize the view.jsp file for the Blogs portlet, you create it here:

```
META-INF/custom_jsps/html/portlet/blogs/view.jsp
```

When you deploy a hook that modifies JSPs, behind the scenes Liferay renames the original JSP file from [*filename*].jsp to [*filename.portal*].jsp. The original file is always still there and still accessible. If you're good at string manipulation, this allows you to make modifications to the page in a way that is easier to maintain than by providing a new implementation. Why is it potentially easier to maintain this way? Well, it depends on what you need to change.

If you need to make a major change to the markup or logic of the JSP, you'll probably want to go ahead and reimplement the JSP. But if you only need to change a header, a field title, or something minor like that (perhaps in conjunction with a change to the language properties), you can do string manipulation on the original JSP and replace the Liferay label with yours. This protects you from Liferay's upstream changes to the JSP. It's not likely that headers and labels will change much; it's much more likely that logic in the JSP will be modified in order to take into account additional bean fields or other business logic. If you've done string manipulation to replace a default label with yours, you can preserve Liferay's logic—however it's implemented—and only update the label. Here is a simple example of how you can do that with the Blogs portlet:

```
<%@ include file="/html/portlet/blogs/init.jsp" %>

<h6>Some Special Header</h6>

<liferay-util:buffer var="html">
  <liferay-util:include page="/html/portlet/blogs/view.portal.jsp" />
</liferay-util:buffer>

<%
html = StringUtil.replace(html, "hello", "hola");
%>

<%= html %>
```

Using the `<liferay-util:buffer />` tag, the entire contents of the original Liferay JSP are placed in a string called `html`. Then there is logic that replaces any instance of the character string "hello" with another value. The result is then written out to the page. Obviously, this can get unwieldy if you need to make a lot of changes, but it's a strategy that has been used successfully.

Now let's look at customizing some interesting stuff: Liferay services.

8.2.6 Customizing services

Remember how you generated your own services for the Product Registration portlet in chapter 3? All of Liferay's services are generated exactly the same way, and you can override them using hooks. You won't do that in a hook by using Service Builder itself; instead, you'll use the decorator pattern to add the functionality you need to the service, while leaving the rest of the functionality alone. This is best done for read-only attributes or attributes that are stored in a separate system, such as LDAP.

Liferay provides a wrapper class for all generated services. This class is aptly named `[Model]LocalServiceWrapper.java`. Because Service Builder uses Spring's dependency injection for much of its functionality, the wrapper class is a convenient place in which to inject an actual implementation of the interface. Liferay uses `[Model]LocalServiceImpl` as this implementation: you created these in chapter 3 when you implemented the service layer of your portlet.

A chain of injections allows you to customize things via the wrapper class: the `-Impl` class is injected into the wrapper defined by your hook, and the -Wrapper class is injected into a Spring AOP Proxy class (replacing the `-Impl` class that was originally injected there), and the Spring AOP Proxy class is injected into the `-Util` class. Figure 8.1 shows this more clearly than describing it does (a picture is worth a thousand words, after all). Of course, the `-Util` class is the one that end users call when they want to access the service. This means you have an opportunity to *decorate* the original implementation with your changes by implementing a wrapper class. When the `-Util` class is called, your wrapper decoration becomes the implementation that is invoked.

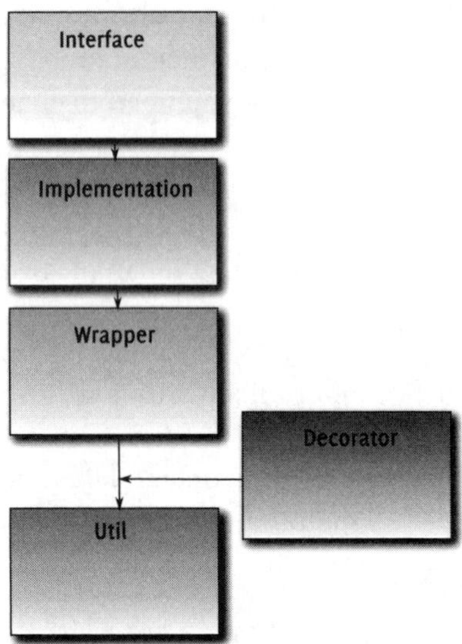

Figure 8.1 This shows how the class inheritance works in Service Builder and how the decorator pattern is used to enable you to customize Liferay's services.

Keeping all this in mind, you now have the tools to implement an override of certain functionality in a service. As with the other features of hooks, the first thing you need to do is define it in your liferay-hooks.xml file:

```
<?xml version="1.0" encoding="UTF-8"?>
<!DOCTYPE hook PUBLIC "-//Liferay//DTD Hook 6.0.0//EN"
➥ "http://www.liferay.com/dtd/liferay-hook_6_0_0.dtd">

<hook>
  <service>
    <service-type>
        com.liferay.portal.service.UserLocalService
    </service-type>

    <service-impl>
        com.liferay.test.hook.service.impl.MyUserLocalServiceImpl
    </service-impl>
  </service>
</hook>
```

You first define the service you want to override and then the implementation class that will contain the new logic you're providing. All that is left, then, is to write the class.

Let's show a simple example. Say you want to add an attribute to the `User` class called `FavoriteColor`. First you create that class:

```
public class MyUserImpl extends UserWrapper {

    public MyUserImpl(User user) {
```

```
        super(user);
    }

       public String getFavoriteColor() {
        return "My favorite color is green.";
    }

}
```

Now you decorate the wrapper class for the service and make sure it returns the new implementation of `User` instead of the default one:

```
public class MyUserLocalServiceImpl extends UserLocalServiceWrapper {

    public MyUserLocalServiceImpl(UserLocalService userLocalService) {
        super(userLocalService);
    }

    public User getUserById(long userId)
        throws PortalException, SystemException {

        System.out.println("## getUserById " + userId);

        User user = super.getUserById(userId);

        return new MyUserImpl(user);
    }

}
```

Because the `MyUserImpl` class is the one being returned instead of the User class, it includes the extra attribute. Of course, this is a simple example that returns a static value. The `getUserById()` method could have created a new `MyUserImpl` object and then queried LDAP, a custom service, or some other system to populate the custom attribute before returning the object.

Speaking of a custom service, you can create services in hooks using Service Builder. This is done in the same exact manner as you would do it in a portlet. But if you want to use the service you create in a hook in a separate plugin, you have to copy the .jar that is generated in the hook's WEB-INF/lib folder to the same folder in the plugin in order to make the classes available to it. This is the same procedure you would use if you had generated the service in your portlet. Alternatively, the .jar files for shared services can be copied to your application server's global classpath, and then the services will be available to all plugins. We'll look at this in further detail in Inkwell's hook, which is the subject of the rest of this chapter.

Now that you have the necessary background on what is possible with hooks, let's take a concrete example and see what the Inkwell development team did with a hook.

8.3 Hooks in action: customizing Inkwell's shopping cart

Inkwell, like other manufacturers of electronic equipment, sells its products through brick-and-mortar retailers, online retailers, and its own web site. One of the reasons

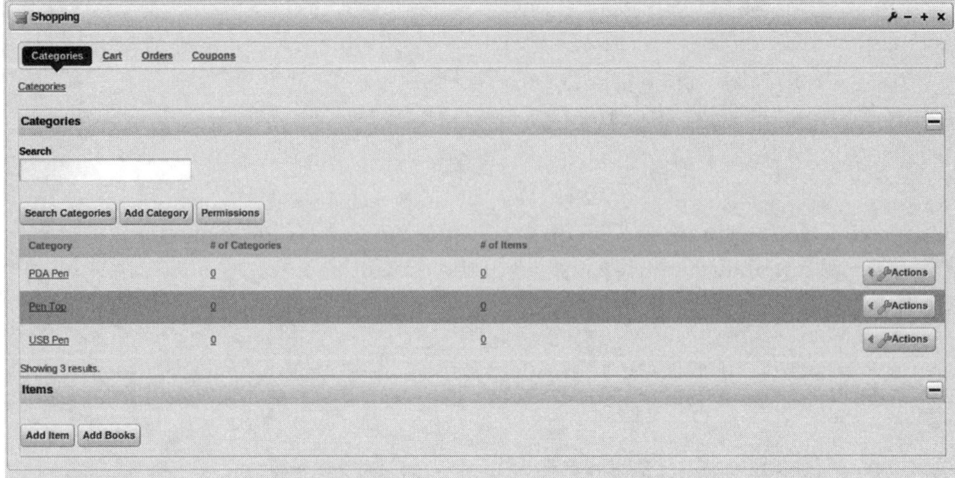

Figure 8.2 This is what Inkwell's shopping cart looks like with the default look and feel. "Flashy" isn't a word I'd use for it, but it's certainly functional.

Inkwell chose Liferay was for its built-in functionality, and this will enable the company to replace its aging PHP-based shopping cart with Liferay's.

The only problem is that Liferay's shopping cart (see figure 8.2) looks like the rest of Liferay's portlets: it uses the search container to display categories of products in a table. The Inkwell design team thinks that this is a little, um, boring. Although the default shopping cart is a good, generic implementation, it isn't the way Inkwell wants to display its product categories. Because Inkwell doesn't have a lot of categories of products, the company wants to display the categories graphically. It's hoped that presenting them this way will make it easier for users to find what they're looking for and will ultimately lead to more orders from the web site.

The design team came up with a mockup for what they'd like the shopping cart to look like, which you can see in figure 8.3.

A hook is a good way to implement this functionality. It allows the development team to package the shopping-cart customization in a single project, it supports every feature the Inkwell team would like to customize, and it's hot-deployable. By using a

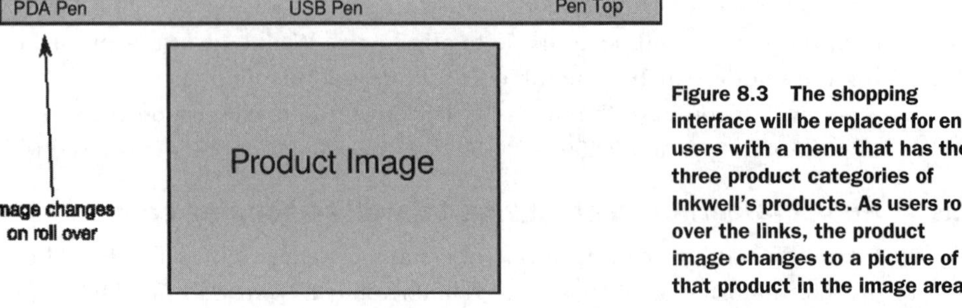

Figure 8.3 The shopping interface will be replaced for end users with a menu that has the three product categories of Inkwell's products. As users roll over the links, the product image changes to a picture of that product in the image area.

hook, all customizations have the benefit of using well-documented Liferay APIs, so the design will be able to be more easily upgraded to future releases of Liferay.

The development team has identified three areas to hook into Liferay's functionality and provide their own customization:

- Create their own version of categories.jspf. This is the file that shows the shopping categories in a search container (shown in figure 8.2). The team will provide new markup to create the more dynamic presentation that they want.
- Add a field to the edit_category.jsp file. This field contains a URL to the category image that will exist in the Image Gallery portlet. To add images that appear in the center area of figure 8.3, users will upload them to the Image Gallery and then paste the URLs to those images into this field.
- Add a small entity called `ShoppingCategoryImage`. This entity will have three fields: a primary key, a foreign-key relationship to the shopping category key, and a field to hold the Image Gallery URL. To make calls to read and store this entity, you'll customize the Shopping portlet's service layer.

You'll do these in the same order in which you built the Product Registration (chapters 3 and 4) and Slogan Contest (chapter 7) portlets: you'll start with the service layer and then move on to the front end.

8.3.1 Generating a service layer in a hook

Let's look at the back-end code first, because the front-end changes depend on the back-end service. You define the `ShoppingCategoryImage` entity using Service Builder. The service.xml file looks like this.

Listing 8.1 Custom shopping service.xml

```
<?xml version="1.0" encoding="UTF-8"?>

<!DOCTYPE service-builder PUBLIC "-//Liferay//DTD Service Builder
➥ 6.0.0//EN" "http://www.liferay.com/dtd/
➥ liferay-service-builder_6_0_0.dtd">

<service-builder package-path="com.inkwell.internet.shopping.sb">

  <author>Rich Sezov</author>

  <namespace>Inkwell</namespace>

  <entity name="ShoppingCategoryImage" local-service="true"
  ➥ remote-service="false">

    <column name="imageId" type="long" primary="true" />

    <column name="categoryId" type="long" />                 ❶ Image fields

    <column name="imageUrl" type="String" />

    <order by="asc">
      <order-column name="imageUrl" />
    </order>
```

```
    <finder name="CategoryId" return-type="Collection">
      <finder-column name="categoryId" />
    </finder>

    <reference package-path="com.liferay.portlet.expando"
    ➥ entity="ExpandoValue" />
    <reference package-path="com.liferay.portlet.expando"
    ➥ entity="ExpandoRow" />

  </entity>

</service-builder>
```

❷ Expando reference

docroot/WEB-INF/service.xml

You've configured a small table with three columns, two of which are keys. You store the category ID from Liferay's shopping cart as a foreign key, and you store the URL to the image in your own field ❶. This requires end users to upload their images to Liferay's Image Gallery first and then copy/paste the URL to the image into the field. Because there are only three categories, this can be done once without much difficulty.

You're using references as you did in chapter 6 to pull in Liferay's Expando services so you can use them in transactions ❷. You're probably wondering what the Expando service is. For now, just know that you need to use the service, and when you get to using Expandos, I'll explain what they can be used for.

As before, when you generate the service, you're given a DTO layer with which to work, and you can add the methods you need to the layer. These methods are shown in the following listing.

Listing 8.2 Shopping image service layer methods

```
public ShoppingCategoryImage addShoppingCategoryImage(
        long categoryId, String url)
    throws SystemException {

    ShoppingCategoryImage image =                          <-- Adds image
        shoppingCategoryImagePersistence.create(
            counterLocalService.increment(
                ShoppingCategoryImage.class.getName()));

    image.setCategoryId(categoryId);
    image.setImageUrl(url);

    return shoppingCategoryImagePersistence.update(image, false);
}

public ShoppingCategoryImage getShoppingCategoryImageByCategory(
        long categoryId)
    throws SystemException {                          <-- Gets image by Shopping Category

    List<ShoppingCategoryImage> images =
        getShoppingCategoryImagesByCategory(categoryId);

    if (images.isEmpty()) {
        return getEmptyImage();
```

```
        }
        else {
            return images.get(0);
        }
    }

    public List<ShoppingCategoryImage> getShoppingCategoryImagesByCategory (
            long categoryId)
        throws SystemException {                        <-- Gets all images by
                                                            Shopping Category
        List<ShoppingCategoryImage> images =
            shoppingCategoryImagePersistence.findByCategoryId(
                categoryId);

        return images;
    }

    public ShoppingCategoryImage updateImage(ShoppingCategoryImage image)
        throws SystemException {                               <-- Updates
                                                                   image
        image = shoppingCategoryImagePersistence.update(image);

        return image;
    }

    public void deleteImage(long imageId)
        throws NoSuchShoppingCategoryImageException, SystemException { <-- Deletes
                                                                           image
        shoppingCategoryImagePersistence.remove(imageId);
    }

    public void deleteImages (long categoryId)              Deletes all images by
        throws SystemException {                        <-- Shopping Category

    shoppingCategoryImagePersistenceremoveByCategoryId(categoryId
    }

    public ShoppingCategoryImage getEmptyImage() {          <-- Gets image object
                                                                for filling
        ShoppingCategoryImage image =
            shoppingCategoryImagePersistence.create(0);

        return image;
    }
```

docroot/WEB-INF/src/com/inkwell/internet/shopping/sb/service/impl/ShoppingCategoryImageLocalServiceImpl.java

As usual, after you've created the methods you need in your `-Impl` class, run Service Builder again; the methods are propagated out to the interface.

Now you need to configure the other parts of your hook.

8.3.2 Creating the configuration file

You now need to glue together all the different parts of your hook by creating a liferay-hook.xml file. If you're using Liferay IDE or Liferay Developer Studio, this file will have already been created for you when you generated the project. Otherwise, create this file in the WEB-INF folder of your project with the following contents.

Listing 8.3 Hook configuration file

```
<?xml version="1.0" encoding="UTF-8"?>
<!DOCTYPE hook PUBLIC "-//Liferay//DTD Hook 6.0.0//EN"
➥ "http://www.liferay.com/dtd/liferay-hook_6_0_0.dtd">

<hook>
  <portal-properties>portal.properties</portal-properties>

  <language-properties>
      content/Language_en.properties
  </language-properties>

  <custom-jsp-dir>/META-INF/custom_jsps</custom-jsp-dir>

  <service>
       <service-type>
        com.liferay.portlet.shopping.service.ShoppingCategoryLocalService
     </service-type>

     <service-impl>
         com.liferay.portlet.shopping.service.
InkwellShoppingCategoryLocalServiceImpl
     </service-impl>

  </service>

</hook>
```

docroot/WEB-INF/liferay-hook.xml

What have you done here? First, you're telling Liferay that you're going to override some portal properties, and those modifications will be in the file portal.properties on the classpath of this project (you'll put it in the src folder, and the build script will copy it to WEB-INF/classes when you build the project). The next thing you're telling Liferay is that you're going to have one or more language keys. This will be for the additional field that will store the URL to the shopping category image—you have to call that field something, via a label. You'll put that something in a language file so it can be translated.

After this, you tell Liferay that you're also going to customize some core JSPs, and you're going to put your customizations in META-INF/custom_jsps. This is where you'll place your customized categories.jspf and edit_category.jsp. And finally, you tell Liferay that you're also customizing a service. You define what service you want to override, and then you define the class—which must extend the wrapper of the overridden service—that will provide the implementation you want. Let's move on to overriding the service.

8.3.3 Overriding Liferay's service

Now comes the fun part. You need to override Liferay's service that deals with shopping categories in order to insert your functionality for adding and removing images. You'll do this by extending the wrapper class that comes with Liferay. Because this class is in the portal-service.jar file, it's on the global class path of the server, so it's accessible from your hook plugin.

There are only three points at which you need to extend the class: adding categories, updating categories, and deleting categories. For adding categories, you'll need to make it so that you create a `ShoppingCategoryImage` object after the category is created. These two objects will be linked by `categoryId`. For deleting categories, you'll do something similar, but in reverse: you first delete the image associated with the category and then call the superclass's method to delete the category itself. Because Liferay's `delete` methods are overloaded twice, you'll need to implement both versions of the method, because you don't know what else in the portal calls them or which version is called.

But wait a minute. All this time you've been assuming that you can get a value from a field on a form all the way down into the service layer. To do that, you need access to the `HttpServletRequest` or the `PortletRequest` object, right? That's where all the form field values from the browser go. But you don't have access to that object in the service layer.

Uh oh. You're in trouble. Your design is flawed.

Or is it?

One thing I've learned while working with Liferay: it's well-designed. The core engineers have already thought of that and have provided a solution. After all, hooks were *designed* to customize Liferay core functionality, so all the tools for doing so are provided. You'll use a service called the `ExpandoBridge`, which can take custom fields and put them into Liferay's `ServiceContext`. This is why you included services for this as references to your entity. We'll come back to this later. The first thing you need to do is to create your extension, as shown in the following listing.

Listing 8.4 Extending Liferay's shopping categories

```
public InkwellShoppingCategoryLocalServiceImpl(
    ShoppingCategoryLocalService shoppingCategoryLocalService) {

    super(shoppingCategoryLocalService);                    <-- 1 Constructor from superclass

}

@Override
public ShoppingCategory addCategory(
        long userId, long parentCategoryId, String name,
        String description, ServiceContext serviceContext)
    throws PortalException, SystemException {
                                                            2 Gets field value from
    String imageUrl = (String)                          <-- ServiceContext
```

```
        serviceContext.getExpandoBridgeAttributes().get(
            "image-url");

    ShoppingCategory shoppingCategory = super.addCategory(
        userId, parentCategoryId, name, description, serviceContext);

    ShoppingCategoryImageLocalServiceUtil.addShoppingCategoryImage(
        shoppingCategory.getCategoryId(), imageUrl);    <-- ❸ Calls service to add entity

    return shoppingCategory;
}
```

docroot/WEB-INF/src/com/liferay/portlet/shopping/service/InkwellShoppingCategoryLocalServiceImpl.java

Make sure you create the class in a package that isn't in the Service Builder hierarchy, so it's packaged with your hook rather than with the persistence classes. A Liferay best practice is to put it in the same package as the service wrapper you're extending, as a reminder of what classes to check when upgrading Liferay.

As you can see here, you've created a class that extends the `ShoppingCategoryLocalServiceWrapper` that ships with Liferay. You're also making sure you call the constructor from the superclass with the implementation that is passed to it ❶ so the base implementation can correctly proxy the service calls. When you have the class set up like this, you can override the methods you need in order to provide extra decorator functionality.

Next, you override Liferay's `addCategory()` method. To get the URL for the image in ❷, you retrieve a map of custom attributes from Liferay's `ServiceContext` by calling `getExpandoBridgeAttributes()`. When you get to the customization of the JSP, you'll use a Liferay tag to render your field so that Liferay treats it as a custom attribute. Liferay takes any fields defined as custom attributes and makes them available in the `ServiceContext`. This is how you get the field value from the form all the way down into the service layer. And finally, when you're finished, you call the service layer ❸ to add the entity to the database.

Why the weird name, *Expando*? The first time I heard the term, I was immediately transported back to my days of reading comic books, and I thought ExpandoMan might be a good name for a superhero who could stretch his limbs like a rubber band. One of Liferay's core engineers has defined Expandos as meaning "to attach additional properties to an object."[1] Liferay has a set of tables that allows developers to do just that.

Because Java isn't a dynamically typed language like JavaScript or Python, Expandos are difficult to implement directly. Instead, `ExpandoBridge` is a helper class that allows for the creation of Expando objects in Java. Additionally, Liferay allows you to persist those Expandos in a set of tables. For your hook, you're borrowing functionality from the Expandos API. This functionality allows you to create an arbitrary attribute in the JSP and get it down to the service layer by embedding it in `ServiceContext`. You'll see how that is done when you get to the JSP. For now, just

[1] Ray Augé, "Expandos - What are they? And how do they help me? (Liferay Portal 5.0.1+)," http://mng.bz/HKAC

understand that the image URL, which is the attribute you're looking for, is in the `ServiceContext` object, so you have access to it. You could do some validation on the value you get, but for this example, you won't do any validation.

After this, all you need to do is add the category, and you do that by calling `addCategory()` from the superclass. This returns to you the category that was added, which makes it a simple matter to add the `ShoppingCategoryImage` object, linking the two by `categoryId`. You then return the `ShoppingCategory` object as the superclass would have.

The `updateCategory()` method in the following listing is similar.

Listing 8.5 Updating a category

```
@Override
public ShoppingCategory updateCategory(
        long categoryId, long parentCategoryId, String name,
        String description, boolean mergeWithParentCategory,
        ServiceContext serviceContext)
    throws PortalException, SystemException {

    String imageUrl =
        (String) serviceContext.getExpandoBridgeAttributes().get(
            "image-url");
                                                    ❶ Get
    ShoppingCategoryImage image =                 <-  image
        ShoppingCategoryImageLocalServiceUtil.
        ➥ getShoppingCategoryImageByCategory(categoryId);
                                                            ❷ Add or
    if (image == null) {                                  <-  update

      ShoppingCategoryImageLocalServiceUtil.addShoppingCategoryImage(
        categoryId, imageUrl);

    }
    else {

        image.setImageUrl(imageUrl);
        ShoppingCategoryImageLocalServiceUtil.updateImage(image);

    }

    ShoppingCategory shoppingCategory =
super.updateCategory(
        categoryId, parentCategoryId, name, description,
        mergeWithParentCategory, serviceContext);

    return shoppingCategory;

}
```

docroot/WEB-INF/src/com/liferay/portlet/shopping/service/InkwellShoppingCategoryLocalServiceImpl.java

The only different things you do here are to ❶ get the `ShoppingCategoryImage` object, ❷ set whatever value is in `ServiceContext` in the object, and then save both the image and the `ShoppingCategory` to the database.

For the delete function, the underlying class provides two implementations. One of these implementations calls for a categoryId, and the other implementation calls for a ShoppingCategory object. Because you don't know what else in Liferay calls these methods, you need to override both:

```
@Override
public void deleteCategory(long categoryId)
    throws PortalException, SystemException {

    ShoppingCategoryImageLocalServiceUtil.deleteImages(categoryId);

    super.deleteCategory(categoryId);

}

@Override
public void deleteCategory(ShoppingCategory category)
    throws PortalException, SystemException {

    this.deleteCategory(category.getCategoryId());

}
```

As you can see, there's nothing special here either. You delete the image first and then call the superclass to delete the category.

Because this is all you need to override, you're done with the service layer and can move on to the view layer.

8.3.4 Overriding the Shopping portlet's interface

Now that you have everything implemented in the back end, you need to implement the front end. Liferay's front end is implemented in JSP files. As you learned earlier in the chapter, if you want to override a core JSP with one of your own, you need to place it in exactly the same path as the one that ships with Liferay. Because you defined the location of your customized JSPs as META-INF/custom_jsps in your liferay-hook.xml file, you'll need to duplicate Liferay's path in this directory.

As you saw earlier, when the development team looked at the Liferay source, they found that in order to do what they wanted, they had to customize two JSPs:

- edit_category.jsp
- categories.jspf

Both of these files are found in the html/portlet/shopping folder, so to start, copy Liferay's version of these files into

META-INF/custom_jsps/html/portlet/shopping

Now you can begin customizing the files. Start with edit_category.jsp, so you can test your service-layer customizations by entering image URLs. In that file, at about line 102, you'll find the following two lines of code:

```
<aui:input cssClass="lfr-input-text-container" name="name" />

<aui:input cssClass="lfr-textarea-container" name="description" />
```

Place the following customization below these lines.

Listing 8.6 Adding the image URL field to edit_category.jsp

```
<%-- Adding Custom URL Field --%>

<%

ShoppingCategoryImage catImage
=
    ShoppingCategoryImageLocalServiceUtil.
    ➥ getShoppingCategoryImageByCategory(category.getCategoryId());


%>

<aui:input name="ExpandoAttributeName--image-url--"      ❶ Define Expando attribute
    type="hidden"
    value="image-url" />

<aui:field-wrapper label="image-url">

  <liferay-ui:input-field                                ❷ Use Expando attribute for field
      model="<%= ShoppingCategoryImage.class %>"
      fieldParam="ExpandoAttribute--image-url--"
      bean="<%= catImage %>"
      field="imageUrl"
  />

</aui:field-wrapper>

<%-- End custom field --%>
```

docroot/META-INF/custom_jsps/html/portlet/shopping/edit_category.jsp

All of this makes sense until you get to the tags, right? Here's where you're borrowing a bit from the Expando API I mentioned earlier. Let's dig in to how this works.

8.3.5 *Expandos, ServiceContext, and tokens, oh my!*

Let's take a short rollercoaster ride that will navigate you quickly through the twists and turns of a couple of Liferay APIs that make developers' lives easier. Picture yourself sitting in a seat next to somebody you really like, with anticipation building because you know this is going to be a cool ride. The operator comes down the line of cars and pushes the restraining loop down over your head, and you feel yourself securely pressed into the seat. After making sure everyone is securely in their seats, the operator goes to a control panel, and you feel the anticipation building.

The operator presses a button, the ride starts on its way, and you feel the pull of gravity as you begin ascending a steep incline in the tracks. It doesn't matter which car you're in; whether you're in the front or in some other car, the incline is such that the view ahead of you is hidden either by the path of the tracks or by the backs of the people's heads in front of you. Soon, however, you feel the car leveling out, and there's a perceptible slowing down as you move from an incline, to being level, to a slight decline, to—

—an HTML input field that's hidden is still a part of the DOM; it's just not displayed to the user. This makes it useful as a convention when processing a form if you want to differentiate some kinds of fields from others. Normally, you use the hidden input field to include data that the user doesn't care about or doesn't need to see. You used it this way in chapter 4, when you needed to include the primary key of a record in a form but didn't want to display it to the user.

Here's the first curve at the bottom of the rollercoaster drop. Liferay's form-processing engine recognizes some patterns in order to implement Expando fields, which are dynamic fields that can be created at runtime by users. If you have ever used Custom Attributes in the Control Panel to add attributes to user records, you've already used this functionality from an end-user perspective. You're in a similar way adding an extra attribute to Shopping Categories: an image URL. You could implement this with the full Expando API, but you instead used Service Builder to create real entities for your images. To support the additional attribute, you're using the part of the Expando API that handles the front end and then persisting the field using a custom service rather than through the Expando back end.

This highlights an important distinction between hooks and Ext. Hooks target specific areas of customization that have been identified by Liferay as the most frequent hot spots of Liferay Portal customization. In this case, you're using hooks both to customize the front end (JSPs) and to override a core Liferay service that manipulates Shopping Categories. In your JSPs, you're having to borrow from the Expando API for one simple reason: in Liferay 6.0, portlet actions aren't customizable by hooks; they can only be customized from Ext. This is one limitation of hook plugins that you'll need to consider as you think about the implementation of your site. As an aside, if you're using Liferay 6.1, this limitation no longer exists—but we want our code to work on both versions. Normally, because you don't have access to the `PortletRequest` object from a hook, you can't retrieve values from a form. You can still accomplish what you want, however, because the Expando API is there. This API provides an easy way of getting your form data from the browser down into the service layer.

TAGGING EXPANDO FIELDS

Let's hit another drop on that rollercoaster so we can build up some speed before getting to the loop. Because Expando fields can be defined at runtime by users, Liferay needs to be able to differentiate them in the front end from the regular fields that are handled in the standard way. In order to do this, a convention has been defined: first a hidden field with the attribute name (the key in a key/value pair) is defined, and then a Liferay tag that maps that key to a Service Builder bean is used. Tokens are used in order to accomplish this. When Liferay processes this form, it looks for any field names that correspond to the predefined tokens. The Expando API defines two tokens:

- `ExpandoAttributeName-- --`

  This token is for the key and is used by the API to tell Liferay what field to look for.

- `ExpandoAttribute-- --`
  This token is for the value and marks the field in the code so Liferay can find it when processing the fields.

> **What are those dashes for?**
>
> The dashes with the token names are used as delimiters to define the field that will be displayed. Liferay once used parentheses for this—because that's a character normally used as a delimiter—but it confused the JavaScript engine of several browsers.

Any fields that are marked as Expando attributes wind up in `ServiceContext`, and the `ServiceContext` is passed down to the service layer by the portlet action for the Shopping Cart portlet.

THE IMPORTANCE OF SERVICECONTEXT

The `ServiceContext` object is like one of those loops on the rollercoaster ride. It's one of the most exciting changes that has been made to Liferay recently. Normally, you wouldn't consider an object used as a parameter on a method to be something exciting. But consider this: Liferay's service methods used to (necessarily) have lots and lots and lots (and lots) of parameters. They had so many parameters that they were an incredible pain to use, especially for developers who had customized Liferay via Ext. Why? Because not only were there lots of parameters, but it was also necessary as features were added to Liferay to *change* the parameters all the time, even between point releases.

What a nightmare. This made it difficult to keep in step with the changes being made in the core (because, as McCoy said about Scotty, engineers love to change things). It was particularly difficult for developers to write code against methods that had 15 parameters in their signatures (no joke). So the Liferay engineers created the `ServiceContext` object, and this solved a lot of these problems. Many of the common parameters that the service layer used to require (such as `companyId` and `scopeGroupId`) can now be found in one object passed down to the service layer. And, as you're seeing in this example, the `ServiceContext` object can also be a handy place to temporarily store custom attributes so they can be persisted, either as Expandos or as bona fide Service Builder entities.

Is that exciting, or what? You don't have to deal with any of the headaches that earlier Liferay platform developers had to worry about. Congratulations! You've successfully hit that rollercoaster loop and gone all the way around without tossing your cookies. And because you did that, you've found that it was the most exciting part of the ride.

Combining the two concepts of `ServiceContext` and Expando tokens, then, Liferay knows that when it encounters a field that uses the predefined token for an Expando attribute, it shouldn't put the field in the `PortletRequest` object where all the regular form fields are placed. Instead, Liferay puts it in `ServiceContext` as a key/value pair. All of this is done by a simple form convention that you can use to put any `String` value you like into `ServiceContext`. You've gained a field-processing engine from the browser down into your service layer, for free.

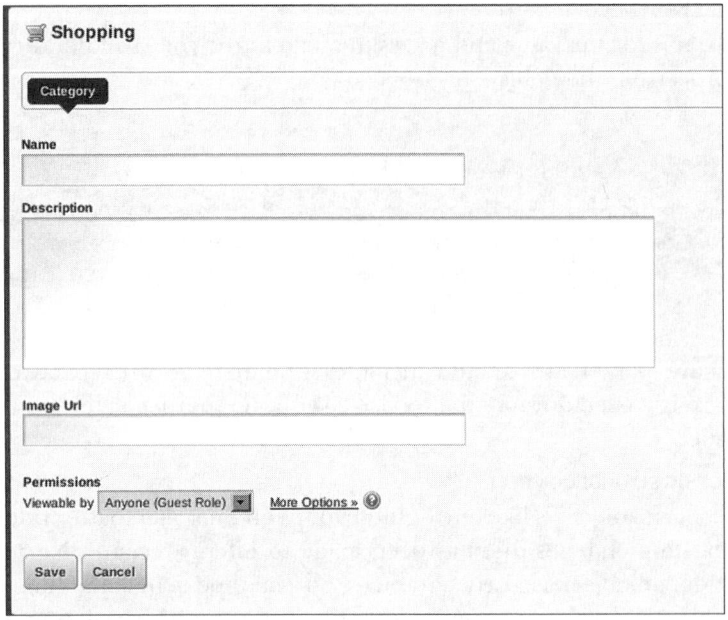

Figure 8.4 Liferay's Shopping portlet now contains an extra field—your field—when a user adds a category.

A LOOK AT THE FRONT END

When you deploy the hook to Liferay, the JSP that Liferay normally uses to display the form for editing shopping categories is replaced, and your form is used instead. That form renders with an additional field, as you can see in figure 8.4.

When a user pastes a value into the Image Url field, that field value gets down into the service layer via the rollercoaster ride. You can then persist the field normally.

> **About validation**
>
> The Inkwell development team elected not to provide any field validation on the Image Url field so that they could finish the project more quickly. This is fine for this particular application: only users with the rights to add products and categories to the shopping cart will ever see this field. But if you're doing something like this for public users of your web site, you'll definitely want to add a validation class to your hook the same way you did with the portlet in chapter 4. If you don't, you're asking for trouble.

The easiest workflow, as defined by the Inkwell development team, is to have the users responsible for the shopping cart add a folder called Shopping Images to Liferay's Image Gallery portlet. After it's added, they can copy/paste the URLs to those images when they create shopping categories. Because there will only be three categories, this should be simple and straightforward.

Now that you can add images to the Image Gallery and paste their URLs into the Shopping portlet, you can turn to how those images are presented to the end user who wants to buy a product.

8.3.6 Presenting the new interface to end users

The Inkwell design team has designed a new user interface for navigating the shopping categories, which you saw at the beginning of this discussion. Users can select product categories from a menu. When they roll their mouse over menu options, an image of that particular product category is displayed. Figure 8.5 shows the user hovering over PDA Pen.

Figure 8.5 Categories appear in a horizontal menu. When users roll over menu items, the product image is displayed. The PDA Pen is by far Inkwell's hottest-selling item, so it appears first in the list.

Figure 8.6 shows the user hovering over USB Pen.

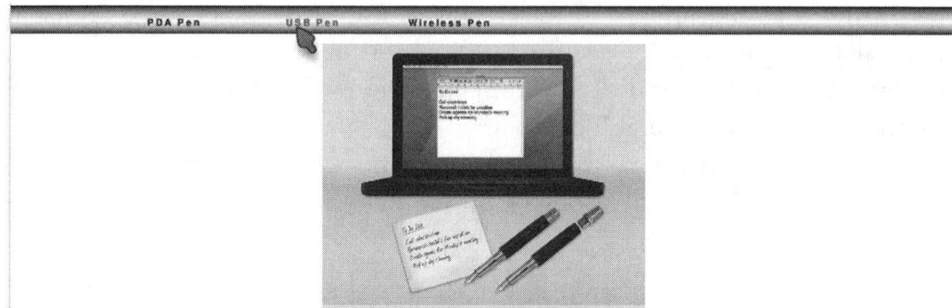

Figure 8.6 The USB Pen is Inkwell's second-best-selling item, so it's second in the list.

And Figure 8.7 shows the user hovering over the third menu item. You can see that this interface can handle a few more categories before it will need to be redesigned.

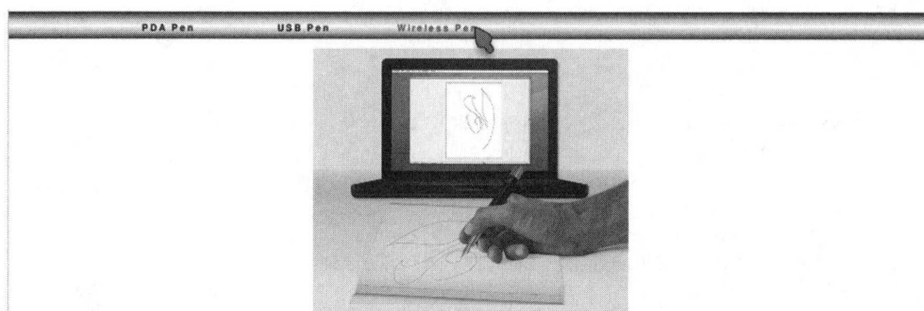

Figure 8.7 The Wireless Pen, which is really a full-fledged computer, is Inkwell's newest item.

The beauty of this design is that it doesn't interfere with the existing interface for categories, which can be reused by administrative users who need to add, edit, and delete categories. You'll see how this is done shortly.

The design team first did a proof of concept of this design in a static web page and then placed the resulting JavaScript in the Inkwell internet theme that was presented in chapter 5. This necessitated the customization of the main.js file, which resides in the _diffs/js folder of the project. In this folder, you have a simple JavaScript function that defines the CSS background image attribute with whatever image URL is passed to the function:

```
function showProduct(p, pic) {

    document.getElementById(p).style.backgroundImage="url('" + pic + "')";

}
```

Because this file is automatically added to a theme's markup, you don't have to do anything other than to add this function to the file and redeploy the theme.

This makes the script available to every page in the portal, so it could theoretically be used anywhere. You'll use it on the page that displays the categories in the Shopping portlet, which is categories.jspf. This page is located in the portal in the folder html/portlet/shopping. Because you'll be overriding this page in your hook, you start by copying this file into your hook project, using the exact same folder structure. Because you've already defined the location of your JSP files as META-INF/custom_jsps in your liferay-hook.xml file, all you need to do is create the proper folder structure there and copy the original file into it.

At approximately line 116, you can implement your new user interface using the code in listing 8.7. Place this code below the following two lines in categories.jspf:

```
boolean showSearch = !results.isEmpty();
%>
```

Listing 8.7 Customizing the shopping interface

```
<%

StringBuilder catMenu = new StringBuilder();                    ❶ Creates String
catMenu.append("<div id='pen-menu'> <ul>");

for (int j = 0; j < results.size(); j++) {                       ❷ Loops through categories

    ShoppingCategory cat = (ShoppingCategory) results.get(j);
    String catTitle = cat.getName();                             ❸ Gets category name
    String catJSTitle = JS.getSafeName(catTitle);
    ShoppingCategoryImage catImage =
        ShoppingCategoryImageLocalServiceUtil.
        ➥ getShoppingCategoryImageByCategory(
cat.getCategoryId());
    String catImageUrl = catImage.getImageUrl();                 ❹ Gets category image URL
```

```
    PortletURL catURL = renderResponse.createRenderURL();        ❺ Creates URL

    catURL.setWindowState(WindowState.MAXIMIZED);

    catURL.setParameter("struts_action", "/shopping/view");
    catURL.setParameter("categoryId",
      String.valueOf(cat.getCategoryId()));

    catMenu.append("<li><a href=\"");
    catMenu.append(catURL);
    catMenu.append("\"
    ➥ onmouseover=\"showProduct('shopping-image','");
    catMenu.append(catImageUrl);
    catMenu.append("');\"
onmouseout=\"showProduct('shopping-image',
➥ '/inkwell-web-site-theme/images/custom/INKWELL_logo_V3.png'
➥ );\">");
    catMenu.append(catTitle);
    catMenu.append("</a></li>");                          ❻ Concatenates String


}

catMenu.append("</ul></div>");                            ❼ Closes tags


%>

<div id="pen-menu-container">

  <%= catMenu.toString() %>                               ❽ Displays String

</div>

<div id="pen-container">

  <div id="shopping-image">

  <%

  if (category != null) {

      ShoppingCategoryImage chosenImage =
          ShoppingCategoryImageLocalServiceUtil.
          ➥ getShoppingCategoryImageByCategory(
          ➥ category.getCategoryId());
  %>
    <img src="<%=chosenImage.getImageUrl() %>"
        alt="Category Image" border="0" />

  <%

  }
  else {

  %>
```

```
         
  <%
  }
  %>

  </div>

</div>
```

docroot/META-INF/custom_jsps/html/portlet/shopping/categories.jspf

Let's look at the overall strategy here, which should help make sense of the code. Think of the algorithm in a step-by-step fashion:

1. Create a `String` to turn records from the database into HTML markup.
2. Loop through each shopping category.
3. Get each category's name, so you can use the name as your link.
4. Get each category's image URL, so you can display the image when the mouse rolls over the link.
5. As you loop, you also create a URL that forms the actual link.
6. When you have all these items, you can concatenate a `String` that can use them in the markup to create the menu. This menu is created as an unordered list in HTML, which is easy to style via CSS.
7. When you're finished with the loop, you close the tags at the end of the `String`.
8. All that remains is to spit out that `String` in the appropriate place on the page.

That's all there is to it. The result is an HTML unordered list that contains menu items built from your database data. After this is a `<div>` that you're calling `pen-container` that contains another `<div>` called `shopping-image`.

The links contain `onmouseover` and `onmouseout` events that call the JavaScript function defined in the theme. This function receives the `shopping-image` `<div>` and swaps the `background-image` attribute with the one passed to the function. Because you built each link as you were looping through the data from the database, each link will contain the image URL that was stored with the `ShoppingCategoryImage` entity. This URL, of course, points to an image stored in Liferay's Image Gallery portlet.

The supporting CSS for this code is also placed in the Inkwell Web Site theme, and it styles the menu and images according to the look and feel defined by the design team.

The `<div>` containing the image also contains some code. The reason is that the same JSP fragment is used to display the categories and to display the category menu. When the category is chosen, you want to display that category's image. For that reason, you fill the `<div>` with the image if the user has chosen a category; if not, you have a nonbreaking space.

You can't just replace the old interface with this one, however. The old interface catered to two audiences: shoppers coming to the site to buy something, and site administrators who need to maintain the site. This new interface caters only to shoppers. You need to preserve the old interface in some way but make sure that shoppers never see it. It turns out that this is easy to do.

Notice that all the way up around line 111, a Boolean called `showAddCategoryButton` is created, based on the permissions of the current user. Obviously, regular users won't be allowed to add categories, so you already have the permission check that you need built in to the page!

The panel that is used to display the search container comes next in the markup. You can wrap that panel in a check on the `showAddCategoryButton` boolean and thereby hide it for regular users and show it for administrators:

```
<c:if test="<%= showAddCategoryButton %>">

[ ... ]

</c:if>
```

At this point, the Inkwell Shopping hook is feature-complete and can be deployed to Liferay. Because it works in conjunction with Inkwell's theme, it will only work when that theme is being used.

> **Bonus assignment**
>
> Now that the customization is complete, a best practice is then to take your string-manipulation skills as described in section 8.2.5 and parse the original JSPs, inserting customizations in the appropriate places. For readability of the example, I haven't done this; but with the hook working, this would be your next step.

If you're going to install this example from the source code, you need to remember something about the Java EE spec: web applications are separated from each other in the JVM by different classloaders. Because you created a service in your hook .war, those classes won't be readable by the customized JSPs running inside the Liferay .war.

This is easy to fix, of course: move (not copy) the service .jar (inkwell-shopping-hook-service.jar) from the hook's WEB-INF/lib folder to the global classpath of your application server (in this case, Tomcat's lib folder) and then restart your application server. Your customized service will then be readable by all web applications that are installed—including both Liferay *and* your hook.

8.4 Summary

You've just experienced a comprehensive presentation on Liferay hooks. Hooks are a powerful way to customize some core Liferay functionality. You can override certain properties and append your own values to list properties, enabling you to define your own Liferay startup events, listeners, authentication events, and more. You can override and define Language properties as well, enabling you to use your own terminology or to provide alternate translations of specific keys.

More powerfully, you can override Liferay's JSP files with your own implementation and also override Liferay's service implementations. Combining these features gives you as a developer some powerful ways to change the core behavior of Liferay by deploying a plugin.

Using the book's case study, you then saw a practical example of how to bring all these concepts together in an example hook that overrides a core Liferay service, provides a new entity of its own, contains a Language property, and customizes core Liferay JSP files in the Shopping Cart portlet.

Now you're empowered to go and create hooks that customize Liferay to your needs. You'll find that this is an easy and convenient way to make Liferay sing to your tune, without ever having to directly modify the Liferay source code.

If you've got a customization you need to make that is just not possible using a hook, read on, because we'll be diving deeper into customizations with Ext plugins next.

9 Extending Liferay effectively

This chapter covers

- Liferay's Ext plugin
- A Liferay architecture walkthrough
- Best practices for Liferay development

I'm sure most of you've seen *Spiderman,* right? Or at least, if you haven't seen the movie, you've had a chance to read the comic book. One of the reasons I've always liked the character of Peter Parker/Spiderman is his humanity. He's reachable. You understand him. He struggles just like the rest of us. And many of the stories are about his struggle to come to terms with this great power he's been given. Sometimes he succeeds in that struggle, and many times he fails. This kind of story rings with a truth that I think most people can relate to, and it's likely a big part of the reason why *Spiderman* has been such a smashing success since the character first appeared on the scene in the early 1960s.

One of the strategies Peter Parker learns to help him use his power wisely comes from his Uncle Ben, who tells him, "With great power comes great responsibility." Of course, Uncle Ben doesn't know the extent to which Peter's struggle with power is a bit more—um—*enhanced* than everyone else's. In a sense, software developers struggle with something similar: they have a skill that most of the rest of the world doesn't understand and that is sometimes viewed alternatively with respect and suspicion. Why is that? Because there are superheroes in the software world, writing good code that helps the rest of humanity, and there are supervillains in the software world, writing bad code, some of which spreads like a virus, stealing and marauding wherever it goes.

I hope you'll be a superhero with what you do with Liferay. There are two ways to do this:

1. Write good software that benefits others.
2. Use the tools Liferay gives you in the right way, creating well-architected and well-written software that is easy to maintain for other developers who may come in contact with it.

In this chapter, we'll focus on 2; I'll leave 1 to you. To get you started, I'd like to help you become a superhero with regard to how you use Ext plugins on the Liferay platform.

Ext plugins are like the great power in the Spiderman story. When given a great power, it's wise to consider how best to use it. Should it be used for everything? Probably not; and if you try, you'll almost certainly make a mess. Can it be abused? Definitely. Can it be used for good and, optimally, so that it provides the best benefit for the most people? Absolutely, but that will take a lot of thought to accomplish.

When I first started working with Liferay, we didn't have all the great plugin types you've already seen. Instead, everything—and I mean *everything*—had to be done using the Extension environment (Ext environment for short). Ext plugins, as they're now called, give you unlimited power within Liferay to do whatever you want. You could implement your entire site using only a single Ext plugin if you wanted to. But that isn't the best way. In fact, more likely than not, if you do it that way, you'll make a big mess. Ext plugins need to be used responsibly.

We'll look at two ways you can use Ext plugins responsibly in Liferay 6.0:

- Customizing Struts actions of internal Liferay portlets
- Modifying core Liferay behavior that can't be done with hooks

For the first use case, I'll be able to show you an example. For the second, because Liferay has so much core functionality, I'll list some common things people do with Ext. Then I'll give you an overview of Liferay's architecture by tracing exactly what Liferay does from receiving a browser request to rendering a page. Because I can't be sure what you may wish to modify, this should hit a lot of internal Liferay code, giving you the tools to determine your strategy for making Liferay do what you want.

After we've looked at Liferay's architecture, we'll discuss some best practices for Liferay development, to help you decide when to use each plugin type. We'll round out this discussion by helping you decide if your changes would be something you could even give back to the product as open source!

Without further ado, let's jump right into Ext plugins.

9.1 Introducing Ext plugins

Liferay's Extension plugin is the ultimate in customizing Liferay. No other portal gives you the level of customization that Liferay does through the Ext plugin. You can literally change *anything* in Liferay, up to and including making it into your own product. The amount of power it gives you is unparalleled. We'll call this Great Power.

Of course, as Spiderman has learned, with Great Power comes great responsibility. Because you have access to all of Liferay's internal APIs when using the Ext plugin, you can also run into trouble, particularly when moving to new versions of Liferay.

"What?!?" you say. "I thought you told me earlier that the Ext plugin was designed specifically *not* to impact upgrades!"

Well, that's true. Liferay's Ext plugin was created to provide a way of separating custom code from Liferay's source, so that developers can more easily tell where their code ends and Liferay's begins. You don't have to modify Liferay's source directly in order to make the changes you want to make: you keep your code separate, and the Ext plugin takes care of overlaying your changes on top of Liferay's source. As a side note, this also allows you to customize Liferay any way you want and not have your code fall under the terms of the LGPL license under which Liferay is released. It also makes upgrading *easier* (note that I didn't say completely pain free), because you can upgrade Liferay and then point your Ext plugin to the new version.

But this is where things can get hairy. The Ext plugin gives you Great Power because it gives you access to all of Liferay's internal APIs. But because these are the *internal* APIs and not the *public* APIs, they're more likely to change when moving from version to version. And boy, do they change. If you're going to use the Great Power that the Ext plugin offers you, you'll need to exercise greater responsibility in writing your code so that it can be updated easily whenever you upgrade to a new version of Liferay. This is why Liferay recommends that you do your best to accomplish what you need to accomplish with other plugin types, rather than through customizations in the Ext plugin, and I heartily agree with that. If you do this, your code is even more isolated from Liferay's code, and you are using publicly available APIs which go through the normal deprecation process when they are changed. All of this makes your life much easier.

With that said, there are some things you can't do with the other plugin types, and this is the role Ext is designed to fill. If I haven't scared you off, this section is intended as a guide for those who want to do extensive customization on top of Liferay Portal. The Ext plugin contains a set of tools that allows developers to customize Liferay out the wazoo. And for Liferay 6, it's another plugin type, although as you'll see, deployment of the Ext plugin needs to be treated differently from that of other plugins.

Another way to think about the Ext plugin is as a wrapper for Liferay's core source—because, in most cases, it mirrors Liferay's core source directories (ext-impl/ for portal-impl/, ext-web/ for portal-web/, and so on). It allows you to develop on top of Liferay portal like a platform.

With that background information out of the way, let's jump right into creating an Ext plugin. As with the other plugin types, all you have to do is navigate to the ext directory in your Plugins SDK and run the `create` script. You'll create an Ext plugin for the Inkwell web site. To do this on LUM, issue this command:

```
./create.sh inkwell-web-site "Inkwell Web Site"
```

And on Windows, use this command:

```
create.bat inkwell-web-site "Inkwell Web Site"
```

When this is done, you should have a new project in your Plugins SDK's ext directory called `inkwell-web-site-ext`.

Let's look at how Ext projects are organized.

9.1.1 Anatomy of an Ext plugin

The structure of an Ext plugin closely mirrors the Liferay source, so as to provide an overlay for Liferay's functions. Table 9.1 describes this structure and what the folders are for.

Table 9.1 Ext plugin structure

Directory	Purpose
/inkwell-web-site-ext /docroot /WEB-INF	The root directory. Because an Ext plugin is organized like a web module, it contains a docroot directory (which contains a WEB-INF directory) as well as a build script. Because all of the folders that make up the plugin are in the WEB-INF folder, the rest of the list will work from there.
ext-impl	Contains all your source and configuration files (except those related to the web application). When an Ext plugin is created, several important files are placed in its subdirectories. The most significant are as follows: ■ */src/portal-ext.properties*—Used to override the values of the properties in the portal.properties configuration file that ships with Liferay Portal. ■ */src/system-ext.properties*—Used to override the values of the properties in the system.properties configuration file that ships with Liferay Portal. ■ */src/content/Language-ext.properties*—Used to add your own internationalized text messages or to override the messages that ship with Liferay Portal, just as you've seen with plugins. You can add variations for other languages using the Java convention for message bundles. For example, the translation to Spanish should be named Language-ext_es.properties.
ext-lib	Contains any extra dependency libraries.
ext-service	Contains the classes that are generated by Liferay's service builder. This works exactly the same way it does with plugins. Note that this functionality is left over for those migrating from older versions of Liferay, is deprecated in Liferay 6, and may be removed in future releases. If you need to create shared services, use a plugin to do it and then place the service .jar on the server's global class path.

Table 9.1 Ext plugin structure *(continued)*

Directory	Purpose
ext-util-bridges	Corresponds to the util-bridges folder in the Liferay source.
ext-util-java	Corresponds to the util-java folder in the Liferay source.
ext-util-taglib	Corresponds to the util-taglib folder in the Liferay source.
ext-web	Contains your JSPs, HTML, images, JavaScript, and all other web application-related files in the docroot subdirectory. Here are some of the most common activities you'll perform from this docroot subdirectory: ■ To add entries to the web application configuration file, edit /docroot/WEB-INF/web.xml. ■ To add a portlet, edit /docroot/WEB-INF/portlet-ext.xml, /docroot/WEB-INF/liferay-portlet-ext.xml, and /docroot/WEB-INF/liferay-display.xml. You may also want to edit /ext-impl/src/content/Language-ext.properties. These *-ext.xml files are read after their parent files are read and override their parent values. Note that I don't recommend adding portlets in the Ext plugin; it's far better to write a portlet plugin instead. ■ If you're customizing some of Liferay's internal StrutsPortlets, the following files will also be of interest to you: docroot/WEB-INF/struts-config.xml and docroot/WEB-INF/tiles-defs.xml.

This is a simple structure, and it's that way on purpose. Next, you'll see why.

9.1.2 *How Ext works*

As you can see, the structure of an Ext plugin closely mirrors that of the Liferay source. This is done on purpose, so your customizations to Liferay can be structured exactly the same way Liferay's code is structured. This way, it's fairly obvious where to place a customization, because you'll place it in the same location where Liferay put the original code.

Using Ext is very simple. You can add your own classes in packages in the src folder in ext-impl. This is patterned after the portal-impl folder in the Liferay source and is designed for you to go ahead and extend those classes. You can modify the behavior of anything in Liferay using this method. We'll get to this in detail in the next section.

The same goes for JSP files. The ext-web folder can be an exact mirror of Liferay's portal-web folder. Any file you place in here will overwrite its counterpart in Liferay, so the only thing you need to be careful to do is to mirror exactly the path and file name of the file you're overriding.

Now, what does Ext actually do? I'm glad you asked. It's different from the other plugin types with which you've been working. Ext plugins replace the parts of the original Liferay installation that you've customized with your own code. Any areas you haven't customized are left alone. Because the changes go into the Liferay installation, the server needs to be shut down and restarted after deploying an Ext plugin. And because you're modifying the original Liferay installation, an Ext plugin isn't all that easy to *un*deploy. This is more of that great responsibility stuff you need to be aware of when exercising Great Power.

Figure 9.1 illustrates how this works.

Because your code becomes part of the Liferay installation, you have the ability to make any call to any API you want, replace Liferay's implementation of something with your own, or implement a new internal service that runs alongside the rest of Liferay's services. Want to replace Liferay's social networking code with your own? Have at it. Need to change how Liferay does deploys? Go for it. All power is yours. Just make sure you're careful to exercise great responsibility with how you implement your changes. The next section will outline a strategy for this.

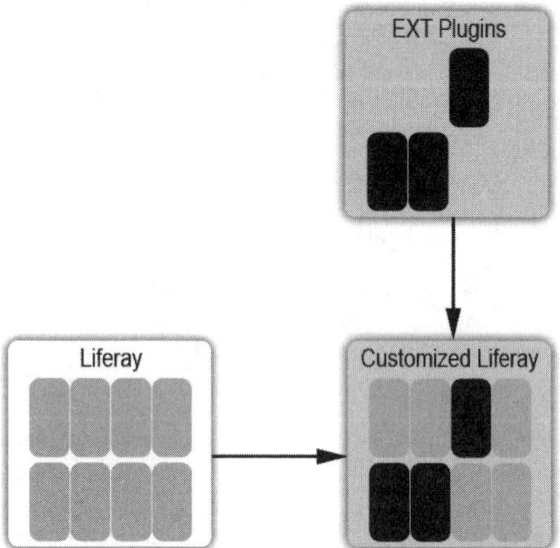

Figure 9.1 When you deploy an Ext plugin, the code therein gets copied *into the Liferay installation itself*. This is different from the rest of the plugin types, where code is loaded dynamically at runtime.

9.1.3 *The Ext strategy*

This is, of course, not the *Exit* strategy: we're not fighting a war here—I mean the *Ext* strategy.

The strategy for using the Ext plugin optimally is simple: *extend, don't modify*. What do I mean by that? Let's look at a common task for which developers use the Ext plugin: customizing Struts actions. If you're using the Ext plugin, I (as Spock would) compute a 99% probability that it's because you need to customize a Struts action in one or more of Liferay's built-in portlets. You can't do this in Liferay 6.0, and in 6.1 (as of this writing), the functionality is still in flux.[1] So we turn to Ext plugins to get the job done.

Let's assume for some strange reason that every time you add a user, you want to save the user's name to a text file. Where could you put that code? If you've read the previous chapter, you know you could put that in a model listener for the User entity, but let's pretend you don't want to do it that way. One place you could put it is in the `EditUserAction` class. If you haven't used Struts, set aside for a moment that I'm using a Struts action as an example: the same rule applies to any class in Liferay that you want to customize. This class is a Struts action class that processes the Edit User form and calls the service layer to add or modify a user. It's easy in the Ext plugin to provide your own implementation of this functionality. To make sure your version is called, all you have to do is modify the struts-config-ext.xml file to make your class the handler for the specific action path (we'll get to this in detail later).

---

1 See Mika Koivisto, "Overriding and adding struts actions from hook plugins," http://mng.bz/HB04

What is one way you could provide your implementation of the action? You could grab a copy of the `EditUserAction` class from Liferay's source, copy it into your Ext plugin, and modify it. That seems like the most simple and straightforward solution, right?

Wrong. Remember: *extend, don't modify.* Why? Because again, you are working with Liferays internal APIs. There is nothing preventing Liferay from adding features and functionality to this particular part of the portal in the next release. When you have to upgrade your code to the next release of Liferay, your added functionality will likely break, and you'll have to paste in the new version of Liferay's class and insert your changes all over again, hoping all along that they integrate well with the new code.

It's far better to extend Liferay's class, do what you want to do, and then call `super.methodName()` on it to invoke Liferay's functionality. That way, all you're doing is piggy-backing on whatever Liferay is doing (which you don't care much about, as long as users are added and modified properly, right?). It's much better to do this instead of reimplementing both what Liferay does and what you want to do in the same class.

This is an illustration of what I meant when I said that Ext gives you Great Power, but you can also get into trouble fast if you're not careful. Control, control, control; you must learn control! Let the Force flow through you, and—well, I'm mixing sci-fi metaphors here, but you know what I mean. Let's next look at what happens when you deploy an Ext plugin.

9.1.4 Deploying Ext plugins

Ext plugins look kind of like the hot-deployable plugins you've seen throughout the rest of this book, but that appearance is deceiving. When deployed, they operate differently than the other plugin types.

There are two ways to deploy an Ext plugin:

- If you're deploying to Liferay running on your developer machine, you can use Ant scripts in the Plugins SDK: specifically `ant deploy` and `ant direct-deploy`.
- If you're deploying to Liferay running on another machine, you can create a .war file via `ant dist` and deploy it manually to Liferay (by copying it into Liferay's deploy folder or using the UI).

No matter how you deploy an Ext plugin, what happens during the deployment is essentially the same, and it's not at all like what happens when other plugin types are deployed. To illustrate the difference, let's look at what the deploy process does (see figure 9.2):

1. The process creates ext-service.jar out of compiled code from ext-service/src and deploys a namespaced copy of that .jar to the global class path. You should know where this is for your application server. The deployer does this after extracting it from the .war, or the Ant script does this as part of `direct-deploy`.
2. The process creates ext-impl.jar out of compiled code from ext-impl/src.

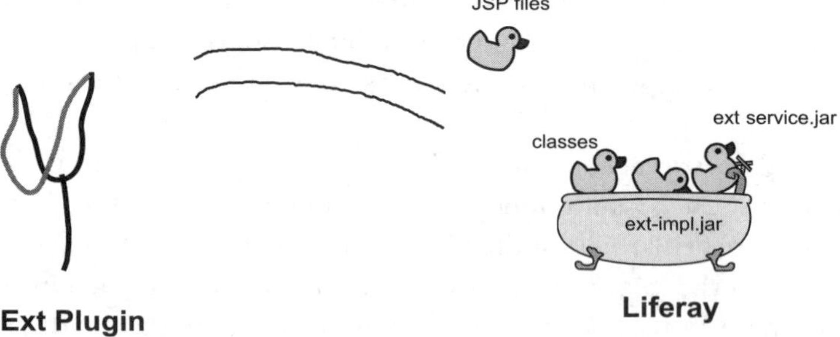

Figure 9.2 Rather than existing as separate applications, Ext plugins are deployed directly into the running Liferay instance, either by Liferay's deployer or by the Ant script.

3. The process creates ext-util*.jar files from the ext-util-* source folders, if you've customized a tag library, a utility, or a portlet bridge.
4. A registry .xml file is built in the WEB-INF folder of the Ext plugin. This registry contains the name of every file in your Ext plugin, so Liferay can keep track of what's been customized. This is to support the possibility of deploying multiple Ext plugins—if one plugin customizes the same thing another plugin has already customized, the deploy will fail.
5. The deployer or Ant script begins to copy files out to where Liferay is deployed. First, it deploys any portal-*.properties or system-*.properties files out to Liferay's WEB-INF/classes folder. It then deploys a namespaced copy of the .jar files that were created above to Liferay's WEB-INF/lib.
6. The deployer or script then copies your ext-web folder into the deployed Liferay's folder, thereby integrating your changes with Liferay's code.

After reading this explanation, I'm sure you understand why you need to restart the server subsequent to an Ext plugin deployment. Regardless of which method you use to deploy an Ext plugin, the end result is the same: your code overlays Liferay's code inside the running instance of Liferay Portal. If you use `ant deploy`, your Ext plugin is packaged into a .war file and then copied into Liferay's deploy folder. If you use `ant direct-deploy`, your Ext plugin is copied directly out to the running Liferay instance, without going through the deployer.

See how this is different from normal plugins? Your code is no longer isolated from Liferay in a different classloader. Instead, it runs as part of the Liferay application, along with the rest of Liferay's code. This brings benefits (Great Power), of course, but it also brings consequences (great responsibility).

The first consequence is that you can't just undeploy an Ext plugin. If you mess something up, you'll need a copy of your original Liferay bundle handy so you can extract a clean Liferay again. Be careful. Deploy in increments, making sure that if you're doing something that—if it goes wrong—can completely break the portal, you have an easy way to revert it out of your Liferay instance without having to resort to extracting a clean bundle. If you're an Eclipse user, I highly recommend that you try Liferay IDE or Liferay Developer Studio, because those products have a way of reverting Ext for you (under the hood they just copy a clean Liferay over your runtime, but every little bit helps).

Additionally, when you upgrade to a new version of Liferay, brace yourself: your code is going to break. That's a consequence of using internal APIs that are subject to change. The great thing is, though, that Ext keeps your code separate from Liferay's, so as long as you follow best practices, you won't have to do all kinds of diffs and merges to integrate your changes back in. All you'll need to do is adjust your code to the realities of the new version of Liferay. These realities will likely include modified method signatures, classes refactored into other packages, replacement of one API with another, or replacement of one internal library with another.

Let's move on to how you use Ext to make Liferay customizations.

9.2 Ext in action

One look at the Liferay source code will tell you that it makes extensive use of Struts 1.x. Let's look at how Liferay uses Struts, and how you can therefore customize Liferay by taking advantage of some of the architecture of Struts.

> **Struts 1.x? Is this 2002, or what?**
>
> Um, no, not the last time I checked my calendar. Why does Liferay use Struts 1.x when there are so many other totally awesome Web 2.0, Ajax-enabled frameworks out there?
>
> Simple. When Liferay was first being developed in 2002, Struts 1.x was totally awesome. And for the use Liferay makes of it, it still is. The thinking in Liferay goes that because Struts 1.x works great, is lightweight and small, is extremely well-tested and stable, and isn't going anywhere, it's okay to use it. The latest stuff isn't always the greatest, after all, or most Fortune 500 businesses wouldn't still be running on Fortran. And besides, as a user of Liferay Portal, wouldn't you rather that Liferay concentrate on building more of the features you want into the product, rather than ripping out an architectural piece that nobody sees and replacing it with—well, something else—for no other reason except that the "something else" is newer? Believe me, there are far better ways for Liferay's engineers to spend their time. Struts 1.x is still in the product and will be for the foreseeable future.

In order to do that, of course, you need to understand Struts 1.x. And if you've ignored it in order to use one of those new, 1337 frameworks out there, you'll need an introduction.

9.2.1 Struts 101

This won't be an exhaustive introduction to Struts; you'll be much better served by picking up a book such as *Struts in Action* (Ted Husted et al, Manning Publications, 2002) for that. This will be something of a whirlwind tour, with notes about how Liferay uses Struts along the way.

STRUTS ACTIONS

The heart of Struts is its actions. Actions are defined as classes and are wired together with pages in a struts-config.xml file that resides in the WEB-INF folder of any web application, including Liferay. In its most basic form, the struts-config.xml file links actions to specific JSP pages, based on whether the action (such as adding a user) succeeded or failed.

Struts actions do something and then return a *forward*, which defines what page the user goes to after the action completes. In this way, the flow of the application can be controlled from a single file, the aforementioned struts-config.xml file.

In a normal web application, Struts actions are linked to paths on the URL. In Liferay, Struts action paths are attributes of the portlet URL. As a developer, it makes no difference; Liferay's extension of Struts handles this for you. These paths are read by Struts and then looked up in struts-config.xml. If a user clicks a link or submits a form that maps to one of these actions, the action class is then loaded and run, and it does its thing (which you define) and then finally returns a forward, which is also defined in struts-config.xml. The forward maps to a page where the user is sent as a result of whatever happened in the action. In this way, Struts enforces a strict MVC paradigm, where Struts itself is the controller.

The page flow logic can be extended with tiles, which Liferay also uses.

STRUTS TILES

Tiles are Struts' way of templating pages. In a web application, you may want to have a consistent header and footer on every page, and use just the center area of the page for content that changes based on user activity. Tiles allow you to accomplish that. You can divide your page into various sections (header, banner, side navigation, and so on) as shown in figure 9.3 and then assemble the various tiles into a whole page.

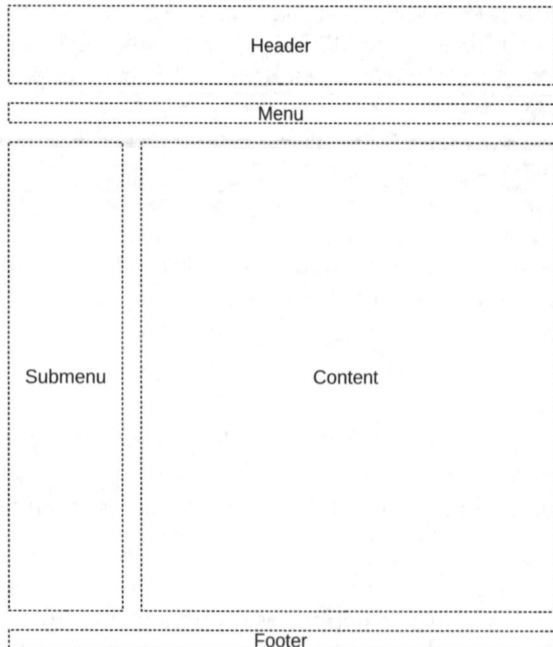

Figure 9.3 In a web application, tiles let you reuse navigation sections while replacing only the content section with the updated content from the Struts action.

Obviously, this makes no sense in a portal, but Liferay uses tiles so you don't have to refer to JSP pages directly. Basically, you can extend a set of tiles called *portlet* (see figure 9.4), which causes your JSP to be inserted into the body of a portlet where it belongs.

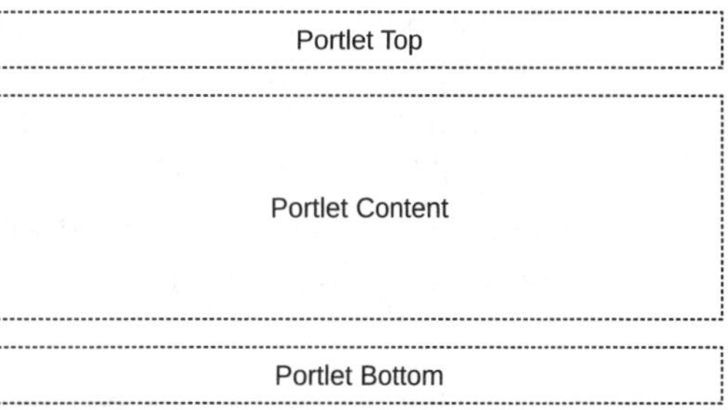

Figure 9.4 In Liferay's internal implementation, tiles are used to replace the portlet content with the markup generated by the portlet. The rest of the tile comes from the theme that draws the portlet window.

Tiles are configured in a separate file called tiles-defs.xml. In turn, you refer in the forward that results from your action to the appropriate tile in struts-config.xml. Struts then does the work of directing your users to the appropriate tile when your action completes.

That was your whirlwind tour. If you need more information about Struts, definitely pick up a good book on the subject. But this covers the basics you'll need for working with Struts in Liferay, so we'll move on to the specifics of customizing Liferay's Struts actions.

9.2.2 *Modifying a core portlet action*

As stated at the beginning of the chapter, the most common use for Ext is to customize the Struts actions used by Liferay's portlets. These actions predate the `MVCPortlet` you're used to from plugins, but they're sort of a precursor of it, because they work on the same principle. There are two differences. First, instead of a `jspPage` parameter, a `struts_action` parameter is generated that points to a Struts action defined in struts-config.xml. Second, each action is implemented as a separate class—although as you'll see in chapter 10, `MVCPortlet` actions can be implemented that way too.

> **Write your portlets as plugins!**
>
> Remember: you're only going to use Ext and Struts to *modify* existing Liferay portlets, right? If you have your own portlets to write, please write them as plugins. You can even write Struts portlets as plugins if you find that you like Struts. Liferay has a sample portlet you can check out to see how that works.

If you look at Liferay's source code, you'll see that all the portlets can be found under the `com.liferay.portlet` hierarchy somewhere. The Struts actions are clearly delineated in their own `action` package for each portlet, which makes it easy to find any particular portlet action. If, for example, you're feeling somewhat punchy and want to modify, say, the `BanUserAction` in the Message Boards portlet so that it emails the banned user, you can find this action in `com.liferay.portlet.messageboards.action`.

Liferay uses this naming convention throughout, so you'll have a consistent experience searching for actions to customize.

Action classes are first declared in struts-config-ext.xml and then implemented in the src folder of ext-impl. Taking our strategy of *extend, don't modify* and applying it to a change to `BanUserAction`, you declare the action in struts-config-ext.xml at the same path as the Liferay action, as shown:

```
<action
    path="/message_boards/ban_user"
    type="com.liferay.portlet.messageboards.action.InkwellBanUserAction">
        <forward
            name="portlet.message_boards.error"
            path="portlet.message_boards.error" />
</action>
```

Then you place the implementation in ext-impl/src:

```
public class InkwellBanUserAction
    extends BanUserAction {

        protected void banUser(ActionRequest actionRequest)
         throws Exception {

            String message = "You're banned, hoser!";
            sendMessage(message);
         super.banUser(actionRequest);

        }

        private void sendMessage(String message) {
            // Implement Java messaging stuff here

        }

}
```

And there you have it. Because you're extending Liferay's implementation (and not replacing it outright), there's not much code, because all you're doing is adding what you want and leaving the rest of the implementation to Liferay.

Beyond Struts actions, fewer and fewer extension points aren't covered by hooks as time goes on. In fact, even Struts actions can be customized in hooks in Liferay 6.1. Although this is the case, there are definitely some things you can't do with hooks, and for those, you should use Ext to get the job done.

9.2.3 Other extension points for the Ext plugin

Let's talk about some of these features that aren't yet supported by hooks. Unfortunately, because they don't break down into easy categories, you'll have to take them as a list. These are some of the most common things that are customized via the Ext plugin.

- *Listeners*—There are some listeners in Liferay that you have to implement in Ext. You'll always find the current list of listeners that are supported in the DTD for hooks. At the time of this writing, that list doesn't include all listeners. Some of the listeners you have to override in Ext are Velocity resource listeners and Journal (Web Content) transformer listeners.
- *Servlet filters*—If you need to add a new servlet filter to Liferay, this isn't supported with a hook. You need to use Ext. Put the configuration for your new servlet filter in Ext's web-ext.xml file. Liferay's deployer will take care of merging your configuration into Liferay's configuration at build time.
- *Permission checker*—You can override Liferay's permission-checking mechanism with a class of your own. This is defined in the property `permissions.checker`, which defines a class that handles permission checking for the portal. If you wish, you can implement a completely different permissions algorithm of your own, but you'll need to use Ext to do it.
- *Portal properties*—Some properties aren't yet supported by hooks, and Ext can help you customize them (the `permissions.checker` property just discussed is one of them). Adding sections to and removing them from the User profile is one of these properties (defined in the users.form.update.* properties). Always check the Hooks DTD to determine whether you can customize a property in a hook instead.
- *Core portlet changes*—We've already talked about changing their behavior through Struts actions, but you can also use the liferay-portlet-ext.xml file to redefine things like whether a portlet appears in the Control Panel and in what order, or to specify a new `AssetRenderer` (that you create). You can also use portlet-ext.xml to modify portlet preferences, such as the default feeds in the RSS portlet.

Many of these concepts should be familiar, because you've already implemented them for your own portlets. For more ideas, you can look at the default portal.properties file that ships with the Liferay source code. In the next section, I'll walk you through some of the internals of Liferay as it builds a page for the user; this discussion will hit a number of internal APIs that you may have a need to customize.

9.3 Delivering a page, Liferay style

As I'm sure you understand by now, Liferay and portal development are different from the traditional way of writing web applications. Instead of being concerned about the entire page, all you need to concentrate on is the portion of your page in which your portlet application resides. Liferay takes care of the rest. You can, of course, control the look and feel through themes and modify core parts of Liferay through hooks and Ext.

In the end, though, Liferay still needs to deliver a complete web page to the user. This page consists of whatever applications and content a user has placed there. How does Liferay do that? What does it go through to compose a page out of all those parts?

Let's raise the hood a bit and look at Liferay's inner workings. We'll start by assuming a user has just clicked a link or typed a URL to a site that is running on Liferay. It will definitely help if you have a copy of Liferay's source code handy; that way, you can follow along.

9.3.1 Struts? Again?

To help you follow this discussion, please refer to figure 9.5. I'm going to try to make it as clear as possible using analogies and whatever else I can, but following the picture will also help a lot. Here we go.

The first thing that happens when a browser hits a Liferay web site is a quick visit to the Friendly URL servlet ❶. This servlet is responsible for parsing the URL and translating the data it finds there into a page, or *layout*, within the site that corresponds to that URL. For example, the URL path /web/guest/home is the default page in a new Liferay installation. The Friendly URL servlet translates this into a call for a particular layout in Liferay. Internally, Liferay stores these as a `plid`, or portal layout ID. You'll see calls for a `plid` throughout Liferay's code, because it's a handy way to get a handle on a particular page. If you're a database person, it also helps to understand that it's the primary key of Liferay's Layout table.

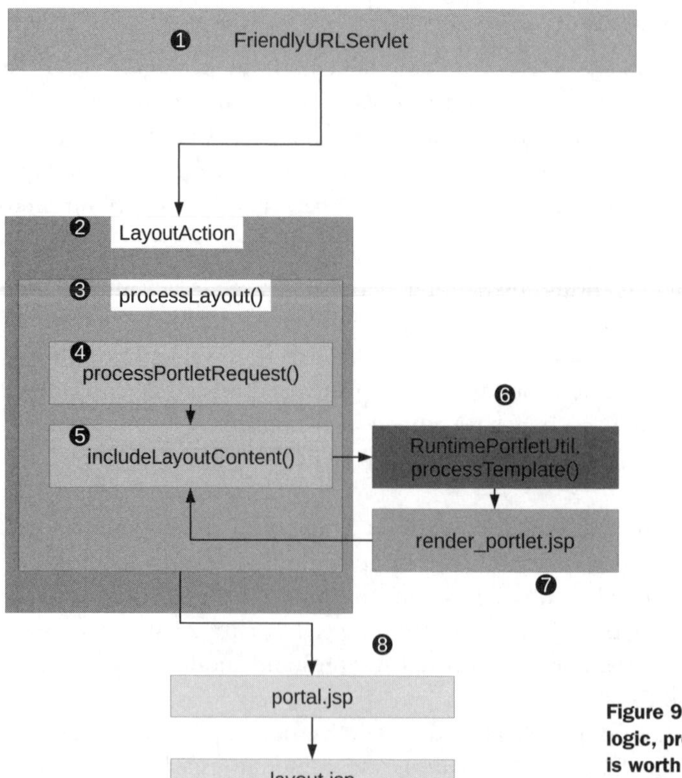

Figure 9.5 Liferay's page-processing logic, proving the old adage, "a picture is worth a thousand words." Well, maybe not in this case.

The Friendly URL servlet—and you'll see more about friendly URLs in the next chapter—translates the friendly URL into something like /c/portal/layout? plid=12345. This, in turn, maps to a Struts action called `LayoutAction` ❷.

> **NOTE** As you can see, Struts 1.x is integrated into Liferay at its core. Of course, this matters not a whit if you're using Liferay as a platform on which to build your site. It does matter if you're planning on customizing Liferay—you'll need to understand Struts. But as you'll see as we get deeper into this discussion, most of Liferay's core is separated into various utility classes that can just as easily be wired together using something other than Struts.

The `execute()`method of `LayoutAction` is called first. This gets the `plid` that had been parsed out by the Friendly URL servlet and passes it to another method (in the same class ❸) called `processLayout()`. When Liferay gets to this method, it finally starts doing something interesting.

The first thing it does is examine the request. Remember that portlets have a life cycle and that a request can be the result of either a portlet action or a render. In order to correctly process the request, Liferay needs to figure out what it is, so it does a check. If it's an action request, it calls another method called `processPortletRequest()` with a parameter called `PortletRequest.ACTION_PHASE` in order to process the action ❹. If it's a render request, it calls the same method with a different parameter indicating that it should do a render.

After the phases complete, the same method (`processPortletRequest()`) calls the `includeLayoutContent()` method ❺. We could stop here, because this method, through various means, processes all the portlets on the page. When this is finished, the Struts action can complete and forward processing to a JSP for final display. Of course, if we stopped here, we wouldn't be doing a very deep dive, so let's examine this method further to see what it does.

9.3.2 Layers and layers

As you can tell (because I keep making analogies to them), I like science fiction movies. Here comes another analogy—if you've seen the movie *Inception*, you'll relate. We're going down deep, through several layers of processing. Hang onto your hat; I'll provide the "kick" you need to wake up from each layer. Your kick for waking up from the first layer is simple: you'll be thrown a huge, heavy ball of data that you'll attempt to catch but that will instead knock you over backward. Let's go down into the first layer, which takes us one level deeper than the Struts action.

PROCESSING LAYOUT TEMPLATES

`includeLayoutContent()` dispatches out to a JSP called portlet.jsp (in the /portal /layout/view folder in Liferay's HTML directory). This JSP is more like a Java class than a JSP: it mainly contains Java code that drives the theme of the page as well as its layout template. After initializing these, it processes them ❻ using a static method of a utility class called `RuntimePortletUtil`. This class contains methods that execute portlets or groups of portlets in a layout template at runtime (hence the name `RuntimePortletUtil`).

The method called in this class is `processTemplate()`. It gets a `TemplateProcessor` based on the layout template for the current page. This is an object that knows how to parse the elements in a layout template—the portlets as well as the order in which they appear in various columns of the template. This object can get a collection of the portlets that are on the page; and when it has that, it can call the portlets one by one in the order in which they appear.

That's exactly what happens next. In a `for` loop, Liferay goes through each portlet and calls `processPortlet()` on it. This method calls `PortalUtil.renderPortlet()` to do the actual render of the portlet; but rather than render the portlet within the method, it requires you to dive deeper into another level, because it dispatches out to a JSP to do the actual render. Your kick for waking up from this next level is that you'll be spun around and around so many times that the resulting dizziness will cause you to become disoriented. As soon as this happens, you'll suddenly be pushed into wakefulness.

RENDERING THE PORTLETS

The JSP that you land in ❼ is called render_portlet.jsp, and it resides in Liferay's /html/portal folder. The actual render of a portlet is implemented as a large script in a JSP in order to easily assemble multiple dynamic UI elements and then wrap the portlet's output in them. Although by the time of publication the line number may have changed, the portlet render occurs at approximately line 720 of this JSP. The rest of the script does a number of things:

- Finds out what portlet modes and window states the portlet supports
- Checks to see whether the user has permission to access the portlet
- Looks up portlet context objects, such as `PortletConfig` and `PortletPreferences`
- Figures out what (if any) portlet window icons (edit, minimize, maximize) should be displayed
- Creates portlet window URLs to invoke portlet modes (edit, help)
- Invokes the portlet class and caches its result in a `String`
- Wraps the portlet's content in the theme's layout

All this processing results in a simple `String` containing the HTML from the theme, the layout template, and the portlet. Remember, render_portlet.jsp is called as part of a `for` loop, which comes back around again and processes another portlet, and around again to process another, and another, and another, in a dizzying stream of HTML spinning into `String` existence until you're not sure whether up is down or down is up and—*kick*! You wake up from this level and look around. Where are you?

DELIVERING THE GENERATED PAGE

You're back in `RuntimePortletUtil` ❻. As you turn around, you see a `for` loop having completed its processing, which resulted in a gigantic, boulder-like ball of data.

This ball is fearsome, because it contains a layout template filled with portlets—a huge mass of HTML and JavaScript, generated by a layout template and multiple portlet developers. The `for` loop whips this ball at you at a speed you thought was impossible. You can't dodge it. You can't deflect it. All you can hope to do is catch it and maybe slow its velocity with your body. At the last second, you brace yourself, and the ball slams into your torso as your arms wrap around it. But it's too fast and too heavy, and you feel its momentum pushing you backward until you lose your balance, falling, falling—*kick*! Your eyes open, revealing a nice, warm, comfortable room. Where are you?

RETURNING THE COMPLETED LAYOUT

You're back in that good old Struts action ❷, where you're safe. All the Struts action needs to do, now that it has all the content it needs, is show that content to the user. The `includeLayoutContent()` method receives all this data and puts it into a request attribute called `WebKeys.LAYOUT_CONTENT` before returning to the `processLayout()` method, which finally forwards to the `portal.layout` tile. Recall from our whirlwind Struts tour that tiles are a way of using templates to create web sites in Struts. The tile you've been forwarded to ❽ is layout.jsp, which inherits from portal.jsp. This combination executes the theme's portal_normal.vm/ftl/jsp and then dumps that huge ball of content by printing the contents of `WebKeys.LAYOUT_CONTENT` onto the page. This page is delivered to the user's browser so the user can interact with it.

That's how Liferay builds a page and delivers it to the user. I understand if perhaps you want to take a break from reading; if so, please do so with the knowledge that the rest of this chapter won't have any code in it. Instead, now that you've been exposed to all of Liferay's plugin types, we can talk about when to use which type. Next, I'll share some best practices for Liferay development.

9.4 Understanding Liferay development best practices

Your Liferay development options largely depend on the kind of project you have. If you're looking to completely customize Liferay, you'll be interested in activities relating to accessing Liferay's functionality. If you want to use Liferay out of the box and add your own portlets and themes to it, you'll be interested in portlet development and the tools and utilities in the platform that can speed up your development. And many developers want to do both. Liferay is unique in that the level of customization it provides is limitless, and it's purposefully designed that way—but you can tiptoe in one step at a time. With that in mind, let's look at some best practices for doing development on Liferay's platform.

9.4.1 Practices for developing applications

Because you're reading this book, your web site requires some custom development to get off the ground—the built-in features of Liferay probably cover a lot of what you want to do, but not all of it. If that's the case, it's best to start your site implementation by writing any applications that are required in order to create a unique user experience. Whether these are social applications, games, or productivity applications, set your unique functionality apart by developing and deploying your applications first. There will be plenty of time to work on configuring message boards, wikis, and web content later.

The next thing you'll want to tackle is your theme. You can easily implement your own web design in a theme project using your HTML, CSS, and JavaScript skills, and then deploy that design to Liferay Portal. As you saw in chapter 8, sometimes you can optimize things by placing reusable JavaScript from your portlet (and hook) applications in your theme. Because you've already finished your applications, you can take time during theme development to make those optimizations. And if any of your portlets are designed to appear on every page, you can go ahead and embed them in your theme.

When you have your applications and your theme humming along, you can then turn to customizations. Whether you use Liferay's Plugins SDK from the command line or in an IDE, my experience is that most portal projects can be implemented without the use of Ext plugins. Liferay's out-of-the-box feature set for organizing your portal's resources, such as users, communities, organization hierarchies, and user groups, plus its robust security and integration features, makes it an ideal development platform for your application and rarely requires customization.

As Liferay evolves, the need for Ext lessens

If you've used previous releases of Liferay, this will seem like a departure. And you're correct, because the old Ext environment had a prominent role in Liferay development. This is no longer the case, and I encourage you to use the other plugin types.

Even if some of these features require customizations, in most instances this can be done with a hook plugin.

9.4.2 Practices for customizing Liferay

Liferay can be customized using either hook plugins or Ext plugins. My advice is to try doing all your customizations as hooks if possible. Hooks provide a much better separation of functionality than Ext does, because they're hot-deployable, they don't overwrite existing Liferay components, and they can be undeployed as easily as they're deployed.

If you find something you can't do in a hook—maybe you need to customize a property that isn't yet supported by hooks, extend an internal Liferay class, implement a custom `PermissionChecker`, or extend a Liferay Struts action—you can use the Ext plugin to do this. Because Ext plugins aren't as easy to use as hook plugins, you should try to keep your code in Ext plugins to a minimum. Yes, technically, you can have more than one Ext plugin if you wanted to, but after knowing what it does (overlays

Liferay code in the Liferay install itself), do you really want to put yourself through keeping track of multiple changes to Liferay through multiple Ext plugins? No, I didn't think you'd want to do that. So try to keep it down to one Ext plugin, and try to keep that plugin relegated to only what is necessary to do in Ext. This won't always be possible, but it's a good goal to shoot for.

Migrate your portlets out of Ext and into plugins

If you're migrating from an older version of Liferay, you can convert your old Ext environment to an Ext plugin. The procedure for doing so is outlined in the *Liferay Portal Administrator's Guide* (6.0) or *Using Liferay Portal* (6.1). Any portlets you've created there will still work for the time being, but you need to be aware that portlets in Ext have been deprecated in the 6.0 release, and support for them is removed in the 6.1 release.

Portlet plugins are a much easier to use option anyway. Portlets written in the Ext plugin aren't hot-deployable like portlet plugins, so you need to restart the server after deploying. And because code from Ext plugins overlays the code in Liferay, you can't have more than one Ext plugin that contains a struts-config-ext.xml file, and you have to put all your portlets into one big, monolithic Ext project.

If you're upgrading from an old version of Liferay, one of the first things you should do as a developer is migrate your portlets out of Ext and into plugins.

Note that if your project requires customization at a deep level, Liferay makes it easier than any other portal product to customize your project to whatever level you may require with Ext plugins. This is the one great benefit of Ext—it truly gives you Great Power. But that power needs to be tempered with great responsibility, which is why I've harped so much on the exact use cases for Ext. You go beyond them to your peril. How do you decide when to use which plugin? I've created a simple way to do that.

9.4.3 *Deciding if you need Ext*

When it comes time to design your portal project, before you write a line of code, you can decide whether your requirements make it necessary to use an Ext plugin or if you can use a combination of the other types of plugins. Remember that extending Liferay's functionality is rarely required, and so it's likely that your project can be implemented using Liferay's core functionality with custom portlets and theme(s) added to it. If at all possible, you should try doing everything without Ext plugins, because that will definitely make your life easier when upgrading. Sometimes this isn't possible, and that's why Ext is there. But you should approach this exercise by seeing what you can do to minimize your use of Ext.

Making this decision is a straightforward process of asking yourself the questions listed in table 9.2. Place a checkmark in the far-right column if you answer "yes" to a question.

Table 9.2 These questions form the decision-making process for your development project. This process enables you systematically to determine how best to approach developing your project on Liferay's platform.

Assessment question	Example	✔
Does your project require integration with other products that Liferay doesn't yet support?	You're writing a new implementation class to connect Liferay's Document Library to another JSR-170 compliant repository, or implementing support for a single sign-on solution that Liferay doesn't yet provide.	
Is the algorithm Liferay uses for a particular piece of functionality inappropriate for your organization?	If Liferay is configured to export a user's account to an LDAP directory, the export occurs every time the user logs in. If this would put undue stress on your LDAP server because you have millions of logins per second (I know this is an exaggeration), you may want to change this behavior.	
Do you need to change the behavior of one of Liferay's built-in portlets in a way that's not supported by a hook?	You need to change the logic of a Struts action in one of the built-in portlets.	
Would your changes be a useful addition to the product?	A change may enhance the product in a way that is usable by other organizations.	

Figure 9.6 illustrates that if you have at least one checkmark, you need to use the Ext plugin to implement at least some of your functionality. But this functionality may be just a small piece of your project. It's still likely that most of your project will consist of custom portlet plugins, a hook or two, and at least one theme.

If you have two checkmarks, you may want to consider one of two options (as shown in figure 9.6):

- *Contact Liferay to sponsor the development of your feature in the core product.* You may want to consider this option you're working on a project with a budget. You may be able save on consulting time or development time by taking advantage of Liferay's Sponsored Development program. You can give your requirements to Liferay, and the company will implement the feature as part of the core portal. Going forward, Liferay will be responsible for maintaining this feature in future versions of the product and will have to fix all the bugs, saving you a lot of work. Many organizations have saved both time and money on their own projects this way.
- *Implement the feature yourself and, because Liferay is open source, contribute it back to the project.* This option gives you the same benefits as sponsored development: if the feature is accepted, Liferay becomes responsible for maintaining it (you can continue contributing to the feature too) in future versions of the product.

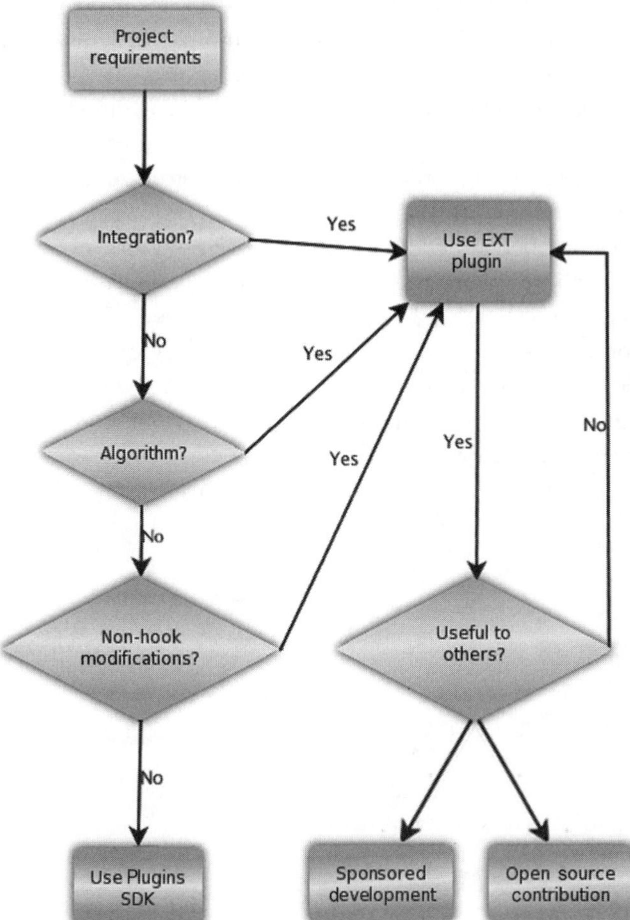

Figure 9.6 Use this flowchart to decide how to approach your development project.

You can find out how to go about either option by looking in appendix D.

If you do need to use the Ext plugin, remember to use it for customizing Liferay only, and only for those customizations that can't be done using hooks.

Regardless of whether you need Ext plugins, Liferay gives you a fantastic platform for creating beautiful, dynamic web sites.

9.5 Summary

Ext plugins provide an unparalleled customization experience for developers, allowing you to change anything in Liferay to operate the way you want it to. Although hooks are powerful, nothing gives you as much power to customize Liferay as Ext plugins. You do need to be careful how you use it, though, in order to create more easily maintained code.

Some of the most common reasons to use the Ext environment in Liferay 6.0 include customizing Struts actions, adding various listeners, adding servlet filters to

Liferay, implementing your own permission checker, and so on. You can deploy Ext to any application server that Liferay supports. You should now feel comfortable navigating the Ext environment and using it to make customizations.

Next, we took a deep dive into Liferay and saw what it does to compose a complete web page out of themes, layout templates, and portlets. The idea is to give you a glimpse of Liferay behind the curtain—there's so much to customize in Ext that a simple list of possibilities isn't enough.

Finally, we looked at some best practices for portal development. You saw how best to begin a project and start implementing the features you need in your site, by using portlets first, then themes, and then hooks and (if you need them) Ext plugins.

We also outlined some ways you can examine a project to determine whether you can accomplish the task with portlets, themes, and hooks only, or if you also need to use Ext plugins. You saw a good strategy for using Ext plugins that keeps complexity down.

You can now handle just about any Liferay project that comes your way. In the final chapter, we'll look at some of Liferay's APIs that you can use in any plugin type to make your life easier.

10 A tour of Liferay APIs

This chapter covers

- Simplifying addresses with friendly URLs
- Organizing larger applications with `ActionCommand`s
- Filtering permissions at the view level
- Using multiple databases with Service Builder
- Sending messages and scheduling jobs
- Indexing data

A couple of nights ago, my daughter was playing with a toy robot that her grandfather gave her for Christmas. It has a remote control, and you can make it move around and do some tricks. It has sensors, so it knows when it bumps into something, and it has a demo mode in which it plays music and dances. As she was messing with the robot and trying to get it to do what she wanted, I began to reflect on how much better the robot *I* had was, when I was a kid. I loved it so much that it was the one and only toy I refused to allow my mother to give to charity when I grew out of it. I've kept it all these years, safely ensconced in my basement. Somewhere.

I began to tell my daughter about my robot, and immediately she stopped what she was doing and wanted to go down into the basement and search for it. Finding the robot was easy. Finding the tape cartridges it used was more difficult, but eventually we prevailed, and up the stairs I went, proudly displaying my prize to my wife: a 2-XL robot, carefully preserved since about 1980.

Figure 10.1 A vintage 2-XL robot. (GPL-ed image courtesy of Wikipedia.) As noted, the face on my robot has yellowed, and I wanted you to see it the way it's supposed to look.

For those of you in the know, a vintage 2-XL robot is nothing more than an 8-track tape player in a plastic robot chassis, with four individual buttons that switch the tracks (see figure 10.1). This system was used ingeniously to create many "programs" that made the robot ask children questions, play games, sing songs, and generally create a lot of fun. To answer a question or provide input to the robot, you pushed one of the buttons, which switched the track on the 8-track tape player; if you were on the right track, the robot told you that you answered the question correctly.

This was easily my most favorite toy I'd ever owned, and I carefully unpacked it. Looking at 2-XL's now-yellowed face brought back some childhood excitement; I took it into the bathroom, where I cleaned the tape head and capstan with alcohol and Q-tips. Hope mounted as I set it up on the dining room table and plugged it in. I inserted the first tape I'd ever used with it (the one it came with), called *General Information*, and then I turned it on.

It worked!

For the next hour, I showed my daughter how to use my old 2-XL and watched the delight on her face as she proceeded to enjoy the toy every bit as much as I had when I was small. As I perused my tape library for the robot (incomplete, but still with some good titles), I began to reflect on the difference between this robot and the one my daughter received for Christmas, now lying on the family room floor, forgotten.

The new robot is filled with sophisticated electronics. It can move, interact with its environment, make all kinds of sounds, and be controlled via remote. In every way, from a technical perspective, it's superior to 2-XL. But it has one major design flaw, which makes it in practical terms far inferior to 2-XL: it's a one-trick pony. After you've exhausted everything it can do (which is kind of limited), it's done. It sits in a pile of other toys, unused, because, well, kids have been known to pretty much define the phrase, "Been there, done that, moving on."

2-XL, however, boasts somewhat different interactivity—it doesn't move, but it talks to you, tells jokes, sings, and is all-around friendly.[1] If you get bored with one tape, you

[1] If you haven't had the benefit of playing with one, I highly recommend the 2-XL simulator, here: www.donationcoder.com/Software/Mouser/2XL/index.html

can try another, and 2-XL becomes something completely different. It's expandable: sports, stories, games, you name it. Even though 2-XL was released in the 1970s and is much simpler than today's robots, it can do much more.

I've been saying throughout this book that Liferay is more than just a product you can download and use: it's an entire development *platform*, filled with functionality just waiting to be tapped. It's not a one-trick pony: when you've exhausted its built-in capabilities, you can use the platform to make Liferay do anything you want. You've already seen a lot of that functionality and how to use it to build applications, rich content stores, and social web sites.

In this chapter, we're going to look at a bunch of APIs Liferay gives you to make your job easier. These include everything from small enhancements to your portlets to unexpected architectural niceties that help you to more easily manage your code. And the cool thing about using the APIs is the simplicity: many of the features in Liferay (as you've seen with the social API and assets) work in the same patterns, making the APIs easy to learn.

Let's get started looking at these APIs. As we go through them, you'll see immediately how they can benefit your applications and web sites. Many of the examples will enhance the Slogan Contest portlet from chapter 7. We'll begin with a couple of things you can use to enhance your portlet applications.

10.1 Making URLs friendly

When I introduced portlets to you, I stated that developers don't have control over the URL in a portal environment in the same way they have control in a regular web application. Of course, that was back when you were a beginner on Liferay's platform. Now you're free to open that up the same way English grammar was opened up to me at the college level. Everybody who took grammar in high school knows that you should never, under any circumstances, end a sentence with a preposition. In reality, this is a rule derived from Latin grammar foisted upon the English language. Those with more experience know that it's more of a guideline than a rule—a thing of style rather than usage. Churchill famously pointed this out by stating, "That is a rule up with which I shall not put." In other words, sometimes following the rule makes things awkward.

Similarly, portal URLs, because they're automatically generated, tend to be pretty awkward, like this:

```
http://localhost:8080/web/guest/home?p_p_id=slogancontest_WAR_slogancontest
➥ portlet&p_p_lifecycle=0&p_p_state=normal&p_p_mode=view&p_p_col_id=
➥ column-2&p_p_col_pos=1&p_p_col_count=2&_slogancontest_WAR_
➥ slogancontestportlet_jspPage=/html/edit_slogan.jsp
```

That's the URL the portal generates when you click the Add Slogan button in the Slogan Contest portlet. As you can see, there are a lot of parameters that tell the portal different things (see table 10.1).

Table 10.1 Anatomy of a Liferay URL

Parameter	Meaning
p_p_id	The portlet ID, derived from the portlet name in portlet.xml.
p_p_lifecycle	The life cycle stage of the current request. Because you just clicked the Add Slogan button, this is a render request (0).
p_p_state	The state the portlet's in: normal, maximized, or minimized.
p_p_mode	The mode the portlet's in: view, edit, or help.
p_p_col_id	References the ID of the column in the layout template where the portlet is located.
p_p_col_pos	The position in the column where the portlet is located.
p_p_col_count	The number of columns in the layout.
[p_p_id]_jspPage	Any parameter prefixed with the portlet ID is a parameter set by that portlet. In this instance, you'd set `jspPage`, which `MVCPortlet` uses to define page flow.

Does the user really need to see all these parameters? No. And it turns out Liferay *does* give you some control over the URL and what it displays. Look at what the Blogs portlet does, using an example entry from liferay.com:

```
http://www.liferay.com/web/raymond.auge/blog/-/blogs/
➥ advanced-web-content-example-with-ajax
```

Human-readable URLs are better, aren't they? At a glance, you can see that this blog entry is on the profile of my friend Ray Augé, it's on his Blog page, and the blog entry is called "Advanced Web Content Example with Ajax." This is a much better URL than the first one, and the great thing is that you can do this just as easily as Liferay does it for the internal portlets.

10.1.1 Declaring the mapper

The first thing you need to do to make your URLs friendly is to declare a friendly URL mapper. As you might imagine, this is done by placing an entry in the liferay-portlet.xml file, and it looks like this:

```
<friendly-url-mapper-class>
    com.liferay.portal.kernel.portlet.DefaultFriendlyURLMapper
</friendly-url-mapper-class>

<friendly-url-mapping>
    slogan_contest
</friendly-url-mapping>
```

```
<friendly-url-routes>
    com/inkwell/internet/slogan/portlet/slogan-friendly-url-routes.xml
</friendly-url-routes>
```

You can place this configuration directly under the `<icon>` tags in liferay-portlet.xml. You're declaring three things:

- Mapper class
- Mapping
- Route

The mapper class defines the logic for how to map friendly URLs to regular Liferay URLs. In 99.9999% of instances, you'll use the `DefaultFriendlyURLMapper` class that Liferay provides, along with a route that you specify in an XML file. For the .0001% of you out there who are gluttons for punishment, you can provide your own implementation by extending `BaseFriendlyURLMapper` the way `DefaultFriendlyURLMapper` does, but I can't see a reason why you would want to do that.

The mapping is a name by which this route can be identified, and the route is a file that describes how to map various parameters to a more friendly look. Let's see how to map your decidedly unfriendly URLs to friendly ones.

10.1.2 Making the unfriendly URL friendly

To do the mapping, you have to look at the URLs you generate in your application. Let's use the Slogan Contest portlet as an example (see figure 10.2).

In this portlet, the main screen has three URLs:

- The Add Slogan button
- The Search container, allowing the viewing of slogans
- The Edit Slogan action button

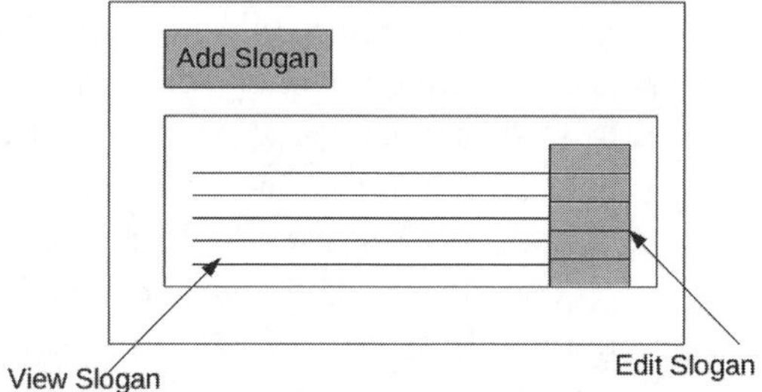

Figure 10.2 These are the three main places you have URLs in the Slogan Contest portlet.

If you click each of these URLs, you'll find that many parameters are generated on the URL that you can map to something friendlier. These are listed in table 10.1. Let's look at how you can map these in your slogan-friendly-url-routes.xml file (see the next listing). By convention, you place this file in the same Java package as your portlet class.

Listing 10.1 Routing URLs

```
<?xml version="1.0"?>
<!DOCTYPE routes PUBLIC "-//Liferay//DTD Friendly URL Routes 6.0.0//EN"
➥ "http://www.liferay.com/dtd/liferay-friendly-url-routes_6_0_0.dtd">

<routes>

  <route>                                                    Edit route
    <pattern>/{resourcePrimKey:\d+}/edit</pattern>
```

```
    <implicit-parameter name="p_p_lifecycle">0</implicit-parameter>
    <implicit-parameter name="jspPage">
        /html/edit_slogan.jsp
    </implicit-parameter>
  </route>

  <route>                                                    <-- Add route
    <pattern>/add</pattern>
    <implicit-parameter name="p_p_lifecycle">0</implicit-parameter>
    <implicit-parameter name="jspPage">
        /html/edit_slogan.jsp
    </implicit-parameter>
  </route>

  <route>                                                    <-- View route
    <pattern>/{resourcePrimKey:\d+}/view</pattern>
    <implicit-parameter name="p_p_lifecycle">0</implicit-parameter>
    <implicit-parameter name="p_p_state">maximized</implicit-parameter>
    <implicit-parameter name="jspPage">
        /html/view_slogan.jsp
    </implicit-parameter>
  </route>

</routes>
```

docroot/WEB-INF/src/com/inkwell/internet/slogan/portlet/slogan-friendly-url-routes.xml

Each route starts with a pattern. This is the URL as it will look to the user. Friendly URLs redefine the query string normally part of a URL into a series of values separated by slashes. Each value, by virtue of its position, can be parsed out by the `FriendlyURLServlet` in Liferay to the real parameter list that normally would be generated by the portlet. The friendly URL must contain all the necessary information the portlet requires for navigating to the data that user is browsing. For example, the `add` URL has nothing but the word *add* in it. This is unique within the routes, and when Liferay sees this route, it can look up the parameters that belong to that route. Because this route maps to the `jspPage` render parameter that `MVCPortlet` requires for navigating to the JSP for adding slogans, this parameter can be supplied to the portlet without showing it to the user, and so the portlet still works correctly.

Notice that you've also added some *implicit parameters.* These are parameters that Liferay tends to add to the parameter list, and they logically have to be there. Why not just tell Liferay to assume they're in the list, so it doesn't have to add them? As the developer of this portlet, you *know* the URL you generated for the `add` function is a render URL. There's no reason Liferay has to generate that on the parameter list—it should assume it. That's why you make `p_p_lifecycle` equal to `0`–the zero means a render request. It's an implicit parameter, because it will always be this way for this URL.

What if you have variable data that you want to pass through?

10.1.3 Passing parameters with friendly URLs

As you can see, the `pattern` tag defines placeholders for various fields that would normally appear in the query string. You can also stick in there a field that normally holds data you use to retrieve stuff from the database. In fact, the `view` and `edit` routes are slightly different because of exactly that.

In both of these, you pass the primary key of the entity from the database through, with either `/view` or `/edit` to denote which URL it is. In order to do this, you declare the original field name that would have been in the query string along with a placeholder for its value, separated by a colon. The placeholder is a regular expression that matches the type of data the value should be. Because primary keys in Liferay are `long`s, you use the regular expression to match only digits.

To make sense of this, let's look at a specific example: the view URL that you generate in the search container of the Slogan Contest portlet. The code for that URL is in the JSP, and it looks like this:

```
<portlet:renderURL windowState="maximized" var="rowURL">
  <portlet:param name="jspPage" value="/html/view_slogan.jsp" />
  <portlet:param
      name="resourcePrimKey"
      value="<%= String.valueOf(slogan.getSloganId()) %>" />
</portlet:renderURL>
```

As you can see, you set several parameters that, in their original form, wind up in the query string: the window state (always set to maximized), the `jspPage` parameter so `MVCPortlet` knows where to direct the user, and the `resourcePrimKey` parameter, which contains the `sloganId` so you can get it out of the database.

Now look at the view pattern you created for the friendly URL from listing 10.1:

```
<route>
  <pattern>/{resourcePrimKey:\d+}/view</pattern>
  <implicit-parameter name="p_p_lifecycle">0</implicit-parameter>
  <implicit-parameter name="p_p_state">maximized</implicit-parameter>
  <implicit-parameter name="jspPage">
      /html/view_slogan.jsp
  </implicit-parameter>
</route>
```

It sets a pattern that places the primary key (the `resourcePrimKey` field) in the first placeholder. The second placeholder is the view label. Implicit to this URL is a render (`p_p_lifecycle=0`) and a maximized portlet state (`p_p_state=maximized`). And of course, this URL should also have `jspPage` set to `/html/view_slogan.jsp`, because that's the view that should be loaded. All these parameters are static except the first one, which contains whatever primary key you're looking for. This route generates a URL like this one:

```
http://localhost:8080/web/guest/home/-/slogan_contest/5/view
```

Much friendlier, isn't it?

I'm sure you can see benefits other than the URLs being friendlier to the user. One benefit of friendly URLs is that they obfuscate the components of your application. Do your users really need to know that the JSP for viewing slogans is view_slogan.jsp and that it's stored in a directory called /html somewhere in your web application? Of course not. Friendly URLs can help you mask the fact that you're using JSPs, Java, or even Liferay, because your URLs become rather RESTful and generic. In fact, if you wanted to add a finder to your application that finds slogans by the text of the slogan, you could generate an even friendlier URL:

```
http://localhost:8080/web/guest/home/-/slogan_contest/pens_are_great/view
```

Although they're optional, friendly URLs are a great addition to your application, after you've completed writing it. I highly recommend that you use them. Next, we'll look at a facility `MVCPortlet` gives you for corralling lots of actions in big applications.

10.2 Organizing larger applications

After all the discussions we've had about frameworks, one thing should be clear: MVC is usually the design pattern of choice for web applications. And as you've seen, Liferay uses MVC internally—with Struts at its core—and also provides its own MVC framework for portlet applications. One thing that's cool about Struts and other MVC frameworks is the ability to move individual actions into separate classes. If you didn't have this ability and you had a large, complex application, all your actions would have to be in your portlet class, resulting in a single, large Java file containing many methods. When you have something like this in an application, it can be difficult for other developers to follow the application's logic. For this reason, it's a good idea to break up larger applications into smaller components that are easier to follow, especially if other developers need to get up to speed on your code. One way to do this is to split your actions out into separate classes. This makes a large application that has a lot of actions much easier to follow.

> **A matter of preference**
>
> Some developers like breaking functionality out into multiple components; some don't. I was once tasked with providing an enhancement to an application that was written by somebody else. Along the way, I also refactored some of the code to break it into smaller parts, because I found it hard to follow the way it was written. Later, I heard that the original developer wasn't pleased with what I had done.
>
> I still maintain that I made the application easier for other developers to understand. But maybe it would've been better to ask first.

`MVCPortlet` has this ability too; I didn't use it previously in this book because the example applications were on the small side, and separating out the actions would've been overkill. But I don't want the limitations of the examples to affect the developer who wants to build something big like an airline reservation system on Liferay. I want to make sure I introduce you to `ActionCommands`.

10.2.1 Conventions instead of configuration

In many MVC frameworks, the framework is configured by creating XML files or by using annotations. Liferay eschews all that by simplifying everything into naming conventions. This is a better philosophy, because once you learn the convention, you know how everything works, and you don't have to clutter your application with unnecessary configuration and noise in your code.

There is, however, one piece of configuration that you need to do in order to turn this on. It's something you've already done in `MVCPortlet` to tell the class which JSP file to load by default when switching portlet modes: add a special initialization parameter. The one you need to add is called `action.package.prefix`, and it points to the package where you'll put your actions.

To take advantage of `ActionCommands`, add the following initialization parameter to your portlet.xml file:

```
<init-param>
  <name>action.package.prefix</name>
  <value>com.myorg.myapp.portlet.action</value>
</init-param>
```

Of course, you would substitute your package in the place of the earlier package. When this is done, you're free to begin implementing your actions.

`MVCPortlet` knows to look for actions in the package you've defined, but there's a two-pronged approach: your actions also need to have the `-ActionCommand` suffix, and they have to implement the `ActionCommand` interface. If you decided to separate out your action that edits slogans, you'd need to name the class `EditSloganActionCommand`.

Let's see what this looks like when you put everything together.

10.2.2 *Implementing an ActionCommand*

Now you have all the information you need in order to separate your actions out into separate classes. Let's look at what one of these would look like, by refactoring one of the actions from the Slogan Contest portlet (see the following listing).

Listing 10.2 A simple `ActionCommand`

```
public class DeleteSloganActionCommand implements ActionCommand {     <-- ActionCommand interface

    public boolean processCommand(
            PortletRequest request, PortletResponse response)
        throws PortletException {                                     <-- Implements processCommand

        long sloganKey = ParamUtil.getLong(request, "resourcePrimKey");

        if (Validator.isNotNull(sloganKey)) {
            try {
                SloganLocalServiceUtil.deleteSlogan(sloganKey);
            }
            catch (PortalException e) {
                SessionErrors.add(request, "error-deleting");
                return false;
            }
            catch (SystemException e) {
                SessionErrors.add(request, "error-deleting");
                return false;
```

```
            }
            SessionMessages.add(request, "slogan-deleted");
            return true;                                    <-- Returns true for success
        }
        else {
            SessionErrors.add(request, "error-deleting");
            return false;                                   <-- Returns false for failure
        }
    }
}
```

docroot/WEB-INF/src/com/inkwell/internet/slogan/actions/DeleteSloganActionCommand.java

As you can see, the action is pretty much the same as it was when it was in the portlet class. The only difference is that when you extract it, you need to place your logic inside a `processCommand()` method, and that method needs to return a simple Boolean for success or failure.

Using `ActionCommands`, you can make larger applications a lot easier for other developers to follow. You should definitely use them if you have a lot of actions, or if you're working on a single, large application with a team of developers.

Next, you'll see how to enhance your portlets to filter content based on permissions.

10.3 Filtering content at the view level

Historically, Liferay's permissions system has been rather complicated. Although it's incredibly robust, it has gone through several iterations to get it to perform well.

The problem has always been that permission checks required a number of JOINs in the database. This, as you might imagine, can become expensive in terms of performance; and so, over the years, newer and better algorithms were developed. With Liferay 6, the product turns to a new permissions scheme that requires far fewer JOINs in the database. If you're starting with Liferay 6 or higher, you get to start fresh with the new algorithm. If you've upgraded from a previous release, no doubt you've had to run through the permissions conversion process outlined in Liferay's *Portal Administrator's Guide* (6.0) or *Using Liferay Portal* (6.1) to convert your installation to algorithm 6. This new algorithm brings some fantastic performance benefits, but it also brings some benefits to the developer. Let me illustrate.

If you have any experience with Liferay as a user, you've probably seen something like figure 10.3 when trying to access a resource that is protected by permissions.

Figure 10.3 You saw an item in a list. You clicked it because you must have access to it, right? Nope. This is what you see instead. Not very friendly, is it?

Because permission checking was such an expensive operation in the past, Liferay didn't support view-level permission filtering. In other words, resources that were protected by permissions were still displayed as the result of a query, and the permission check happened only when a user clicked the resource.

This, obviously, isn't optimal, nor is it expected by the user. Who wants to see something that's clickable, only to find out you don't have permission to view it after you click it? Well, this doesn't have to happen anymore, now that you have algorithm 6 and Service Builder that's fully integrated with it. This functionality isn't turned on by default, to preserve existing expectations on the part of Liferay developers. But if you need this feature in your application, it's easy to add view-level permission filtering with a few simple modifications to the methods you call in the service layer. If you have a use case that requires view-level permission filtering, you can easily modify your queries to support it. Let's again use the Slogan Contest portlet as an example.

In the service layer, you made the following call in `SloganLocalServiceImpl` to get `Slogans` out of the database:

```
List<Slogan> slogans = sloganPersistence.findByG_S(groupId, status,
➥ start, end, obc);
```

This is how you retrieved `Slogans` by `groupId` and `Status`. And this is how you change it so that view-level permission filtering is enabled—I almost wish I could be there to see your reaction, because it's so easy:

```
List<Slogan> moreSlogans = sloganPersistence.filterFindByG_S(groupId,
➥ status, start, end, obc);
```

That's all there is to it. The hard work is done for you by Service Builder and algorithm 6. As Forrest Gump would say, that's all I have to say about that. When users view a search container powered by this query, items that they don't have permission to see won't appear in the list.

Next, you'll look at how you can use Service Builder to help with data in another database.

10.4 Accessing other databases

When building your web site, I hope you've appreciated how incredibly convenient it is to use Service Builder. This utility is fantastic when building your site from scratch. But what about existing data? Can you access existing data with Service Builder? Of course you can! It's not as easy as starting with your application from scratch, but considering the alternatives, it's still a time saver that will help you get to production faster.

The first part of this involves some Spring configuration. This will be familiar to those who have done the Spring/Hibernate thing before—and I'm sure many of you have.

10.4.1 Building the service.xml file

One difference is that as with Liferay, you also define the data source with Spring. It's done this way because of Liferay's open source philosophy. That philosophy says you should be in control of your environment, so Liferay does its best to not lock you down to a particular piece of software. You should be free to swap in and out various components of your infrastructure. With that in mind, Liferay doesn't default to using application server data sources (although you can use them if you wish). Instead, they're by default configured through Spring, using a separate, open source data source.

The first thing you need to do is build your service in service.xml and generate the Java code and Spring/Hibernate configuration. Your service might look like the following listing.

Listing 10.3 Service configuration in another database

```
<service-builder package-path="com.inkwell.legacy.db">
  <author>Rich Sezov</author>
  <namespace>legacy</namespace>

  <entity
      name="LegacyEntity"
      local-service="true"
      data-source="myAppDataSource"
      session-factory="myAppSessionFactory"
      tx-manager="myAppTransactionManager">        <-- Reference to Spring beans

    <column name="legacyId" type="long" primary="true" />
    <column name="legacyName" type="String" />
    <column name="legacyThing" type="String" />
    <column name="legacyOtherThing" type="String" />

    <!-- Foreign Keys -->

    <column name="companyId" type="long" />
    <column name="groupId" type="long" />
    <column name="userId" type="long" />

    <!-- Finders -->

    <finder name="GroupId" return-type="Collection">
      <finder-column name="groupId" />
    </finder>

    <finder name="CompanyId" return-type="Collection">
      <finder-column name="companyId" />
    </finder>

  </entity>
</service-builder>
```

Service Builder allows for the configuration of a different data source *per entity*. It doesn't work without some manual configuration of Spring and Hibernate, but building the service gets you mostly there. After you've got this entity in a service.xml file and you build the service, you'll get the usual Spring and Hibernate configuration files in the META-INF folder of your src tree.

Next, you need to create the data source.

10.4.2 Wiring the data source up with Spring

You create a data source in one of two ways: you can create it in your application server and access it through JNDI, or you can do it the cross-platform, Liferay way and put the configuration in your Spring configuration files. Because the second method works the same regardless of application server, this is the way you'll do it.

In the META-INF folder described earlier, create a file called ext-spring.xml. Make it look like the next listing.

Listing 10.4 Spring configuration of separate data source

```
<?xml version="1.0"?>
<!DOCTYPE beans PUBLIC "-//SPRING//DTD BEAN//EN"
➥ "http://www.springframework.org/dtd/spring-beans.dtd">

<beans>
  <bean class="
org.springframework.beans.factory.config.
➥ PropertyPlaceholderConfigurer">
    <property name="location">                          ❶ JDBC
      <value>/WEB-INF/jdbc.properties</value>             information
    </property>
    <property name="placeholderPrefix" value="${jdbc." />
  </bean>

  <bean id="myAppDataSourceTarget"                         Data source
     class="org.springframework.jdbc.datasource.         ❷ target
     ➥ DriverManagerDataSource">
    <property name="driverClassName"
value="${jdbc.driverClassName}" />
    <property name="url" value="${jdbc.url}" />
    <property name="username" value="${jdbc.username}" />
    <property name="password" value="${jdbc.password}" />
  </bean>

  <bean id="myAppDataSource"
      class="org.springframework.jdbc.datasource.          ❸ Data source
      ➥ LazyConnectionDataSourceProxy">
    <property name="targetDataSource">
      <ref bean="myAppDataSourceTarget" />
    </property>
  </bean>
  <bean id="myAppHibernateSessionFactory"
      class="com.liferay.portal.spring.hibernate.
      ➥ PortletHibernateConfiguration">
    <property name="dataSource">
      <ref bean="myAppDataSource" />
    </property>
  </bean>                                                ❹ Session
  <bean id="myAppSessionFactory"                            factories
      class="com.liferay.portal.dao.orm.hibernate.SessionFactoryImpl">
    <property name="sessionFactoryImplementor">
      <ref bean="myAppHibernateSessionFactory" />
```

```
    </property>
  </bean>
  <bean id="myAppTransactionManager"
      class="org.springframework.orm.hibernate3.
      ➥ HibernateTransactionManager">                    ◁ ❺ Transaction manager
    <property name="dataSource">
      <ref bean="myAppDataSource" />
    </property>
    <property name="sessionFactory">
      <ref bean="myAppHibernateSessionFactory" />
    </property>
  </bean>
</beans>
```

Here, you define a properties file to hold your JDBC information ❶, the data-source target ❷, the data source ❸, session factories ❹, and a transaction manager ❺. Normally, they're generated for you when you use the Liferay database. You're redefining them for an entity that wants to use a different database.

The JDBC properties file goes in your `WEB-INF` folder, and the properties look like the ones in Liferay's portal-ext.properties file:

```
jdbc.driverClassName=
jdbc.url=
jdbc.username=
jdbc.password=
```

Of course, you supply the information for your database.

You've defined the JDBC information directly here, but as mentioned before, you can also use JNDI for this. If you want to use JNDI, substitute the earlier data-source target section with a JNDI lookup:

```
<bean id="myAppDataSourceTarget"
    class="com.liferay.portal.spring.jndi.JndiObjectFactoryBean"
    lazy-init="true">
  <property name="jndiName">
    <value>jdbc/myAppPool</value>
  </property>
</bean>
```

You can now code for this entity as normal. You'll have one extra step, though, when you test the code: Service Builder won't create the tables automatically. You'll have to do that yourself. Thankfully, Service Builder makes this easy. If you run `ant build-db` on your project, Service Builder generates SQL files for all the databases Liferay supports, and you can run the appropriate file manually on your database to create the tables.

> **NOTE** A regression bug in Liferay EE SP1 prevents the SQL files from being generated. This will likely be fixed by the time this book is printed.

As you can see, Service Builder fits nicely into this scenario. It doesn't streamline your work as much as it does when using Liferay's database, but it still helps an awful lot to get your service code in shape quickly.

Next, we'll look at something many people probably don't realize is a part of Liferay: a lightweight message bus that you can use to handle certain tasks asynchronously.

10.5 Sending messages over Liferay's message bus

I'm sure you can tell by now that Liferay has a track record of going its own way. From the earliest days of the product's existence, Liferay's engineers have pushed more and more into the product. When I first encountered it, the company was running Liferay on its web site, but the forums were phpBB forums and the wiki was powered by MediaWiki, even though Liferay already had both a Message Boards portlet and a Wiki portlet.

Over time, those portlets became more and more powerful until they reached a modicum of parity with those other products, and then Liferay went ahead and migrated over to its own software for its web site. This keeps happening. Sometimes the team starts with something else and then writes their own and migrates to it, and sometimes they out and out implement their own version of something that may already exist, because the current solutions aren't the right fit.

This is exactly what happened with the message bus. There are open source Enterprise Service Bus solutions out there, but they were too heavyweight for Liferay, because Liferay only wanted a small, internal bus that would perform quickly. Certain scenarios within the portal required one component to be able to send a message to another component to do something, independent of the request/response model of the web. Rather than use something that was too heavy or wasn't quite the right fit, Liferay built its own message bus.

What is it used for? Here's an example: remember those message boards I was just talking about? One feature involves subscribing to various threads. Users can start a discussion and then subscribe to that discussion so they can be notified via email when somebody replies. This is a pretty standard feature of forum software.

If you stop to think about it for a moment, though, how you would implement this isn't so straightforward. Ideally, you want the emails to go out to subscribers as soon as a new message is posted, so you can place the message-sending code in the action that saves the new thread. But this design has problems. Say a popular thread has 50 people subscribed. What happens to that request?

You can probably see where I'm going. The user submits the new post and then has to wait for a response back from the server saying that the post was successful. Meanwhile, the forum is churning through a list of 50 email addresses, and it's communicating with a separate mail server (that may also be busy with other tasks) to do this. Should users have to wait until all that processing completes in order to see that their posts are saved successfully? Of course not! Saving a post and sending 50 emails are two separate tasks, and they should be handled separately. But how do you do that? Enter the message bus. It's clean, fast, it'll be a smooth ride, and there are no tolls.

The Message Boards portlet sends a message to a listener over the message bus and then returns the response to the user, who can continue interacting with the portal in

Figure 10.4 The message bus is pretty simple. Applications can send a message over the bus to a listener. The listener, by virtue of its being a listener for this particular type of message, can hear the message and knows what to do with it.

any way he or she chooses. Meanwhile, the listener that receives the message can act on it on a separate thread (see figure 10.4). In the case of subscriptions, there's a listener that can receive a primary key of a Message Boards thread, go look up the subscribers to that thread, and send them emails.

Do you have a scenario in your application that would require something like this? It's possible that you do, so let's look at how to work with the message bus.

10.5.1 Configuring the bus to send your messages

As you did with pointing Service Builder to another database, you need to add some Spring configuration to your WEB-INF/src/META-INF folder. This configuration file declares three things that you need in order to make the message bus work for you:

- One or more *listeners* to listen for messages and take action
- One or more *destinations* so the bus can deliver your messages
- A *configurator* (yes, I know that's not a word) that links the destination(s) to the listener(s)

That's not too bad, is it? Let's dig in and see what it looks like. Again, you'll need to have some familiarity with Spring, but you've done enough of this by now that it should be a snap. The Spring configuration in listing 10.5 goes in a file called messaging-spring.xml, in the META-INF folder in src. You'll add the sending of a small message to the Slogan Contest portlet.

Listing 10.5 Spring config for message bus

```
<?xml version="1.0" encoding="UTF-8"?>
<beans default-destroy-method="destroy"
➥ default-init-method="afterPropertiesSet"
➥ xmlns="http://www. springframework.org/schema/beans"
➥ xmlns:xsi="http://www.w3.org/2001/XMLSchema-instance"
➥ xsi:schemaLocation="http://www.springframework.org/schema/beans
➥ http://www.springframework.org/schema/beans/spring-beans-3.0.xsd">


  <bean id="messageListener.slogan_listener"                ❶ One or more listeners
      class="com.inkwell.internet.slogan.portlet.
      ➥ SloganConsoleListener" />

  <bean id="destination.slogan"                             ❷ One or more destinations
      class="com.liferay.portal.kernel.messaging.ParallelDestination">
    <property name="name" value="inkwell/slogan" />
  </bean>

  <bean id="messagingConfigurator"
      class="
com.liferay.portal.kernel.messaging.config.                 ❸ Configurator
➥ PluginMessagingConfigurator">
    <property name="messageListeners">
      <map key-type="java.lang.String" value-type="java.util.List">
        <entry key="inkwell/slogan">
          <list
value-type="com.liferay.portal.kernel.messaging.
➥ MessageListener">
            <ref bean="messageListener.slogan_listener" />
          </list>
        </entry>
      </map>
    </property>

    <property name="destinations">
      <list>
        <ref bean="destination.slogan"/>
      </list>
    </property>

  </bean>

</beans>
```

docroot/WEB-INF/src/META-INF/messaging-spring.xml

This is pretty straightforward Spring stuff. You first define the classes that will be your listeners and your destinations. In this case, I'm keeping it as simple as possible, but you can have as many listeners ❶ and destinations ❷ as you want. The configurator ❸ is where you wire them together. This tells the message bus that for the destination inkwell/slogan, the listener that should be injected into the call is the one defined as the messageListener.slogan_listener, which of course maps to your Slogan-ConsoleListener. And the destination type is Liferay's implementation of a parallel destination, because you want this to execute as soon as possible, rather than wait in a queue for other jobs to complete. Now all you have to do is code your sending and listening functionality.

10.5.2 Implementing the sender and the listener

Next, let's implement the listener class and make sure you send the message in the event you've defined, which is adding a slogan. This event is in the SloganLocalServiceImpl class, specifically in the addSlogan() method. You can add a small method there called sendMessage() to build the message and then send it across the bus:

```
private void sendMessage(
    Slogan slogan, ServiceContext serviceContext) {


    Message message = new Message();
    message.put("userId", serviceContext.getUserId());
    message.put("slogan", slogan.getSloganText());
    MessageBusUtil.sendMessage("inkwell/slogan", message);

}
```

The message, as you can see, consists of the userId of the user who submitted the slogan as well as the slogan text. You can, of course, include as much or as little information as you have on hand. For example, if you wanted to act on the slogan entity in your listener, you might want to include the primary key of the slogan entity so you could go grab it and manipulate it. For demonstration purposes, you don't need that, because all your listener is going to do is display the slogan in the console. Let's see how that works in the following listing.

Listing 10.6 Receiving a message

```
public class SloganConsoleListener implements MessageListener {

    public void receive(Message message)
        throws MessageListenerException {

        try {
            doReceive(message);                    ❶ Receives and processes message
        }
        catch (Exception e) {
            _log.error("Unable to process message " + message, e);
        }
    }

    protected void doReceive(Message message)      ❶ Receives and processes message
        throws Exception {
```

```
        String slogan = message.getString("slogan");
        System.out.println("Slogan Entered: " + slogan);

    }

    private static Log _log =
        LogFactoryUtil.getLog(SloganConsoleListener.class);
}
```

docroot/WEB-INF/src/com/inkwell/internet/slogan/portlet/SloganConsoleListener.java

Again, this is simple, isn't it? The only thing you have to implement is a `doReceive()` method ❶ in which you place the logic for receiving the message and then doing something with it. The `Message` class provides many convenience methods for getting various Java types, and you can send your own classes across the message bus as well.

You have one last component to configure. In order to find the Spring configuration file, you need to tell Liferay where to look for it. This is done by adding a context configuration location to your project's web.xml file:

```
<context-param>
    <param-name>portalContextConfigLocation</param-name>
    <param-value>
        /WEB-INF/classes/META-INF/messaging-spring.xml
    </param-value>
</context-param>
```

All that's left now is to test it. If you deploy the Slogan Contest portlet and enter a slogan, you should see something like the following in your Liferay server log:

```
01:12:43,558 INFO  [PortletHotDeployListener:382] 1 portlet for
➥ slogan-contest-portlet is available for use
Slogan Entered: Not your grandfather's pen.
```

I hope you can see how you might use the message bus. You can do all kinds of cool things with it. For example, with the Slogan Contest portlet, you might send an email to everyone with the role that approves slogans in the workflow. That way, those users are notified when a new slogan is entered, and they can go right in and approve or reject them as fast as they're entered. You could write another listener that updates a web content article with a count of the number of slogans entered. The list is endless.

Next, we'll look at another general-purpose utility in Liferay: a job scheduler.

10.6 Scheduling jobs

Liferay, because it's a platform, contains functionality for running various jobs on a schedule. You can make these jobs do pretty much anything you want, because they have the same access to all of Liferay's APIs as any other plugin. You can, for example, write a mailing list manager application that lets users subscribe to receive email newsletters. These newsletters can be composed and then sent on a schedule—say, at midnight on Monday morning, so the newsletters are waiting in subscribers' inboxes first thing on the first workday of the week.

Depending on the application, there can be any number of use cases that require a scheduler. Liferay's Calendar portlet uses it to send event notifications. Some enterprises use it to import users from other systems. Of course, you can use Liferay's scheduler to run whatever jobs you may need to run on a regular basis.

Now that you know about the message bus, using the scheduler will be a piece of cake, because it uses the message bus to get the jobs done. The jobs are `MessageListener` classes, just like the ones you'd write to receive a message sent across the message bus. All the scheduler does is kick off one of those `MessageListener` classes on the schedule you define.

The schedule is set up declaratively in the liferay-portlet.xml file, in `<scheduler-entry>` tags inside the `<portlet>` tag:

```
<scheduler-entry>
  <scheduler-event-listener-class>
      com.myapp.messages.MyScheduledJobListener
  </scheduler-event-listener-class>
  <trigger>
    <simple>
      <simple-trigger-value>1</simple-trigger-value>
      <time-unit>day</time-unit>
    </simple>
  </trigger>
</scheduler-entry>
```

You declare the listener you want to trigger, and how often you want to trigger it. You have the option of using simple values as in this example; or if you're a 1337 Unixhead, you can use `<cron>` and `<cron-trigger-value>` tags and specify cron values for the schedule instead of the simple ones. You'll need to do this if you want to set specific times, like midnight on Monday morning.

Liferay's scheduler is remarkably easy to use, but it gives you a powerful facility for running jobs at a frequency you define. We now have only one more API to go through before your Liferay journey comes to an end, so we'll end with a bang and talk about indexing and searching for data in Liferay.

10.7 Indexing and search

Liferay uses indexing and search throughout the portal. In fact, we could argue that a portal isn't worth much *without* indexing and search, because after filling it with content, you need a way of finding that content, right? Thankfully, Liferay gives you an easy way to do that, by providing a robust API to use to index data and search for it.

Liferay uses Lucene by default under the hood. This is a feature-rich search engine provided by Apache that is so widely used that most likely you're not surprised that Liferay uses it. Lucene was originally written in Java but has been ported to .Net, C, Python, Perl, Delphi, Ruby, LISP, PHP, Objective-C, and probably grandma's home-cooked programming language to go, by now. If you need to do search, and you're not Google, you can't go wrong by using Lucene.

It's kind of amazing to find such widespread support for something like Lucene, but there's a good reason: its API is *awesome*. In fact, it's so awesome that Liferay's search API is pretty much just a wrapper around it. When you find something this awesome, why fight it?

But you aren't tied to Lucene if for some incredible reason you don't want to use it. You can still write your portlet to Liferay's search API, and if you're an enterprise customer using one of Liferay's search plugins for commercial search servers, it'll work. You *still* get great search performance and features with the same API, no matter what the underlying implementation is.

I think the reason everybody likes this particular API is that it lets you search anything by abstracting everything into only two components: `Documents` and `Fields`. You translate the data (or the system translates well-known formats, such as PDFs, Open Document files, or Word documents) into a `Document` with `Fields` on it, and then you pass that `Document` on to the indexer, which happily churns through it and makes the data searchable.

This also helps to avoid weird database queries. Instead of searching the database, you can search the index, and then retrieve the proper entity through a `Document-to-entity` conversion (see figure 10.5).

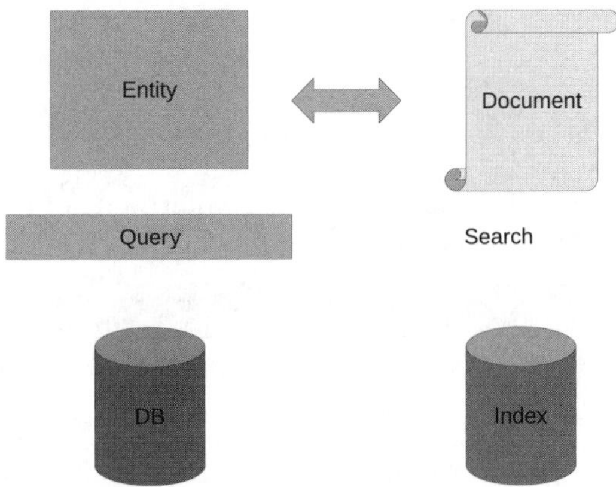

Figure 10.5 You can get the same data by querying for it or by searching for it.

Similarly, you do the same thing in reverse to do the indexing. At the same time you save the entity into the database, you can convert it into a `Document` and then kick off the indexer to get its content into the index. And I'm betting you can already guess how this happens on a separate process outside of the browser request and response. Under the hood, again, the message bus is used to make it happen. But this time, you don't have to do any configuration or implement any listeners—it's all done for you, by creating an indexer. Let's get to the code to see how this is done.

10.7.1 Indexing your data

To index data, you need to implement an interface for translating entities to `Documents` and back. The first step is to declare an indexer in liferay-portlet.xml with a single line in the `<portlet>` block:

```
<indexer-class>
    com.inkwell.internet.slogan.search.SloganIndexer
</indexer-class>
```

After you've declared it, you can implement the indexer. This class needs to extend Liferay's `BaseIndexer` class; and when you do that, you'll find that there are five methods you need to implement, described in table 10.2.

Table 10.2 Indexer methods

Method	Purpose
`getSummary`	Builds a `Summary` object out of a `Document`, a snippet, and a portlet URL. The URL should have a `jspPage` parameter that points to the JSP in the application that views your entity.
`doDelete`	Accepts an `Object`, which you cast to the entity. You then convert this to a `Document`, which you tell the indexer to delete.
`doGetDocument`	Accepts an `Object`, which you cast to the entity type. When you have this, you build a `Document` out of fields from the entity that you would like to index. You should also include context information, such as the `companyId`, `groupId`, and so on.
`doReIndex`	Overloaded three times. Indexes a `Document` passed to it, an entity (from its primary key), or all of the `Documents` associated with the `companyId`.
`getPortletId`	Returns the portlet ID.

Let's look at the most interesting of these methods, starting with `getSummary()` in the following listing.

Listing 10.7 Getting a summary

```
public Summary getSummary(
    Document document, String snippet, PortletURL portletURL) {

    String title = document.get(Field.TITLE);

    String content = snippet;

    if (Validator.isNull(snippet)) {
        content = document.get(Field.DESCRIPTION);

        if (Validator.isNull(content)) {
            content = StringUtil.shorten(
                document.get(Field.CONTENT), 200);      <-- 1 Specifies summary size
        }
    }

    String resourcePrimKey = document.get(Field.ENTRY_CLASS_PK);

    portletURL.setParameter("jspPage", "/admin/view_slogan.jsp");
    portletURL.setParameter("resourcePrimKey", resourcePrimKey);

    return new Summary(title, content, portletURL);
}
```

docroot/WEB-INF/src/com/inkwell/internet/slogan/search/SloganIndexer.java

This method is called when the search runs, in order to show the results of the search. Although it's not needed for slogans, in the previous code, I used one of Liferay's convenience methods in `StringUtil` ❶ to make the summary a certain size (200 characters, to be exact—60 more than Twitter gives you), so you can see another utility class Liferay's platform gives you as a convenience. Later, you'll use a `SearchContainer` that iterates through these `Summary` objects.

Deleting a `Document` is even shorter:

```
@Override
protected void doDelete(Object obj)
    throws Exception {

    Slogan slogan = (Slogan)obj;
    Document document = new DocumentImpl();

    document.addUID(PORTLET_ID, slogan.getPrimaryKey());

    SearchEngineUtil.deleteDocument(
        slogan.getCompanyId(), document.get(Field.UID));

}
```

The unique ID of the `Document` is created through the portlet ID and the primary key of the entity. Otherwise, this method is pretty straightforward.

Next, here's how to convert an entity into a `Document` object.

Listing 10.8 Converting an entity into a `Document` object

```
@Override
protected Document doGetDocument(Object obj)
    throws Exception {

    Slogan slogan = (Slogan)obj;
    long companyId = slogan.getCompanyId();
    long groupId = getParentGroupId(slogan.getGroupId());
    long scopeGroupId = slogan.getGroupId();
    long userId = slogan.getUserId();                          ❶ Fields from entity
    long resourcePrimKey = slogan.getPrimaryKey();
    String title = slogan.getSloganText();
    String content = slogan.getSloganText();
    String description = slogan.getSloganText();
    Date modifiedDate = slogan.getSloganDate();

    long[] assetCategoryIds =
        AssetCategoryLocalServiceUtil.getCategoryIds(
            Slogan.class.getName(), resourcePrimKey);
        String[] assetCategoryNames =                           ❷ Categories and Tags
            AssetCategoryLocalServiceUtil.getCategoryNames(
                Slogan.class.getName(), resourcePrimKey);
    String[] assetTagNames = AssetTagLocalServiceUtil.getTagNames(
        Slogan.class.getName(), resourcePrimKey);

    Document document = new DocumentImpl();                     ❸ Create the Document
```

```
    document.addUID(PORTLET_ID, resourcePrimKey);

    document.addModifiedDate(modifiedDate);

    document.addKeyword(Field.COMPANY_ID, companyId);
    document.addKeyword(Field.PORTLET_ID, PORTLET_ID);
    document.addKeyword(Field.GROUP_ID, groupId);
    document.addKeyword(Field.SCOPE_GROUP_ID, scopeGroupId);
    document.addKeyword(Field.USER_ID, userId);
    document.addText(Field.TITLE, title);
    document.addText(Field.CONTENT, content);
    document.addText(Field.DESCRIPTION, description);
    document.addKeyword(Field.ASSET_CATEGORY_IDS, assetCategoryIds);
        document.addKeyword(
           Field.ASSET_CATEGORY_NAMES, assetCategoryNames);       API
    document.addKeyword(Field.ASSET_TAG_NAMES, assetTagNames);  4 difference

    document.addKeyword(Field.ENTRY_CLASS_NAME,
        Slogan.class.getName());
    document.addKeyword(Field.ENTRY_CLASS_PK, resourcePrimKey);

    return document;
}
```

docroot/WEB-INF/src/com/inkwell/internet/slogan/search/SloganIndexer.java

The first thing you do is retrieve everything you need to index: the fields from the entity ❶ and the categories and tags (if any) associated with the entity ❷. Then in ❸ you create the `Document`. One of the things you'll notice right away is that Liferay has standardized the field names in constants for context within the portal (company ID, group ID) as well as for things like categories and tags. Using these predefined field names allows you to add search for these portal capabilities in a standard way in any application you wish to write. And when you search for a particular tag—say, "contest," if all slogan contests are tagged that way—you should get back all entries with that tag, because the tag was indexed.

I've called out ❹ because there's a difference between current builds of Liferay Community Edition and Liferay Enterprise Edition at the time of this writing. The code ❹ will work fine in Enterprise Edition. In Community Edition, for whatever reason, the Field for category names has not been backported to the code, so you'll have to substitute that line for this:

```
document.addKeyword("assetCategoryNames", assetCategoryNames);
```

You only need to look at one of the `reIndex` methods to see how reindexing is done—I'm sure you can do things like loop through all of your entities by `companyId` in the overloaded versions of these methods at this point (if you aren't sure how to do that, you may want to flip back to chapter 3 on Service Builder):

```
@Override
protected void doReindex(Object obj)
    throws Exception {
```

```
    Slogan slogan = (Slogan)obj;
    SearchEngineUtil.updateDocument(
        slogan.getCompanyId(), getDocument(slogan));

}
```

All that's interesting here is a single call to update the document.

When the Indexer class is complete, you're free to implement search in the user interface. To do that, you'll add a search form to the existing JSP and add another JSP for viewing the results.

10.7.2 Searching your data

Searching for data and displaying it isn't different in Liferay from querying for data and then displaying it. In both cases, you make a call to the back end and display the results in a search container.

In this section, you'll add a search feature to the Slogan Contest example. When run, the Search page looks like figure 10.6.

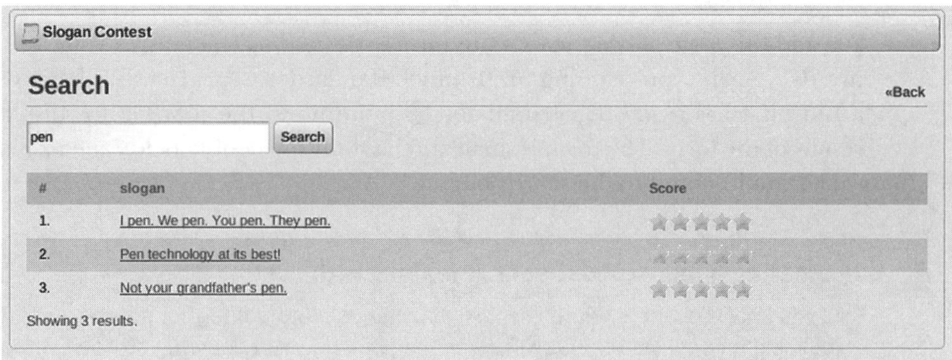

Figure 10.6 If you search for *pen*, you get slogans with that word, which is different from what you get if you search for *pens*.

This is probably the simplest search form you could have, in the tradition of Google. The implementation is straightforward; you add a search form to view.jsp, and then you create a JSP to display the search results. The following listing shows the code to add the search form to view.jsp.

Listing 10.9 Adding a search form

```
<liferay-portlet:renderURL varImpl="searchURL">
    <portlet:param name="jspPage" value="/html/search.jsp" />    ❶ URL to search results
</liferay-portlet:renderURL>

<aui:form action="<%= searchURL %>" method="get" name="fm0">
  <liferay-portlet:renderURLParams varImpl="searchURL" />
  <aui:input name="redirect" type="hidden" value="<%= currentURL %>" />
```

```
    <aui:input name="groupId"
        type="hidden"
        value="<%= String.valueOf(scopeGroupId) %>" />

    <div class="portlet-toolbar search-form">

      <span class="aui-search-bar">
        <aui:input inlineField="<%= true %>"
            label=""
            name="keywords"
            size="30"
            title="search-entries"
            type="text" />                              ❷ Search field

        <aui:button type="submit" value="search" />
      </span>

    </div>

</aui:form>
```

docroot/html/view.jsp

You add this form above the existing form for switching the tabs, as you can see in figure 10.7. Again, you're doing pretty much standard `MVCPortlet` stuff here: you create a URL that has a `jspPage` parameter ❶ pointing to the new JSP for displaying the results of the form. The form is small and has only one visible field called `keywords` ❷, which you'll submit to the search engine.

> **Creating a more robust search feature with Lucene**
>
> If you know Lucene's search syntax, you can use it to refine your search. And if you're building an application that will be centrally focused on search, you can even provide your own advanced search JSP that abstracts out some of the syntax for the user into separate fields. Then, after the search is submitted, all you have to do is cobble the submitted information back together into Lucene syntax that you can submit to the indexer just as you're doing here.

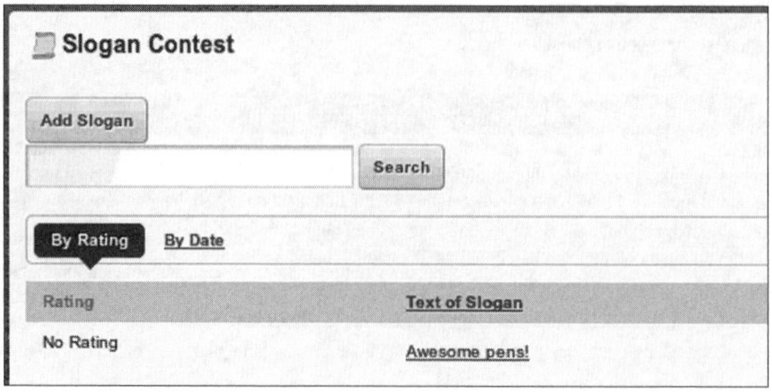

Figure 10.7 The search form appears above the tabs so it can be used regardless of which tab is selected.

Listing 10.10 shows the JSP that displays the results. I'm sure you'll notice that this code is doing everything, and I mean *everything*, right in the JSP. As such, you're violating all that code layering and separation stuff I talked about earlier in the book. But I have two reasons for doing this:

1. You'll see code like this in Liferay all the time, so I want it to look familiar to you. If it helps you feel better, any code you see written like this wasn't written by me.
2. I wanted to show you several things, and, for pedagogical reasons, it's a lot easier to encapsulate it in one file.

After all we've been through together, I'm asking you to please give me a break on this one. I agree: it would be better to separate your concerns and follow MVC, having the search in Java and display-logic only in the JSP. I'll leave it to you to separate it properly; for our purposes, it's much more understandable if I show you the entire thing this way in the next listing.

Listing 10.10 Showing search results

```
<%@ include file="/html/init.jsp" %>

<%
String redirect = ParamUtil.getString(request, "redirect");

String keywords = ParamUtil.getString(request, "keywords");
%>

<liferay-portlet:renderURL varImpl="searchURL">
  <portlet:param name="jspPage" value="/html/search.jsp" />
</liferay-portlet:renderURL>
```

(1) Creates search URL

```
<aui:form action="<%= searchURL %>" method="get" name="fm">
  <liferay-portlet:renderURLParams varImpl="searchURL" />
  <aui:input name="redirect" type="hidden" value="<%= redirect %>" />

  <liferay-ui:header
      backURL="<%= redirect %>"
      title="search"
  />

  <%
  PortletURL portletURL = renderResponse.createRenderURL();

  portletURL.setParameter("jspPage", "/html/search.jsp");
  portletURL.setParameter("redirect", redirect);
  portletURL.setParameter("keywords", keywords);

  List<String> headerNames = new ArrayList<String>();

  headerNames.add("#");
  headerNames.add("slogan");
  headerNames.add("score");
```

```
SearchContainer searchContainer = new SearchContainer(
    renderRequest, null, null, SearchContainer.DEFAULT_CUR_PARAM,
    SearchContainer.DEFAULT_DELTA, portletURL, headerNames,
    LanguageUtil.format(
        pageContext,
        "no-entries-were-found-that-matched-the-keywords-x",
        "<strong>" + HtmlUtil.escape(keywords) + "</strong>"));     ❷ Creates search container

try {
    Indexer indexer =
        IndexerRegistryUtil.getIndexer(Slogan.class);     ❸ Gets indexer

    SearchContext searchContext =
        SearchContextFactory.getInstance(request);

    searchContext.setEnd(searchContainer.getEnd());
    searchContext.setKeywords(keywords);
    searchContext.setStart(searchContainer.getStart());

    Hits results = indexer.search(searchContext);     ❹ Does search

    int total = results.getLength();

    searchContainer.setTotal(total);

    List resultRows = searchContainer.getResultRows();

    for (int i = 0; i < results.getDocs().length; i++) {
        Document doc = results.doc(i);

        ResultRow row = new ResultRow(doc, i, i);

        // Position

        row.addText(
            searchContainer.getStart() + i + 1 + StringPool.PERIOD);

        // Slogan

        long sloganId =
            GetterUtil.getLong(doc.get(Field.ENTRY_CLASS_PK));

        Slogan slogan = null;

        try {
            slogan = SloganLocalServiceUtil.getSlogan(sloganId);

            slogan = slogan.toEscapedModel();
        }
        catch (Exception e) {
            if (_log.isWarnEnabled()) {
                _log.warn("
                    ➥ Slogan search index is stale and contains entry " +
                    sloganId);
            }
```

```
                continue;
            }

            PortletURL rowURL = renderResponse.createRenderURL();

            rowURL.setParameter("jspPage", "/html/view_slogan.jsp");
            rowURL.setParameter("redirect", currentURL);
            rowURL.setParameter("resourcePrimKey",
                String.valueOf(slogan.getSloganId()));

            row.addText(slogan.getSloganText(), rowURL);

            // Score

            row.addScore(results.score(i));

            // Add result row

            resultRows.add(row);
        }
        %>

    <span class="aui-search-bar">
      <aui:input inlineField="<%= true %>"
label=""
name="keywords"
        size="30"
title="search-entries"
type="text"
        value="<%= keywords %>" />

      <aui:button type="submit" value="search" />
    </span>

    <br /><br />

    <liferay-ui:search-iterator
        searchContainer="<%= searchContainer %>" />

    <%
    }
    catch (Exception e) {
        _log.error(e.getMessage());
    }
    %>
</aui:form>

<%
if (Validator.isNotNull(keywords)) {
    PortalUtil.addPortletBreadcrumbEntry(
        request, LanguageUtil.get(pageContext, "search") +
            ": " + keywords, currentURL);
}
%>

<%!
```

❺ Row URL

❻ Search container tag

❼ Breadcrumb entry

```
private static Log _log =
   LogFactoryUtil.getLog("slogan_contest.docroot.html.search_jsp");
%>
```

docroot/html/search.jsp

To allow users to search again right from this JSP, you create a URL pointing back to the same JSP ❶. Before, I showed you the search container tags so you could see how easy it is to create a search container inside your JSP declaratively. If it's more your style to create it programmatically, you can do it as you see in ❷. There's nothing stopping you from creating a search container in your portlet class and placing it in the JSP where you want it using the tag in ❻. But we're getting ahead of ourselves. Before you place the search container in your JSP, you have to fill it with content.

The call in ❸ instantiates the `SloganIndexer` class you created earlier, and ❹ uses that indexer to do the search. You don't have to implement this method because the implementation is in the superclass. The only things you need to do are to tell the indexer how to create `Summary` objects as well as how to convert entities into `Documents` and back again. The URL for the row is in ❺, and this code is similar to the code you used in view.jsp back in chapter 7 when you created the Slogan portlet. The search container is placed on the page in ❻, and this is followed by a cool little piece of code ❼ that adds the search keywords to the breadcrumb in the theme.

Search is pretty easy to implement in Liferay, but it's extremely powerful. Because building a web site is all about getting the right content to your users, you can use search effectively to make sure that happens.

10.8 Summary

Liferay Portal is filled with APIs and utilities that are designed specifically to help you to build your site on Liferay. In this chapter, we spent some time looking at useful APIs. Friendly URLs make it easy for users to navigate your site and share links. And because they're implemented not by code but by pattern matching in an XML configuration file, they're simple to add to your completed application.

Action commands give you a way to separate `MVCPortlet` actions into multiple classes to make larger applications easier to follow. You can use them to build large applications in Liferay while also allowing for easy maintainability of those applications.

Liferay's implementation of its sixth algorithm for permissions lets you take advantage of view-level permission filtering. This makes it easy to check permissions at the query level, rather than when you're retrieving an entity, which provides for a much better user experience. In this case, the sixth time really was the charm.

Flexibility is key to fitting into multiple environments, from the small web site to the large enterprise, and Service Builder gives you that by allowing you to connect not just to Liferay's database, but to any database. There are a few extra things to configure, and tables aren't generated automatically, but you can use Service Builder to generate the service layer just the same.

Underlying many of Liferay's features is the message bus. You can now send messages across the bus to listeners, which can act on the messages they receive to perform jobs outside of the browser's request/response model. You can send messages across the bus in response to user actions, and you can also use Liferay's scheduler to send a message to kick off a job on a schedule. And in the case of the scheduler, you need do nothing but add the schedule to the application's liferay-portlet.xml file.

Finally, you saw how easy it is to implement indexing and search in Liferay, because Liferay takes advantage of the excellent search API provided by Lucene. By implementing your own indexer and calling it to do the search, you can provide a powerful search capability for your applications with minimal effort.

This ends not only this part, but also the entire book. I'm glad you've made it this far, and I hope you've enjoyed it as much as I have. Working with Liferay is a pleasure for me, because it does so much—it's a one-stop shop for anything you'd want to do with a web site. I hope this book has helped you be as effective as possible while working with the platform. If that's the case, then I succeeded in my job, and, God willing, maybe we'll get to do this all over again on a future version of Liferay.

Until then, may you go on to build great things on Liferay's platform!

appendix A *Liferay and IDEs*

Although there are developers today who prefer nothing more than a command-line interface to a build tool such as Ant coupled with a good text editor, they aren't me, even though I hope someday to aspire to such guru-ship. It can be argued that most developers use an integrated development environment (IDE) to produce code. IDEs offer several benefits over a command-line interface and text editor:

- Code lookup and completion
- Project and file browsing
- Refactoring support
- Integrated debugging
- Integrated interface to source code management (SCM) software, complete with diff tools
- Quick, built-in interface to Javadoc and inline documentation
- Depending on the IDE, more—sometimes much more

From the information in chapter 2, it should be easy to see how to use Liferay's SDKs with just a text editor and a command-line interface to Ant. Because many if not most developers today use an IDE, it's important to spend some time covering how you set up Plugins SDK projects in an IDE, but the topic isn't necessarily germane to Liferay specifically. This information is useful, but didn't fit well into the book itself, so it appears here. I'll demonstrate how to work with Liferay using the two most popular open source IDEs available at the time of this writing: Eclipse (www.eclipse.org) and NetBeans (www.netbeans.org), as well as with Liferay's flavor of Eclipse, Liferay IDE/Developer Studio.

Another note about agnosticism: because developers are most effective when using the tool of their choice, I'm not recommending any IDE over another; I chose Eclipse and NetBeans because they're both open source IDEs and thus both represent zero barrier to entry solutions for state-of-the-art development (and it should be obvious why I chose Liferay IDE). With regard to the two generic IDEs, I'll attempt to be fair and present them in alphabetical order, making no recommendations as to which may be most appropriate for your project; both are adequate and are ideal solutions in their own right. I'll present Liferay IDE after Eclipse, so you can see what it adds to a generic Eclipse install.

All of these products have documentation of their own, so if you plan on using one of these IDEs to create portlets or themes, or to extend Liferay, you'll be best served by referring to the documentation for these projects. I'm assuming you already know how to use your IDE, so we'll cover only the basics of getting up and running. If you're using a commercial IDE such as IntelliJ IDEA, Borland JBuilder, or Oracle JDeveloper, the concepts in this chapter apply as well, and you should be able to use this information to do Liferay development in your IDE of choice.

A.1 Eclipse

Eclipse is an open source IDE that was originally created by IBM to replace its aging Visual Age for Java product. IBM's goal is stated as follows:

> We wanted to establish a common platform for all IBM development products to avoid duplicating the most common elements of infrastructure. This would allow customers using multiple tools built by different parts of IBM to have a more integrated experience as they switched from one tool to another. We envisioned the customer's complete development environment to be composed of a heterogeneous combination of tools from IBM, the customer's custom toolbox, and third-party tools. This heterogeneous, but compatible, tool environment was the inception of a software tools *ecosystem.*[1]

IBM built the initial version of Eclipse and released it in 2003. Afterward, the company created the Eclipse Foundation for two reasons:

- To provide an open, collaborative organization to oversee the future development of Eclipse
- To remove the perception that Eclipse was under IBM's control, because the goal was always to provide an open platform that was vendor neutral

This strategy worked, and today Eclipse in some incarnation (whether Eclipse itself or one of many rebranded versions—such as Liferay IDE and Liferay Developer Studio—that ship with various plugins) is one of the most widely used IDEs on the market.

Eclipse comes in several downloadable versions for various operating systems. Because Liferay is a Java web application, I recommend that you download the version that is labeled for Java EE Developers. This gives you the basic features you need for Java EE applications like Liferay.

---

[1] http://mng.bz/pmPo

If you're going to work with Liferay's source code, you may find it useful to have Subclipse or Subversive, which are Eclipse plugins that interface with Subversion code repositories. Liferay's source code is stored in a Subversion repository, so it can be more convenient to update from the repository from within the IDE. You may also want to check out the egit plugin, because Liferay has switched to Git for managing core development.

Speaking of plugins, yes, Eclipse like Liferay also has the concept of plugins. These have nothing to do with Liferay's plugins but are instead ways of extending Eclipse to do things other than what it does when you first download it. For example, Red Hat provides a business-modeling tool based on Eclipse plugins.

It's beyond the scope of this book to go over all the Eclipse plugins you might want to use as a developer. Suffice it to say that there are plugins for Facelets, Velocity templates, additional application servers, diagramming, and much more. With the configuration outlined here (Eclipse for Java EE plus optionally a plugin for managing source code in a repository), you should be able to do everything from implementing your own projects to contributing to Liferay's core.

A.1.1 Eclipse and workspaces

Eclipse uses the notion of *workspaces* (something it inherited from Visual Age for Java) to store Java projects. Unlike Visual Age for Java, an Eclipse workspace is just a folder on your file system with projects in it. Eclipse creates various hidden folders (using UNIX-style dot notation) that make the IDE look at the folder structure as a workspace. Eclipse also allows you to import projects from your file system. In that case, only Eclipse's configuration files for the various projects are stored in the workspace. I think it's better to use Eclipse this way, because you're free to put your projects anywhere you wish, which frees you to organize your projects the way you want.

The first time you launch Eclipse, it will ask you for a workspace location. If you're developing on a Windows platform and you plan to store projects in the workspace, I recommend that you place your workspaces somewhere close to the root folder of your drive in [Code Home], for reasons mentioned in chapter 2. Users of LUM operating systems don't have this problem.

Longtime Eclipse users generally have the practice of keeping separate workspaces for separate groups of projects. For example, if a developer were working on a set of portlets that made up a Customer Relationship Management system, that set of projects might exist in one workspace. Say a bug was found that affected another set of projects the developer completed a month ago. This developer could then switch workspaces and open the other set of projects all at once.

Developers who use Eclipse have learned to do this because Eclipse compiles code in the background occasionally. If there are a lot of projects in the workspace, this process can take a long time and slow down your system. Liferay is a very large project with thousands of source-code files, so you can imagine how Eclipse might be affected by having the Liferay source-code project in its workspace. If you're writing applications on top of Liferay, this won't affect you as much, because you won't necessarily need access to the Liferay source. But if you're customizing Liferay or want to hack on Liferay itself, it can be an issue, especially if you mix Liferay and a bunch of other projects in your workspace.

One other way to accomplish almost the same thing is the concept of *working sets.* These are sets of projects that can be opened and closed as a group. If you use working sets, you can generally keep all your projects in one workspace and only open the group of projects with which you're working at any one time.

More recently (as mentioned earlier), Eclipse allowed developers to open projects that exist outside the workspace. In this case, Eclipse keeps only its own configuration files in the workspace, and the source code files stay wherever they are. Because we use the Plugins SDK to generate portlet, theme, layout template, and other projects, we won't be using Eclipse to create new projects. For this reason, I recommend that you use Eclipse to point to projects in your Plugins SDK, rather than putting your entire Plugins SDK in the workspace. You can still have different workspaces for different project sets; you'll just need to install a different Plugins SDK somewhere else on your system and point to those projects in a new workspace.

This may sound complicated to the uninitiated, but it's not. You'll see how to get all this set up in the next section.

A.1.2 Server runtime

Launch Eclipse, and connect to the workspace of your choice. If you've never used Eclipse before, the default location is generally fine, unless you're on a Windows system—remember that 256-character limit on the total path of an NTFS file system.

Your first task in Eclipse will be to connect Eclipse to your installed Liferay bundle. You need to do this so that you can start it in debug mode in order to debug your code.

If you've installed Eclipse for Java EE developers, then Eclipse will by default start in the Java EE perspective. This is a version of the Eclipse UI that's optimized for writing Java EE applications. Eclipse has many other perspectives (which can be defined as versions of the UI), but this one is the most appropriate for writing portlets. Follow these steps:

1. At the bottom of the perspective is a Servers tab. Click this tab to activate it, and then right-click in a blank space in the body of the tab. Select New > Server. From the dialog box that appears, choose the type of server bundle you have installed. If you're following along with our recommended setup, this will be a Tomcat v6.x bundle, but you can use any bundle that Eclipse supports. If your server isn't listed, click the Download Additional Server Adapters link and install an adapter for your application server of choice.
2. At the bottom, change the server name so that it better reflects what server it is (see figure A.1). For example, for a Tomcat v6.x bundle (the default at the time of this writing), you can change the name to Liferay-Tomcat 6.0.

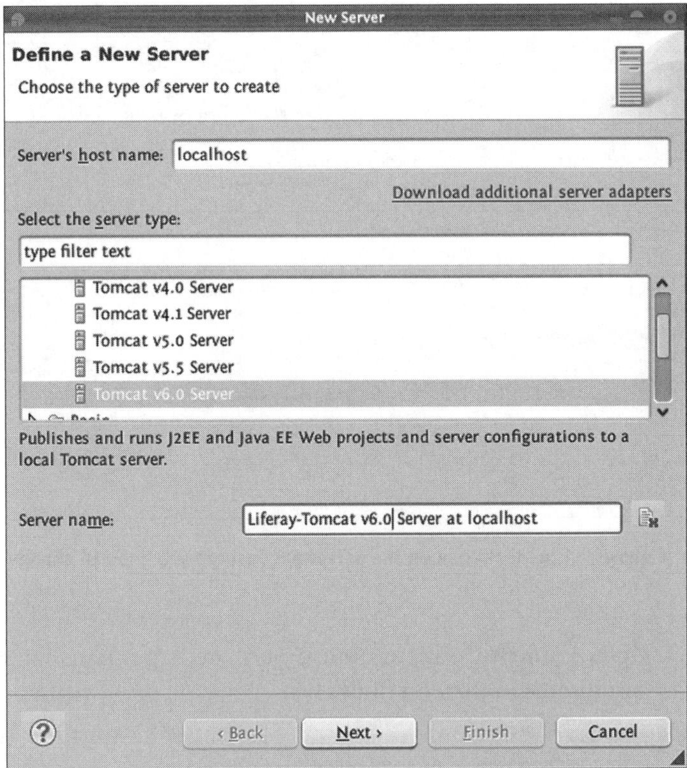

Figure A.1 Setting up your Liferay runtime is easy because Eclipse contains support for many different kinds of application servers, including the one in the default Liferay bundle.

3 Click Next. In the dialog box that follows, click the Browse button and browse to the location where you have installed your Liferay bundle. Then, click Finish. The dialog disappears, and the server runtime appears in the Servers tab.
4 Right-click your new server runtime, and select Open. You see the Eclipse Configuration page for your application server. By default, Eclipse creates a separate configuration for your application server in its workspace. You don't want it to do that; you want it to use the server configuration that already exists in the application server, because the bundle is preconfigured to run Liferay. This configuration screen is complicated; the changes you need to make are pictured in figure A.2.
5 Under Server Locations, select Use Tomcat Installation. Under Deploy Path, click the Browse button, and browse to your bundle's webapps folder.
6 On the right side of the screen, open the Publishing section, and select Never Publish Automatically. Open the Timeouts section, and change both the start and stop timeouts to 300 seconds.

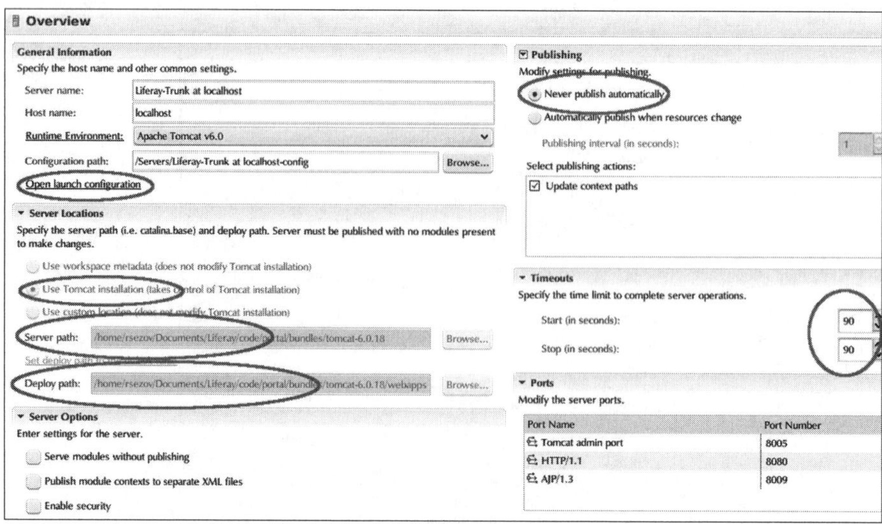

Figure A.2 This figure shows all the locations on the server page where you need to change settings in Eclipse.

7 At left, click Open Launch Configuration. Select the Arguments tab, and add the following arguments to the end of the list:

```
-Dfile.encoding=UTF8 -Duser.timezone=GMT -Xmx1024m -XX:MaxPermSize=256m
➥ -Dexternal-properties=portal-developer.properties
```

8 Click Apply and then OK. Close and save the configuration window by clicking the X icon in the tab.

You're now ready to start your Liferay bundle in Eclipse! Right-click it, and select Start; or select it, and click the green play icon in the Servers window border. You should see the server startup messages scroll in Eclipse's console window. When Liferay has finished starting, the console window switches back to the Servers tab, and the server's status is labeled "started." You can always switch back to the Console tab to see the server console messages. In fact, Eclipse will do this automatically if another message is generated.

For now, right-click the server in the Servers tab, and select Stop. Doing so shuts down Liferay.

A.1.3 *Setting up a plugin project*

In chapter 2, you generated a portlet project called Hello World in the Plugins SDK (to jog your memory a little more, it eventually became the Hello You project). Let's set up that project for use in Eclipse:

1 In Eclipse, select File > New > Dynamic Web Project. A new dialog box comes up, asking you for the name of your project. Type `hello-world-portlet` in the Project Name field, and deselect the Use Default Location check box.

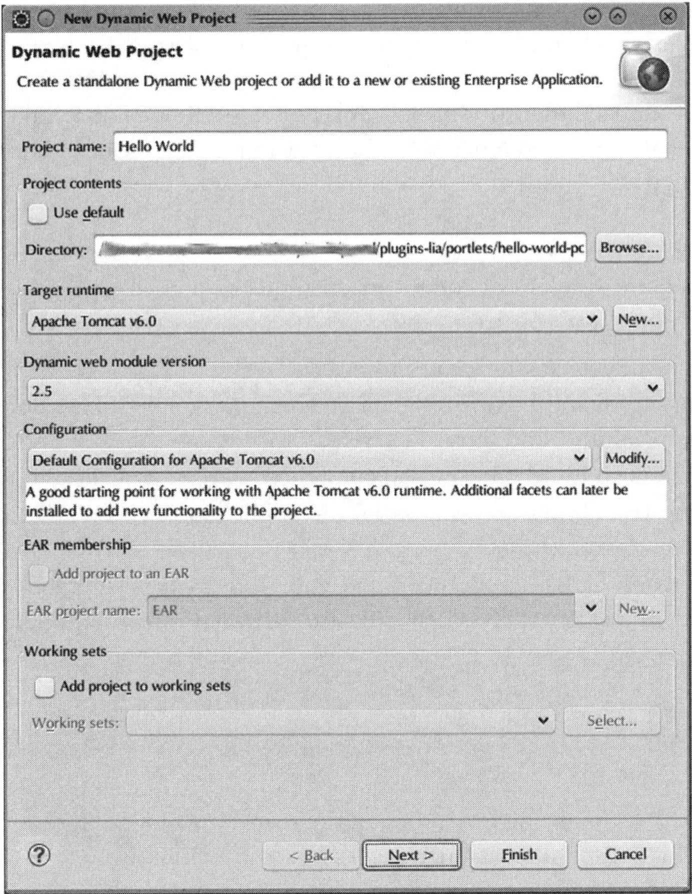

Figure A.3 The first dialog box in setting up your Hello World project in Eclipse. I've smudged out the actual path on my system because I'm paranoid. Please don't be offended.

2 Use the Browse button to navigate to the new project you just generated in your Plugins SDK. When you're finished, you should have a dialog box that looks like figure A.3.
3 Select the web module version appropriate for your application server, and click Next.
4 Eclipse guesses where your source code folder is and gets the guess wrong. In the dialog box, select the source folder, and click the Edit button. In the dialog box that appears, type `docroot/WEB-INF/src` and click OK. At the bottom of the dialog box, change the output folder to `docroot/WEB-INF/classes`. Click Next.
5 You're given an opportunity to select your project structure. Plugins SDK portlet projects differ from Eclipse's default project structure in that the name of the web module content folder is docroot. Eclipse by default uses WebContent. Under Content Directory, type `docroot`. If the Generate web.xml check box is checked, deselect it.
6 Click Finish.

Eclipse opens your project, and you see it in the Project Explorer window on the left. You can use the same technique to set up a Liferay theme, layout template, web, or hook project.

You've probably noticed that your project as-is in Eclipse shows that it has errors in it. The reason is that the dependencies for the project haven't yet been configured. Let's see how to fix that.

A.1.4 Fixing project dependencies

Portlet projects require several dependencies on the class path. Eclipse has an easy way of setting this up for your project:

1. Right-click your project, and select Properties.
2. In the resulting dialog box, from the list on the left, select Java Build Path. Select Server Runtime, and then click Next.
3. Select the Liferay bundle runtime you configured earlier, and click Finish.
4. This puts the Java classes that will be on the application's classpath at runtime on the project classpath.
5. Click Add External Jars, and browse to your Liferay-Tomcat bundle folder. Browse to webapps/ROOT/WEB-INF/lib, and then select the following .jars:
   - commons-logging.jar
   - util-java.jar
   - util-taglib.jar
   - util-bridges.jar
6. Click OK to clear the dialog box. After a brief pause (to allow Eclipse to attempt to compile the source code again), the errors should disappear.

If you have errors in JSP or TLD files in your project, don't worry about them; sometimes Eclipse can't parse them properly. Finally, everything is set up. Now let's see how to get some work done.

A.1.5 Debugging and deploying

You can now use Eclipse to debug and test portlet projects. You already have a Liferay bundle set up as a server in Eclipse. You can start this server in debug mode, set a break point in your portlet code, and step through to watch the functionality. Doing so is as simple as right-clicking your server in the Servers tab and choosing Debug instead of Start as you did earlier.

One other thing to note is that you should never use Eclipse to build and deploy your projects. Always use the Ant script generated with the project. Eclipse has good integration with Ant. You can enable the Ant view by selecting Window > Show View > Other > Ant. Doing so places an Ant tab in the same location as your Servers and Console tabs. To use it, drag the build.xml script from your project to this view. It's automatically parsed, and you can select any Ant task to run by double-clicking it.

Eclipse users should now be comfortable working with Liferay projects—to say any more here would start us delving into documenting Eclipse, and you would be much better served by official Eclipse documentation. Suffice it to say that the Eclipse IDE is a great environment for working on Liferay projects, and lots of Liferay developers use it every day for that purpose.

A.2 Using Liferay IDE and Liferay Developer Studio

Liferay began to hit critical mass in 2010 and has only accelerated since. When you reach critical mass and your product begins to get more and more popular, it becomes important to create tools to help developers get going quickly. Liferay did that by starting to build a team with expertise in tooling. Eclipse is an ideal platform on which to build, because it's designed from the ground up to be extended. Lots of developers use it every day, and so there's lots of Eclipse expertise out there.

Liferay IDE's first release happened during the writing of this book, and it's been getting regular updates all along. It adds a host of features to Eclipse to make working with Liferay straightforward. As I'm sure you gathered from the earlier material about vanilla Eclipse, getting Eclipse and the Plugins SDK to work together isn't the smoothest process in the world. Liferay IDE makes them fit together well into a workflow that's natural for the developer.

Liferay Developer Studio is the "productized" version of Liferay IDE that bundles Eclipse and Liferay's Eclipse plugins in one package. It also includes a few extra features meant for the enterprise developer, including support for proprietary application servers such as WebLogic and WebSphere. If you're a Liferay EE customer, you get a copy of Liferay Developer Studio with your EE license. Because we aren't concerned with proprietary application servers in this book, I'll just refer to Liferay IDE from here on—plus it's a lot less to say (and type). Everything I say about Liferay IDE also applies to Liferay Developer Studio.

Let's see what it's like to get things going in Liferay IDE. Because you just read about Eclipse, it's a great opportunity to do this so you can see how much easier it is to work with Liferay and Eclipse using Liferay IDE.

A.2.1 Getting started with Liferay IDE

The first thing you want to do is get Liferay IDE installed. You can do this two ways. The first way is to visit Liferay's product page[2] and follow the instructions there. Doing that gets you access to both the stable builds and the nightly builds if you like to live on the bleeding edge.

Alternatively, if you're using Eclipse you can grab Liferay IDE from the Eclipse Marketplace, by launching Eclipse and then choosing Help > Eclipse Marketplace. Once you're there, search for Liferay. Liferay IDE will show up in the search, and you can install it.

---

[2] You can find that product page here: http://mng.bz/7ep3

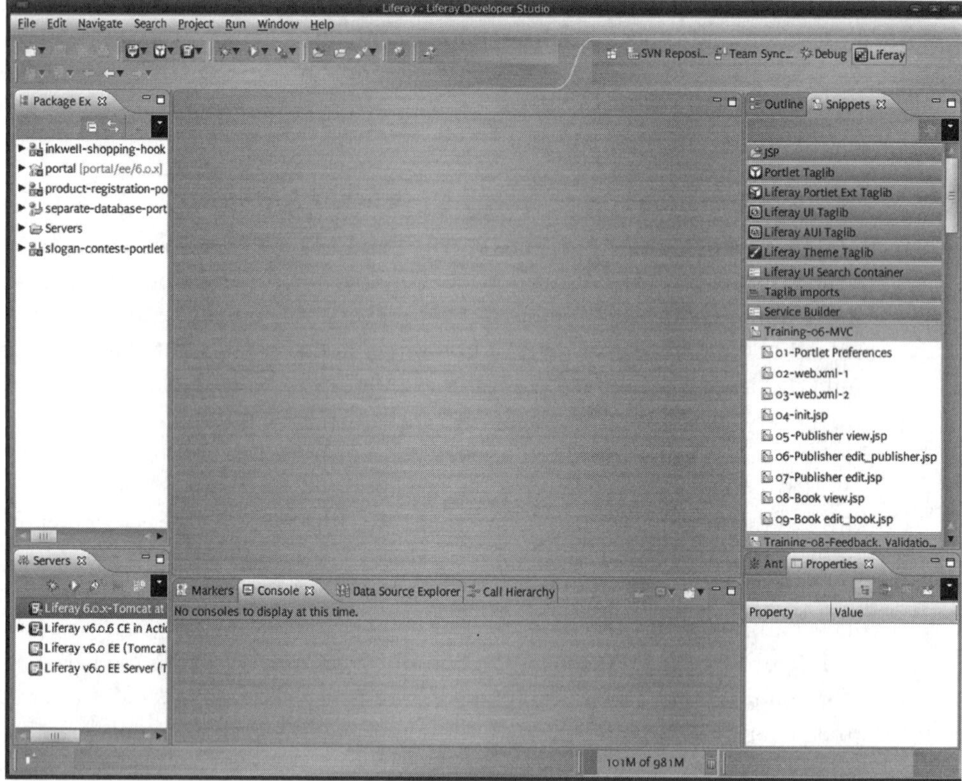

Figure A.4 This is the new Liferay perspective that comes as part of Liferay IDE. As you can see, the projects from this book are populated in the package explorer. I thought that would be cool.

After you've installed Liferay IDE, you'll have a new Liferay perspective (see figure A.4), some new menu and toolbar entries, and some useful snippets that support many tags from Liferay's tag libraries. The Search Container snippet alone is worth its weight in gold. Let's see how Liferay IDE can make working with Liferay in Eclipse a lot easier.

A.2.2 *Adding runtimes*

As of this writing, Liferay IDE supports Liferay/Tomcat bundles, and Liferay Developer Studio supports those as well as WebSphere runtimes, with more to come. Adding runtimes is extremely easy: right-click in the Servers view at bottom left, and select New > Server. Figure A.5 shows the server support provided by Liferay IDE: you can point to a Tomcat bundle directly, and you won't have to edit the server once you add it.

This is much easier than adding a runtime in vanilla Eclipse—in fact, if this was all Liferay IDE offered, it would probably be enough to recommend its use. But let's see how it also helps you work with the Plugins SDK.

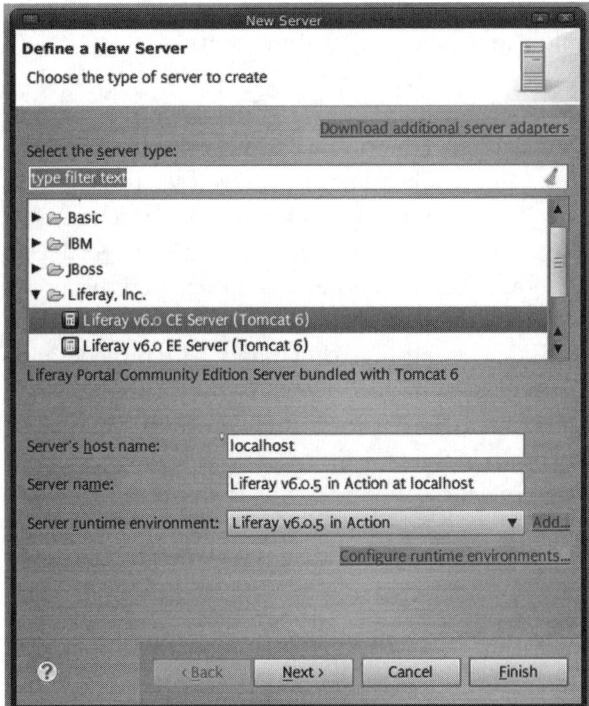

Figure A.5 Liferay servers are directly supported. Point to where your Tomcat bundle is installed, and away you go.

A.2.3 Working with the Plugins SDK

Liferay IDE has direct support for the Plugins SDK. This means you won't have to drop to the command line, run an Ant task to create a project, and then import it into your IDE. Instead, you can register a Plugins SDK with the IDE and easily use it to create new projects or bring existing projects into the IDE without ever leaving the IDE. Let's see how that works.

The first thing you have to do is register a Plugins SDK:

1. Select Window > Preferences, and then expand Liferay in the list on the left.
2. One of the links that appears is Installed Plugin SDKs. Select it, and you see an interface for adding Plugins SDKs in a similar fashion to the way you added a runtime: all you have to do is point to it.
3. Click Add, and browse to the location of your Plugins SDK, as shown in figure A.6.

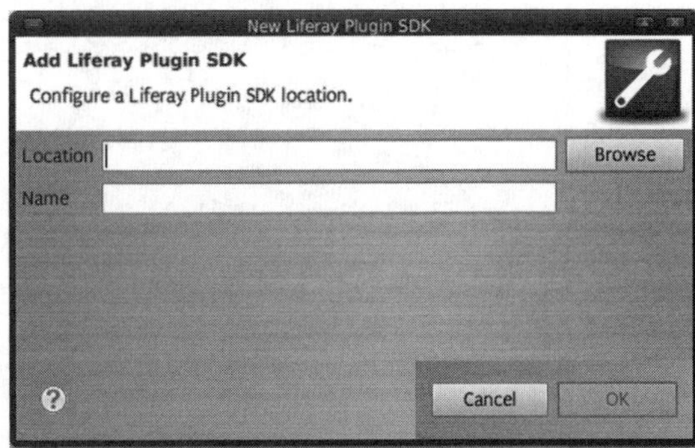

Figure A.6 Adding a Plugins SDK is as easy as browsing to it and giving it a name.

After you register a Plugins SDK, you can begin adding projects to the IDE. You do this in a natural way, as you would expect it to work within the IDE.

A.2.4 Creating and importing projects

In contrast to the way you'd have to do it in vanilla Eclipse, importing existing projects from your Plugins SDK is easy. Choose File > Import, and you see two choices in a Liferay category: Existing Liferay Project and Liferay Plugins SDK Projects. You'd use the first option if you created a project in another IDE that supports portlet projects or from a Plugins SDK that you don't want to register. I've never used this option myself. The second option lets you import projects from Plugins SDKs that you've registered. You just select them from a list, click Finish, and blammo! The projects are imported into Eclipse, with all their dependencies intact.

Creating new projects benefits from a wizard interface that you'd expect to see with full IDE integration, as shown in figure A.7.

The cool thing about the project-creation wizard is that it uses the Plugins SDK to generate the project. This means the project is created in the Plugins SDK as it should be, but it's available in Eclipse as a normal Eclipse project. If you're sharing a Plugins

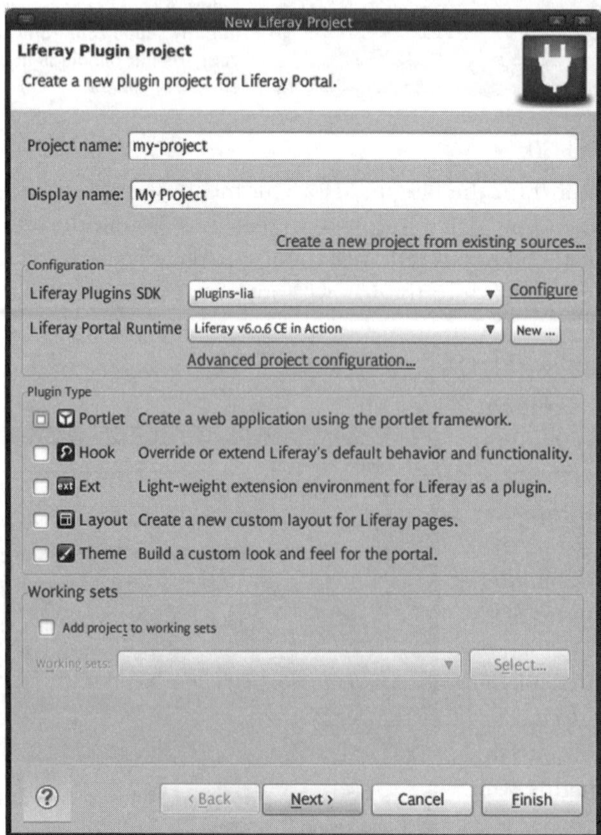

Figure A.7 Liferay IDE lets you create plugin projects of every type covered in this book.

SDK in your source-code repository, you can participate using Liferay IDE in a seamless fashion with other people using other tools.

I could go on about all the shortcuts you get with Liferay IDE—a visual layout builder, service generation, code snippets, and more—but I think you get the picture: if you're an Eclipse user, you'll be best served by installing Liferay IDE and working with that. It streamlines your work nicely.

But enough about Eclipse. Other open source IDEs are available, and I definitely don't want to leave out the users of another incredibly popular IDE, NetBeans.

A.3 Using NetBeans as a development environment

NetBeans is an open-source IDE that is dual-licensed under the Common Development and Distribution License (CDDL) and the GNU Public License version 2 (GPLv2). Originally created by students at Charles University in Prague as a closed-source product, the IDE was purchased by Sun in 1999 and subsequently open-sourced.

NetBeans has gone through many changes since its humble beginnings, and it has become the flagship IDE offered by Sun, often bundled along with Java Development Kit downloads. At the time of this writing, Oracle has announced continued support for it, so it isn't going anywhere.

NetBeans is powerful and supports all the features you need for Liferay development out of the box. NetBeans, like Eclipse, can also be extended by using plugins. Plugins are available from its plugin repository to support additional application servers, importing projects from other IDEs, Facelets, UML diagramming, and more. It's a cross-platform project, implemented in Java, using Swing as its widget set for its graphical user interface.

Projects in NetBeans are configured using its GUI, and settings are stored in XML files in a special nbproject folder that is created in the root folder of the project. You can store projects anywhere on your system and open them by choosing the typical File > Open Project command. Ant is integrated with the IDE at all levels: if you create a new project using NetBeans, it will use Ant to build it behind the scenes. You can use your own Ant scripts as well, and this is how you'll use NetBeans, because projects built out of the Plugins SDK already have their own Ant scripts.

To install NetBeans, download the installer and run it on your system. It's best that you download either the Web and Java EE distribution or the All distribution. On all operating systems, the installer is a typical wizard-based installation routine, and it allows you to install NetBeans anywhere on your system. When the installer has finished, you should have a NetBeans icon on your desktop. Double-click this icon to start NetBeans.

A.3.1 Server runtime

Your first task in NetBeans is to set up a Liferay bundle. Follow these steps:

1. On the left side of the NetBeans work area are three tabs: Projects, Files, and Services. Click the Services tab. The bottom node in the tree is labeled Servers.

Open it, and you see that one or more application server runtimes are already registered with NetBeans, depending on which version of NetBeans you downloaded. You'll add another one specifically for your Liferay-Tomcat bundle.

2. Right-click the Servers node, and select Add Server. Because the bundle you're working with uses Tomcat 6.x as an application server, choose that. Note that you can also choose any application server for which NetBeans supports a runtime, but this example sticks with Tomcat.
3. Change the server's name to something that will help you recognize it, such as Liferay-Tomcat-6. Click Next.
4. In the dialog box that follows, click the Browse button, and browse to the location of your Liferay bundle.
5. At the bottom of the dialog, you're asked for a username and password for the Tomcat manager role. Enter `tomcat` for both. When you're finished, the dialog box looks like figure A.8. Click Finish.

The Liferay bundle is now listed in the tree under Servers. To start it, right-click it and select Start. You should see the Liferay server console messages begin to scroll in the console window at the bottom of your NetBeans screen. When the server has completed its startup sequence, it's marked with a green "play" icon in the Servers tree.

For now, right-click your server and select Stop. Liferay shuts down, and the green "play" icon disappears. Now that you've got the runtime configured, you can move on to creating projects.

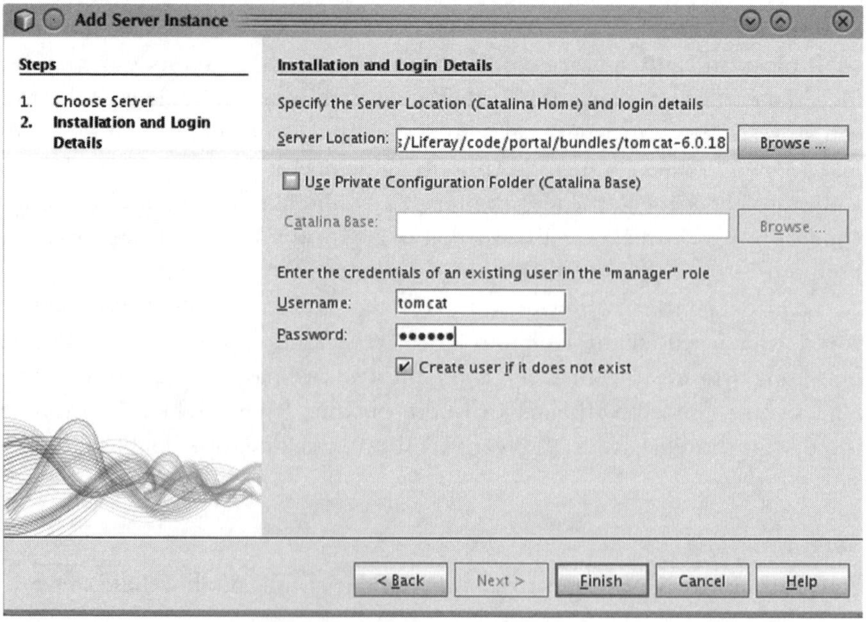

Figure A.8 One plus for NetBeans: setting up a server runtime is a lot easier than it is in Eclipse, but not any easier than Liferay IDE.

A.3.2 Setting up a project

Because you already generated the Hello World project in the Plugins SDK, let's get it set up in NetBeans:

1. Select File > New Project, and the New Project Wizard appears. From the left column, choose Java Web; from the right column, choose Web Application with Existing Sources. This indicates to NetBeans that you want to create a project that already exists. Click Next.
2. In the dialog box that follows, click the Browse button next to the Location field. Browse to the location of the hello-world-portlet project inside your Plugins SDK. The rest of the fields should then be automatically filled out. The dialog looks like figure A.9.
3. A new dialog box appears telling you that an Ant script already exists in the project. NetBeans uses Ant internally to build projects, so every NetBeans project needs to have an Ant script. This dialog box says that because the project already has an Ant script called build.xml, the IDE will generate one for NetBeans called nbbuild.xml. Click OK to let NetBeans do this—you'll likely never use the script that NetBeans generates anyway.
4. The dialog box that follows asks you to map the project to a server runtime. Choose the Liferay runtime that you created previously. Choose the Java EE version that your application server of choice supports. Click Next.

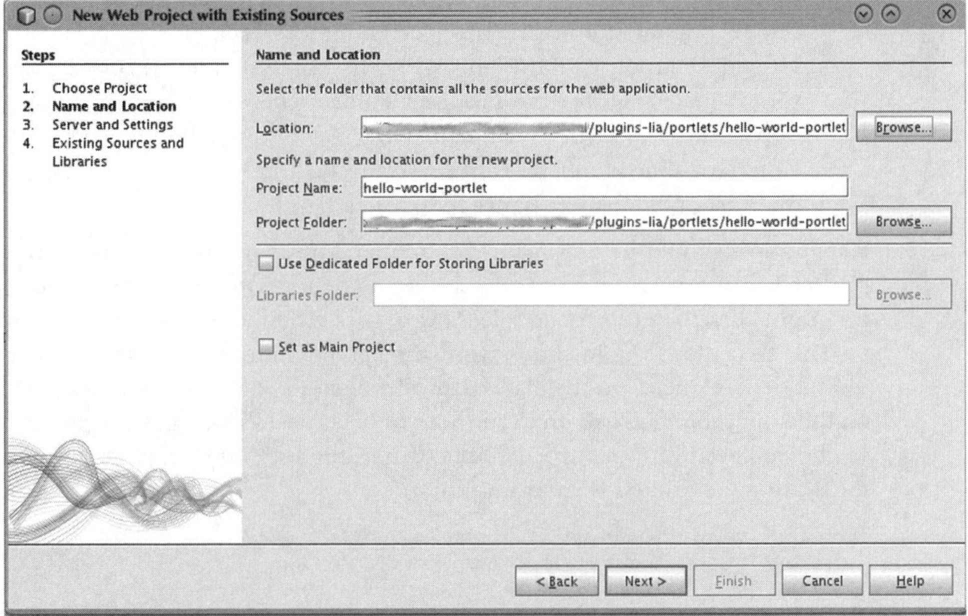

Figure A.9 Browse to the path of your project, and the rest of the fields are filled out automatically. Again, I have smudged out the actual path on my system because I'm paranoid. Please don't be offended.

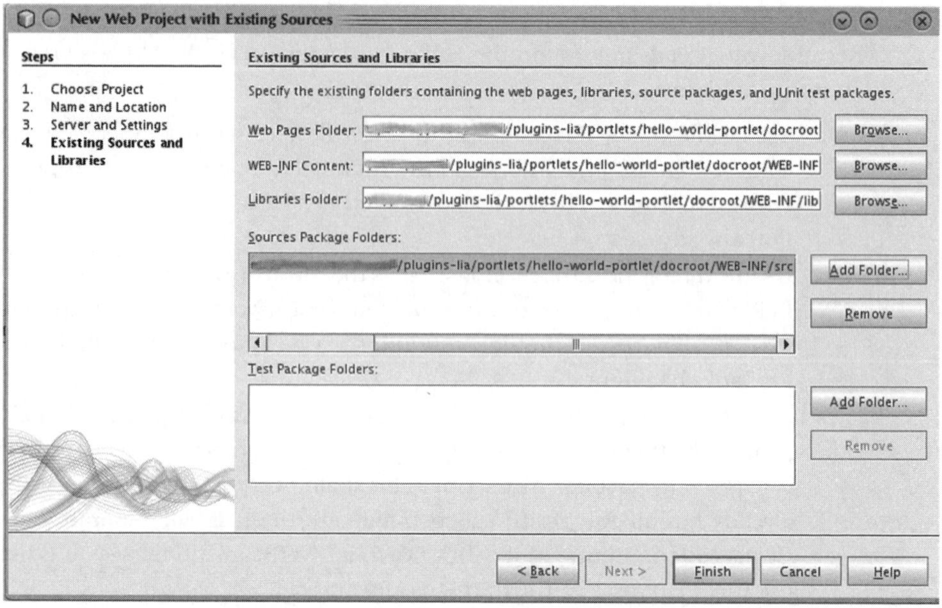

Figure A.10 This is the final dialog for creating a project in NetBeans. Even if you get these folders wrong, you can always correct them later.

5 The final dialog box is prefilled with values for the location of your web pages folder and your WEB-INF content. The wizard generally guesses these correctly, but the values should be [Project Home]/docroot for Web Pages, [Project Home]/docroot/WEB-INF for WEB-INF Content, and [Project Home]/docroot/WEB-INF/lib for the Libraries Folder, where [Project Home] is the location of the project in your Plugins SDK. You also need to add the folder where your Java source will be stored: [Project Home]/docroot/WEB-INF/src. The dialog should look like figure A.10. Click Finish.

Your project should be automatically created. You may, however, have errors in the project because it requires certain .jar dependencies to be on the classpath. To fix this, right-click the project and select Properties. Then, click the Libraries category.

This area allows you to choose your project dependencies. Portlet projects require several dependencies on the class path. You need to place the Java classes that will be on the application's classpath at runtime here, as well as any other dependencies that will be deployed with the project. Following is the list of dependencies required. Add these using the Add Jar/Folder button:

```
[Liferay Install Location]/lib/servlet-api.jar
[Liferay Install Location]/lib/jsp-api.jar
[Liferay Install Location]/lib/ext/portal-service.jar
[Liferay Install Location]/lib/ext/portlet.jar
[Liferay Install Location]/lib/ext/activation.jar
[Liferay Install Location]/lib/ext/hsql.jar
[Liferay Install Location]/lib/ext/jms.jar
```

```
[Liferay Install Location]/lib/ext/jta.jar
[Liferay Install Location]/lib/ext/mail.jar
[Liferay Install Location]/lib/ext/mysql.jar
[Liferay Install Location]/lib/ext/postgresql.jar
[Liferay Install Location]/webapps/ROOT/WEB-INF/lib/util-taglib.jar
[Liferay Install Location]/webapps/ROOT/WEB-INF/lib/util-bridges.jar
[Liferay Install Location]/webapps/ROOT/WEB-INF/lib/util-java.jar
[Liferay Install Location]/webapps/ROOT/WEB-INF/lib/jstl-impl.jar
[Liferay Install Location]/webapps/ROOT/WEB-INF/lib/jstl.jar
[Liferay Install Location]/webapps/ROOT/WEB-INF/lib/commons-logging.jar
```

After you've added these dependencies and clicked Ok, all the errors in your project should disappear. You're now ready to work on the project in NetBeans.

A.3.3 Debugging and deploying

You now have a portlet project set up properly in NetBeans, and you can begin using the IDE to build your application. At some point, you'll want to deploy the application to your Liferay server in order to debug it. This is easy to do in NetBeans.

Start your server in debug mode by clicking the Services tab on the left side of the screen, right-clicking your server, and selecting Start in Debug Mode.

1. To deploy your portlet, click the Files tab on the left side of the NetBeans window. Expand your project, and click the build.xml file, which is your Ant script. The Navigator window displays all the Ant tasks. Right-click the Deploy task, and click Run Target. Your project is deployed to Liferay.
2. To debug your code, set a breakpoint in a source code file by clicking in the margin of the Java editor on the line of code you wish to begin debugging. Then add your portlet to a page in Liferay.

Debugging in NetBeans is a two-step process. First you start the server in debug mode, and then you attach the debugger. The console window contains a log of your server's startup. At the top of this log, the debugging port is displayed. You'll likely have to scroll all the way to the top of the log in the console window in order to see it. Make a note of this port number; then choose Debug > Attach Debugger, and enter this number into the Port field. Click OK, and the IDE goes into debug mode, where you can step through code, view variables, and so on. When your portlet reaches the code at which you have set a breakpoint, processing stops and you can use the IDE to step through the processing.

A.3.4 Project settings

If you need to change the settings of your project (for example, to add a source-code tree for unit tests), you can right-click the project and select Properties. Here, you can step through some of the dialog boxes you used in the New Project Wizard. This allows you to easily set up new project dependencies, map IDE tasks to Ant tasks, and more.

Beyond this, you'll be much better served by the documentation NetBeans provides. As with Eclipse and Liferay IDE, my goal is to point users who are already familiar with these IDEs to some quick instructions for getting Liferay projects set up.

appendix B *Introduction to the Portlet API*

To help you understand the foundation undergirding Liferay's platform and get started writing portlets according to the Java Portlet Standard, this appendix takes a closer look at the Portlet API. Because many reading this book may have never worked with portlets before, I want to make sure that I at least give you a quick and dirty introduction to the portlet specification to show how it differs from the servlet specification. Of course, this discussion didn't fit well into the book, so it's here. For a more in-depth view of the Portlet API, see *Portlets in Action* by Ashish Sarin (Manning, 2011).

B.1 Portlets as fragments of a web page

Portlets are web applications that run in a portion of a web page. Rather than being responsible for (and taking up) the whole page, they're instead responsible only for their own functionality. If you were expecting me to say something more profound or mysterious, I'm sorry to disappoint you: that's all they are. But this gains you a lot.

As a developer, you're free to concentrate only on your application and its functionality, and you don't have to worry about ancillary things like users, user management, registration, layout, permissions, and the like. That stuff is built into the portal, and you get to take advantage of it in your application. Figure B.1 shows four portlets running in a single web page.

Having that stuff taken care of for you by the portal also gives you freedom in the way you think about your application. If you write a full web application, you have to be responsible for every page and its layout; portions of the page that need to update each other are things you'll have to manually handle. With portlets, you can approach the design of your application differently. Suppose you want a search bar at the top of the page that shows results below it. But searching and displaying

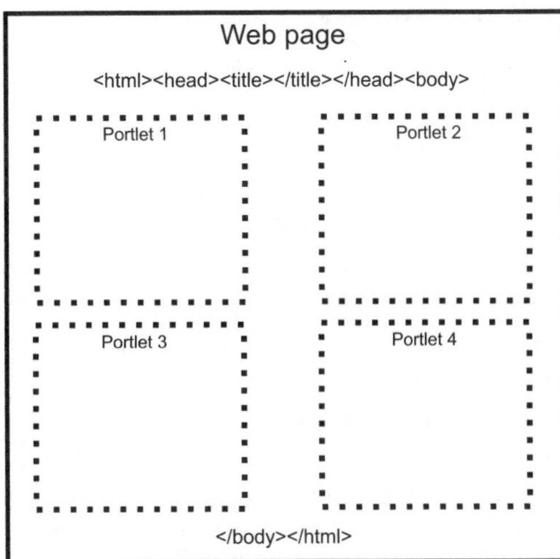

Figure B.1 Portlets appear within the body of a web page and thus are only responsible for producing the markup that makes up their individual section of the page. The portal will compose the page based on the theme, the layout, and the portlets that make up the page.

results are two separate functions, aren't they? In a web application, you'd have to compose that page manually to include both functions, which is unnatural. Imagine you've done this and then you show your client what it looks like. What if the client doesn't like it and wants the search moved to the left side instead? You then have to go back and modify the page styling to move the search element.

With portlets, you can write a search portlet that takes the search request and passes it to a separate display portlet as an event, which then displays the result. If your client doesn't like the search at the top, fine: before their eyes, while you're in the midst of the demo, drag that search portlet over to the left and drop it there. No code has to be modified. Why? Because the portal is responsible for aggregating the portlets on the page. You've saved yourself some work—especially if you can think of other ways to break up the functionality of your application.

The heart of any portal implementation is its portlets, because portlets are where the portal's functionality resides. Liferay's core is a portlet container, and the container's job is to manage the portal's pages and to aggregate the set of portlets that are to appear on any particular page and display them properly to the user. All the features and functionality of your portal application must reside in its portlets.

Portlet applications, like servlet applications, have become a Java standard, which various portal server vendors have implemented. The JSR-168 standard defines the Portlet 1.0 specification, and the JSR-286 standard defines the Portlet 2.0 specification. A JSR-168 or JSR-286 standard portlet should be deployable on any portlet container that supports those standards. Portlets are placed on the page in a certain order by the end user and are served up dynamically by the portal server. And, of course, you can lock down pages so that portlets can only be moved around by administrators.

I can almost hear your next question: what about my favorite framework? I don't want to give that up! Rest easy: you don't have to.

B.2 Portlets, frameworks, and other languages

A lot of developers nowadays like to use certain frameworks to develop their applications because those frameworks provide both functionality and structure to a project. For example, Struts enforces the Model-View-Controller design pattern and provides lots of functionality, such as custom tags and validation, that makes it easier for a developer to implement certain standard features. With Liferay, developers are free to use all the leading frameworks in the Java EE space, including Java Server Faces (JSF), Struts, and Spring MVC. This allows developers familiar with those frameworks to more easily implement portlets and also makes it easy to port an application that uses those frameworks over to a portlet implementation.

Additionally, Liferay allows for the consuming of PHP and Ruby applications as portlets, so you don't need to be a Java developer in order to take advantage of Liferay's built-in features (such as user management, communities, page building, and content management). You can use the Plugins SDK to deploy your PHP or Ruby application as a portlet, and it will run seamlessly inside Liferay. Liferay has plenty of examples of this; to see them, check out Liferay's plugins project (which is just a Plugins SDK prepopulated with sample portlets) from Liferay's public code repository.

Does your organization use any enterprise planning (ERP) software that exposes its data via web services? You could write a portlet plugin for Liferay that can consume that data and display it as part of a dashboard page for your users. Do you subscribe to a stock service? You could pull stock quotes from that service and display them on your page, instead of using Liferay's Stocks portlet. Do you need to combine the functionality of two or more servlet-based applications on one page? You could make them into portlet plugins and have Liferay display them in whatever layout you want. Do you have existing Struts, Spring MVC, or JSF applications that you want to integrate with your portal? It's a straightforward task to migrate these applications into Liferay; then they can take advantage of the layout, security, and administration infrastructure that Liferay provides.

Let's drop down from this high level and see what components make up a portlet.

B.3 Understanding the structure of a portlet

I said that portlets are really just web applications that run in only a portion of the page. That's a high-level way of looking at it. At a lower level, portlets are web components that process requests and generate content fragments that are then aggregated into a full web page by a portal server. They're written according to an overall standard (JSR-168 for Portlet 1.0, and JSR-286 for Portlet 2.0), and this standard is implemented by multiple portal vendors. In this way, portlets can be cross-platform and deployed on any number of servers that adhere to the standard.

From a deployment standpoint, an application server considers a portlet application to be a web application packaged in a web archive (.war file). Although the file structure inside this archive is the same as that of any web application, a portlet application contains at least one more deployment descriptor than a standard web application. This deployment descriptor is called portlet.xml and is stored in the WEB-INF directory along with the web.xml file. This descriptor tells the portlet container what portlets are included in the application, what portlet modes they support, and more.

Portlets, unlike servlets, have more than one phase of operation. In a servlet, the `service()` method processes all requests, often divided between `doGet()` and `doPost()` requests. A portlet has several phases:

- *Render phase*—Runs whenever the portlet needs to redraw itself on the page.
- *Action phase*—Called as the result of an `ActionURL`. This allows the portlet to do some processing to change its state, which is then reflected when the portlet is rendered again.
- *Event phase*—Called as the result of an event being fired. Events can be fired in the action phase of the portlet and are processed during the event phase.
- *Resource-serving phase*—Called by the `serveResource()` method. This is used for directly serving a particular resource without calling any other part of the lifecycle, and was designed with AJAX in mind.

Liferay 5.0 and greater support the Portlet 2.0 specification (JSR-286). This standard was approved and published on June 12, 2008. It retains backward compatibility with the first version of the specification while also adding new features. This means any portlet that ran on a Portlet 1.0 container ought also to run on a Portlet 2.0 container. The event and resource-serving phases are new features added to the specification. The event phase in particular is a welcome addition to the spec, because it provides a standard method of doing inter-portlet communication (allowing two or more portlets to communicate with one another).

Portlets have additional characteristics that make them different from servlets. Portlets have three standard *portlet modes*, which indicate the function the portlet is performing:

- *View mode*—The standard mode of the portlet when it's first displayed. This can consist of one or more screens of functionality in the portlet window.
- *Edit mode*—A mode in which portlet configuration can be done. For example, a weather portlet can be placed into edit mode to allow a user to enter a zip code that causes the portlet to show the forecast for that location when it's in view mode.
- *Help mode*—A separate mode that can be used to display help text about the portlet.

Portlets also have *window states* in which they can be displayed. Portlets can be maximized, minimized, or in normal mode. A maximized portlet takes up the entire page area. A minimized portlet shows only its title bar. And a portlet in normal mode can be on a page with several other portlets at the same time.

There is much more to the portlet specification than has been mentioned here, but this is a good introduction to the concept of a portlet without getting too detailed. For further information, you can read the specification—particularly if you're looking for a cure for insomnia.[1]

[1] You can find the specification here: http://mng.bz/9JnG

appendix C Inter-portlet communication

This appendix exists because I really wanted to cover inter-portlet communication (IPC) in the book. I think it's a core portlet skill, because much of the power of making portlet applications is the ability to make your applications modular. You can write one portlet that shows customers in a list, have a user click one of those customers, and then have their orders show up in another portlet on the page. The portal framework gives you the power to drag these portlets around and arrange them on the page any way you like. It's very powerful.

Unfortunately, the chapter I came up with didn't fit nicely into the book. The code wasn't Liferay-specific (because this is a core portlet skill), the example had nothing to do with Inkwell, and there was no good place to put the chapter. But I still wanted to put it in the book, somehow—so here it is, in an appendix.

You may have seen how easy it is to write a portlet. You may have been introduced to the basics of the Portlet API and used features from Portlet 1.0 to achieve this. We're now going to look at some of the things that Portlet 2.0 brings to the table. Of course, the best way to do this is by example. But first, I want to give you a little history of the portlet specification.

C.1 History of the portlet specification

I want to start with a mental exercise. If it helps, you can close your eyes. Wait: no you can't, because then you wouldn't be able to read what I'm about to tell you. Well, *imagine* your eyes are closed, or that you're doing whatever you need to do to help you visualize things.

The year is 2003. The internet bubble has burst, tech stocks have tumbled, and many, many internet startups have failed, their assets having been auctioned off to the highest bidder. You may be sitting in one of those trendy Herman Miller Aeron chairs, originally purchased by a hopeful entrepreneur using VC funds, and acquired at auction by your company for a fraction of its original price. But even if you're not, you're well aware of the downturn in the industry.

As a Java developer, you're looking for direction. Thankfully, Apache recently released the Struts framework, and you've been looking to implement it in your next project. Although a framework like Struts goes a long way toward enabling you to better manage and organize your web-development projects, it's for web applications only. You're aware of web services and SOAP and, although they're fairly new technologies, they hold some promise as a loosely coupled connection between various disparate (and mostly proprietary) systems. But again, that only solves part of the problem. You and the industry need a solution that brings all aspects of your application architecture together: security, infrastructure, and front-end web access to all those back-end processes. What is it?

C.1.1 Portlet 1.0: promising the stars and delivering ... what?

The original Java Portlet Specification (JSR-168) was finalized in October 2003. It was created to "define a Portlet API that provides means for aggregating several content sources and applications' front ends. It will also address how the security and personalization is handled."[1]

This was exactly the thing you and the industry were looking for. You read tons of press releases and articles about it—by all initial accounts, JSR-168 or Portlet 1.0 succeeded in giving the industry a solution to bringing everything in their enterprises together. There was now a standard in Java for applications that could reside in portions of a page. These applications could exist on their own or connect to back-end systems to expose data to the end user in combinations that had not been possible before. The applications would be aggregated together by a portlet container that adhered to a standard API, allowing these applications called portlets to run on a variety of application servers provided by multiple vendors. Everyone hailed the Day of the Portal. Or something like that. Open your eyes (or whatever)—you're about to get a dose of reality.

C.1.2 Portlet 2.0: a bit of a reboot

As developers began to implement applications using the JSR-168 standard, however, they soon found that the standard had some limitations. Perhaps the biggest limitation at the time was that there was no mechanism in the standard for allowing portlet applications to communicate with one another. This was a necessary feature to allow portals to serve complicated ERP, CRM, and workflow applications composed of multiple portlet windows.

Of course, the lack of a standard for this feature didn't stop innovative developers, who soon came up with multiple methods of doing this. The only problem was that

[1] http://jcp.org/en/jsr/detail?id=168

there was no consensus on how to make portlets talk to each other, and this affected the portability of applications. Liferay was no exception and had two methods for enabling this communication: a custom tag library for Java developers and custom JavaScript functions, which allowed the client-side developer to jump into the fray. Other portal vendors followed suit, with the result that there were multiple methods for IPC, but none of them were portable across portal servers. And this was just one problem with the standard.

The Portlet 2.0 standard process began in November 2005 with solving this problem as one of its goals. Three years later, the standard was finalized, and Liferay Portal was one of the first portal vendors to provide an implementation. This means we can finally begin writing new (or porting old) portlet applications to take advantage of true, cross-platform IPC!

The new standard provides for (among other things) portlet events. Portlets can send events with payloads of data that other portlets can then receive and act upon. Multiple portlets can listen to multiple events, and the portlets don't need to be on the same portal page in order to communicate in this fashion. This opens the door to the creation of robust portlet applications whose various portlet windows can remain in sync with the navigation of the user. These portlet applications can be written to the standard, allowing them to be deployed on any portal server that supports the standard.

What follows is an introduction to the event-driven method of providing inter-portlet communication in the new Java Portlet Standard (JSR-286). We'll go in and create a couple of portlets that can talk to each other.

C.2 Portlets conversing about baseball

You'll be creating a simple demonstration of IPC using baseball—well, at least, part of baseball. Your project will contain two portlets: a Pitcher portlet and a Catcher portlet. You can see the Pitcher portlet in figure C.1: it will randomly generate a pitch and then send the name of the pitch as the payload of a portlet event. To cause the portlet to do this, you'll provide a simple link.

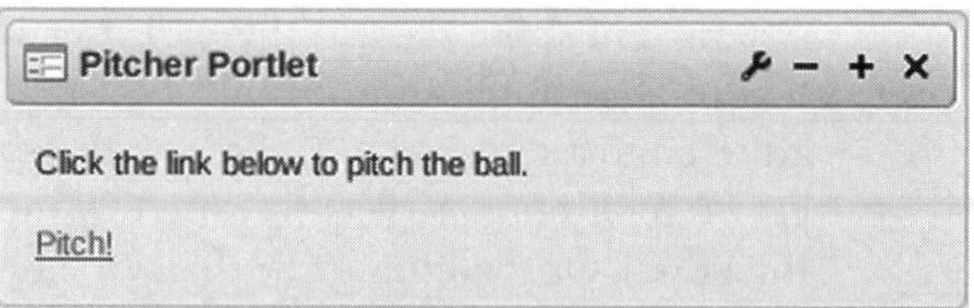

Figure C.1 Click the Pitch link to pitch the ball. This will send an event with the type of pitch to any portlets listening for that particular event.

The Catcher portlet will listen for the event. When it receives the event, it will display the name of the pitch it received from the Pitcher portlet (see figure C.2). It doesn't

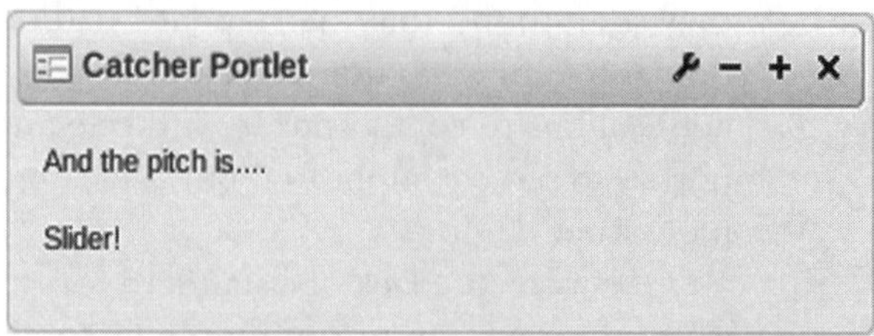

Figure C.2 The Catcher portlet receives the event and displays it. Because your event is a `String` that denotes the type of pitch, the catcher portlet displays the event payload.

do anything other than that, but you might be able to create an entire portlet-based baseball game, if you wanted to.

There is no `BatterPortlet`. Yes, this makes for a rather boring game; but hey, there's nothing stopping you from implementing the batter yourself. You'll start by creating the project in the Plugins SDK. Because the Plugins SDK makes certain assumptions when generating a project, you'll have to refactor what it creates by default.

C.3 Creating and refactoring the project

To create your portlet project, start from a command prompt, and then navigate to the portlets directory in the Plugins SDK. If you're using LUM, type

```
./create.sh ipc-baseball "IPC Baseball"
```

If you're using Windows, type

```
create.bat ipc-baseball "IPC Baseball"
```

The Plugins SDK automatically generates a blank portlet project with the name ipc-baseball-portlet. This project will reside in the portlets directory of the Plugins SDK. If you use a text editor, you can begin working right away. If you use an IDE, you'll need to import the project and set up its dependencies. See appendix A for further information about this.

When Liferay's Plugins SDK generates a portlet project, it makes an assumption that your project will have one portlet in it and that the portlet will have the same name as the overall project. IDEs that support portlet projects do the same thing. For this example, however, this isn't the case. You'll have two portlets: a `PitcherPortlet` class and a `CatcherPortlet` class in one project. You need to modify the project so it's set up the way you want it.

The first thing to do is create your two portlet classes. Create a package in the src folder of your project and create `PitcherPortlet` and `CatcherPortlet`. Both of these classes should extend the `GenericPortlet` class.

Next, you need to modify the portlet.xml file. This file resides in the WEB-INF folder along with the web.xml file that defines a web module. When the project was generated, this file was generated with an entry to the default portlet, and you need to modify it to point to your two portlets. Because you created the two portlet classes you need, these changes need to be reflected in the portlet.xml file.

First, change the portlet name, the display name, and the portlet class:

```
<portlet-name>pitcher-portlet</portlet-name>
<display-name>Pitcher Portlet</display-name>
<portlet-class>com.liferayinaction.ipc.PitcherPortlet</portlet-class>
```

Next, modify the `init-param` for the view mode of this portlet so that it points to a JSP stored in a directory for the portlet:

```
<init-param>
  <name>view-jsp</name>
```

```
  <value>/pitcher/view.jsp</value>
</init-param>
```

The JSP will be in a subfolder.

Finally, modify the `portlet-info` tag so it reads as follows:

```
<portlet-info>
  <title>Pitcher Portlet</title>
  <short-title>Pitcher Portlet</short-title>
  <keywords>IPC Baseball Pitcher</keywords>
</portlet-info>
```

Next, you need to add a new portlet declaration for the `CatcherPortlet` class, which you can see in the following listing.

Listing C.1 `CatcherPortlet's` entry in portlet.xml

```
<portlet>
  <portlet-name>catcher-portlet</portlet-name>
  <display-name>Catcher Portlet</display-name>
  <portlet-class>
      com.liferayinaction.ipc.CatcherPortlet          <-- Portlet class
  </portlet-class>

  <init-param>
    <name>view-jsp</name>
    <value>/catcher/view.jsp</value>          <-- JSP in folder
  </init-param>
  <expiration-cache>0</expiration-cache>
  <supports>
    <mime-type>text/html</mime-type>
  </supports>
  <portlet-info>
    <title>Catcher Portlet</title>          <-- Title in portlet window
    <short-title>Catcher Portlet</short-title>          <-- Short title in portlet window
    <keywords>IPC Baseball Catcher</keywords>
  </portlet-info>
  <security-role-ref>
    <role-name>administrator</role-name>
  </security-role-ref>
  <security-role-ref>
    <role-name>guest</role-name>
  </security-role-ref>
  <security-role-ref>
    <role-name>power-user</role-name>
  </security-role-ref>
  <security-role-ref>
    <role-name>user</role-name>
  </security-role-ref>
</portlet>
```

docroot/WEB-INF/portlet.xml

C.4 Configuring the event definition

The event definition is placed at the bottom of the file, outside the two portlets. Your event is a simple one: the `PitcherPortlet` will randomly generate a pitch (a number from 1 to 3), which will be translated into a `String` denoting what kind of pitch it is. This `String` object will be sent as the payload of the `Pitch` event. The `PitcherPortlet` will be configured to send the event, and the `CatcherPortlet` will be configured to receive the event.

First you define the event itself, and then you define which portlet sends the event and which portlet receives it. Below the last portlet in the portlet.xml file, add the following code:

```
<event-definition>
  <qname xmlns:x="http://liferay.com/events">x:ipc.pitch</qname>
  <value-type>java.lang.String</value-type>
</event-definition>
```

A QName is a *qualified name*. Using a QName allows events to be name-spaced properly so that no two event names are identical. This definition declares an event called `ipc.pitch` within the namespace http://liferay.com/events. You also declare that your payload is a `String` object.

Now that you have the event, you need to identify who can send it and who can receive it.

C.4.1 Identifying the event sender

The portlet standard defines a way of telling the portlet container (in this case, Liferay Portal) which portlet is responsible for sending an event. This is `PitcherPortlet`. Place the following code in the `PitcherPortlet` definition in portlet.xml, below the last `<security-role-ref>` tag:

```
<supported-publishing-event>
  <qname xmlns:x="http://liferay.com/events">x:ipc.pitch</qname>
</supported-publishing-event>
```

This tells Liferay that `PitcherPortlet` supports the publishing of the event you defined earlier. Next, you need a receiver.

C.4.2 Identifying the event receiver

The portlet standard allows one or many portlets to receive events. This might allow you to later create a `BatterPortlet` that also listens for the ipc.pitch event and determines whether the ball is hit. For now, you have only one event receiver: `CatcherPortlet`. Add the following code below the last `<security-role-ref>` tag in the `CatcherPortlet` definition:

```
<supported-processing-event>
  <qname xmlns:x="http://liferay.com/events">x:ipc.pitch</qname>
</supported-processing-event>
```

You've defined everything you need to define in the portlet.xml file. Save and close the file; it's time to begin implementing the event.

C.5 Structuring the Pitcher portlet

`PitcherPortlet` and `CatcherPortlet` will have the same basic structure as the Hello You portlet in chapter 2. Let's add that structure to the portlets first. You can see this overall structure in the following listing; this code should be inside the class declaration for each portlet.

Listing C.2 Portlet code structure for Pitcher and Catcher portlets

```
public void init()
    throws PortletException {

    viewJSP = getInitParameter("view-jsp");
}


public void doView(RenderRequest req, RenderResponse res)
    throws IOException, PortletException {

    include(viewJSP, req, res);
}


protected void include(
        String path, RenderRequest req, RenderResponse res)
    throws IOException, PortletException {

    PortletRequestDispatcher prd =
        getPortletContext().getRequestDispatcher(path);

    if (prd == null) {
        _log.error(path + " is not a valid include");

    }
    else {
        prd.include(req, res);
    }
}

protected String viewJSP;

private static Log _log = LogFactory.getLog(PitcherPortlet.class);
```

Notice that there is no `processAction()` method in this code. One of the enhancements in the Portlet 2.0 standard is the use of Java 5 or above. Because Portlet 2.0 is based on Java 5, it can use annotations to make things easier. In the past, developers were encouraged to extend the `GenericPortlet` class and override the `processAction()` method to determine which portlet action to run. For a complicated portlet, this could result in a long if-then-else statement inside the `processAction` method.

With Portlet 2.0, methods that process specific actions can be created without having to override the `processAction()` method; you do this through annotations, as you'll see next. You'll notice that it results in a much cleaner portlet class.

The `PitcherPortlet's` processing is simple:

1. The view.jsp file displays a URL to the Pitch action.
2. When a user clicks the URL, the Pitch action is called.
3. The action generates a pitch and then publishes the pitch as an event.

Let's implement this totally awesome (random) pitching algorithm, shown in the next listing.

Listing C.3 Totally awesome pitching algorithm

```
@ProcessAction(name="pitchBall")
public void pitchBall(ActionRequest request, ActionResponse response) {
    String pitchType = null;

    Random random = new Random(System.currentTimeMillis());
    int pitch = random.nextInt(3) + 1;
    switch (pitch) {
    case 1:
        pitchType = "Fast Ball";
        break;
    case 2:
        pitchType = "Curve Ball";
        break;
    case 3:
        pitchType = "Slider";
        break;

    default:

        pitchType = "Screw Ball";

    }

    QName qName = new QName("http://liferay.com/events", "ipc.pitch");
    response.setEvent(qName, pitchType);
}
```

docroot/WEB-INF/src/com/liferayinaction/ipc/PitcherPortlet.java

Notice that the event starts with an annotation. Because you're extending `GenericPortlet`, you're using that portlet's `processAction()` method. The implementation of `processAction()` in `GenericPortlet` uses annotations to call any method with the same name as the action name. When the user clicks an action URL with the name `pitchBall`, this method is called.

The `pitchBall()` method generates a random number between 1 and 3 and translates this number into a String describing the type of pitch. You then send an event with the name you defined in portlet.xml containing the `String` payload that has the pitch type. As you can see, it takes only two lines of code to look up the event type, set the payload, and send the event.

Let's turn to the `PitcherPortlet`'s view, which is implemented in view.jsp. The Pitcher view is very simple: it displays a short message and a URL (see listing C.4). Create this file in the location you defined earlier in portlet.xml (docroot/pitcher/view.jsp).

Listing C.4 `PitcherPortlet's` view.jsp, which lets the user pitch a ball

```
<%@ taglib uri="http://java.sun.com/portlet_2_0" prefix="portlet" %>

<portlet:defineObjects />

<p>Click the link below to pitch the ball.</p>

<a href="<portlet:actionURL name="pitchBall" />">Pitch!
</a>
```

docroot/WEB-INF/pitcher/view.jsp

As you can see, you do something a little different this time to create the `ActionURL`. You create the URL directly in the JSP using portlet tags, whereas in the Portlet 1.0 example (the Hello You portlet from chapter 2) you created the URL in the portlet class and sent it to the JSP as a bean in the request. Either way is fine; most developers find using the tags to be easier. I wanted to show you both ways of doing it so you can decide which way works best for you. The action URL you created is named `pitchBall`, which corresponds to the method name and annotation. When a user clicks this link, your action method is called.

The pitcher is now implemented. You now need somebody to catch the ball.

C.6 Structuring the Catcher portlet

The Catcher portlet is even simpler. It doesn't do anything except receive the event sent to it by the Pitcher portlet and then display the payload. This is a much more basic application of this particular technology than you might normally use events for. If you were doing this in a real application, you might instead examine the payload of the event and then perform some action on it. For example, a portlet could receive an event that contains a customer number. This event might have been sent by a search portlet or a portlet that lets you browse customers. After the portlet received this event, it could take that number, query a database for all orders the customer has placed, and then display those orders. In this way, a developer could write one portlet that does customer lookups and another portlet that does order lookups. If these portlets communicate with each other using events, they could be used to assemble an invoicing application fairly quickly, using the portal container to lay out the pages.

In this case, all the Catcher portlet does is display the type of pitch the Pitcher portlet generated. As you did with the Pitcher portlet, place the following method below the `include()` method in CatcherPortlet.java:

```
@ProcessEvent(qname="{http://liferay.com/events}ipc.pitch")
public void catchBall(EventRequest request, EventResponse response) {
    Event event = request.getEvent();
```

```
    String pitch = (String) event.getValue();
    response.setRenderParameter("pitch", pitch);
}
```

As in the earlier case, you're using annotations. `GenericPortlet`'s `processEvent()` method works like its `processAction()` method and directs the processing to your `catchBall()` method. In this case, the name of the event is the parameter to the annotation. The only processing you do is to take the value of the event payload and set it as a render parameter so it can be displayed to the user during the render phase of the portlet. A portlet's render phase occurs when the portlet redraws itself according to whatever parameters are set.

As shown in the next listing, the Catcher view takes the render parameter you set (which has the pitch payload in it as a `String`) and displays it on the page.

Listing C.5 Displaying the catch to the user

```
<%@ taglib uri="http://java.sun.com/portlet_2_0" prefix="portlet" %>

<portlet:defineObjects />

<%
String pitch = (String) renderRequest.getParameter("pitch");
%>

<p>And the pitch is....</p>

<p>
<%
if (pitch != null) {
%>
    <%= pitch %>!
<%
}
else {
%>
    ... waiting for pitch.
<%
}
%>
</p>
```

docroot/WEB-INF/catcher/view.jsp

Remember, this file should be created in the folder you defined earlier in portlet.xml (docroot/catcher/view.jsp). As you can see, the page attempts to retrieve the render parameter. If it's null, the page displays a message stating that it's still waiting for the pitch event.

You've configured everything that's necessary to deploy this project on any Portlet 2.0 standards-compliant portlet container. You could build the project right now and deploy it, but there are some extra things you can do to package the project better for Liferay.

C.7 Other deployment descriptors

Three other deployment descriptors were generated when you generated this project:

- liferay-portlet.xml
- liferay-display.xml
- liferay-plugin-package.properties

These are Liferay-specific deployment descriptors that let you specify settings that the Liferay portlet container can act on. Because they don't exist in the portlet standard, they will be ignored by other containers.

C.7.1 liferay-portlet.xml

This descriptor lets you tell Liferay some extra things about the portlet. Some common things you'll want to set here for your own portlets are the location of CSS and JavaScript files and the location of the icon for the portlet and also link Portlet API roles to Liferay roles. The following listing contains the entirety of this file.

Listing C.6 IPC Baseball's liferay-portlet.xml configuration file

```
<?xml version="1.0"?>
<!DOCTYPE liferay-portlet-app PUBLIC "-//Liferay//DTD Portlet Application
➥ 6.0.0//EN" "http://www.liferay.com/dtd/liferay-portlet-app_6_0_0.dtd">

<liferay-portlet-app>
  <portlet>
    <portlet-name>pitcher-portlet</portlet-name>         <-- Name must map to portlet.xml

    <icon>/icon.png</icon>                    <-- Icon in portlet window

    <instanceable>true</instanceable>          <-- Portlet instanceable?

    <header-portlet-css>/css/test.css</header-portlet-css>    <-- Defines CSS per portlet
<header-portlet-javascript>
   /js/test.js
</header-portlet-javascript>                   <-- Defines JS per portlet
     </portlet>
     <portlet>
    <portlet-name>catcher-portlet</portlet-name>
    <icon>/icon.png</icon>
    <instanceable>true</instanceable>
    <header-portlet-css>/css/test.css</header-portlet-css>
<header-portlet-javascript>
   /js/test.js
</header-portlet-javascript>
  </portlet>
  <role-mapper>                                <-- Maps JSR-286 roles to Liferay roles
    <role-name>administrator</role-name>
    <role-link>Administrator</role-link>
```

```
  </role-mapper>
  <role-mapper>
    <role-name>guest</role-name>
    <role-link>Guest</role-link>
  </role-mapper>
  <role-mapper>
    <role-name>power-user</role-name>
    <role-link>Power User</role-link>
  </role-mapper>
  <role-mapper>
    <role-name>user</role-name>
    <role-link>User</role-link>
  </role-mapper>
</liferay-portlet-app>
```

As you can see, each portlet in this file must map to the same entry in portlet.xml; this is how Liferay knows which portlet to apply these settings to. All of these settings are optional and Liferay-specific, but they help Liferay to better aggregate the portlets on a page. For example, telling Liferay where the CSS and JavaScript files are for this portlet enables Liferay to declare these files in the `<head>` section of the HTML that is returned to the browser. This ensures that browsers process your JavaScript and your styles correctly. Otherwise, they would've been inserted wherever you inserted them in your markup, leading to strange behavior in the browser (because a proper HTML page requires that they be declared in the `<head>` of the page).

C.7.2 liferay-display.xml

Use the liferay-display.xml descriptor to place the portlet in a category of your choosing in the Add > More window. You'll place your portlets in their own category, which you'll call IPC (see the next listing).

Listing C.7 IPC Baseball's liferay-display.xml configuration file

```
<?xml version="1.0"?>
<!DOCTYPE display PUBLIC "-//Liferay//DTD Display 6.0.0//EN"
➥ "http://www.liferay.com/dtd/liferay-display_6_0_0.dtd">

<display>
  <category name="IPC">
    <portlet id="pitcher-portlet" />
    <portlet id="catcher-portlet" />
  </category>
</display>
```

docroot/WEB-INF/liferay-display.xml

This code results in a new category called IPC, and this category will contain both portlets from this project.

C.7.3 liferay-plugin-package.properties

Liferay-plugin-package.properties allows you to define metadata about the portlet for Liferay's Software Catalog (see listing C.8). You can also define dependency .jar files, which are copied from the Liferay installation to the portlet .war at deploy time.

Listing C.8 IPC Baseball's liferay-plugin-package.properties configuration file

```
name=IPC Baseball
module-group-id=liferay
module-incremental-version=1
tags=
short-description=
change-log=
page-url=http://www.liferay.com
author=Liferay, Inc.
licenses=MIT

portal.dependency.jars=\
    jstl.jar,\
    jstl-impl.jar
```

docroot/WEB-INF/liferay-plugin-package.properties

These three files go in the WEB-INF folder of the project with the other deployment descriptors. Default versions were generated, but you should replace what is in them with the code shown here.

C.8 Deploying and testing the portlets

To deploy the portlet, run the *deploy* Ant task. This can be done from the command line (on any OS) by entering the project folder and typing the following command:

```
ant deploy
```

If Liferay is running, it will automatically deploy the portlet. If Liferay isn't yet running, start it; when it has finished starting, the portlet will be deployed.

To test the portlets, log into Liferay with the default administrative credentials:

User Name: test@liferay.com
Password: test

Go to the Dockbar, and select Add > More. A new window will pop up with categories of applications in it.

From the IPC category (which you created in liferay-display.xml), drag the Pitcher and the Catcher portlets onto the page and drop them there. Click the Pitch link in the Pitcher portlet. The pitch event will be received by the Catcher portlet, and the pitch will be displayed there (see figures C.1 and C.2).

C.9 Some notes about events

Portlet events have some qualities that can make them interesting to implement. Here are a few things you should be aware of when working with portlet events. I love how the portlet spec words these things sometimes, so for the first one, I'll give you a quote:

> Portlet events are not a replacement for reliable messaging (see other JavaEE APIs, like Java Message Service, JMS, for providing reliable messaging). *Portlet events are not guaranteed to be delivered* and thus the portlet should always work in a meaningful manner even if some or all events are not being delivered.[2] [emphasis mine]

It's worded to induce panic, isn't it? What's the point of using events if they're not guaranteed to be delivered? Rest assured; this isn't as bad as it sounds. What the JSR committee means here is that a portlet event is part of a request. Events don't go into a queue where they can be collected if there's trouble delivering them, and they don't have any way of handshaking with their receivers to verify that they've been received. They're sent with the hope that someone out there is listening (see figure C.3). If you need guaranteed delivery, queuing, polling, and/or handshaking, it behooves you to use a more robust API like JMS or Liferay's message bus.

You made `CatcherPortlet` work in a meaningful manner by providing a default message in case there was no event. This is the kind of thing you should do whenever you're writing portlets based on events.

Events are like broadcasts. They go out, but they're only heard if another portlet is listening (again, see figure C.3). The portlet spec says sure, you can use the `setEvent()` method programmatically without declaring the event in the deployment descriptor. But the individual portlet container may decide not to deliver the event—this is left up to the individual portal vendor to decide. In Liferay's case, Liferay will deliver all events that are listened for. You definitely have to declare ahead of time that a portlet is listening for an event, but you don't necessarily have to declare that a portlet is going to send a particular event. It's still a good practice to declare what events your portlets will send, as it prevents someone else who might have to maintain your code from having to

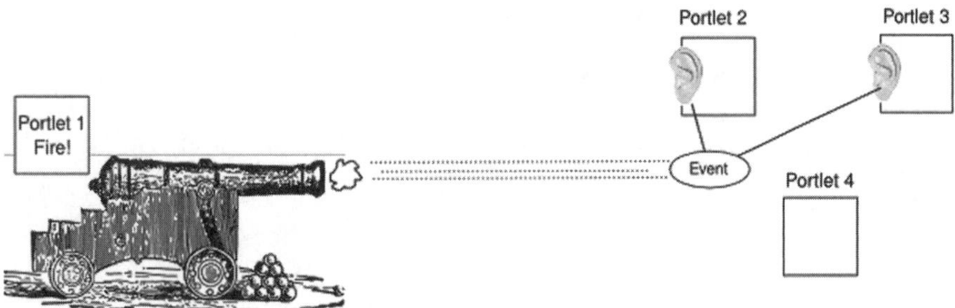

Figure C.3 Portlet events are fired by the portlet that is configured to send the event. Only the portlets that are configured to listen for the event receive it. In this example, portlet 2 and portlet 3 would receive the event, but portlet 4 wouldn't.

[2] JSR-286 Portlet 2.0 specification, http://jcp.org/en/jsr/summary?id=286, page 109.

search the code for events. If they're declared, all that person has to do is look at your portlet.xml file.

The spec also says that portlet events can be heard by portlets that aren't on the same page as the portlet that sent the event. Liferay implements this in a couple of different ways. Remember that portal-ext.properties file you used in chapter 2 to connect Liferay to a database? There's a property you can use in that file to define how you want Liferay to handle events:

```
portlet.event.distribution=layout
```

You can set this property to either `layout` (the default) or to `layout-set`. If set to `layout`, portlets have to be on the same page as the sender in order to receive any of its events. If it's set to `layout-set`, portlets in the same group of pages—either the public or private pages of a community or organization—will be able to receive events sent by any portlet within the same layout set.

Events can also be sent between portlets residing in different .war files. This is one of the features of the design. Just because you put both portlets in one project for this example doesn't mean you have to. In fact, if you wanted, you could turn Hello You into a portlet that responded to the Pitch event in some way (maybe by yelling, "He's no batter! Swing!").

The last thing I want to mention about events is that you can't predict the order in which other portlets will hear events, so it's best not to chain events or make them depend on each other in some way; you can't guarantee which events are sent when or which portlets hear events first or last.

appendix D
How to contribute to Liferay

Liferay Portal is an open source project. Yes, it has a company behind it that supports it and provides training, documentation, consulting services, and anything else you might imagine to foster its use and help people be successful with it. But it also has a vibrant community of thousands of users and developers who contribute to the product and help make it better by writing the features *they* need—which are likely also the features *you* need—and then contributing those features back to the product. This successful mixture of a commercial entity and open source works because open source as a philosophy of how to do software is something that the founders of the company (and many of the employees, like me) believe in at the core of our being.

I can't point to just one thing that won me over to the open source mindset. I switched to Linux when Windows 98 kept crashing and making me lose my data. I moved from proprietary systems over to the Java world to escape being placed in the same niche as the products in which I had expertise. And I can't tell you how many times an open source project has saved my bacon in various projects over the years. But for the founders of Liferay, it goes deeper than that.

Around the year 2000, a very young software developer named Brian Chan volunteered to create a web site for his church. He wanted to make it dynamic and fully featured, as well as easy to update for end users who couldn't tell an HTML tag from a .gif file. Looking around at what was available, though, he found that his financially strapped, nonprofit organization would have to fork over thousands of dollars to purchase software to do the kinds of things he wanted to do. What does a good software developer do in that circumstance? That's right—he rolled up his sleeves and got to work writing it himself.

During the first few years of Liferay's existence, there was no company behind it. It was a small open source project that was slowly gaining a community. Soon, one company became interested in using it for their web site, and Brian found that he needed help—he couldn't both work on enhancing Liferay and work on customizing it for customers at the same time all by himself. He asked for help from some of his friends—people he knew and trusted. Some he met while getting his degree, and some he met in other ways. These became the founders of Liferay the company, and they all took great leaps of faith in quitting jobs to join what was, by all definitions, a very risky endeavor.

Pretty soon, Brian had another customer. His wife began handling the administration and finances of the fledgling company. Another customer, and the company needed a team of consultants. Liferay rented an apartment in a bad neighborhood in LA, and a team of guys—most of whom didn't even know each other before being hired—lived there, meeting with customers by day and coding by night.

Meanwhile, the community grew. Because Liferay was an open source project, it received contributions from all over the world. Key contributors came not just from LA, but from Canada, Spain, Hong Kong, and all over the US. A major system built on Liferay was implemented in the school system in Madrid. Liferay received internationalization code from a developer in Canada. And Liferay continued to gain customers—customers who first downloaded the product for free and then paid the company for support and customization. This allowed more people to be hired, and these people could do things like enhance the product, run the company, start offices in China, manage projects, coordinate training, and yes, write documentation. But even those people are bolstered by the members of the community who add to the product every day—features and ideas that those who are close to the product might never have thought of.

Open source built not only Liferay Portal the product, but also Liferay the company. Now the customizations are easy: if you've read this book, you can see how Liferay is designed to be customized, to have applications built on it, to be made in *your* image. This only happened because, by a leap of faith, the product was made available to all, and the best way I can say this is that God put the right people in place to make it a success. It's the people who matter—people like you, who use Liferay to make your business more successful, to make sites that entertain and educate children and adults, or to design a system that tracks relief efforts for those in need, making the world a better place.

Whatever you use Liferay for, if it's something you think could or should be part of the product, you can contribute that feature back to the product. Of course, giving back to the product makes the product better, but if your feature goes in, Liferay then becomes responsible for keeping it up to date. It's a win-win situation for you.

Let's see how you can contribute back to Liferay. We'll start with contributing code either by yourself or as part of a community program, move to contributing documentation, and finally look at contributing bug reports and new feature requests.

D.1 Making a code contribution

If you've got code to contribute, that's fantastic! A lot of what's in Liferay came from contributions like this. There's a procedure to follow that makes sense when you think about it:

1. Make sure the feature doesn't already exist. It almost sounds humorous to say that, but I figured I'd mention it anyway. You might post a message about the feature on Liferay's message boards to see if there's wider interest in it, too.
2. Optional: if you're implementing the feature for your organization, you should implement it in Ext first, so that you and your organization can take advantage of the feature right away.
3. Grab Liferay's source as a download or clone it from Liferay's Github repository (https://github.com/liferay/liferay-portal), and make your changes in the source. Your source should follow Liferay's code-development guidelines, which I've modeled for you in the source for this book.[1]
4. Create a patch for your features. Your patch should include only differences and should not include any differences generated from Service Builder, because the services will be regenerated anyway by Liferay's engineering team.
5. Go to Liferay's issue management system at http://issues.liferay.com, and add a New Feature issue describing the feature in detail. Attach to this issue the patch you created in the previous step, and name the patch according to the issue number you receive from the system and the SVN revision number against which you wrote the code. Example: LPS-12345-build-54321.patch.
6. Click Contribute Solution on your issue. If you've reported the issue, you can also click Accept Contribution to change the state to Community Resolved. If somebody else added the ticket, that person will have to accept the contribution.

After you've got your contribution in this state, you'll likely be contacted by one or more of Liferay's core engineers as they work through your contribution.

Of course, these steps describe the most complicated of scenarios: the implementation of a new feature. There's absolutely nothing stopping you from following the same procedure to report and fix bugs.

There are other ways in which you can contribute too; let's look at those.

D.2 Taking advantage of community programs

If you want to be more involved, you can become part of a community team that focuses on issues that the community agrees need to be addressed. This is called Liferay's 100 PaperCuts program[2]. The idea is to create a team of people to address the most annoying issues—or paper cuts—within Liferay. These are the kinds of issues that aren't showstoppers or bugs, but instead are those annoying sorts of things that people learn to work around. They're called paper cuts because they're like small

---

[1] The complete list of guidelines is here: http://mng.bz/MWcO

[2] You can find information on the 100 PaperCuts program at http://mng.bz/9pto

injuries: they don't stop you from accomplishing what you need to do, but they're irritating when they happen.

If you use Eclipse for Liferay development and you've developed a particularly productive way of doing so, you can also help out with Liferay IDE.[3] This is a set of Eclipse plugins (covered in appendix A) that makes it easier for developers to work with Liferay and Liferay projects. The procedure for adding features and fixing bugs is the same as for Liferay.

Let's turn to a contribution that's a little different: documentation.

D.3 Contributing documentation

Found a hole in Liferay's docs? Want to document that new feature you just contributed? You can contribute documentation to Liferay as well. Liferay's wiki is replete with community documentation that helps users every day make the most out of Liferay. Look at the editorial guidelines,[4] and then go ahead and add your documentation.

There are a lot fewer steps involved than contributing code, and documentation is of great use to people who are implementing Liferay installations around the world. Perhaps you've got a working configuration of Liferay and SSL, or you've successfully connected Liferay to a single sign-on implementation. You can document that configuration in the wiki for the benefit of others who are working on a similar setup.

Liferay's official documentation is Creative Commons licensed and is also available on Github. Would you like to create a translation into your native language? Clone the repository, make your translation, and send me a pull request. Think something's poorly written or not covered as exhaustively as it could be? Make your change and send me a pull request. It's that easy.

Finally, if you're strapped for time, you can still contribute bug reports and feature suggestions.

D.4 Contributing bug reports and feature suggestions

If you're not a programmer, don't know anything about Eclipse, and don't like writing—or are strapped for time due to the constraints of your own projects—you can make a valuable contribution by submitting bug reports and feature suggestions to Liferay. You do so using the same issue-management system you'd use to contribute code to Liferay.[5]

The first thing you'll want to do is a search to make sure the bug or feature hasn't already been reported. If you don't find anything, you can create the issue and mark it as a bug or a feature request. It's simple to do this; and often, someone from Liferay or from the community will pick up your feature or bug report and get it implemented.

As you can see, there are many ways you can contribute back to the open source project. If you have time to do so, I strongly urge you to get involved. Everybody can make a contribution, and the product becomes better every time someone new brings their gifts and ideas to the table.

---

[3] You can find out more about contributing to Liferay IDE at http://mng.bz/z6qV

[4] Editorial guidelines are here: http://mng.bz/M78f

[5] http://issues.liferay.com

appendix E Liferay 6.1 Documents API

You may have noticed a glaring omission from the body of this book. Liferay has an API that its Document Library uses to manage, store, and retrieve files to and from the file system; yet there was no mention of it anywhere. Why is this?

It's for a good reason. This API changed significantly between Liferay 6.0 and Liferay 6.1; and because I wanted the book to apply to both versions, I thought it best to relegate covering this API to an appendix, where we can look at the commonalities and the differences in both versions of Liferay. This way, you can be empowered to use the API regardless of which version you're on. You won't encounter code in the body of the book that doesn't apply to your copy of Liferay, and you still get to find out about the API and how to use it. Hey, I'm looking out for you.

Let's look at Liferay's Documents API to see where it's been, where it's going, and what it can do for you.

E.1 Reviewing document handling in Liferay

When Liferay first started working with documents, it was out of a necessity to have a way to store files in a file system type of structure on the Web. These files would be displayed in a Document Library portlet that gave users the ability to upload and share documents. Early versions of Liferay had only the Liferay repository as a design goal, so the initial API reflects this design.

Later, as more features were added to the API, it grew. The concept of *hooks* was added first. These allowed developers to change the back end of the Document Library to point to different file-storage repositories. They predated Hook plugins, still exist in Liferay 6.0, and have been renamed to Stores in Liferay 6.1 to avoid confusion with Hook plugins. For this reason, if you're on 6.0, you have to be careful sometimes to clearly state what kind of hook you're talking about if you're in a heavy technical conversation with a fellow Liferay developer.

The most famous hook that a lot of developers know about is the `JCRHook`. At one time, it was the default hook for the Document Library, because it turned the Document Library portlet into a Java Content Repository (hence the name `JCRHook`). Using the open source Jackrabbit repository from Apache as the implementation of the JCR, Liferay was able to ship with a complete implementation of the JSR-170 standard.

Recent releases relegate the `JCRHook` to an option rather than the default, because the file system–based hooks perform better, and the JCR standard hasn't caught on as expected. But other document-storage options are available, and Liferay's Document Library can connect to them.

E.1.1 Connecting to repositories in 6.0 and below

Liferay 6.0 and below use Document Library hooks (again, not to be confused with Hook plugins) to connect to various repositories. This means administrators can choose which kind of repository the Document Library will use, and then users can happily upload documents to that repository (see figure E.1).

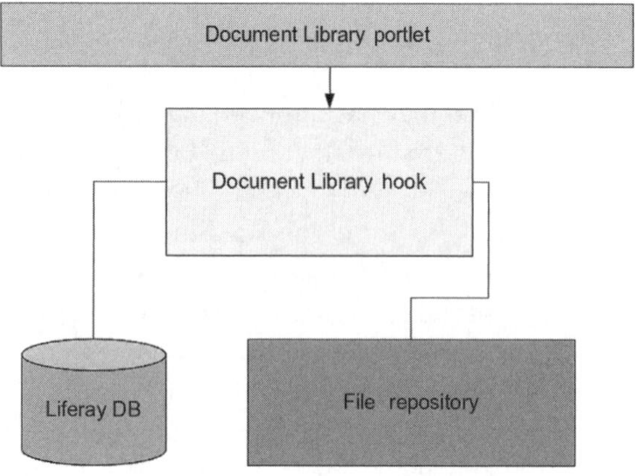

Figure E.1 The Document Library portlet can be connected to any repository for which there is a Document Library hook to support it.

Liferay supports several different Document Library hooks for various repositories:

- *File System Hook*—For connecting to disk-based file systems
- *Advanced File System Hook*—For better performance and scalability on disk-based file systems
- *CMIS Hook*—For connecting to a CMIS repository
- *JCR Hook*—For connecting to a JSR-170 Jackrabbit repository
- *S3 Hook*—For connecting to a file store on Amazon's S3 service

As you can see, the Document Library hooks system provides the Document Library portlet with flexibility in choosing its data store. When the data store is hooked up, users can store files using the portlet or using other portlets that implement the Document Library API. For example, Liferay's Message Boards portlet supports attaching files; the portlet uses the Document Library API to make this happen.

Speaking of the API, let's look at what Liferay gives you for storing and retrieving documents.

E.1.2 Storing and retrieving documents: the low-level API

Okay, so it's not really a low-level API. I get that. Java's API for files is lower-level for sure. But because the way documents are handled has been enhanced in Liferay 6.1, we need some way of referring to the older API, which is still there and still relevant for some use cases. This API follows the same pattern you see everywhere in Liferay: it has a model and it has services. The model objects are as follows:

- `DLFileEntry`—Represents a file
- `DLFileRank`—Represents the most recently accessed files per user
- `DLFileShortcut`—Represents a shortcut to another file entry
- `DLFileVersion`—Represents a particular version of a file
- `DLFolder`—Represents a folder

In 6.0 or earlier, to store and retrieve documents, you use the matching service layer (such as `DLLocalServiceUtil`) to persist these objects to Liferay. The Document Library hook takes care of how the files get persisted and how the metadata is loaded into Liferay. This API can be used anywhere in Liferay, including your plugins. The following listing shows how it's used in Liferay's Message Boards.

Listing E.1 Adding attachments to messages

```
if (files.size() > 0) {
    long companyId = message.getCompanyId();
    String portletId = CompanyConstants.SYSTEM_STRING;
    long dlGroupId = GroupConstants.DEFAULT_PARENT_GROUP_ID;
    long repositoryId = CompanyConstants.SYSTEM;                  ❶ Value: 0 in LR 6.0
    String dirName = message.getAttachmentsDir();

    try {
        dlService.deleteDirectory(
            companyId, portletId, repositoryId, dirName);
    }
    catch (NoSuchDirectoryException nsde) {
        if (_log.isDebugEnabled()) {
            _log.debug(nsde.getMessage());
        }
    }

    dlService.addDirectory(companyId, repositoryId, dirName);     ❷ Adds folder

    for (int i = 0; i < files.size(); i++) {
        ObjectValuePair<String, byte[]> ovp = files.get(i);

        String fileName = ovp.getKey();
        byte[] bytes = ovp.getValue();

        try {
            dlService.addFile(                                    ❸ Adds attached files
                companyId, portletId, dlGroupId, repositoryId,
                dirName + "/" + fileName, 0, StringPool.BLANK,
                message.getModifiedDate(), new ServiceContext(), bytes);
```

```
        }
        catch (DuplicateFileException dfe) {
            if (_log.isDebugEnabled()) {
                _log.debug(dfe.getMessage());
            }
        }
    }
}
```

You can see that this is similar to any other service call either inside Liferay or as generated in your portlet applications. You have a `repositoryId` ❶ that on Liferay 6.0 has a value of 0 (more on this later). Folders are added to store files ❷, and files are added to those folders ❸. You pass in values from Liferay like the `groupId` so that the content is scoped to the community or organization to which it should belong, the one the message board portlet is on.

The way this works is very Liferay-specific. It follows all of the Liferay patterns, making it easy for those who are familiar with Liferay to create folders and manage documents. It works well and is consistent across the portal.

When examining this design, however, I'm sure you can foresee some limitations. Let's look at those.

E.1.3 *Limitations of the Document Library in 6.0 and below*

I bet one limitation jumps out at you right away when you look at figure E.1: you can connect to only one data store at a time, and that connection has to be made by administrators. What if you wanted some files to use the Liferay data store and some others to go into a CMIS repository? You wouldn't be able to do it.

Another limitation is in the metadata for the files. Note that document information is stored in the Liferay database, whereas the file is stored in the repository in a way that the file can be connected to the metadata. That connection works great for Liferay repositories, but it's not so great for other repositories.

Generally, if you're using a third-party repository, you want to browse it with third-party tools. But Liferay stores documents the Liferay way in these repositories, meaning they don't always get natural names. Instead, they're named according to an algorithm that allows for a way to point back to the metadata in the Liferay database. For example, the Advanced File System hook uses an algorithm that uses the filename to create a structure for versioning the file. If you have a file called tps-report.pdf, that hook will create a structure like this:

tp/tps-report.pdf/tps-report_1.0.pdf
tp/tps-report.pdf/tps-report_1.1.pdf

This works great behind the scenes for Liferay, but if you were to browse, say, your CMIS repository with a different client, this structure isn't the most intuitive. Still, it's great that Liferay supports many different kinds of repositories in versions 6.0 and below, and you should feel free to use them. But these limitations needed addressing, and this is exactly what has happened in Liferay 6.1.

E.2 Managing documents in Liferay 6.1

Document management and the Document Library portlet got a major overhaul in Liferay 6.1. You now have the notion of *document types* (see figure E.2), which can denote various file formats as well as *metadata sets* (see figure E.3).

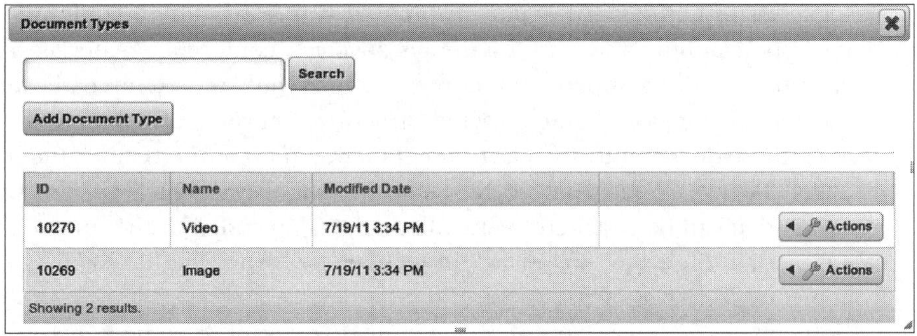

Figure E.2 The Document Library in Liferay 6.1 is a lot more flexible and can handle any document type you want to throw at it.

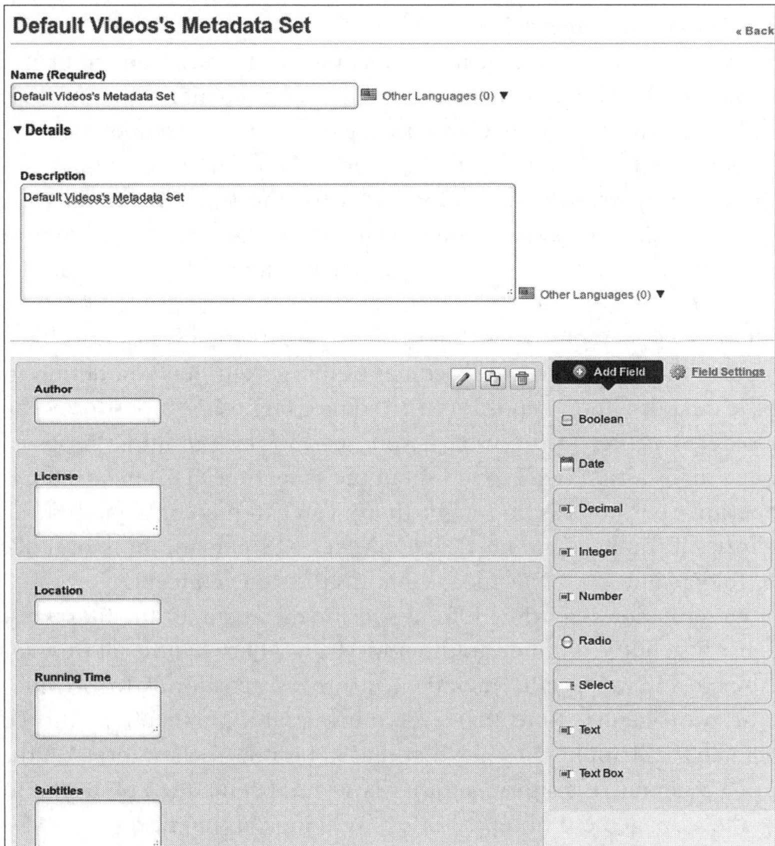

Figure E.3 You can define any metadata you like for any file type you want to define. This one ships with Liferay 6.1 and contains metadata that would be useful for video files.

This gives you the ability to attach whatever metadata you want to any file type that users may submit. This metadata, of course, can be categorized and tagged, as well as indexed for search, making Liferay a fantastic platform for dealing with uploaded assets (such as videos) from users.

A common business requirement is that users want to be able to establish metadata associated with business rules. For example, if you're running a conference, you're going to be handling a lot of files: quotes, invoices, conference materials and handouts, graphics, video snippets, and more. Of course you'll want to upload your files for the conference into a common directory structure. But you'll also want to set up metadata for those documents, such as the region, the quarter, the year, or the marketing manager. Liferay 6.1 lets you create a new document *type*, which consists of a set of metadata that can be attached to any file that gets uploaded to the system. Or, in the case of certain file types, metadata can be extracted from the file, such as EXIF data from pictures or ID tags from MP3s.

Sometimes you'll have sets of metadata that you want to come in across different document types, such as legal requirements. A particular file, whether a document, picture, or video, might have data such as the representing law firm or a pointer to a license under which the content may be used. Similar legal requirements might be applied to a sales event somewhere else.

In programmer's terms, this means a document type has a one-to-many relationship to metadata sets. The metadata set can have a one-to-many relationship to metadata. And there's a one-to-one relationship between a file and a document type.

The flexibility of this system makes it powerful. You can, for example, attach workflows to document types, so that if a document has the *legal* document type, it has to go through the legal workflow. Folders can be configured so that any document added to, changed in, or deleted from a particular folder triggers a workflow that can set a particular document type.

In addition to document types, Liferay 6.1 also has the idea of multiple repositories that can be mounted into the Document Library. This lets you define some folders using the default Liferay repository and some using other repositories, but show a seamless folder structure to the user. If you need to have multiple repositories, you can mount as many as you need to mount at the same time. This means the limitation of one repository per hook is no longer there: you can mix and match several different repositories if you have the need. If you're a UNIX person, think of it like mounting shared folders into the UNIX file system. It's the same concept.

The other limitation regarding Liferay-specific metadata for the files is also no longer there, because of the addition to the underlying API to handle all this. You no longer have to use Liferay-specific metadata in other repositories to provide the link between the two systems. Note that everything I said earlier about the Document Library API in 6.0 still applies, it's just that that API is now the low-level API that is used for mounting a Liferay repository. Another layer has been added on top of it in order to abstract the management of repositories. We'll look at that next.

E.2.1 Handling multiple repositories in Liferay 6.1

Liferay 6.1 adds a new layer called the Document Library Application API (`DLApp` in the code) on top of the existing Documents API. The other API (`DLFolder`, `DLFileEntry`, and so on) is still there; it's been abstracted so that a single API at the top level can be used to talk to any repository. The old API now handles the Liferay Repository only and is one of several repository implementations. Figure E.4 shows how this works.

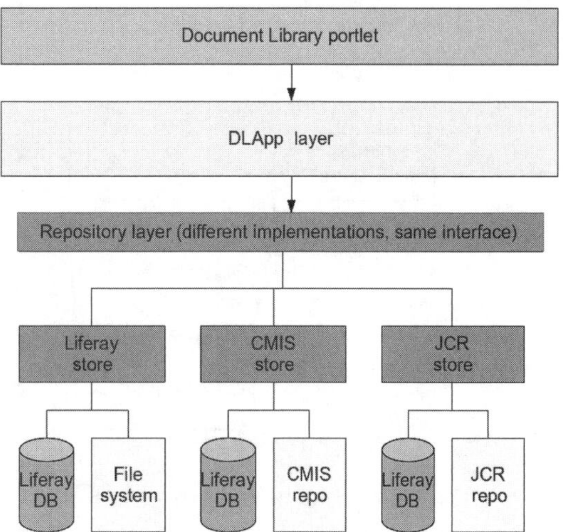

Figure E.4 In Liferay 6.1, there's a layer of abstraction above the level of the repository, and Liferay's older API has been demoted to one of many possible Store implementations.

As a developer, you now have a choice: if your application needs to store files, you can still use the older API with which you may be familiar. Nothing's been removed, and it's used internally by Liferay for things like the Message Boards portlet, so there's no reason to believe it's going anywhere. Your files will be stored in Liferay's repository just as they always have been. But if you need more than this, you may want to use the new `DLApp` API. If so, here's a short tour of that API to help get you started.

E.2.2 Using the Document Library Application API

The new `DLApp` classes add a layer of abstraction on top of the existing classes. Simplifying things for the developer, the API aggregates the different service classes into one service: the `DLAppService`. Here, you'll find all the methods you need for adding and managing files, checking in and checking out files, adding and managing folders, and dealing with mounted repositories. Everything is in one place, and it's all convenient for the developer. How does the API do this? Through repositories.

REPOSITORIES

The new Document Library Application API is based on repositories. You'll need a handle to a repository in order to be able to do anything with a file. `Repository` is an interface that has several implementations, based on which type of file store users are connecting to. For example, figure E.5 shows the class inheritance model for the `LiferayRepository` implementation of this interface.

Repositories have IDs that uniquely identify them. In the instance of a `LiferayRepository`, the ID is a groupId. In the instance of other repositories, they're unique constructs that get their own entries in the Repository tables in the database. It's here that the metadata is stored.

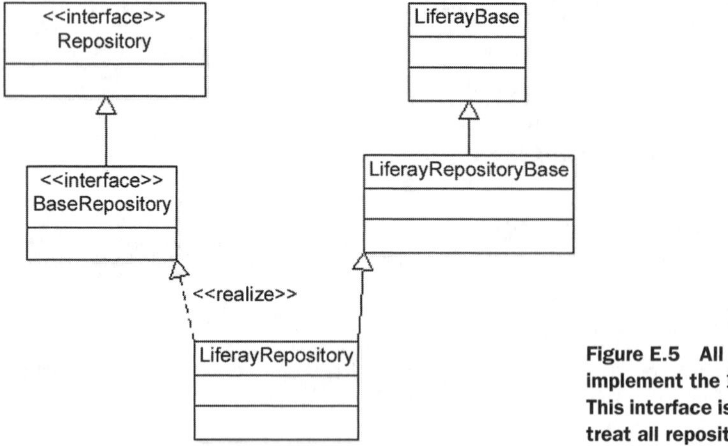

Figure E.5 All repository objects must implement the `Repository` interface. This interface is what enables `DLApp` to treat all repositories the same.

Not pictured here is the existence of the `LocalRepository`. This is a parallel set of classes and interfaces like the other local services you see in Liferay: their method signatures are simpler because you can pass complex objects like `ServiceContext` to them. The Liferay repository is the only repository in 6.1 that implements both the local and remote interfaces.

RAMIFICATIONS OF THE NEW API

As you can see, this is all nicely designed, clean, and extensible. But you, of course, just want to get something done with it. How? I can offer you some advice.

If you're using the basic Liferay repository, you can call the `DLApp` layer with the same options you used to use with the old API, and it will work. In that case, your `scopeGroupId` is your `repositoryId`. The only difference you should encounter is the objects you'll receive back: instead of `DLFileEntry`, `DLFileVersion`, and `DLFileFolder`, you'll receive higher-level wrapper classes: `FileEntry`, `FileVersion`, and `Folder`. They effectively do the same thing, although they can wrap different implementations.

If you're using CMIS or another remote repository (Liferay EE 6.1 comes with connectors for Documentum and SharePoint), you need a repository ID for the remote repository instance. In the UI, you can specify this ID when mounting the repository for the first time. This allows you to access the repository through `RepositoryServiceUtil`. What you get back is data from the new Repository table in Liferay, which is a mapping table for all new non-Liferay repositories.

There's one other thing to mention if your use case is attachments in a custom portlet. You can continue to use the older API for this, as Liferay does with the Message Boards portlet. But if you opt to use the new `DLApp` API, your folders will be visible within the Document Library portlet. If this matters to you, you can stick with the old API, but you'll lose the flexibility to enable *your* application to talk to multiple repositories. A future enhancement to the new API will enable you to hide folders programmatically so they don't appear in the Document Library.

index

Symbols

Numerics

A

E

F

G

H

I

J

K

L

M

N

O

T

U

RELATED MANNING TITLES

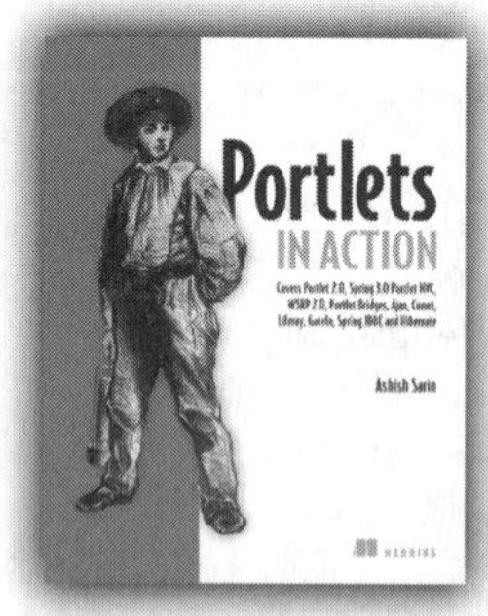

Portlets in Action
by Ashish Sarin

ISBN: 978-1-935182-54-2
550 pages, $49.99
September 2011

Spring in Action, Third Edition
by Craig Walls

ISBN: 978-1-935182-35-1
424 pages, $49.99
June 2011

Ext JS in Action
by Jesus Garcia

ISBN: 978-1-935182-11-5
496 pages, $49.99
November 2010

jQuery in Action, Second Edition
by Bear Bibeault and Yehuda Katz

ISBN: 978-1-935182-32-0
488 pages, $44.99
June 2010

For ordering information go to www.manning.com